W9-DFN-918

THE CORRESPONDENTS

THE CORRESPONDENTS

SIX WOMEN WRITERS ON
THE FRONT LINES OF WORLD WAR II

JUDITH MACKRELL

THORNDIKE PRESS
A part of Gale, a Cengage Company

Copyright © 2021 by Judith Mackrell.
Originally published in hardcover in Great Britain as *Going with the Boys* by Picador, an imprint of Pan Macmillan, London, in 2021.
Thorndike Press, a part of Gale, a Cengage Company.

ALL RIGHTS RESERVED
Thorndike Press® Large Print History Fact and Fiction.
The text of this Large Print edition is unabridged.
Other aspects of the book may vary from the original edition.
Set in 16 pt. Plantin.

**LIBRARY OF CONGRESS CIP DATA ON FILE.
CATALOGUING IN PUBLICATION FOR THIS BOOK
IS AVAILABLE FROM THE LIBRARY OF CONGRESS.**

ISBN-13: 978-1-4328-9659-1 (hardcover alk. paper)

Published in 2022 by arrangement with Doubleday, an imprint of The Knopf Doubleday Publishing Group, a division of Penguin Random House LLC.

Printed in Mexico
Print Number: 01   Print Year: 2022

In memory of my father

CONTENTS

7

AUTHOR'S NOTE AND ACKNOWLEDGEMENTS

The Second World War was the most sprawling conflict in modern history, fought on many geographical fronts and ignited by long-festering territorial, political and ideological issues. It contains a multitude of narratives, and, in presenting the war from the perspective of these six women correspondents, I have confined myself to a necessarily partial view of its events.

Each of the women in this book were journalists of courage and distinction, and they ranked high among the valiant group of female correspondents who fought hard, and sometimes painfully, to earn their place on the front line between 1939 and 1945. Their individual experiences of the war were inevitably constricted, however, both by time and circumstance. Aside from Martha Gellhorn's tour to China in 1941, none of the six were able to report on the brutal fighting in Burma, Singapore and elsewhere in the Far East, nor did they see much of Russia. As journalists too, they were given only restricted access to the political and military issues at play — Helen Kirkpatrick, the best informed, knew more than she could publish, but even she acknowledged there was much that she learned about in retrospect.

For more thorough accounts of the war there are, of course, many scholarly histories, to whose expertise and rigour I'm hugely indebted. A selected number of these appear in the bibliography, along with very fine individual biographies of Martha Gellhorn, Lee Miller, Clare Hollingworth and Sigrid Schultz, without whose research and insight I could not have written this book.

Many people have been extraordinarily generous with their time and expertise, and, as always, praise must go to the archivists and librarians who helped in the accessing of material, especially those at Smith College and Göttingen University, the latter going beyond the call of duty in reviving some dinosaur microfilm technology. Huge thanks also to Harriet Crawley and Antony Penrose for sharing memories of their mothers, Virginia Cowles and Lee Miller; to Patrick Garrett for answering my questions about his great-aunt, Clare Hollingworth, and also to Westport historians John Suggs, Morley Boyd and Wendy Crowther for their fabulous detective work into the life of Sigrid Shultz.

My publishers and I would like to thank

the following for their generous permission to quote from published and unpublished works: the Sophia Smith Collection, Smith College Special Collections, for extracts from Helen Kirkpatrick's letters and personal papers; the Washington Press Club Foundation for extracts from the Helen Kirkpatrick Milbank interview with Anne Kasper; The State Historical Society of Wisconsin for extracts from Sigrid Schultz's papers; Hodder and Stoughton for extracts from Patrick Garrett's *Of Fortunes and War;* Faber and Faber for extracts from Virginia Cowles' *Looking for Trouble;* Grove Atlantic and Eland Publishing for extracts from Martha Gellhorn's *The Face of War;* Alexander Matthews for permission to quote from Martha Gellhorn and Patrick Garrett for extracts from Clare Hollingworth's *Front Line.* Full permissions acknowledgements can be found on p. 435.

Thanks and love to all my friends, who had to accommodate my obsession with war over the last three years, and in particular to Debra Craine for her generous and meticulous first reading of this book.

My agent Clare Alexander and my editors George Morley and Cara Reilly have been the best and wisest of champions, and the editorial team at Picador have been patient, kind and eagle eyed — I bow down to Chloe May, Penelope Price, Rachel Wright and

Marissa Constantinou whose fortitude has been all the more remarkable during this year of Covid.

To Simon, Fred and Oscar, all my love and gratitude as always.

INTRODUCTION

When Virginia Cowles flew into Berlin on 31 August 1939, she knew that this assignment could be one of the most hazardous of her career. Gleaming black enfilades of Nazi fighter planes were parked along the runways of Tempelhof Airport, the Berlin skyline was spiked with anti-aircraft guns and the city centre looked, to her, like an "armed camp" — its streets clogged with military trucks, its hotel lobbies jostling with Nazi storm troopers. Europe was now so close to war that every British journalist had been recalled home, and staff at the British embassy had been ordered to pack. Even the weather felt ominously on edge. A dry, dusty wind blew through the city, which, to Virginia's ears, had the "queer sound of a death rattle" as it "caught up bits of paper and rubbish and sent them scraping along the pavement."[1]

Yet Virginia, an American correspondent for the *Sunday Times,* was determined to remain in the city long enough to scoop what would probably be her paper's final report before Germany became enemy territory. Ambitious, inquisitive, wilful, and not a little ruthless, she'd always had faith in her ability to survive. It was stubborn self-belief that had lifted her, first, out of the ghetto of New York society columns, and had subsequently taken her to Italy, to interview Mussolini on the launch of his invasion of Abyssinia, and then to Spain, where she became one of a tiny minority to cover the civil war from both sides. Yet, if Virginia appeared fearless in the advancement of her career, the most powerful weapon in her armoury was charm. Wide-eyed and slenderly built, disconcertingly glamorous in lipstick and high heels, she could walk into a military mess or a politician's office, and coax the toughest, most recalcitrant of men to talk.

Her job in Berlin was to analyse the mood of the German public, and, the following morning, when Virginia awoke to the news that Adolf Hitler had sent his troops into Poland, she expected to find the city in a state of high agitation. The invasion was in clear violation of the peace agreement which Hitler had signed with Britain and France the previous year, and it was a deliberate provocation to war. Most of the ordinary Berliners to whom Virginia spoke that day, however, seemed unaware of the crisis they faced — the reception clerk at her hotel had been incredulous when she suggested that his country might soon be in conflict with half of Europe: "Poland is Germany's affair," he'd protested. "What's it got to do with anyone else?"[2]

But Dr. Boehmer, the Chief of Foreign Press in Berlin, had burst into tears when he'd heard the morning's news: "nothing can save the situation now," he'd lamented, "the whole world will soon be involved."[3] As one of the saner Nazis in power, Boehmer understood the catastrophe that Hitler was courting. And Virginia, too, had to acknowledge that her own situation was now precarious. It might be only a matter of hours before Britain and its allies responded to the gauntlet Hitler had thrown down, and, once they did, it might take her weeks, even months, to find her way home.

In fact, she was safely back in London in time to file her report for the next day's paper. But while she'd escaped Berlin, the war was to become the story of Virginia's career, and she would face far greater dangers in covering it. She would report on the Russian invasion of Finland, the blitzing of London, the occupation of France, and she would get deeper into the desert war in Tunisia than any other correspondent.

At first, newspaper editors would try to make Virginia a part of the stories she filed — an attractive young woman who was willing to brave bullets and bombs, a former "society girl" who could muck in with the men in trenches. Female correspondents were still a novelty when the war started in 1939. Yet, despite the fuss and publicity that was made of Virginia and a few women like her, a very small but determined contingent of women had actually been reporting from the world's battle zones for close to a hundred years.

Jane Cazeneuve may have been the first, reporting on the Mexican–American war in 1846, but two years later she was followed by Margaret Fuller, hired by the *New York Tribune* to cover the Italian uprisings against Austria; in 1897, the war between Turkey and Greece was covered by Cora Taylor Crane for the *New York Journal,* and, in 1899, Lady Mary Howard reported on the South African war for the *Daily Telegraph.* By 1914, when editors across Europe and America had become alerted to the size and profitability of their female readership, many were keen to report World War One from a woman's angle. And while those who were assigned to the battlefields were meant to be limiting their reports to nurses and hospitals, a doughty few did manage to send back dispatches from the front.

It was the Second World War, though, which was to become the defining opportunity for female correspondents. As the battle lines spread and the story grew to encompass both civilians and soldiers, editors had to increase their global coverage, and, by the end of the war, around 250 of the reporters and photographers accredited to the Allied armies were women.*

Prominent among them was Clare Hollingworth. Although she'd been a virtual novice when she talked her way into a stringer's contract with the *Daily Telegraph,* she was armed with a self-belief that was even more foolhardy than Virginia's. Having been sent to Katowice, in south-west Poland, the first assignment she set herself was to borrow a car from the British consulate and drive into Germany to go scouting for troop activity. It was 29 August 1939, and the escapade was madness — Clare could have been apprehended as a spy, even shot by jumpy guards. But she was very ambitious to prove her reporter credentials and her initiative would be rewarded with an astonishingly lucky scoop. Driving close to the border, she found herself on a road that was lined with broad hessian screens; and when a gust of wind blew one of them aside, she was able to see straight down to the valley below, where nine Panzer divisions were massed in battle-ready

* The majority were North American, while those from Britain and the Commonwealth included sixteen Australians, accredited in 1942.

formation.

It was clear evidence of an invasion force, and the story Clare phoned through from Katowice was splashed over the *Telegraph*'s front page the following morning. In London, there was still hope that war could be averted, but, on 1 September, Clare was awoken at dawn by the heavy crump of anti-aircraft fire, and she had a clear sight of warplanes circling in the distance. The attack on Poland had surely begun and, as she phoned in the second headline story of her new career, the adrenalin pumping through Clare's veins was not so much fear as the certainty that she'd found her life's vocation.

One of the bravest of all women correspondents, Sigrid Schultz, would not report from an active battle zone until January 1945, yet she'd been covering her own, personally fraught, front line since 1933. As Berlin bureau chief for the *Chicago Tribune,* Sigrid had made herself a heroically persistent opponent of the Nazi regime. Tiny, combative, with a fluent grasp of five languages and the best sources in Berlin, she had withstood surveillance, interrogation and death threats in order to publish the truth of Germany's descent into a criminal, fascist state.

William Shirer, who reported from Berlin for CBS radio, would credit Sigrid as the bravest and best informed of the foreign press corps. On 1 September 1939, he noted in his diary that it was she who alerted him to the invasion of Poland: "At six a.m., Sigrid Schultz — bless her heart — phoned. She said: 'It's happened.' I was very sleepy — my body and mind numbed, paralyzed. I mumbled: 'Thanks, Sigrid,' and tumbled out of bed."[4]

Although Sigrid was dedicated to keeping the world informed about Nazi Germany, she could publish only a fraction of what she knew, and there were others outside Berlin who were also tracking the spread of fascism through Europe. When Martha Gellhorn went to Madrid in March 1937, it was with the conviction that the civil war in Spain represented a historic battle between freedom and totalitarianism. Objectivity is "shit," she declared, and in her coverage for *Collier's* magazine she was passionately partisan in her support for the Republicans and their fight against General Franco's coup. Her duty as a journalist was to harness opinion on the side of the angels, she believed, and she would cling to that conviction as she followed the course of the war from Czechoslovakia to Italy, France, Germany, and finally to the gates of Dachau.

Lee Miller held herself to similarly high standards, although she came to war, and even to journalism, much later than Martha. As a professional photographer, she'd been a celebrity of the New York fashion world, a star of the Parisian avant-garde, and she'd never been interested in covering hard news. Yet, after she'd settled in London in 1939, Lee experienced a kind of epiphany. As Germans bombed the city night after night, she found a new and urgent use for her camera. The war was her true métier, she believed; and, learning the skills of a photo-journalist, adding a Baby Hermes typewriter to her professional kit, she went on to report from the battlegrounds of northern France, the Allied push through Germany, the liberation of Paris and the concentration camps. In both her writing and photography, Lee produced some of the war's most haunting coverage, and all of it, extraordinarily, was published in *Vogue.*

Helen Kirkpatrick would always say that she'd been a professional reporter for whom the war "got in the way."[5] She'd begun her career in Geneva, reporting on the League of Nations, and had initially been a committed pacifist. But, as she'd witnessed the warmongering aggression of Hitler, Mussolini and Franco, she'd become convinced that Europe's triumvirate of dictators could only be stopped by force. She moved to London, where, as the first female correspondent for the *Chicago Daily News,* she reported on the progress of war from the thick of the Blitz. So accurate and shrewd was her coverage that Helen became much admired by the military and, by express order of General Eisenhower, she was the first woman to report from an Allied war zone with equal privileges to men.

Back in September 1939, when Europe first went to war, it was widely assumed that women would only cover the civilian angle — the evacuees, the rationing, the stories of life in the air-raid shelters. It was assumed they lacked the authority for hard military news. Betty Wasson, an American radio journalist who risked near-starvation to cover the German invasion of Greece, was actually barred from broadcasting her own material because her voice was considered too feminine. It was also assumed by those in charge of official protocol that women would be unable to endure the blood, violence and noise of battle, and, for most of the war, female correspondents were officially prohibited from all combat zones under British or American jurisdiction.

But far more entrenched than concerns about women's safety and their tolerance for war lay the belief that a lone female journalist, embedded within a division of male soldiers, must be an inevitable source of trouble. Not only was she likely to arouse sexual or emotional unrest among the battle-wearied troops, but, far more embarrassingly, to create difficulties in the matter of toilet facilities.

It was apparently beyond the squeamish

military imagination to conceive of ways in which a woman might decently, and practically, relieve herself in a war zone, and the "cloakroom question," or what the Americans more briskly termed "the latrine business," would become the issue dominating all discussion concerning the admittance of female correspondents to the army press corps. For the women themselves, who were fully capable of ducking behind a bush, or even braving an open latrine, it felt both demeaning and absurd that a fuss over sanitary arrangements could get in the way of them doing their jobs. It seemed obvious to them that the issue was a smokescreen, a way for the conservative military to conceal its fear of a "female invasion." The British would continue to hide behind "the convenience question" until very late in the war, barring accreditation to all women. The Americans, however, were a little more flexible, and when they entered the war in December 1941, Clare Hollingworth was one of several women who transferred herself to an American news organization in order to secure her accreditation with the U.S. army.

Even the U.S. War Department, however, had rules written in "invisible ink," which limited the freedom of women reporters. While they might be permitted to the rear of a combat zone, they were to be kept at a strict distance from the front, and they were to be treated rather like an amateur, auxiliary press corps — prohibited from using official transport and facilities, and excluded from the army's briefing sessions.

By November 1944, America would ease its restrictions, but until then, every woman who attempted to report from an Allied combat zone had to do so by illicit or ingenious means. When Virginia Cowles went to cover the fighting in Italy, she attached herself to the Free French Expeditionary Corps, whose attitude to protocol was infinitely more relaxed. When Martha Gellhorn learned that she was barred from covering the Normandy landings, she hid herself on board a hospital ship and sailed stowaway. She spent a night on Omaha Beach, helping with the transportation of injured soldiers, and the stories she filed were far more authentic, far more detailed than those of her husband, Ernest Hemingway, who, like most of the official press corps, had witnessed the invasion from the relative security of an assault craft.

Over and over again, it was the restrictions imposed on women which, ironically, led to their finding more interestingly alternative views of the war. Forced to dodge around the public-relations officers, or PROs, who controlled the media's movements, they set up their own informal contacts with soldiers, found their own pockets of war action, their own human interest stories. And, as a consequence, their reporting often had a different colour and a different heartbeat from that of their male colleagues. Dorothy Thompson, the celebrated American journalist, would always insist that women made the best reporters, as well as the best spies, principally because "[they] are more naturally inquisitive, trained to listen and far more likely to retain social contacts."[6]

There were other qualities that united the women who battled to cover this war. As a group, they were smart, ambitious, reasonably educated and white (there was just one African American, Elizabeth Murphy Moss, a reporter for the *Baltimore Afro-American,* who was accredited to the U.S. army in 1944, but whose war career was cut short by illness). As a group, they were also quite conscious of each other's work. When Helen Kirkpatrick was learning to be a foreign correspondent in Geneva, she read everything she could of Sigrid's Berlin coverage; and her own war reports were subsequently read, and admired, by Martha and Lee. On the brief occasions when their reporting paths crossed, most were also grateful for the female companionship. When Virginia and Martha were together in Spain, Czechoslovakia and Italy; when Lee and Helen shared a flat in liberated Paris, or a freezing billet in bombed-out Cologne, it was a rare opportunity for them to bitch about idiotic PROs, sexually predatory officers or over-entitled male journalists. It was an even more luxurious opportunity for them to relax their professional guard; sharing stories of trauma and discomfort which they couldn't admit to men, or simply feeling free to ask a colleague for the loan of a tampon, a sanitary towel, a bar of army-issue soap.

Outside of these chance interludes, however, the women did not care to be viewed as a professional, female sorority. They might share each other's frustrations, and face the same obstacles, but they were so ambitious to be ranked on equal terms with the men, so anxious to avoid the slur of the "woman's angle," and the need for "special treatment," that they preferred to fight most of their battles alone, without any fuss. Self-reliant and extremely competitive, they were operating solo for most of the war, following wherever the action took them, and developing their own distinctive angles. Lee and Martha, whose magazine work allowed them to focus on the human stories of conflict, would make their names as passionately subjective writers, closely and vividly involved with their subject matter. Clare, Sigrid, Helen and Virginia wrote for daily newspapers, and their reporting, by contrast, was driven by the exigencies of deadlines, and the breaking of news.

After the war, the achievements of these women did not go unrecognized. Helen was honoured with the American Presidential Medal of Freedom, the French Legion of Honour and the Médaille de la Reconnaissance Française; Virginia was awarded an OBE by the British government; and Martha and Lee were feted as media celebrities. However, once the honours had been distributed, and the speeches made, their future was not to be easy. Many female correspondents faced professional redundancy, as editors began scaling down their foreign news desks, and allocating work to returning servicemen. A far greater number, however, became lost in a very personal struggle to make the transition from war back into peace.

The cost of the last five and a half years had been high. Pursuit of a combat career had forced a number of women to sacrifice their closest relationships, with lovers, husbands, even children. And, as they returned to their broken lives, they also brought with them the nightmares — the flashbacks to all the horrors they'd seen. As Martha Gellhorn put it, the war had damaged most of them, left them "shredded up inside." Yet however "hated and perilous and mad" the experience had been, it was also very difficult to relinquish. War had become a kind of home to these correspondents, a home where "everyone had something to do, something that looked necessary."[7] The idea of settling back down into a civilian existence, of living without that sense of urgency, was almost impossible to imagine.

Emotionally displaced, professionally uncertain as they were, it was not yet possible for these women to know that, in decades to come, they would be emulated and admired as a generation of pioneers. They could not know that, when conflicts developed in Vietnam, Israel, the Balkans and the Middle East, the battles they'd fought, the standards they'd set, would pave the way for many more women to cover front-line news. The *Sunday Times* correspondent Marie Colvin would always carry a volume of Martha's collected journalism when she went to the wars of the late twentieth and early twenty-first centuries. And if that volume was Colvin's talisman and inspiration, it was also her reminder that the authority with which she and her peers were able to speak and to write was an authority which had been handed down by Martha Gellhorn, Clare Hollingworth, Lee Miller, Helen Kirkpatrick, Sigrid Schultz, Virginia Cowles — women who, along with the rest of an exemplary regiment of female correspondents, had fought to cover the Second World War.

■ ■ ■ ■

THE CORRESPONDENTS

■ ■ ■ ■

CHAPTER ONE:
BERLIN, 1936

"I want to give readers all
the dope there is"
SIGRID SCHULTZ[1]

In the autumn of 1936, Sigrid Schultz was
starting to feel like a stranger in her own city.
Less than a decade ago, the Berlin she'd
known and loved had been crackling with wit,
colour, deviance and dissent. Painted boys
with nipped-in waists had sauntered through
the stylish crowds along Kurfürstendamm;
girls in suits and monocles had drunk cocktails at the Eldorado ballroom. Satire — the
city's native genius — had flourished in
cabarets and bars, and, as a very dazzled
young William Shirer had noted, Weimar
Berlin had felt like "a wild open city full of
crazy poets and homosexuals," a place for
adventure and self-reinvention.[2] It had been
a city of violence, too — scarred by Germany's recent defeat in the 1914–18 war, rocked
by political battles within the newly democratic Reichstag and growling with a savage

underbelly of poverty, drugs and prostitution. Yet, to an ambitious young journalist like Sigrid, it was the darkness in the glitter of Berlin that made it the most engrossing city in the world in which to make her career.

Then, in 1933, Hitler and the National Socialists had seized power, and the Nazification of Berlin began. The brown-shirted muscle of the *Sturmabteilung* (SA) and the black-uniformed elite of the *Schutzstaffel* (SS) had bullied most of the satirists into silence and forced the radical artists to skip town. Formerly emancipated women had been told to wipe off their lipstick and produce babies for the Fatherland, while the children were dragooned into the Hitler Youth or the League of German Girls. As fledgling Nazis paraded through Berlin in their crisp little shirts and neckerchiefs, it seemed to Sigrid as though the city itself was in uniform. Scarlet and black swastikas rippled from every public building and the streets were loud with Party messages, broadcast daily over public loudspeakers.

The harsh metallic tones of Adolf Hitler and the hectoring bark of his Propaganda Minister Joseph Goebbels had become almost as familiar to Berliners as the voices of their family and friends. And, to all those who'd become principal targets of the regime — the trade unionists, the communists, the homosexuals and, above all, the city's Jews — these

32

voices were also a daily reminder of the threats they faced, whether of violence or arrest.

As bureau chief of the *Chicago Tribune,* Sigrid had made it her mission to keep America informed about Germany's decline into totalitarianism, to expose every stage of its draconian dismantling of democracy and the rule of law. According to Gregor Ziemer, her former assistant and fellow journalist, she was "one of the most talented foreign correspondents" of her generation, publishing more damning information about the Nazis than any of her colleagues, facing off Gestapo spies and interrogation until she was finally forced to leave.[3] Hitler's Berlin had been her personal war zone, and if it had made her as expert as any combat journalist in arming herself against danger, it had also forced her to keep very close the fact that, by Nazi reckoning, she was a Jew.

Sigrid Lilian Schultz had settled in Berlin late in 1913. She'd been a pretty, intellectually pugnacious twenty-one-year-old, with a command of several foreign languages and a headful of ambitions to sing in opera or practise law. She also considered herself a cosmopolitan, for, despite her Germanic-sounding name, her father had been born in Norway and she herself had been born in Chicago, where Herman Schultz, a society portrait painter, had moved in 1891 to advance his career. His plan had been to put down "deep roots in prairie soil" to create his version of the American dream, and, after his eighteen-year-old wife, Hedwig, had given birth to Sigrid, on 5 January 1893, he'd settled his family in a spacious house in the suburb of Summerdale, with a garden over-looking miles of open ground.[4]

Sigrid was a tiny blonde scrap of a child for whom Herman had high ambitions. She was to be raised in the modern American way, encouraged to run freely around the country-side with the family's huge St. Bernard dog. But she was also to be raised as a European, to speak German and French as well as English, and, until she was eight, she lived in the centre of a charmed little world, petted by her parents, admired by the busy stream of friends who came to the house. Then, in 1901, that world broke apart as a sharp downturn in the Chicago economy coincided with a temporary decline in Herman's own health, and the Schultz family felt they had to pack up their home and return to Europe, where a commission awaited Herman in the royal court of Stuttgart.

The two years Sigrid spent in Germany were, for her, a period of angry exile. While her father was painting in Stuttgart, she and her mother were sent to Hedwig's family in

Wiesbaden, where, for the first time in her life, Sigrid encountered disapproval. Her Jaskewitz relatives might have descended from a vivid ancestral mix of Spanish, Polish, Balkan, Russian, Central European and Jewish stock, but they'd adopted the mindset of snobbish, provincial Germans. They'd never cared for Herman and they greatly disliked the "fresh" American ways which he'd allowed his daughter to develop. Sigrid was thus sent away to Munich, "to a school for little princesses," and, missing her parents, mocked for her "Yankee" accent, she turned from petted child to aggressive little waif.[5]

Years later, she recalled that she'd never hated that school more deeply than when news filtered through of her father's favoured position at court, and "suddenly the teacher became so nice and all the little girls wanted to carry my books home."[6] But, once Herman had fulfilled his commission, he was able to move his family to Paris, and there Sigrid flourished. She attended an excellent lycée, she had teachers to develop the sweetly melodious voice that she'd inherited from her great-grandfather Joseph Jaskewitz, a former director of the Wiesbaden Opera, and she finally got to meet her father's Norwegian family. They were ebullient, "crazy" — and she adored them, just as she adored Herman himself. But the most charmed hours of her life were the weekly lunches with her father, when he introduced her to Parisian restaurants, taught her about good food and wine, and recounted the stories of when he'd been a nineteen-year-old dreamer and had bicycled all the way from Norway to Paris to become an artist.

To Sigrid, Herman seemed marvellous; he was funny, flamboyant, gallant, and he could light up a room with his anecdotes. "He never lost the faith that life was thrilling," she wrote, "and always knew how to make others share his joy." It was only as she reached puberty that she realized how promiscuously Herman was spreading that joy; and while she would loyally excuse his philandering — "Poor man, he couldn't help it the way women were running after him"[7] — she could see the pain it caused her mother. Later, she would admit how badly she was affected by these dark sexual ructions — "I was really scared of marriage" — and in her troubled, confused state, the teenage Sigrid was also starting to worry about her parents' finances.[8]

Herman's career had remained volatile, boomeranging between celebrity and penury, and it had become apparent to Sigrid that neither of her parents had any talent for managing money. Hedwig, girlishly pretty and guileless, had never mastered the art of the household budget, while Herman, a man always hoping for better times, could squander lavish sums in a restaurant, even when there were only scraps in the larder at home. At one point, they were living in a studio on the Place Pigalle, a "ramshackle, terrible and colourful district," and, noting the squalor of other failed artistic careers, Sigrid studied to become the watchful adult of the family, teaching herself to cook and attempting to practise small domestic economies.[9]

"I probably missed out on a lot of fun," she acknowledged. But she had no intention of sacrificing her own ambitions and, having graduated from the lycée with high honours, she not only began professional singing lessons, but was enrolled at the Sorbonne for courses in history and international law. Already, she was displaying the stubborn application that would drive her reporting career, and, even though she'd inherited Herman's weak chest and had to be admitted to a Lucerne sanatorium with possible TB, she remained open to new horizons. When her parents wrote with news that they were temporarily setting up a home and studio in Berlin for Herman's work, she was eager to join them as soon as she was well.*

Berlin seemed full of possibilities when

* Her voice, now a coloratura soprano, won her a scholarship at the Paris Conservatoire, but acceptance required her to relinquish her American citizenship and she turned it down.

Sigrid arrived: it had a fine university and "it was *the* place" to study singing, if she could only scrape together the funds.[10] Yet it didn't take her long to become aware of an unsettling edge to the city. The newspapers she read were strident with xenophobic editorials, calling for the Kaiser to defend Germany against the expansionist greed of its European rivals; meanwhile, her parents' Jewish friends spoke of an alarming surge of anti-Semitic feeling in the city, their businesses boycotted and hate mail sent to their homes. Even though the Schultzes themselves had made little of Hedwig's ancestry (it's not even clear when Sigrid was told that she herself was half-Jewish), the family could not ignore these signs and could not but feel that Berlin in early 1914 was a potentially hostile city.

Sigrid's own response to these uncertain times was typically self-denying and typically practical. It was obvious that she and her parents needed a reliable source of income, so, abandoning her own studies, she gained a rudimentary teaching certificate and advertised for work as a private language tutor. Herman, who'd had such fine plans for his daughter, was grandly and unreasonably disappointed in her, yet, by 3 August, he had to acknowledge Sigrid's prescience. The Serbian bullet that assassinated Archduke Franz Ferdinand had sparked a dramatic unravelling of the already fragile European peace, and the Central Powers of Germany, Austro-Hungary, Bulgaria and the Ottoman Empire were now at war with Russia, France and Britain.

Initially, the war made little impact on the Schultzes. They trusted that their dual American and Norwegian citizenship would keep them safe (both countries were still neutral at this point); Herman was earning unexpectedly good money from high-ranking Germans who wanted to be painted in their uniforms; and Sigrid was particularly buoyant because a Norwegian-American naval officer, whom she'd known for several years, had proposed to her while on leave in Berlin. Guarded as she later was about the details of her private life, she didn't identify her fiancé by name, but she did imply that he'd been the love of her young life, that he'd helped to overcome her fears of marriage and that she'd hoped to become his wife as soon as the war was over.

Two and a half years and several million casualties later, however, the war showed no signs of ending, and, in April 1917, when America joined forces with Allied powers, Sigrid's own situation became extremely grave.

Like all American citizens, she and her parents had been encouraged to leave Germany, yet their departure had been delayed because Herman had been offered a last-minute and very lucrative commission in

Hamburg. His decision to accept would then prove fateful for the whole family because, once there, he was diagnosed with TB and placed under strict quarantine, which left Sigrid and Hedwig stranded in Berlin, not only scared about Herman's health, but, even more frighteningly, re-categorized as enemy aliens, required to report twice a day to the police and to remain confined to their immediate neighbourhood.

Life for Sigrid now shrank to a series of small survival strategies, as she dodged the military police to teach her few remaining pupils and bred rabbits on the apartment balcony, bartering them for flour at a local bakery. Then, in the summer of 1917, she heard that her fiancé had been lost at sea, his ship almost certainly torpedoed by German U-boats. At that moment, she all but buckled under the weight of despair. "I thought [it] was the end of my emotional life," she recalled.[11] Yet her parents still needed her support, and, in the autumn of 1917, when she learned that the mayor of Baghdad was in Berlin and was looking for an interpreter who was fluent in English, German and French, Sigrid forced herself to rise above her misery and apply for the post.

Her new job was to have a transformative effect on her world. Réouf Bey Chadirchi was rich, aristocratic and clever, and while he'd come to Berlin on diplomatic business, he

40

was planning to supplement his own private law studies at the city's university, and was expecting Sigrid to assist him in lectures as well as in meetings. After three years of anxious, menial work, it was thrilling to feel her brain re-engaged: "Can you imagine," she wrote, "the joy of continuing studies that seemed all important to me, and being paid for that privilege." But so intimately did Réouf come to depend on Sigrid, for her intelligence as well as her interpreting skills, that he began to entrust her with some of his more politically tricky affairs.[12]

If there was a moment when Sigrid first got her taste for investigative journalism, it may have been the confrontation she engineered with Réouf's most formidable adversary, the right-wing nationalist and anti-Semite, General Ludendorff. Ludendorff had come up with a plan to scapegoat the nation's Jewish community for Germany's failing performance in the war and he was pressuring Réouf to drum up support for his scheme among the Arab states. Réouf had been repelled by the idea, but his position in Berlin was delicate and he was ready to accept Sigrid's proposal that she interrogate Ludendorff further, on his behalf.*

* Ludendorff was planning an international propaganda campaign, which castigated the Jews for their supposedly "treacherous" business links with

Later she would admit that her strategy for questioning the general was intrepid, but naive; for, while she'd provided herself with cigarettes and canned sardines to bribe her way up to Ludendorff's hotel suite, she had no way of compelling him to listen and, as she recalled, "an onlooker would have been amused to see me firing questions at the stony faced general while he tried to walk away as fast as possible without actually breaking into a trot."[13] Yet, even though Sigrid failed to assist Réouf in his dilemma, he was captivated by the courage she'd shown, and in November 1918, when the war ended and he was recalled to Baghdad, he asked her to accompany him as his wife.

"Our relations, which were indifferent at the beginning, became more and more intimate, you supported and advised me in every way," Réouf fondly reminded Sigrid when he wrote to her fourteen years later.[14] But, while she cared for Réouf, she had no interest in marrying him, not least because she was still in mourning for her fiancé and would continue to be so for "years and years."[15] Nevertheless, Réouf's departure would leave an emotional as well as a financial void in Sigrid's life, and she would feel his absence

America, their alleged hoarding of war profits and their "poor" military record.

even more keenly when Germany's defeat in the war was followed by months of revolutionary chaos.

Disillusioned soldiers and a radicalized workforce had taken to the streets to fight for a socialist leadership, and, during the long hard winter of 1918–19, Berlin became a battleground. "I saw a ravenous mob slaughter a starving horse where it fell," Sigrid wrote. "I hurried through the Berlin streets under a crossfire of Red guns on one side and Republican soldiers on the other."[16] It was almost impossible to reach the homes of her pupils, and, eking out the meagre savings she'd put by, she and her mother were often cold and hungry. Even though she didn't write much about this period, the toughness, the scrappiness that Sigrid developed would stay with her for the rest of her life.*

But her luck turned again with the offer of a second job, and with it the discovery of her future career. In February 1919, the American journalist Richard Henry Little was appointed Berlin bureau chief for the *Chicago Tribune,* and having been recommended Sigrid as his German interpreter, he was as

* Germany's communist party had mobilized a surge of populist anger that had followed the nation's defeat — anger against the incompetence of the generals and against the ruling classes who'd grown rich on war profits.

quick as Réouf to spot that her talents ranged far beyond translation. He began to favour her with small investigative tasks and to take her with him on assignments outside Berlin — "I trotted by his side, an eager cub reporter," she recalled.[17] And Little's hunch that Sigrid had the brains, belligerence and instinct of a potential journalist was confirmed when she managed to argue her way past guards at the Naval Office to secure an audience with the notoriously reclusive Admiral Reinhard Scheer. In January 1920, when the *Tribune* was looking to expand its international coverage, Dick Little and his lead reporter Floyd Gibbons between them pressed for Sigrid to be hired as the paper's junior foreign correspondent in Berlin.

There were very few women, at the time, who had staff jobs with American publications, and far fewer who were allowed to escape the feminized sphere of society columns and fashion. The *Tribune* had its offices in the Hotel Adlon, whose vast marbled lobby, interior garden and extravagantly carved Japanese fountain made it one of the most luxurious establishments in Berlin. But far more beguiling to Sigrid was the clatter of typewriters and the shrilling of telephones upstairs in the paper's offices, and the busy news conferences over which Dick Little presided. She was conscious of being gifted a rare privilege, of being valued over the squad of competitive young men who might have expected to land this plum Berlin posting, and she was impatient to justify Dick's faith with her first substantial scoop.

Friedrich Ebert, the first elected President of the new Weimar Republic, had been holding on to power by a thread. The catalogue of humiliations which had been imposed on Germany by the Treaty of Versailles — the punitive war reparations, the ban on rearming, the loss of key territories — were felt as a national shame and a wound. Officers who'd served in the war believed that the Germany for which they'd fought no longer existed. And, as Ebert and his fragile government were made scapegoats for that loss, a faction of Prussian aristocrats, army generals, völkisch right-wing nationalists and supporters of the exiled Kaiser had organized an armed coup to bring down the Republic and impose an autocratic government in its place.

On 13 March, as Sigrid had listened to the first crack of artillery fire in the streets of Berlin, she'd been mad with frustration. It was too dangerous to leave her apartment, the telephone lines were closed to all but emergency calls, and she could think of no way of getting an angle on the unfolding putsch. But then a close friend and useful source named Dr. Johann had burst into her apartment, claiming that he'd run through bullets to bring her information about the

45

coup and the names of some of its leading players. Terrified that he'd been followed, that there would be rifle butts battering down the door, Johann locked himself inside Sigrid's bathroom. But she went directly to work: and, by passing herself off as a nurse, pretending that the names on Johann's list were doctors with whom she needed to speak, she had her interviews done and her article written and ready to file by the time it was safe to return to the office.

It was Sigrid's first headlining story and, over the next three years, the volatile Republic would yield many more. The German economy was floundering; by 1923, inflation had spiralled to such unreal levels that a loaf of bread cost 200,000,000,000 marks and people had to transport their cash in wheelbarrows. Millions of jobs were lost; beggars and crippled war veterans starved on the streets. And, as Sigrid and her colleagues kept track of the economic crisis, they were alerted to a pale, stuttering, but eerily magnetic young war veteran who was converting the nation's fear and unrest into the fuel for his own political ascent.

Adolf Hitler became front-page news when he led his "Beer Hall Putsch" against the Munich state government on 8 November 1923. The *Tribune* ran with the story for days, analysing the crude but potent vision with which he'd mesmerized his followers, the vision of a resurgent and racially pure Germany that would be forged from blood, soil and steel. When Sigrid was sent to Munich to investigate Hitler's power base she learned how broad it was — an unlikely, and alarming, alliance between the populist NSDAP or Nazi Party, patrician Junkers, disaffected students, right-wing military and wealthy industrialists like Fritz Thyssen, whose iron-fisted views matched those of his ally, General Ludendorff. Only three years earlier, Dr. Johann had warned her never to underestimate the arrogance, fanaticism and xenophobia of the nationalist right wing, explaining that she hadn't lived in Berlin long enough to realize how ruthless they were. Back then Sigrid had thought he was being melodramatic. But now, even though the Beer Hall Putsch was quashed, the Nazi Party banned and Hitler put behind bars, she could see that the threats to the young democratic Republic were very real, and had only gone underground.

So absorbed was Sigrid in the daily business of news, she had no idea that her boss Dick Little had fallen in love with her and had actually gone to her father to discuss the possibility of marriage. Herman was back in Berlin, but his TB was advancing to its terminal stage and he was fearful of losing his daughter, who was also his provider and nurse. Querulously, he insisted she was too young to marry, that she needed first to "learn to become an independent woman." Yet Dick had no better luck when he proposed to Sigrid directly. She had come to revere him as a mentor and friend, and a decade later, when an inquisitive young journalist asked why she remained unmarried, she implied it was because she'd never found another man to match Dick's intellectual stature — that he had been an irreplaceable "giant" to her. In 1923, however, marriage had still seemed impossible, to Dick or anyone else. Sigrid was still in thrall to the memory of her dead fiancé and still burdened by her parents — a weak and fractious couple now, unable to take care of themselves. "I had to support my Father and Mother," she explained, "and I was not going to load the expense for my parents onto whomever I married."[18]

The absence of a man in Sigrid's life was a subject of much speculative gossip in the *Tribune* office. According to one of her assistants, she was, in her early thirties, a very attractive woman: "She was lovely to look at when she bothered to put on a frilly dress and manipulate that golden hair of hers [or] use some make-up. She knew how to make the best of her small compact lively body — when she wanted to — which was not always."[19] But, while Sigrid would eventually allow herself to fall in love again, there were good professional reasons why it suited her to remain independent in Berlin. She knew that very few women possessed the levels of freedom she currently enjoyed: the freedom to work long hours in the office and to socialize with colleagues. There was a tradition among the foreign press corps to meet for evening drinks at the Adlon bar, or for plates of spaghetti at Die Taverne — a faux-Italian restaurant that was always pleasantly fuggy with smoke, gossip and beer fumes. These sessions were convivial but also combative: George Seldes, who worked for a brief time at the *Tribune*'s Berlin office, recalled, "we were friends yes . . . but we were all competing . . . at the Adlon we could keep our eyes on each other"; and it was much easier for Sigrid to stay the course knowing there was no husband or lover waiting up impatiently for her return.[20]

Most of the Berlin press corps were of course men and, in her determination to integrate herself, Sigrid took to smoking a little white clay pipe, while her colleagues puffed collectively on their Chesterfields and cigars. Since she barely tipped the scales at ninety pounds, she couldn't keep pace with their drinking, and instead persuaded the bar staff to serve her orange juice with just a whisper of gin. Yet there were subtle advantages, she was learning, to being a lone female in this very masculine club. No one ever guessed how sober she remained during these late-night drinking sessions, nor how beadily she scrutinized the increasingly lax, boozy conversation for information and leads. And Sigrid was not above exploiting her femininity when she needed to. In February 1925, when President Ebert fell suddenly ill, she faked a flutter of heart palpitations to get herself admitted into the clinic where the President was being treated, and, once there, was able to flirt the attending doctor into revealing that Ebert was suffering from a ruptured appendix, and was not expected to recover. By the time his death was announced, Sigrid had her story ready to file, hours ahead of her rivals.

According to one *Tribune* reporter, Sigrid was now breaking so many stories that she was unofficially acknowledged as "the man behind the guns" in the Berlin office, her talents all the more evident because Dick Little had moved on, leaving the bureau in the hands of a far less capable newsman, Parke Brown.[21] Her achievements had also been noted by Colonel Robert McCormick, the paper's Chicago publisher. McCormick was a tough Midwesterner, a former army officer of deeply conservative and anti-Semitic views, and Sigrid might well have been sacked had she revealed her own Jewish ancestry. But his overriding concern was circulation numbers. He could see that Sigrid was driving the headlines and, later that year, when he was moving around his chiefs of staff, McCormick chose to give her Berlin, making her the first-ever woman to run an American foreign bureau.*

Over the next sixteen years, Sigrid would have to learn how to tolerate the Colonel's aggressive editorial style, his readiness to spike any story that bored him, or that ran too counter to his own political views. She would also have to accommodate the fact that, like many right-wing Americans, he would be fascinated and impressed by Hitler's rise to power. In 1933, when McCormick visited Berlin, Sigrid was alarmed by his dazzled admiration for the Nazis' parades: "his soldier's heart [was] throbbing — the way they marched was just absolutely beautiful."[22] But, back in 1925, she was simply grateful for what the Colonel had done for her. Her new eminence came with a personal suite at the Adlon, a team of secretaries and assistants and, above all, the freedom to choose what stories she wanted to report. All these were things to glory in, and while Sigrid inevitably encountered those who regarded a female bureau chief as a freak of nature, she met them full on. According to one of her colleagues, she was at her most happily

* Her predecessor, Parke Brown, was relocated to Rome, much against his will.

pugnacious when "protecting the reputation and rights of her sex."[23] Once, when the Minister for Foreign Press tried to ban her from covering a gathering of business leaders, Sigrid scribbled him a scornful note: "Are 200 men afraid of one woman?" Not only was she allowed into the room, but she claimed that every "big boss" had made a point of talking with her.

Sigrid always boasted of that triumph; yet, quick though she was to enlist in a battle for equal rights, she could be wary of sharing the field. Dorothy Thompson was the most celebrated female correspondent of her generation, and her arrival in 1927, as temporary Berlin chief for the *New York Tribune,* caused Sigrid a niggling competitive grief. Not only had she been ousted from her position as the city's top woman journalist, but certain media reports were claiming that Thompson, not she, was the first woman to be given charge of a foreign bureau.

Her friend and colleague Bill Shirer would later fault Sigrid for her lack of generosity: "she had that small side to her," he thought. But she'd fought so hard for the *Tribune* job and she was always fearful that it could be taken away. She believed that she and her Berlin office had to outclass all the competition, to put themselves beyond reproach, and in pursuit of perfection she became easily frustrated. Gregor Ziemer recalled that "hot waves of anger, often articulated in French" used to emanate daily from her office, if ever a junior reporter failed to match her high standards, or if one of the female employees came into work wearing too much rouge, or was caught in indiscreet gossip.[24]

But, if Sigrid could be quick to anger, she'd also learned from her father how to charm and, according to Ziemer, she had the most diverse circle of contacts of anyone in Berlin. Like any good reporter, she knew the importance of keeping her contacts close, and every month she held large informal dinners, where she mixed teachers, trade unionists, musicians, artists, politicians and aristocrats, as well as the occasional celebrity, like the fighter pilot turned film star Ernst Udet. These dinners were held in the flat which she still shared with Hedwig, and they were always cooked by Sigrid herself; a succession of mid-European delicacies — caviar on miniature potato pancakes, slivers of bone marrow on melba toast — which were served, as Herman had taught her, with their appropriate wines.

By the late 1920s, Sigrid had become somebody in Berlin. Her by-line was famous, invitations to her monthly soirées were sought after and, as she smoked her little clay pipe, conversing brilliantly and caustically with friends, she bore little resemblance to the angry, uneasy teenager who'd fretted over her parents' marriage. Her heavy, honey-blonde hair had been cut short to frame her strong oval face, highlighting the brilliance of her deep-set eyes, and, if her clothes were carelessly worn, they'd nonetheless been bought from the fashionable boutiques along the Ku'damm. Young though she still was, Sigrid had become formidable enough for the younger correspondents, freshly arrived in Berlin, to call her "the boss."

If Sigrid was on the rise, so, it seemed, was Germany. Fat American loans had shored up the economy, there were jobs to be had, and a popular package of welfare and employment reforms had weakened support for the political extremes on both the left and the right. The neon-lit centre of Berlin, meanwhile, was embracing its own *Goldene Zwanziger* moment, outclassing even Left Bank Paris as a capital of culture and fun: Josephine Baker was dancing naked on the Theater des Westens stage; Fritz Lang's hallucinogenic *Metropolis* was playing in the cinemas; Kurt Weill and Bertolt Brecht's raunchily subversive *Die Dreiggroschenoper* (*The Threepenny Opera*) was breaking box-office records; and the gaudy bars and cabarets along Nollendorfplatz were doing a roaring business, day and night.

The bubble glistened; it gave the illusion of permanence. But, in 1928, Sigrid was warned by the liberal-minded Foreign Minister,

Gustave Stresemann, that she needed to watch out for Hitler and his recently re-formed Party. Not only were the Nazis back from their period in exile, they had a new manifesto, *Mein Kampf* (*My Struggle*), in which Hitler had outlined his blueprint for rebuilding Germany: overthrowing its "craven and corrupt" democracy; expanding its borders to provide *Lebensraum,* or living space, for every citizen; and, most chillingly, purging the nation of all its "degenerate" racial elements.

These were policies of extreme, unconstitutional violence, written in a rabid jumble of mysticism and xenophobia, yet Stresemann warned Sigrid that the Nazis were now dangerously attempting to reframe themselves as a democratic organization. Politics rather than putsches were to be the way forward and, by slow degrees, the Nazis were grooming candidates for election. In 1928, they gained only twelve of the Reichstag's 491 seats, but their nationwide campaign had won them a fanatical following. When the American stock market crashed, pushing the German economy into freefall, the moment was ripe to mobilize their support.

During the run-up to the 1930 elections, Hitler criss-crossed the country in a tireless programme of rallies. The speeches he gave made little sense, as he randomly blamed the economic crisis on Russian-backed communists, American capitalists and an international conspiracy of Jews. But his promise to reinvent Germany, to create a world superpower, a Third Reich that could dominate Europe for a thousand years, was exactly what the most frightened, angry and ignorant members of his audience needed to hear. Their current government, led by President Hindenburg, seemed only to stand helplessly by as Germany slid back into the abyss of the early 1920s, the cities once again rife with beggars and prostitutes, the homeless once again gathered in cardboard shanty towns. In September, when Germany went to the polls, Sigrid reported that the Nazis had achieved "a smashing victory," gaining almost a quarter of the Reichstag's seats.[25]

She could not yet take Hitler seriously as a politician: he seemed to her a crude "fascist bugbear," a demagogue "drunk on his own words," and she turned down the offer of an exclusive interview with him, partly because the Nazi press officer had actually tried to charge her — ten cents a word.[26]

The Party itself, however, she would not underestimate, and she asked one of her assistants, a thin, monocle-sporting Prussian named Alexander von Schimpff, which of the Nazi officials had "manners good enough to invite . . . to lunch,"[27] so that she could learn more of their plans and their policies. Schimpff recommended Hermann Göring, the decorated fighter pilot, now the Party's leading elected deputy, because he was both susceptible to women and a notorious glutton. When Sigrid put on her good dress and met Göring at the most expensive restaurant her budget could afford, she found him exactly as Schimpff had promised. A vain man, with a sprawling belly and a saccharine smile, he readily accepted a second invitation, this time to one of her soirées — and he reacted just as she hoped when she sat him next to the beautiful and brilliant American writer Katherine Anne Porter. Desperate for a repeat invitation so that he might "try his luck" with Porter, he readily acceded to Sigrid's suggestion that the two of them continue to meet up, for informal discussions of his Party's politics.

Göring was "worth more to me than anything else," Sigrid acknowledged.[28] By flattering his ego, by promising that the paper would retract anything he considered a lie, she managed to draw him into revealing nuggets of extraordinarily sensitive information. The relationship she built up with him was especially useful too because it was beyond her powers of deception to make a similar connection with Hitler. The first time she encountered the Nazi leader face to face was while she was sitting with Göring at the Kaiserhof Hotel. A small commotion in the lobby had signalled that Hitler had arrived for tea and cakes (his favourite meal), and Göring had lumbered to his feet to make the introduction. This could have been Sigrid's moment to ingratiate herself. But she admitted that, when Hitler leaned in to kiss her hand, his eyes staring "soulfully" into hers, she'd been unable to disguise her instinctive distaste. "I just froze up with him," she wrote, repelled as much by the "vulgar" flourish of the kiss as by the flop of hair over his pasty forehead and the forced intensity of his pale blue gaze. She knew, immediately, that Hitler had registered her recoil — "he had superb instincts for whether people responded to him" — and she was correct to predict that he would not forgive or forget. At all of their subsequent meetings, Hitler would dismiss her with the coolest of handshakes, and when she was given her first formal interview, he insisted that his personal adjutant, Rudolf Hess, remain in the room to monitor the conversation. "There was . . . a weird transference between them," Sigrid wrote. "Hess just stared at Hitler as if he were trying to hypnotize him."[29]

If Hitler remained closed to Sigrid, Göring helped ease her access to other prominent Nazis. "One can make glorious creepy stuff out of the Hitlerites," she wrote to the paper's cable editor, George Scharschug; but, however tempted she was to file sensationalist copy, she knew it was more important to understand how the Party operated.[30] She learned to get the measure of Joseph Goebbels, a dark, thin man with a limping gait, whose messianic brilliance as propaganda chief was driven by his thwarted literary ambition and his pathological hatred of Jews. She taught herself, almost, to like the Party's press officer, Ernst "Putzi" Hanfstaengle, a lanky, Harvard-educated man, whose clownish jokes and amiably earnest attempts to reconcile the demands of his bosses with those of the foreign press made Sigrid regard him as one of the more tolerable of all the Nazis — although she despised his predatory approach to women.

It was frequently astonishing to her how easily she could lead these Nazis astray, and her early coverage of the Party was supported by startlingly frank admissions of how they planned to seize absolute power for themselves and to wage a "bloody" war against the Bolsheviks and the Jews. At this early stage of their Reichstag career, Göring and his circle were too avid for publicity to be aware of the harm they were doing their Party in supplying such quotes. More experienced politicians, however, were alarmed by the antagonistically astute trend of Sigrid's reporting. In 1932, the patrician German Chancellor Franz von Papen and his self-styled Cabinet of Barons were seeking Nazi support for a political coup, by which they planned to dismantle the German constitution and restore Junker rule. When Sigrid exposed that plan, the repercussions were swift. An anonymous death threat was delivered to her home and, in the autumn, a formal ultimatum came from the Foreign Ministry that, unless she moderated her coverage, she would be deported.

Sigrid refused to be intimidated. Under recent legislation it had become possible for the state to expel any foreigner deemed threatening to Germany's reputation, but, as she wrote to McCormick, she didn't believe they would risk applying it to her; it would make a too "dramatic story and leave no doubt in anybody's mind that Germany was run by Junker government."[31] She was still assuming, however, that the country was run by men who cared about international opinion and the basic rule of law, and she had no idea how fast the political landscape could change. Although von Papen had been obliged to resign the Chancellorship, he still wielded immense political influence and he was able to persuade President Hindenburg that his best chance of remaining in power lay in facilitating an alliance between the Nazis and the Junker elite. To that end he proposed giving Hitler the post of Chancellor, arguing that, once in office, the Nazi leader would prove easy to manipulate, especially if he, von Papen, were appointed

Vice Chancellor and could pull the strings.

So, on 30 January 1933, Hitler was promoted to the second most powerful office in Germany. A number of journalists and politicians were quick to praise von Papen's shrewdness, his playing of the long game, but they had failed to take the measure of Hitler's amoral genius, and it took less than two months for the Nazi leader to demonstrate he would serve no agenda other than his own. After an arson attack had conveniently been made on the Reichstag — possibly stage-managed by Göring, but blamed on "a deranged Dutch communist" — Hitler used the ensuing panic to pass an emergency Enabling Act that would allow him to act outside the constraints of parliamentary consent and constitutional law.* It was presented to the Reichstag as a temporary strategy for "restoring calm," but, in reality, it would become Hitler's free pass to eliminate his opponents and assume total control.

Members of the communist party, the KPD, were the first to be targeted, as SA thugs were sent on an orchestrated rampage, vandalizing properties and beating and incarcerating communist leaders. Other groups came under attack, among them liberals,

---

* Göring boasted that he had orchestrated the fire, but subsequently denied it when he was questioned at the Nuremberg Trials in 1945.

intellectuals, prominent trade unionists, even priests — and the law courts and universities were purged of anyone deemed hostile to Nazi interests. On 22 March, Heinrich Himmler announced the opening of a new concentration camp at Dachau, where enemies of the Reich could be contained without trial or legal redress. In April, hundreds of thousands of "anti-German" books were burned in the centre of Berlin; by July, all political parties other than the Nazis had been disbanded and power had been transferred from the Reichstag to Hitler's own Chancellery. German democracy had been obliterated, Sigrid wrote, with "an enthusiasm and thoroughness that is breathtaking"; even Goebbels admitted that it had "been achieved much more quickly than we had dared to hope."[32]

Less than half the population actually voted for Hitler when a spring election was held to ratify his accession to Chancellor, yet, even among those who'd voted against him, there was a reluctance to confront exactly what he and his party were doing. Six million Germans were now unemployed and the twin spectres of hyperinflation and revolution loomed large; if Hitler could deliver on his promise to give every man a job, a house and a car, then most of the country was willing to give him a chance. Decent people were learning to turn away from the occasional bloodied body left lying in the street, from the screams of the occasional individual being bundled into a prison van. It was better to believe that genuine criminals were being targeted. And, in August, when the death of Hindenburg allowed Hitler to combine the posts of President and Chancellor and become absolute ruler of Germany, there was no one to stand in his way.

Germany was, de facto, a dictatorship now, and Sigrid knew what danger this spelled for the Jewish communities. Ever since she'd lived in Berlin, she'd seen how precariously they were positioned — at best tolerated, at worst scapegoated for every national failing. Germany's defeat in the 1914–18 war had been blamed on "Hebrew corruptors of the Reich," just as the economic depression of 1923 had been blamed on "profiteering Jews." During the second recession of 1931, a thousand Nazi supporters had rampaged down the Ku'damm, attacking Jewish-owned restaurants and shops. And, during the last decade, pro-Nazi publications like *Der Stürmer* had dripped anti-Semitic poison into the national psyche, publishing crude cartoons of hook-nosed bankers, of greasy, dwarfish characters threatening the modesty of Aryan girls.

Even with this backlog of violence and hate, however, the Jewish population hadn't understood how horrifically fast their world could be overturned. By July 1933, laws had been passed which restricted Jewish business, barred Jews from the legal professions and stripped all recently naturalized Jews of their citizenship rights. No less terrifying was the Nazi campaign to bully as many Jews as possible into leaving the country. SA and SS troops were sent into Jewish neighbourhoods to daub swastikas on buildings, burn down synagogues, vandalize businesses and commit random acts of violence. A number of high-profile Jews were taken to secret prisons, in basements, sheds or cinemas, where they were subjected to vile forms of punishment — forced to drink emetic quantities of castor oil or branded like animals with red-hot irons. "Racial science" was introduced to the school curriculum, teaching children how to discriminate between those of Aryan and degenerate origin; new identity documents were required to show proof of non-Jewish identity, and the very word *Juden* became an insult. By the time the Nuremberg Laws were passed in September 1935, to remove every last vestige of their civil rights, Jews were officially designated a "subhuman race."

Göring expressed no shame when Sigrid challenged him over the abhorrence of his party's policies. "You people try to understand with your heads. We must be understood with the heart," he replied, arguing that there was a romantic yearning for purity in the German soul that Americans could never comprehend.[33] Sigrid knew that Göring had a certain fastidiousness when it came to acknowledging Nazi policy, that he preferred to deal in sentimental platitudes, to let others do his dirty work. But she also understood his capacity for ruthlessness. In April 1933, he'd created the Gestapo, a nationwide secret police force that was designed to keep watch on every German citizen and to keep tabs on Göring's own political rivals. The foreign press was not exempt from surveillance, certainly not Sigrid, and, during the last year, she'd become accustomed to the flat, sinister click of her phone line being tapped; to the car that shadowed every taxi she took; to the spying vigilance of her cleaner. She knew that her letters were opened, that a dossier had been assembled on her private and professional life, and she was working on the assumption that someone in her office had been co-opted as a Party informant. In December, when she wanted to write "a few uncensored notes" to Colonel McCormick, she had to ask a friend who was travelling outside Germany to post the letter on her behalf.[34]

The muzzling of the media had begun almost immediately when the Nazis took power. As Minister of Propaganda, Goebbels had made his first moves on the domestic press, replacing serious journalists with men whom Sigrid scornfully described as "low ranking state officials," under orders to regurgitate the Party's own communiqués.[35] The foreign correspondents could not be interfered with so directly, but they too were subjected to a campaign of subtle and not so subtle harassment. Daily press briefings were now delivered exclusively in German, making it difficult for all but the most fluent to follow; they were also issued by two entirely separate bodies — the Foreign Office (which had its own chief of foreign press) and Goebbels' Ministry of Propaganda and Public Enlightenment, a system that deliberately hampered journalists in the sourcing and checking of facts. Meanwhile, everything they did publish was scanned by an army of minor officials, checking for evidence of what Goebbels described as "editorializing." Threats were issued to those whose commentary was deemed unacceptable: in 1933, two of the most outspoken Americans, Hubert Knickerbocker and Edgar Mowrer, were ordered to leave Berlin, and, early in 1934, the Czech reporter Ludwig Popper was incarcerated in Columbia House, an informal SA prison, which, as Sigrid reported, was "one of the best known beating up quarters in town."[36] Even the revered Dorothy Thompson was not immune. In August 1934, she returned to Germany after an absence of three years and, when she reported with incautious disgust on the changes she observed, she was given forty-eight hours to leave the country voluntarily, or else face deportation by the police.

Sigrid — her animosity forgotten — filed a blistering response to Thompson's expulsion, but she rightly predicted that it would be followed by increased difficulties for the resident press corps. Her own reporting on the regime was now assisted by two "very, very good" informants, a brilliant Munich doctor named Johannes Schmitt, who treated a number of very high-profile Nazi patients, and Schmitt's "great friend" General von Hammerstein, one of a small but courageous number of military officers opposed to Hitler's methods and agenda.[37] So accurate and so damaging were some of her exposés that Sigrid had not only been hauled up for reprimand, but had begun to experience mysterious "glitches" in the cabling of her dispatches. At first she hadn't been unduly alarmed. She still had powerful friends in Berlin, not least the American ambassador William Dodd, and she believed that Goebbels had too high a regard for her Chicago publisher to risk an overt attack. McCormick's admiration for the Nazis hadn't simply been based on their military parades. Like many Western businessmen, he admired their political nerve in crushing the communists and trade unionists, their efficiency in force-starting the economy. Even though the Colonel gave Sigrid space to criticize the regime, he ensured that the *Tri-*

bune's overall coverage remained balanced, either by burying the most hostile of Sigrid's articles deep in the paper, or by offsetting them with more positive editorials of his own.

This even-handed stance was valuable to the Nazis, and it offered Sigrid some protection. But, by the autumn of 1934, Goebbels had lost patience with her dangerously well-informed reports. Sigrid came out of his office one day with "threats of expulsion sizzling around my ears," simply because the phone operator transcribing her copy had misheard a word and had made the tone of her article more critical than she had intended.*[38] The time had come for a more cautious strategy; from this point on, whenever she wanted to publish her most damning exposés, Sigrid would not only file her copy outside Germany, but would further thwart surveillance by redacting her own name and falsifying the dateline (which gave the time and location of filing).

There were others, of course, who pushed hard against the regime. Frederick Birchall of

* The operator was at the Press Wireless Centre in Paris, to which most foreign correspondents wired their reports, in order to have them transmitted on to their relevant desks. She had simply heard the word "cowardly" as "comradely," a mistake that implied Sigrid had approved of the alleged assassination of a German officer.

the *New York Times* spoke for many when he wrote, "No decent man can sit . . . close to this thing for long without becoming in a sense a crusader for freedom, decency and the rights of the weak"; Norman Ebbutt of the London *Times* and the American broadcaster William Shirer were among the most informed and outspoken critics in Berlin, while a young British journalist, Elizabeth Wiskemann, made regular investigatory trips to Germany until she was arrested by the SS and warned never to return.[39] For Sigrid, though, the secret fact of her Jewishness made her attacks on the Nazis both more personal and more perilous.

Had Goebbels, Göring, or even McCormick discovered that secret, it's probable she would no longer have been able to function as bureau chief; it's even possible that her life might have been in danger. But Sigrid was also pressing her luck because she was now working on the fringes of the Berlin underground, giving assistance to the increasing number of Jews who were trying to get out of Germany. Some kind of modesty kept her from elaborating on the exact nature of this work, but much of it seemed to centre on helping Jews to sell or smuggle their goods and properties before they departed. Even though the Nazis were pressuring them to leave, officials were charging a very high price for their exit papers and, in some cases, were using the Reich Flight Tax — imposed during the 1931 depression — to justify seizure of their assets before they left. "I swindled a good deal of stuff out of Germany for them," Sigrid acknowledged, hinting that she'd made use of her extensive contacts to source sympathetic purchasers and had even bought one family's library with her own money.[40]

More clandestinely still, Sigrid was also working on behalf of individual community leaders — rabbis, lawyers and intellectuals — whom the regime wanted to arrest. She was part of a group who found them safe hiding places, but she was also helping to divert a small number of official exit permits their way; in fact, according to one of her friends, Ruth Steinkraus Cohen, some of these permits may, amazingly, have come through Göring.

Compared to many of his fellow Nazis, Göring was not a hardened racial zealot. Before the Party came to power, he'd enjoyed profitable relations with a select group of Jewish businessmen and artists, and Cohen's suggestion that he might have been helping some of those individuals to either get out of Germany or disguise their racial identity was based on his frequent boast that he had it in his power to "decide" who was Jewish and who was not.[41] If Cohen was correct, Göring was presumably charging a high price for his services, but whatever opportunistic quid pro quo he'd arranged with Sigrid, it was not one he could sustain for long. By the spring of 1935, Göring had beaten off his rivals to become a Nazi potentate, second only to Hitler. And, to safeguard his position, he not only had to dissociate himself from Sigrid, he ideally had to get her out of the way.

One afternoon in April, Sigrid was working in her office when Hedwig phoned to say that a stranger had delivered a sealed envelope to their apartment, marked for Fräulein Schultz's "urgent attention." Sigrid had heard of attempts to plant incriminating documents on Party enemies and, racing back home, she discovered that the contents of the envelope were exactly as she feared. They were plans for an aeroplane engine — possession of which, she wrote, "would have finished me"[42] — and she barely had time to burn the offending papers before she saw three men approaching her building. Two of them she recognized as Gestapo agents, and, knowing that her next actions would be critical, she confronted the trio in her most assertively patrician German, assuring them that they would find nothing of interest in her apartment, and that she would be going directly to the American ambassador to report this attempted breach of her rights.

The agents were left standing as Sigrid sailed off in a taxi, and had she been more cautious, she would have let the matter rest.

But she could never stand to be bullied — even as a tiny child in Chicago, her father had caught her shouting furiously at a boy who had tried to scare her with his parents' axe. Convinced, now, that Göring had attempted to frame her, Sigrid was determined to expose him in public, and she chose to do so at a lunch held by the Foreign Press Association, on 2 May, to celebrate Göring's marriage to the pretty, plump and amiable actress, Emmy Sonnemann. Sigrid, seated at one end of the long table, had remained silent as all of her colleagues had proffered their good wishes. She'd said nothing as Göring, in a filthily ungrateful temper, had used the occasion to castigate the assembled journalists for the lies which he claimed they continued to peddle. He'd been an intimidating presence, his meaty paws clenched into fists and his bulky chest puffed up with rage. But when he'd eventually run out of words, Sigrid was ready with her own attack, and, in a voice so deceptively casual she might, according to one witness, have been "exchanging chitchat about the opera," she described to the room how the Gestapo had attempted to incriminate her. It had been a clear abuse of power, she stated, and she continued to argue her case even as Göring began pounding on the table and letting fly a hysterical volley of abuse, calling her a "dragon woman," a female gangster from "the crime ridden city of Chicago," a privileged guest of Germany who'd never attempted "to show proper respect."[43]

Later, Sigrid would swear she'd been as proud of her intervention as if she "had scored a scoop and netted gratifying headlines."[44] It resulted in a six-month moratorium on press intimidation, and she was able to use that relative freedom to report on the Nazis' escalating persecution of Jews and on Hitler's increasingly arrogant disregard of world opinion. This was the period when the regime began its open flouting of the Versailles treaty, first speeding up its illicit programme of rearmament and then, in March 1936, sending in troops to reoccupy the Rhineland — the wealthy, westernmost area of Germany, which, in 1919, had been placed under Allied control. Sigrid and her colleagues had been shocked by the gall of this second contravention; Hitler himself had admitted it was the gamble of his career. Yet any hopes they'd had that the Nazis had overreached, that France and Britain must be galvanized to a military response, were dashed. Memories of the 1914–18 war were still too painful for the western democracies to willingly contemplate force, and economic links with the newly dynamic Germany were too profitable to risk. The reoccupation of the Rhineland was referred to the League of Nations, where the matter was kicked around the council chamber, endlessly but uselessly debated.

"Hitler has got away with it!" wrote Bill Shirer grimly in his diary; and, although he accused France and Britain of venality, cowardice and inertia, he knew as well as Sigrid how adept Hitler had become at the diplomatic lie.[45] When challenged over Germany's illegal rearmament, he would insist, with righteous sincerity, that he only wanted his country to play a proper role in "a collective system for safeguarding European peace." When challenged over the Rhineland, he would claim that he was taking only what was German by rights, and had no designs on any additional territory. In the summer of 1936, when Berlin was host to the Olympic Games, the entire city was drafted into that diplomatic lie: anti-Jewish graffiti was scrubbed off the buildings, anti-Jewish notices removed, and the SA thugs were kept on an unusually tight leash.

As soon as the foreign dignitaries had left, however, the violence and the intimidation returned. When Sigrid was approached by a man who claimed to be an American university lecturer, who wanted to know her opinion on whether Hitler intended to provoke a European war, she rightly guessed he was a Nazi agent, attempting to trap her into incriminating statements. Mindful of the sharp rise in mysterious accidents in Berlin, she avoided travelling by car and began to vary the routes that she walked home at night. And as threats against the foreign press intensified, she realized that she had to take more extreme measures to protect herself. The strategy of redacting her byline had been of limited use — the style and accuracy of her articles had pointed too obviously to her — and she decided now to armour herself with an alias, an invented alter ego, to whom she could attribute her most damning copy.*

"I want to give our readers all the dope there is but am perfectly willing to hide behind somebody's name or coat," Sigrid explained to Scharschug, and, with the paper's permission, she launched the career of a new "roving correspondent": a man named John Dickson, who was based in Paris and, according to a carefully placed announcement in the *Tribune,* was "specially trained" to obtain facts about the Nazis that were inaccessible to the press in Berlin.[46] Sigrid had chosen the surname as an oblique tribute to Dick Little, and in honour of her former mentor and chief, the very first article she wrote as John Dickson was also one of

* She wasn't the only journalist to try this strategy; the *New York Times* correspondent also deployed it from time to time, his own position uniquely vulnerable because his paper was owned by a Jewish publisher.

the most incendiary of her career. Published on 1 November 1936, and headlined "Democracy Surrenders: Dictatorship Crushes Freedom in Germany," it analysed the stages by which the Nazi inner circle had consolidated their power, starting with the "night of the long knives" in June 1934 when the Party had purged itself of dissenting voices, and tracing the sophisticated advance of surveillance, interrogation and torture which had been used to terrorize the rest of the nation.

"Even the rumour of mysterious disappearances is enough to enforce the silence desired by the men in power," wrote Sigrid, and, relishing the shockwaves her article created, she remained stubbornly on the attack, using her new alias to write about the card-index system by which the Reich kept tabs on the employment history, political attitudes and racial background of all its citizens, and about the schools and youth groups in which Hitler was grooming his new generation of Nazis. To strengthen the fiction of Dickson's existence, Sigrid created a careful paper trail, fabricating a correspondence, and making casually disingenuous references to him in her diary: "Trib. front page by that fellow Dickson . . . wonder who he is." She would not even admit the subterfuge to her colleagues and friends, and, although many of them guessed the truth, they understood it was safer not to speak of it.[47]

But there were moments when Sigrid wondered if she and Dickson were having much effect, and whether the daily subterfuges and the constant prickle of apprehension were a price worth paying. It was hard not to feel isolated in what Shirer had dubbed "Hysterical Nazi Land"; hard not to wonder why the rest of the world was not raising its voice against Hitler's criminal policies at home, nor showing more concern for his ambitions abroad.[48] To Sigrid, it was obvious that the German war machine was being geared up for much larger targets than the Rhineland. Even if she hadn't had this confirmed by General von Hammerstein, her military source, Hitler himself had written openly about his mission to subdue Eastern Europe, the Balkans, Ukraine, even France under the yoke of his Thousand Year Reich.[49] It was astonishing to Sigrid that the diplomats and politicians who nodded along to all of Hitler's pieties about "international cooperation" seemed ignorant of the passages in *Mein Kampf* where he dismissed pacifism as the "philosophy of weaklings," and advocated "total war" against all of Germany's enemies.* She'd already predicted privately to McCormick that, once Hitler's army was up

* Even though Hitler issued an official ban on foreign translation, numerous private translations were in circulation.

to strength, he would begin his "great push eastwards." Yet, agonizingly, even with her Dickson alias, this was not a fact that she was free to publish.

History would bear Sigrid out. But, accurate though her predictions were, she failed to anticipate that the first significant rupture to European peace would come not from Hitler, but from the right-wing Spanish general, Francisco Franco, when he launched his coup against Spain's newly elected Popular Front government. By the autumn of 1936, that coup had swelled into an international and ideological war. The army of the Spanish Republic — the Loyalists — was reinforced by a brigade of foreign volunteers, many of them civilian writers, intellectuals and socialists, who believed they were fighting for freedom and democracy. Franco's Nationalists, or Insurgents, were supported by the Catholic Church, by rich landowners and by a romantically conservative core of Hispanophiles. And, despite an internationally agreed neutrality pact, both sides were also supported by foreign governments, with Soviet Russia sending covert assistance to the Loyalists, while Mussolini and Hitler jointly supplied Franco with troops, guns and planes.

Sigrid wrote what she dared about the trafficking of German military aid to Franco, describing how Luftwaffe pilots were officially "demobbed" so that they could cross into

Spain on tourist visas. Yet it was impossible to publish what most concerned her, which was the near-certainty that Hitler was using Franco's war as a testing ground for his own armoury of weapons, that he was gauging their destructive potential before turning them elsewhere. To even hint that the conflict in Spain might be a prologue to Hitler's "total war" was to risk everything. Trapped as she was within the tentacles of Nazi surveillance, Sigrid had to trust that others would understand where Germany was heading, and that others would report the danger on her behalf.

CHAPTER TWO: MADRID, 1937

"The best thing I have
ever seen or lived through"
MARTHA GELLHORN[1]

"We knew, we just knew that Spain was the place to stop fascism. It was one of those moments in history when there was no doubt."[2] During the spring of 1937, Martha Gellhorn was in Madrid, learning how to write about war. Sitting in her unheated hotel room, she was searching for the right voice with which to articulate the glory and gravity of this turning point in history — a point at which it was still possible to believe the Loyalists could triumph over Franco. She was trying to write sentences that could hold the horror of a small boy dying in his grandmother's arms; the stoicism of young Spanish soldiers, cold and hungry at the front. She was trying to understand the speed with which war could become a way of life — violent, heroic and staggeringly normal. She was also examining the effects of sharing this most intense experience with Ernest Hemingway, the writer whose photograph she'd had pinned to the wall of her college bedroom, on whose prose she'd tried to model her writing, and who was now, in Spain, her lover.

The two of them had met three months earlier, in a world very far from both embattled Madrid and Nazi Berlin. Martha had been vacationing in the Florida Keys with her mother, Edna, and her brother Alfred, and the trio had sought shade from the unseasonably hot December sun in Sloppy Joe's, a sleepy local bar with a fierce brand of rum and a sawdust-covered floor. At the far end of the counter, a large grizzled man had been reading his mail, dressed like a fisherman in a pair of "somewhat soiled white shorts."[3] It was Hemingway, and, once Martha had introduced herself, she'd been entranced by the ease with which he'd insisted that she and her family sit and drink with him.

Hemingway had struck Martha, then, as "an odd bird, a marvellous story teller, very loveable and full of fire."[4] Although he was only nine years her senior, his torso was running slightly to fat, his features were becoming blurred by drink, and she was far more attracted to an athletic Swede with whom she'd just been flirting on the beach. But Ernest had already set his sights on Martha. At twenty-seven, she was a golden girl —

made beautiful by the expressive quickness of her face, and by the burnish of her long, tanned legs and tawny hair. She was also a woman of interestingly vehement moral certainties, with such a witty ironic lash to her humour that by the end of the evening, he'd vowed to have her.

It took Ernest more than the three days he'd bet himself to seduce Martha — a proposition that was complicated by the fact that he was living at home with his wife Pauline and two young sons. But, for two weeks, he made himself her attentive companion, talking about life, love and literature, the novel Martha was writing and, above all, about Spain. Ernest had always loved the Spanish, and, outraged by Franco's insurgency, he was already planning to get himself out to the Loyalist stronghold of Madrid to report on the war for the North American Newspaper Alliance (NANA), and to assist on a pro-Loyalist propaganda film, *The Spanish Earth.*

He believed it was his moral duty to bear witness to this conflict, yet he also craved the adventure, for cushioned within the elegant life that Pauline had made for him, he'd begun to fear that his imagination and his prose were running to middle-aged slack. Spain could rekindle the fire in his belly, and the more enthusiastically he spoke about his plan to Martha, the more eager she was to become part of it. Like many of her generation, she'd been an instinctive pacifist, committed to the hopeful, humane principles enshrined within the League of Nations. But she'd travelled sufficiently widely through Europe to understand the fascist threat, and, knowing how many other writers were making the pilgrimage to Spain, she'd already wondered how she might join them. When Ernest offered to pave her way to Madrid, she barely hesitated, even though she guessed she would likely end up there as his lover.

Guiltlessly, Martha chose to ignore the inconvenience of Hemingway's marriage. "We are conspirators and I have personally got myself a beard and dark glasses," she wrote with half-mocking complicity, after she'd left Florida to prepare for her journey.[5] It seemed to her that history was approaching a crisis and that it was both her right and her duty to experience it to the full, whatever moral lines she might have to cross: "time is getting shorter and shorter," she told herself, "one has to work all day and all night . . . and love as many people as one can find around and do all this terribly fast."[6]

The route to Spain would not be simple, though. Strict controls had been imposed on the border to slow the incoming flood of foreign volunteers, and a formal letter of accreditation was required to confirm that Martha was not a combatant but a journalist.

Since she spoke no Spanish and was entirely ignorant of military matters, she had no idea how to get such a letter — "I believed that all one did about a war was go to it as a gesture of solidarity and get killed or survive if lucky until it was over."[7] But she had a friendly contact at *Collier's* — a magazine with a wide readership and an eclectic coverage of world affairs — and, although he, Kyle Crichton, could promise nothing beyond a willingness to read whatever she submitted, he wrote a letter which named Martha, somewhat vaguely, as *Collier's* "Special Correspondent in Spain." By early March, she was ready to leave: "I am going to Spain with the boys," she wrote jubilantly to a friend. "I don't know who the boys are but I am going with them."[8]

It took unusual confidence for Martha to launch herself at a world so alien from everything she'd known, but, like Sigrid, she'd been raised with high expectations. Born on 8 November 1908, she was the only girl among three siblings, adored by her mother and held to exacting intellectual and moral standards by her father. Both of her parents were progressively minded: Edna Gellhorn was a college-educated suffragette, while George Gellhorn was an eminent obstetrician and professor of medicine. And Martha's early childhood, growing up in a prosperous, tree-lined neighbourhood of St.

Louis, was happy. George gave a penny to the child who made him laugh the loudest when telling the story of their day, and it was nearly always Martha, impish and clever, who won. Later, as an awkwardly tall and rebellious teenager, she would chafe against her role as the precocious, cherished daughter, but she would not fundamentally doubt herself. When she spent the summer of her seventeenth year in France, smoked her first cigarette, kissed a boy and discussed philosophy with a group of Oxford students, Martha knew for certain that a luminous future awaited her, somewhere far from St. Louis.

She was high-minded enough to believe she would have to work at that future: it was her theory that "you can do anything you like if you are willing to pay the full price for it."[9] After spending two reluctant years at Bryn Mawr College, largely to please her parents, she moved to New York in the summer of 1929 to earn her own money and experience her own life. The work was mundane — mostly drudge-reporting for the *Albany Times Union* — and there were moments, fending off the advances of middle-aged journalists, when the life of the literary free spirit seemed very distant. But, by early 1930, Martha had saved enough money to sail to Paris, where she planned to write her first novel. With her typewriter in her suitcase, and just seventy-five dollars in her purse, she felt exhilarated, even purified as she watched the American coastline recede. "I knew now that I was free," she wrote. "This was my show, my show."[10]

It was, inevitably, much harder to stage that show than she'd hoped. Martha looked very young and very provincial in her tweed skirt and college coat; she was laughed out of the *New York Times* bureau when she applied for a job and the work she eventually found as a copy taker with the United Press news agency was uninspiring. But she was only twenty-one, and, making friends with other aspiring writers, breathing in the bohemian air of Left Bank Paris, she still believed it was possible to "go everywhere and see everything and . . . write my way."[11] By the middle of the summer, she'd not only plotted the draft of her first novel but had embarked on her first love affair.

Bertrand de Jouvenal was a successful journalist — a slender, handsome, nervously energetic man, who seemed to Martha the embodiment of European sophistication. His father was editor of *Le Matin* and his stepmother was the celebrated novelist Colette — a fact all the more dizzying to Martha because Bertrand had been seduced by Colette when he was a boy of just sixteen. Even though Martha agonized when Bertrand first pressured her to make love — he was married and she was bound more tightly to her

father's morality than she cared to admit —
to be in France and to be losing her virginity
to a brilliant intellectual made her feel like
the heroine of a modern novel.

But love and sex were not exactly as Martha had imagined. She was an American
idealist, with a core of sturdy good sense, and
there was something about Bertrand's sensu-
ality and his very Parisian finesse that offended her. She was dismayed, too, to discover that his lovemaking left her cold,
stranded in his bed like a "caught fish."[12]
Naive as she was, Martha assumed the fault
must be hers, that she'd formed unrealistic
expectations of sex or that she suffered from
some physical defect which made her "not
quite like a woman."[13] Her confidence in
running her "own show" was starting to
falter, and in December, when she discovered
that she was pregnant, it collapsed. Despairing melodramatically that she "did not have
whatever it took to live," she believed she had
no option but to return home, to get an abortion and put Paris and Bertrand behind her.[14]

But home felt like failure, and when Bertrand followed her out to St. Louis, swearing
that he would get a divorce if she would only
come back to him, Martha eventually agreed.
George Gellhorn was harsh in his disapproval: "There are two kinds of women,"
he said, "and you are the other kind."[15] Martha, however, aspired to be the kind of

woman whose body and morals were her own, and, returning to Paris as Bertrand's mistress, she was resolved to liberate herself, fully, from her father's stern influence.

Now that she and Bertrand were living openly together, she was able to go with him to restaurants and theatres, to meet his Parisian friends. She took a new job, as assistant to the fashion editor of *Vogue,* and was given a couture wardrobe to wear, from Schiaparelli and Chanel. Never had Martha felt so elegantly expensive; yet, even in the middle of this pampered existence, she remained focused on her writing. Her debut novel, *What Mad Pursuit,* was now in its final draft and she was editing herself with a passionate scrupulousness, attempting to write only "straight clear sentences" and suppress what she knew to be her weakness for "the beautiful mellow phrase and the carefully chosen strange words."[16] Journalism, too, was becoming more important to her. Back in October 1930, Martha had been commissioned by the *St. Louis Post-Dispatch* to write about a group of women who'd risen to prominence within the League of Nations, and the period she'd spent in Geneva, following the League's debates and mixing with the foreign press corps, had been a revelation. Reporters here were a higher breed than the hacks at the *Albany Times Union,* they were writing about issues of international importance, they had the power to shape public opinion, and it dawned on Martha that the writing of really fine journalism could be as profound an endeavour as fiction. From that point on, she worked hard on her own portfolio, running around Paris like a "crazed squirrel" to pitch articles for American publications and, at Bertrand's suggestion, going to London in 1933 to cover the World Economic Conference.

Under Bertrand's influence, too, Martha was attempting to further her political education. She'd always considered herself a "reforming liberal," unquestioningly committed to a just society and unquestionably opposed to war. Bertrand, however, lived and breathed politics with an academic rigour that made her own ideas feel like "intellectual jelly."[17] He was part of a clever, bookish, pacifist group in Paris who believed that the political divisions in Europe could be healed through bonds of mutual assistance and understanding. And so impressed was Martha by their conviction that, when the group planned a visit to Berlin, to seek out kindred spirits and find converts to their cause, she signed up as an enthusiastic participant.

Berlin, however, would seed the beginnings of Martha's disillusionment, both with Bertrand and his politics. It was January 1934, and while the young, blond and very clean-cut Germans who took charge of the group disclaimed all connection with the Nazi regime, they were clearly members of the Hitler Youth movement. During the day, when they escorted the Parisians around model factories and schools, they spoke with pre-scripted enthusiasm about the miracle of Hitler's new Germany; at night, after several tankards of beer, they let rip with anthems to the sacred Fatherland.

Martha was appalled, contemptuously judging them to have only "one parrot brain" between them.[18] But, while Bertrand, too, was shaken by aspects of the Berlin visit, he believed it was better to establish contact with Hitler's Germany than simply condemn, and, once back in Paris, he devoted himself to the launch of a new magazine, *La Lutte des Jeunes,* which would promote his vision of an enlightened, unified Europe. Martha was still sufficiently loyal to assist with the launch, but she had grave doubts about the magazine's value, and because she resented the time it took from her own work, she inevitably began to resent Bertrand. As a lover he now seemed cloyingly dependent, demanding too much of her attention, and Martha, who needed, so much, to feel in charge of her own show, began to regard him as an intolerable constraint. "He is so weak that it is like cancer," she admitted privately to a friend, "it is an incurable and a killing sickness."[19] Even now she couldn't summon the courage to end the affair, and finally it was Bertrand who took the initiative. He loved Martha deeply — for the sharpness of her intelligence and the long-boned elegance of her body — yet he could see that he was making her miserable. "Take this chance, little one. Escape," he wrote to her, with fatalistic tenderness, and, by October 1934, Martha had returned home to America.[20]

Later, in a rush of corrosive self-knowledge, she would worry that there was something implacable and aloof in her own nature that made it impossible for her to fall unconditionally in love. "[I] HATE people unless they are free of me. I want nothing to do with anyone except my superiors. I have a real physical loathing of people who are morally weak. A man is no use to me, unless he can live without me."[21] At the time, however, escape from Bertrand had felt purely liberating. "What an eagerness and energy I have to live," she wrote joyfully in her diary, and, within a month of her return to America, she'd found a political cause of her own to which she believed she could whole-heartedly commit.[22]

When Franklin D. Roosevelt had been elected President in March 1933, it was on a ticket to bring America back from the brink of social and economic collapse. The stock-market crash of 1929 had not only sent shock waves around the world, it had plunged America into a prolonged depression. With seventeen million workers unemployed and many more facing abject poverty, Roosevelt had created a new body, the Federal Emergency Relief Administration, to distribute welfare among the nation's neediest. It was an unprecedented move in American politics, and Martha, deeply impressed by its humanitarian potential, applied to join the team of writers who'd been hired by FERA's director, Harry Hopkins, to report on the problems facing individual communities. Grandly assuring Hopkins that she was "vastly experienced and very well known in Europe," Martha was accepted onto the team,[23] and, packing her typewriter and her warmest Parisian cast-offs, she left for her designated tour of New England, the Carolinas and other devastated regions.

She had no idea how bleak it would be. All her life, Martha had been taught to care about injustice, yet she'd never been exposed to the stink and grind of actual poverty; as the bus drove her through landscapes that were "ugly, horribly ugly . . . spread with the haphazard homes of a shifting unrooted grey people," she encountered squalor beyond her imagination.[24] She talked to families who were squeezed together in filthy shacks, their children rickety with hunger; she saw mill girls sagging with exhaustion, proud working men in beggars' rags, and she listened to teachers, doctors and union organizers explain how hard it was to defend their sinking communities from the greed of unprincipled bosses and the extortion of loan sharks.

The more she saw, the more guilty Martha felt about her own privileged good fortune, but the more disillusioned she became, too, about FERA's ability to help. In Idaho, she was so affected by the stories of some brutally exploited and underpaid workers, she rashly suggested they draw attention to their plight by smashing the windows of their local FERA office. That act of mild sedition got Martha fired from Hopkins's programme. Yet, even though she was glad to be done with it, the information she'd gathered was already transforming, in her mind, into material for a book and, early in 1935, she began work on *The Trouble I've Seen,* a quartet of stories extrapolated from the lives she'd observed and from the people she'd interviewed.

The most harrowing of them all centred on a child prostitute named Ruby, a guileless eleven-year-old who'd been persuaded to turn tricks by the older girls in her neighbourhood, who'd promised her that sex "only hurt the first time really" and could earn her enough money to buy the roller skates for which she'd always longed. Yet, painful though these stories were to write, they were burning in Martha's imagination and they came faster, more easily than any of her more autobiographical fiction. When they were eventually published, in September 1936, they were championed by the First Lady, Eleanor Roosevelt — an old acquaintance of Edna Gellhorn's who'd latterly become Martha's own particular friend and confidante — and they were acclaimed as some of the most powerful writing to have emerged from the Great Depression.

Several reviewers expressed surprise that so young (and attractive) a woman could have handled such challenging material with such trenchant clarity. The English novelist Graham Greene pronounced it "quite amazing" that Martha had displayed none of the usual "female vices" of sentimentality and that her "masculine characters [were] presented as convincingly as her female."[25] Martha was irritated by Greene's facile chauvinism, irritated even more by the fuss that was made of her youth and her sex: "it's awful when women [writers] go feminine publicly," she complained to Eleanor Roosevelt.[26] But she was entranced by the success of her stories and she was profoundly grateful that her father had been able to read them, in manuscript form, just before he died.

George Gellhorn had been unsparing of Martha's debut novel. What she had prized as a sophisticated modern narrative of adultery, drink and venereal disease, he had dismissed as evidence of her worst failings, her inability to apply herself to serious matters, her belief that she could get by on her "precocious" charm — "her yellow hair and lively spicy conversation."[27] But *The Trouble I've Seen* had gained his respect and — aside from the story about Ruby, which he found too agonizing to read — he'd sped through the rest "with breathless interest." That acknowledgement from her father was precious to Martha and it allowed her to make some kind of peace with him before he died, late in 1935, from a heart attack.

Having expended so much creative energy and anger on her Depression stories, Martha sagged in the months that followed. She yearned to write "great heavy swooping things, to throw terror and glory into the mind," but had no idea what her next subject might be.[28] Instead, she went travelling, and, having spent the early summer of 1936 in London, gently rebuffing the venerable but incorrigibly lustful novelist H. G. Wells, she went to Paris to seek a reconciliation with Bertrand. The city itself felt alien to her though, for, despite the recent election of France's first socialist Prime Minister, Léon Blum, the loudest voices seemed to be those of the "greedy rich" and the crypto-fascists who were calling for their own Hitler, to rid them of their own Bolsheviks and Jews. Fascism was casting its dark spell on the City of Lights and Martha considered it her duty to revisit Nazi Germany, and investigate more deeply. Travelling on her own to Stuttgart and Munich, she could see the ugliness of the Reich in plain view, and, observing the graffiti and the hateful newspaper headlines, Martha felt a sudden sickening consciousness of her own racial ancestry. George Gellhorn's side of the family were Jewish, and while that was something to which she'd previously paid little attention, she was now aware of what it could have meant if she'd been born and raised here, in Germany. Europe seemed very sick to Martha, and, in early December, when she sailed back to America, she believed she was done with it.

Then she met Hemingway, and Europe was very far from over. By 24 March 1937, Martha was trudging across the Spanish border, hugging herself against flurries of unseasonal snow. She'd got rid of her bulkier luggage in Paris, entrusting it to Ernest's friend and fixer, an American bullfighter named Sidney Franklin, who'd also helped arrange her onward visa. But she'd resisted any suggestion that Franklin travel with her. It felt necessary to Martha that she make her own way into Spain, that she embark on her adventure alone and in the raw; and she knew her instincts were correct when she caught a slow, cold train to Barcelona, and her carriage was invaded by six Loyalist recruits, excited fervent young men who sang their revolutionary songs to her and shared out their modest military rations of "garlic sausage and bread made of powdered stone."

Barcelona itself was "bright with sun" and revolution, and already, Martha had lost her heart to Republican Spain. She had no idea yet of the factional violence that was destroying it from within, as Kremlin-backed communists sought to purge the Loyalist army of all those anarchists, Trotskyists or merely mild liberal moderates whom they deemed "enemies of the people." All Martha saw was a carnival of youthful conviction, the red Republican banners that rippled from every building in Barcelona, the throngs of animated men and women who strolled down Las Ramblas, all of them kitted out in workers' berets and overalls, their rifles hefted nonchalantly across their shoulders.[29]

"It is the loveliest atmosphere going," she wrote, and her euphoria persisted as she hitched a ride south in a munitions truck and met up with Sidney Franklin in Valencia.[30] Ernest had arranged for the two of them to be driven to Madrid in a Republican press car, and, even though Franklin proved to be a silent, sullen companion — loyal to Pauline, he disapproved of Martha's presence — the austere beauty of the La Mancha landscape and the crystalline purity of the light were intoxicating compensation. Spain was like coming home, she thought, but to a place that "you hoped would exist but were never quite sure." Occasionally, Martha heard the distant thunder of artillery fire, and her heart raced every time she was asked to show her improvised letter of authorization to checkpoint guards. But the war itself remained largely abstract, and it was only when the car drew close to the outskirts of Madrid that she sensed the enormity of what lay ahead.

The city had endured a long winter of siege, pounded by German bombers and bombarded by Nationalist shells, and it looked to her now like a "battlefield waiting in the dark."[31] As the car inched a precarious route through cratered streets, and Martha craned to stare at the bomb-gutted buildings rearing against the sky, she felt suddenly anxious for Hemingway. He'd told her they would both be staying at the Hotel Florida, along with the rest of the foreign press, but, when she reached the hotel, a building whose marble and wrought-iron décor had clearly seen better days, Ernest was nowhere to be found. Eventually, she located him in the basement restaurant of the Gran Vía Hotel, sitting at a long trestle table and immersed in boozy conversation with an American airman. But, even now, it was very far from the reunion she'd imagined. Rather than embracing her, congratulating her on her safe arrival, Ernest had simply called out with a lordly casualness, "I knew you'd get here daughter, because I fixed it up so you could."[32]

Martha flinched. She'd become accustomed to "daughter" — it was the term Ernest used for all attractive young women — but she minded very much his easy dismissal of her own initiative in getting to Spain. She tried to excuse his arrogance as a "foible of genius," but later that night it took a far more disconcerting turn. Just before dawn, Martha was jerked awake by a terrifying noise: a series of high crescent screams and convulsive blasts, which she knew must be enemy shells. She could hear loud footsteps clattering down the stairs, her fellow guests seeking shelter in the lobby, but, when she tried to yank open her door, it would not budge. Bewildered and very much afraid, she called for help and as her room bucked and rattled from nearby explosions, it seemed like hours before anyone came. Her immediate instinct, then, was to check on Ernest's safety, but, to her confusion, she discovered him sitting calmly in his room, playing poker, and cheerfully ready to admit that it was he who'd locked her in. The Florida was lousy with pimps, drunks and whores, he said, and, given that Martha's bedroom was at the back of the building, he'd decided she would face far less danger from enemy shells than she would from some inebriated punter.

Ernest's presumption was astonishing: "I should have known at that moment what doom was," she later acknowledged.[33] Out in Madrid, she would notice other small signs of danger — the unattractive swagger with which he claimed precedence over the rest of the press corps, the exaggerated air of expertise with which he discussed strategy with Loyalist officers. But Martha was new to this world, new to the war, and it was easier to concentrate only on the generosity with which Ernest was subsidizing her expenses (NANA was paying him up to $1,000 per dispatch) and on the generous care he was taking with her education as a war correspondent.

It was Ernest who held Martha steady when she witnessed her first casualty — a man so violently decapitated by an exploding shell that his blood sprayed hot and red over the street outside their hotel. "It wasn't you, or anyone you know," he reminded her tenderly, warning her that she could not allow herself to mind about every death.[34] It was Ernest who tutored Martha in the language of weapons, ordnance and military rankings; he who introduced her to the people who mattered — the Loyalist officers and Republican press censors, the most experienced of the correspondents. And it was, most crucially, through Ernest's advice that she found her own way of writing about the war itself.

■ ■ ■ ■

When Martha first arrived in Madrid, she was so overwhelmed by the newness of it all, she could not imagine committing her experiences to paper. War had long become a way of life in the city; it was actually possible to take a tram to the nearest front, constructed out of what had recently been the university quarter. Early on in the siege, the Loyalists had dug out a maze of defensive trenches from which they were able to fire at the Nationalists on the opposite side of the river, and on Martha's first tour of "University City," she was startled by the traces of its former life — abandoned textbooks piled into gunners' nests, and lecture-room doors used to shore up the mud of the trench walls.

It felt relatively safe to visit this front, aside from the blood-chilling seconds it took to sprint from the final tram stop to the entrance of the trenches, bent double to avoid enemy bullets. However, Martha was exposed to far greater risks when she drove with Ernest to the distant mountain fronts, and their jeep came under fire. And she was far more conscious of actual death and destruction when she toured the military hospital and saw soldiers whose faces were raw and ridged with scar tissue, whose limbs had been sawn down to bandaged stumps.

Martha strove to conceal her horror when she talked to the injured men, just as she strove to suppress her fear when Madrid was shelled. But, while she was learning how to pass herself off as a war-seasoned journalist, she had no idea how to write like one. "What made a story?" she fretted. "Didn't something gigantic and convulsive have to happen before one could write an article?"[35] Even though she'd looked at battles through binoculars, had seen pin-sized soldiers pitched against each other with tommy guns and grenades, she had too little knowledge to describe these things with any authority. She knew she needed a different angle and, in the end, it was Ernest who helped her find it. None of her readers, he pointed out, had any idea of what it was like to live in a city under siege, and if Martha could make herself the eyes and ears and hearts of Americans back home, this was the story she could own.

It was the most liberating advice of her career. Martha trained herself to note the "exact sound, smell, words and gestures" of everything she experienced, and the two essay-length features she eventually filed for *Collier's* — "High Explosive for Everyone" and "The Besieged City" — read more like travel diaries than war reports. She described how unreally simple it was to get to the university front, "No matter how often you do it, it is surprising just to walk to war, easily from your own bedroom where you have been reading a detective story or a life of Byron, or listening to the phonograph or chatting with your friends." She re-created the moment when the Hotel Florida took a direct hit, when "the noise was in your throat and you couldn't feel or hear or think." And she emphasized over and over again the sheer oddity of being in a city where the war had become so intimate a part of daily life.[36]

There was an almost surreal gaiety, she wrote, to the ease with which the Madrilenians had adapted to war, accepting as normal the dry choke of cordite, the whistle of shells, the constant backdrop of gunfire. The cinemas were still showing Marx Brothers' comedies, bright yellow trams still rattled down the streets and, after each fresh bombardment, cheerfully stoic work crews gathered to trundle away the rubble and the broken glass, to board up shattered windows and fill the worst of the craters. When Martha herself went to Bar Chicote for a glass of the "frankly fatal" gin which passed for a Madrid cocktail, she didn't think twice about stepping over the corpse of a stray dog, or skirting around rusty splashes of blood that had dried on the pavement.

She never once allowed herself to become blasé about the casualties, however, and at the heart of her Madrid reporting was the fine, furious account of the afternoon she saw a small child killed during an enemy bombardment. Her eye had been caught by an elderly woman dragging a thin little boy by the hand as the attack had begun and Martha had instantly felt the woman's fear as her own: "You know what she is thinking, she is thinking she must get the child home, you are always safer in your own place, with the things you know." Then as shells rained down, one had exploded close by and a "small piece of twisted steel, hot and very sharp," had lanced the boy's throat. Writing in an urgent, cinematic present tense, Martha tried to concentrate the full shock of that moment — her own dazed helplessness and the grandmother's uncomprehending grief: "The old woman stands there, holding the hand of the dead child, looking at him stupidly, not saying anything, and men run out toward her to carry the child."

It wasn't only that Martha wanted her readers to know the pity and the horror of the boy's death; she wanted them to feel, as she did, the sheer wickedness of this war — the unjustified brutality of the Nationalist assault on free Spain, and the complicity of the Americans who, as signatories to the international non-intervention pact, were refusing to come to the Loyalists' aid.[37]

"I think I must have imagined public opinion as a solid force," Martha acknowledged, "something like a tornado, always

104

ready to blow on the side of the angels."[38] She fully believed that, if she wrote about Spain with sufficient clarity and power, America would be persuaded to drop its neutral stance and would help to bring this war to a just conclusion. Later she would admit to the naivety of this belief, yet she would also acknowledge that, during this first visit to Madrid, she had never felt more purposefully alive.* Exactly as Ernest had promised, there was no past and no future here, only the urgent present tense. When the two of them lay in bed together, playing records of Chopin piano music to mask the distant sputter of gunfire, or when they drank rough red wine with soldiers near the front, Martha believed she was getting "something out of history that is more than anyone has a decent right to hope for . . . that fusion . . . of body and soul; of living one's life and believing with one's whole heart in the life around one."[39] She felt that too when Ernest read her very first piece on Spain — a broadcast script for Republican radio — and gave it his admiring blessing, "Daughter, you're

* The Americans, like the British and French, were reluctant to get embroiled in a "foreigners' " war, but there was also a strong body of right-wing policy-makers who believed Franco was acting as a useful bulwark against the spread of socialism and communism in Europe.

lovely."[40]

"I like writing," Martha observed in her diary. "In the end, it is the only thing which does not bore or dismay me or fill me with doubt. It is the only thing I know absolutely and irrevocably to be good in itself, no matter what the result."[41] She was confident now that hers was an authentic war voice, a natural progression from the detailed novelist's style that she'd developed in *The Trouble I've Seen,* and she believed it was no less accurate or tough than the more military-focused approach of her male colleagues. When NBC radio asked Martha to broadcast a piece from the "women's angle," she reared back in affronted disgust.

Yet, as Martha found her niche as a war correspondent in Spain, she realized that the excitement and the drive were only intermittent. Physically, the life was hard; Madrid's supply routes were under regular attack and there was little food in the shops beyond beans, bran-bulked bread, the occasional oily grey sausage or tough mule steak. None of the press corps went hungry: Sefton "Tom" Delmer, writing for the *Daily Express,* had laid in private supplies of whisky and chocolate; Ernest was able to magic fresh ham and eggs from his excellent contacts and to shoot the occasional partridge. But Martha dreamed longingly of the abundance and variety she'd taken for granted in America, and, ever mindful of her figure, she fretted over the starchiness of her wartime diet.

Harder still was the boredom. Days passed when there was little new to write about and Martha growled anxiously in her diary, "I do nothing here but eat, sleep, grow fat, spend money and loaf."[42] She was disappointed by the mediocrity of some of her fellow correspondents, the boys she'd been so impatient to join. Herbert Matthews, a long, thin, scholarly and compassionate reporter for the *New York Times,* was the exception (also, he was flatteringly half in love with her), but Martha thought George Seldes was "unpleasant" and dismissed Tom Delmer as a lazy cynic, far too happy to recycle his stories from the daily press briefings.[43]

She was unsettled, too, by the realization that the others didn't necessarily share her own moral certainties. Passionate in her commitment to the Loyalists, Martha was deaf to any suggestion of their failings: she dismissed the stories of civilian Spaniards who'd been persecuted, even tortured, for disloyalty to *La Causa;* she brushed away rumours of factional violence; and she fully endorsed the strictness of the Republican censors, who scanned all copy for negative comment before allowing it to be sent from Madrid. Objectivity counted for "shit" in Spain, Martha believed. With so much at stake, she thought that writers were justified in skewing the truth or omitting unpalatable facts from their reports, and she deeply distrusted those colleagues who were asking harder questions than her about the war.[44]

The American novelist John Dos Passos was one of them. He'd been an active supporter of the Republicans from the start and was close friends with one of their officers, Colonel José Robles Pazos. Back in December 1936, however, the Colonel had been arrested as a Nationalist spy and Dos Passos was convinced he'd been framed. Robles Pazos had started to raise concerns about the number of Russian aviators, gunners and training officers who were arriving in Spain, and who were, he could see, fomenting unrest within the Loyalist ranks. Simply to talk about the Russians was dangerous, however, since their very presence in Spain was in violation of the non-intervention pact; and it was infinitely more dangerous to hint as the Colonel had done at the truth of their underlying mission — which was not to defeat Franco but prepare the way for a communist Spain.

Clearly, Robles Pazos' enquiries had led to his arrest, and Dos Passos had begged for Ernest's help in clearing his name. Hemingway, however, refused to believe that the Loyalists and their Russian allies could ever stoop to incriminating an innocent man. And when the Colonel was executed, without even the pretence of a fair trial, Ernest had no sympathy to give Dos Passos, dismissing his anguish as the sentimentality of a "typical American liberal." The incident sent ripples of unease throughout the press corps, but, for Martha, it had been too unthinkable to doubt the veracity of the Loyalists, and too difficult to question Ernest's judgement.

Their relationship, as lovers, was already complicated. She'd had no doubt that it was Ernest's passion for Spain that had first "hooked" her into the affair, and some of their happiest times in Madrid were the hours they lay together in his room, talking over the day's battle news and trying to invent words that best described the "rot-pop-pop" rattle of machine-gun fire or the arcing whine of a shell. Martha didn't particularly worry that the lovemaking which preceded these talks was invariably disappointing; having been assured by doctors that there was nothing medically wrong with her, she'd resigned herself to faking her orgasms and to the simpler pleasures of having "arms around me and the illusion of tenderness."[45] In April, less than a month after arriving in Madrid, Ernest announced that he wanted to divorce Pauline and marry her, and in her diary she wrote, "Note to H. I love you very much indeed."[46]

But Martha was also conscious that she'd allowed a dangerously dominating force into her life, a lover with a volatile temper and an imperious sense of his own entitlement. One day, at the front, when there was no action to report, he'd picked up a rifle and — roaring, "This is all too quiet!" — had begun to fire pointlessly at the enemy. Martha was learning how to manage Ernest in public, puncturing his bluster with irony, shrugging off his hubris. But she often felt emotionally at sea, unable to predict from moment to moment whether he would choose to charm her with his sweetness, his boisterous gifts for pleasure and intellectual curiosity, or whether he would retreat from her into arrogance, indifference and bluff insensitivity.

She never knew, for instance, how he would react to the other men who found her attractive. As one of a tiny number of women journalists in Spain, and "just about the only blonde in the country," Martha had got used to being the centre of male attention.[47] Mostly, she enjoyed it, but on one occasion the flirtation spun upsettingly out of her control. Randolfo Pacciardi, a handsome Italian Loyalist in command of the Garibaldi Brigade, had always been attentive to Martha — eager to escort her around his section of the front, eager to buy her dinner. But, when they were being driven back to the Florida one night, Pacciardi had tried to force himself on her, grabbing her hand and pressing it against his groin. She'd fought him off, had told herself the assault fell far short of rape. Yet it had still felt like a gross violation, and when Martha had gone shakily to Ernest, she'd expected some sympathetic outrage on her behalf.

Instead, he'd barely listened — Pacciardi had been acting like any normal man, he implied, Martha was behaving like a small-town prude. And as hard as it was to listen to Ernest's cold, cavalier dismissal, it was additionally humiliating because there had been other occasions when even the scent of a rival flirtation had aroused him to near murderous levels of jealousy. Once at a party at Gaylord's Hotel (the Soviets' unofficial HQ), Martha had got a little drunk on the excellent vodka and fallen into an agreeably bantering conversation with an attractive Spanish general. Evidently, Ernest had taken offence, for, bearing down on them both with "an ugly shark smile," he challenged Juan Modesto to a duel of Russian roulette.[48] A flurry of official intervention had defused the situation, but Ernest and Martha were hustled, humiliated, from the room. And it was at moments like these, when Madrid felt rampant with male ego, that Martha found herself wishing for the balm of some female company.

For much of her life, she'd done without close women friends. She loved and admired the saintly Eleanor Roosevelt, and adored her mother, Edna, but most women were too cloyingly intimate for her taste, too tentative in their opinions, too lacking in the bracing robustness of men. In Spain, though, the sexual imbalance could be exhausting, and when Martha first began looking around for a female ally, the most obvious candidate was Josephine Herbst, an older American freelancer, who'd known Ernest many years ago, in Paris. But Josephine herself was not disposed to friendship. She greatly disliked the man Ernest had become, affronted by the "splurging magnificence" with which he was showing off his celebrity in Madrid, and, by association, she came to dislike his mistress too, resenting the seemingly privileged air with which Martha was whisked to the front in Ernest's specially designated jeep, elegantly outfitted in "beautiful Saks Fifth Avenue pants, with a green scarf wound around her head."[49]

Martha, stung by Josie's hostility, dismissed the older woman as "ugly and vulgar" and turned hopefully to Ilsa Kulcsar, a clever, cultured woman who ran the censor's office with her lover, Arturo Barea.[50] But Ilsa was working exhaustingly long hours and, when Martha had tried to confide the difficulties she was having with Ernest, Ilsa simply gave her a weary smile and suggested that, with all the advantages she'd gained from her lover, Martha should consider herself somewhat

112

"spoiled."[51]

It was almost by default that Martha sought out the company of Virginia Cowles, a young American journalist who'd appeared in Madrid a fortnight or so after her own arrival. In any other context, Martha might have dismissed Virginia at a glance. Fine-boned and slender, her eyes wide and dark in a neatly shaped face, she had arrived at the Hotel Florida as though dressed for afternoon tea in Manhattan — her tailored woollen dress accessorized with a black fur jacket and a matching pair of high-heeled shoes. But Martha had discovered that, beneath her absurd wardrobe, Virginia — "Ginny" — had unexpected steel. There was a flicker of cool calculation in her gaze and she was clearly no less resolute than Martha to prove her mettle as a war correspondent.

Most immediately appealing, though, was Virginia's talent for fun. There were pockets of pre-war luxury still in Madrid, and it was at Ginny's prompting that Martha allowed herself to enjoy them. The two women went window-shopping together, comparing the prices of Schiaparelli perfumes, silver-fox furs or handmade shoes, and growing "desperately greedy wanting them"; they went to one of the city's last remaining beauty salons in Madrid to have their hair washed and their nails manicured.[52] And while Ernest was talking battle strategy with his Loyalist friends, Martha and Ginny sat together in the Miami Bar, gossiping, drinking afternoon cocktails and listening to the owner's small and very scratched collection of American jazz records.

For Martha, these outings were a reprieve from Ernest, a regression, almost, into easy girlishness, and she assumed the friendship with Ginny was nothing more than a temporary expedient. Politically, the two of them were worlds apart, for Ginny was not only writing for *New York Sunday America,* a title belonging to the conservative Hearst empire, she'd actually come to Madrid without any real commitment to the Loyalist cause. Frankly she admitted she had no "line" to take, but only an interest in what she called the "human side — the forces that urged people to such a test of endurance."[53] And it was her interest in the "human side" that had also determined Virginia to get into Franco-held territory once she'd left Madrid.

This was, in fact, a recklessly brave endeavour. Very few journalists had attempted to cover the war from behind both Nationalist and Loyalist lines; paranoia was so rife that anyone crossing from one side to the other was assumed to be engaged in espionage, and liable to arrest. Martha, however, saw nothing to admire in Virginia's plan. The very notion of balance was morally bogus to her, as if reporting on the Nationalists were a form of endorsement. Grateful though she was for Ginny's company, Martha could only regard her as a lightweight, and, once they'd moved on from Madrid, she had no expectation of meeting her again. Only gradually, as the fighting spread across Europe and the two women's paths continued to cross, would Martha come to realize how gravely she'd underestimated Virginia, and how unexpectedly she would come to depend on her as a friend.

CHAPTER THREE:
MADRID AND SALAMANCA,
1937

"NY society girl sees
fighting in the trenches"
VIRGINIA COWLES[1]

Virginia's charm, her natural ability to engage with strangers, was assumed by most people, Martha included, to be the gift of privilege and wealth. In reality, however, it was one of several weapons with which she'd fought her way out of an unhappy childhood, and had escaped from the effects of her parents' disastrous marriage.

Beautiful, patrician Florence Wolcott Jacquith had been nineteen when she scandalized Boston society by eloping with a handsome young doctor, Edward Spencer Cowles, and she'd been married to him for less than a decade when she discovered he was an adulterer and sued him for divorce. For the couple's small daughters, Mary and Virginia (the youngest, born on 24 August 1910, in Vermont), the consequences were terrifying. Edward was so vengefully outraged by his wife's divorce suit that he kidnapped the two little girls from their school and hid them away at his mother's house. When they were found by Florence and taken back home, he then refused to pay the alimony which had been set by the courts. Florence's own family were unwilling or unable to offer financial support, and, pushed to the brink of poverty, Florence not only had to move herself, Mary and Virginia into a tiny apartment, but then find herself a job. On the strength of her Jacquith name, she was hired as a society columnist for the *Boston Herald,* but the pay was so meagre she also had to work long shifts as a typesetter. Unable to care properly for her daughters herself, the final blow for Florence was having to send the girls away to boarding school where, as charity pupils, they had to do kitchen chores in lieu of fees.

Virginia was traumatized by the upheavals to her little world. She would never forget the moment when Florence, haggard and distraught, came to rescue her and Mary from their grandmother's house. She would never forget the misery of her first year at boarding school, when, homesick for her mother, she hid under her dormitory bed and screamed. Even when Florence was earning enough to have the girls back in her care, Virginia could not settle. She was inattentive at school and, by the age of fourteen, had already begun sneaking out, after dark, to explore Boston's nightclubs.

Yet, even while Virginia was veering towards adolescent rebellion, she was making practical plans for her future, determined to make herself independent so that a man like her father could never control her life. At school, she was voted "the girl most likely to succeed," and at sixteen she got her first job, selling copies of *Harper's* magazine over the telephone. Within weeks, she had been promoted to the advertising sales department, and, within a year, she'd earned enough money to buy a second-hand car and take a solitary road trip across America. It was a wilfully rash venture for a teenage girl, but Virginia had decided to try to follow her mother into journalism, and during that long drive she kept a travel diary, filling its pages with zingy local colour, which she hoped to put to future use. Once back in Boston, she allowed Florence to throw her a modest debutante's tea party (even in reduced circumstances, Jacquith girls were expected to "come out"). But none of the Boston bachelors held any interest for her and, as soon as the season was over, she moved to New York, where, like Martha, she imagined she would find her route into a brilliant career.

Edward Cowles was now based in Manhattan, too, running a brilliant, if controversial, practice as a "nerve doctor." Virginia was unable to forgive his cruelty to Florence, but she warmed to his second wife, Nora, a friendly woman from the South, and, when Edward offered to help her settle in New York, Virginia was not too proud to accept. In 1928, it was hard enough for any woman to succeed in the hard-knuckled world of New York journalism, even harder to do so without money and contacts; and as Virginia took her first professional steps, writing photo captions for *Harper's,* pitching her first by-lined articles, she was pragmatically grateful for Edward's support.*

The skills she developed, however, were all her own. Virginia was a natural journalist, her prose rattling along with a fashionable snap, and, although she wanted, ultimately, to write about world events, she was sensible enough to accept that her most immediate asset was her youth. It was as a "flapper reporter," a "society-girl columnist," that she wrote her way to success, turning out sassy debunking pieces about divorce, drink and the death of

* Edward Cowles' experiments with hypnosis and pep pills were believed to work wonders, where conventional mental-health treatments had failed, and, while he was willing to treat his most afflicted patients for free, he was also much sought after by the rich and famous. Later, when Edward merged his practice into his newly founded Mind and Body Foundation, he would be investigated for breaches of medical ethics.

romance in 1930s Manhattan. Her work appeared in *Harper's Bazaar, Collier's, Boston Post* and *New York America,* and one of her articles, a witty takedown of the debutante system, was syndicated widely across the States.

In the photograph that accompanied her columns, a pixie hat perched rakishly on her short, dark hair, Virginia looked the embodiment of Manhattan chic. She was described in her byline as "a member of the New York Social Register and the daughter of Edward Spencer Cowles," and the elegance of her professional image was not so far from the life she was leading. Even after the stock-market crash of 1929, parts of New York remained awash with careless money, and, despite the introduction of Prohibition laws, the city was buzzing with nightclubs and parties. This was the glossy, rackety milieu in which Virginia sourced most of her material and made most of her friends — years later, her husband would recall that he'd had his first glimpse of her on a Long Island dance floor, a fashionable "It Girl" being "rushed" by a crowd of wealthy young men.

Privately, however, Virginia was keeping herself at a watchful distance from this world of easy privilege. She disliked its drunkenness and promiscuity (she would wait until she was twenty-five and believed herself in love before having her first affair), and she was impatient to report on more substantial matters than the idiosyncrasies of America's gilded youth. As yet, she knew of only a tiny number of women who'd graduated to hard news, and, by comparison with her heroine, Dorothy Thompson, she knew herself to be an amateur. But she was determined to find some way of expanding her journalistic skills, of broadening her knowledge of the world, and, by the most tragic of ironies, it was the death of her mother that provided Virginia with the opportunity and the means.

Florence's health had never been good. Worry and hard work had aged her prematurely and, late in 1932, when she'd developed an acute case of appendicitis, her death had been rapid. For Virginia, as for Mary, the loss had been awful, for the two young women had adored their mother, and been deeply protective of her. Yet, when Florence's estate was settled the following year, they learned that her modest life-insurance policy had yielded an inheritance of $2,000. This was a fabulous, potentially life-altering sum, and rather than putting it in a bank Virginia persuaded Mary that they would best honour their mother's memory by using it to see the world. For $500 apiece, they could travel to Japan and back, taking in northern India and parts of the Far East; and, for Virginia herself, the trip had the additional lure of furnishing her with a very new brand of copy. Just before she and Mary set sail in late 1933, she went to an editor at Hearst to pitch the idea of a travel column for their Sunday "March of Events" supplement. Even though he would not commit to giving her a regular slot, he agreed to read whatever she sent, and this was all the incentive she required. During the next eleven months, Virginia cabled back a series of spirited columns about the feminist movement in Burma, about the effects of purdah in India, the commercial marriage bureaus of Tokyo, the pirate crews on the China Seas. Although she was writing as a tourist — her research skimpy, her analysis superficial — she had an eye for the surprising incident, the piquant human detail, and she was very good at getting strangers to confide in her. So lively, direct and funny were her stories that Hearst published all of them, and when Virginia returned to New York, she was ready to build on her new credentials, and persuade editors to start seeing beyond her flapper image. By the autumn of 1935, when Mussolini was threatening to invade Abyssinia (now Ethiopia), Virginia was so confident of her ability to tackle what she called "more vigorous subjects," that she begged her editor at Hearst, a man named T. V. Rank, to send her to Rome to report on how the Italians were reacting to their leader's imperialist plans.

Rank was understandably skeptical. But

Virginia had become expert at selling herself and, while she admitted that her knowledge of foreign affairs was negligible, she was able to convince him that the "few descriptive pieces" she'd envisaged might be a colourful alternative to Hearst's more specialist political coverage.[2] Although Rank could not agree to fund her travel, he was curious to see what she would produce, and, on 3 October, the same day that Mussolini launched his invasion, Virginia arrived in Rome as a freelance "roving correspondent."

Already, she wrote, "the ghost of war was walking and the air was tense with apprehension."[3] Young army recruits crowded the streets, raw and self-conscious in their uniforms; newsreels of the first Italian manoeuvres were showing in the cinemas; and the cafes were raucous with pro- and anti-war debate. But, even as Virginia scribbled down notes for her descriptive stories, she was plotting to impress Rank with some very different coverage. En route to Rome, she'd spent a few days in Paris, where one of her increasingly international network of friends had promised to secure her an invitation to fly out to the Italian colony of Libya and to dine with General Air Marshal Italo Balbo, who, as head of the Italian Air Force and Governor General of Libya, ranked only second in command to Mussolini himself.

An interview with Balbo was a scoop in

itself, but Virginia was also hoping to get some inside information on developments in Abyssinia. When she arrived in Tripoli on 6 October, she was gratified to see a number of high-ranking Italian officers gathered at the Air Marshal's opulent Moorish villa, and she assumed that the war must be their main focus of concern. Yet, to Virginia's surprise and frustration, these Italians seemed to regard their Libya posting as a holiday. All they talked about at dinner was food and pheasant hunting, and, as for Balbo, he spent the entire evening flirting with Virginia, urging her to take a ride in his private plane so that he could show her the beauties of the Libyan desert.[4]

Still hopeful of acquiring some military gossip, Virginia agreed. The following afternoon, she posed for Balbo's photographer, looking svelte and assured in a borrowed flying suit. The plane, however, turned out to be an antiquated, two-seated Breda, which wheezed and buckled so effortfully Virginia feared it would fall apart. During the flight she was far too frightened to register the spectacle of the desert sunset, and when Balbo started to angle the Breda's joystick in preparation for some aerial stunts, she faked a weak heart and begged him to land. The "famous and dashing air marshal" was clearly offended by her lack of enthusiasm, and when she refused his offer of a second excursion, he turned childishly petulant, demanding to know if Virginia found him physically unattractive. But nothing would induce her to risk her life with Balbo again, and, while she was able to inform her readers that her three days in Tripoli had been "an extraordinary interlude," it was largely because of the insight she'd gained into the unwarrior-like insouciance of the Italian military and the "rough, easy going charm" of their commanding officer.[5]

But Virginia had come away with some entertaining copy — copy no male correspondent could have obtained — and, shortly after returning to Rome, she was able to pair it with an even more unlikely exclusive. On first arriving in the city, she'd been introduced to a charismatic and very well-connected Italian journalist, and, giddy, perhaps, with the adventure of her assignment, she'd fallen into bed with him. The journalist, gallantly stricken by the discovery that he was Virginia's first lover, had then gone out of his way to help her, not only providing her with background to the Abyssinian War, but wangling her onto the guest list of a high-level political dinner.

Given her schoolgirl Italian and sketchy political knowledge, Virginia didn't expect to elicit more than a few quotes and some general context from this Roman dinner. It was only as a matter of form that, on finding herself seated next to Dino Alfieri, the Italian Minister of Propaganda, she asked if it would be possible to get an interview with Mussolini. She had no expectation of being taken seriously, and was thus completely appalled when she woke the next morning to a message that Mussolini would see her at six p.m. sharp. "The fact that I was to speak to the Napoleon of the day, at a moment when he challenged the peace of the entire world, seemed to be stupendous," she recalled. Unable to eat, convinced she'd be struck dumb in his presence, Virginia spent the entire day writing and rewriting the list of questions she should ask.[6]

That list turned out to be redundant. While Mussolini, in person, looked nowhere near as daunting as the "solemn black-uniformed dictator" she'd imagined, his ego made up for his unimpressive physique.[7] His notion of an interview was simply to bludgeon Virginia with an impromptu rant as, in rapid, ungrammatical English, he outlined the glorious destiny he had planned for Italy, and his contempt for the "weakling" League of Nations and the "treacherous" British who tried to stand in his way. Only once did she manage to interrupt, asking why Mussolini chose to remain a member of the League, if he despised it so much. At that point, an expression of coy boastfulness crossed his face. "Because I'm a very clever man," he replied.

"Politics is a difficult game and, the way I'm playing, it's my best chance to win."[8] Then, as abruptly as he'd begun the interview, he shut it down, rising to his feet and ordering Virginia from the room.

The entire audience had been little more than a propaganda exercise, yet Hearst still claimed it as a scoop, and the report Virginia filed was syndicated across their entire stable of publications. She minded that she was still being billed as a news dilettante, her byline referring to her as the "New York Social Registerist who is now touring Europe and Africa," but her credentials had been bolstered by this Italian assignment and, in early 1937, when half the world's media were converging on Spain, Virginia was convinced she could join them. She'd formulated a careful sales pitch, assuring Rank that she could become the first-ever reporter to cover the war from both sides. And, while he doubted this was true, he knew there was a story in Virginia simply making the attempt. When she started out for Madrid in mid-March, she'd not only been given a full travel budget from Hearst, but had been promoted to its elite cadre of special correspondents.

Finally, she was approaching the ranks of professional luminaries like Hubert Knickerbocker, Dorothy Thompson and Edgar Murrow; finally, she could claim to be a serious journalist. However, the friends with whom

Virginia broke her journey in Paris were unsympathetically quick to puncture her triumph. Conditions in Madrid were atrocious, they said. People were starving, the streets were littered with corpses and Virginia herself was equally likely to be "bumped off," since the only wardrobe she'd packed was her three good wool dresses and her fur jacket — clothes which, in Spain, would only be worn by a Nationalist.

She'd scoffed, then, at the idea of kitting herself out with some workers' overalls. But when her plane landed in Valencia, now the temporary seat of the Republican government, she did become aware of some very "dark stares" as she used her few Spanish phrases to ask directions to a decent hotel. In fact, it was principally her suitcase that was causing offence — its red and yellow stripes an exact match of Franco's flag — and, when she presented herself at the Republic press office to ask for a press car to take her to Madrid, Virginia encountered no further hostility.

Two days later, she was on the road. Sharing the car was a shabby, nicotine-stained priest who'd been hired to rebut stories of Loyalist attacks on the Catholic Church; also, a young American woman with "a monkey face and thick horn-rimmed spectacles," who was volunteering her services to the Madrid press office.[9] Virginia was greatly entertained by this idiosyncratic couple, and even more so by their anarchist driver, who stopped to donate all of their petrol to a stranded comrade, forcing his own passengers to wait by the road for more supplies. Like Martha, two weeks earlier, Virginia was so absorbed in the unfolding novelties of Spain that it was not until she saw the outskirts of Madrid, looking cold, forbidding and dark in the gathering dusk, that she felt a twinge of apprehension. And it was not until she booked herself into the Florida and was breezily assured by the reception clerk that a shell would only ever hit the hotel "by mistake" that Virginia realized she might have come to Madrid to die.[10]

The following morning, that realization returned with a shattering force. Virginia was being shown around the neighbourhood by a helpful and slightly flirtatious Tom Delmer, when a high-pitched sound, like ripping fabric, came rushing through the air. It was the start of a bombardment, and after the first of the shells smashed into the Telefónica Building at the end of the street, a second plunged into the pavement ahead of them, and a third hit a nearby block of flats. To Virginia it seemed that the city was collapsing around her in a slow-motion dance of brick, timber and dust. She and Tom dived for shelter into the nearest shop, and when they emerged, half an hour later, it was clear they were lucky to have survived. As Virginia wrote afterwards, "The pavements were strewn with bricks and shrapnel and a telegraph pole leaned drunkenly across one of the buildings. The second floor of a hat shop had a gaping hole and at the corner an automobile was a twisted mass of steel. Nearby, the pavement was splattered with blood where two women had been killed."[11]

Never had she experienced such "intense fear."[12] Yet, this first experience of enemy shelling also taught Virginia how quickly that fear could pass. Once the bodies had been removed and the dust had cleared, normal life surged back onto the streets of Madrid, and when she and Tom resumed their walk, she realized that the gouged and blackened buildings felt no more menacing to her than "if we were parading through a movie set."[13] This was how you coped with war, Virginia realized: you allowed your panic to galvanize you in a crisis, but afterwards you suppressed the memory of it. It was how the Spanish people were surviving and she was determined to measure up to them, writing admiringly in her first report for Hearst how "[they] have not lost their sense of humour but are as quick and changing as the country they live in."[14]

Those who failed to adapt had a grim time. As Virginia acquainted herself with other journalists in Madrid she noted that Josie

Herbst, in particular, struggled to recover from the panic of each bombardment, that she dreaded a tour to the front, and that her fears affected her standing with her colleagues. Beneath the convivial drinking and the trading of gossip, the correspondents "studied one another like crows," and it was clear to Virginia that one didn't readily admit to weakness in so competitive a crowd.[15] It was equally clear to her, though, that however brave a front she was personally able to assume, it would be foolish to claim more experience than she actually possessed, and that she would gain most assistance from her colleagues by trading on her status as a war ingénue.

Not everyone warmed to Virginia immediately. Ernest was irritated by her determined elegance, as she clicked her way through the war debris of Madrid in her heavy gold bracelets and high-heeled shoes. Mendaciously, he claimed that, when she'd passed a lorryload of soldiers singing "The Internationale," she'd had no idea it was the great socialist anthem, and had innocently enquired, "What is that divine tune?" But most of the other men were disposed to look out for her. Tom Delmer instructed her in basic press strategy: how to put in a request for a trip to the front; how to forge an official permit, if one was not forthcoming (few of the sentries could read, so they tended to wave through any remotely convincing piece of paper). The eminent British scientist J. B. S. Haldane, who was in Madrid to advise on antidotes to poison gas, was no less generous, offering himself as Virginia's escort when she took her first tour of University City.[16]

Haldane, sporting an ancient army tin helmet, evidently liked to think of himself as a seasoned war professional. Saluting the soldiers like old friends as he led the way through the first of the sandbag-lined trenches, he was delighted when the Loyalists began returning Nationalist fire and bullets started whizzing overhead. Virginia would see some real action, he boasted, and she was lucky to do so, because no previous war had allowed women so close to the front. He beamed when one group of Spaniards actually offered Virginia a rifle so that she could take a crack at *los facciosos* herself.

Virginia was less convinced of her good fortune. The bullets were flying so low she had to start crawling on her hands and knees, then, just as she was wondering exactly why she'd wanted to come to Spain, the trench they were following came to a sudden dead end and Haldane confessed he hadn't the "foggiest idea" where they were. He instructed her to stay put while he looked for an alternative route, but, now that she was alone, trying to shield herself from the geysers of mud thrown up by exploding mortars,

Virginia gave way to panic. When a mortar detonated just twenty feet away from her, she assumed the next must surely kill her. Yet, almost as though summoned by her distress, a Spanish officer appeared and, whistling jauntily, guided her through a concealed tunnel, which led to a disused farm shack where he and his unit were taking a break from the fighting.[17]

The shack seemed alarmingly crowded, full of very young soldiers, who fired questions at Virginia in fast, incomprehensible Spanish or broken French. However, they were touchingly concerned for her welfare, begging her to take a share of their dry bread rations, urging her to get warm by the little wood stove, even attempting to clean the sticky trench mud from her shoes. The men's simple gallantry charmed away her fears and, during the rest of her stay in Madrid, she would experience that gallantry in many forms. Out near the fighting in the Guadarrama Mountains or the fields of Guadalajara, the soldiers she met would offer small tributes of songs, poems and flowers; they would compete to share their battle stories and personal confidences; and one especially devoted young Loyalist would offer to drive her through a fusillade of enemy fire so that she could know the thrill of hearing fascist bullets crack against the sides of his armoured truck.

Only twice did Virginia feel threatened as a

woman. The first time, she and Hemingway were trapped in the basement of the Gran Vía Hotel, sheltering from an unusually prolonged bombardment. Pepe Quantillana, the head of the Republican secret police, was trapped in the basement too, and, when he insisted on sitting at their table, his behaviour towards Virginia became aggressively lascivious. He wanted her to share his very expensive bottle of wine, he suggested he could throw her a "very special party," and then, most bizarrely, he proposed marriage. Placing his hand heavily over Virginia's, his long, sinister face corrugated with smiles, he swore it would be a most practical and enjoyable arrangement: "I already have a wife but it's all for the best. She will do the cooking for us. What an excellent idea that is."[18]

Quantillana's sense of humour was known to be lethal — his nickname, "The Executioner of Madrid," reflected the ruthless good cheer with which he dispatched his victims. But he was only toying with Virginia, and far more hazardous was the romantic interest she attracted from a Soviet general who was stationed close to Madrid. It was mid to late May, Martha and Ernest had already left Spain, and, before Virginia departed too, she wanted to make one last trip to Morata, where units from the International Brigade were holding out against the enemy. A press car was supplied for her and two others, but their driver took a wrong turn and, when they asked for directions at a ramshackle-looking mill and were, suddenly, surrounded by uniformed guards, they realized they had inadvertently stumbled upon a secret Russian HQ. This was forbidden territory, and when the commanding general emerged to order them back to Madrid, none of the journalists were inclined to protest.

By the following week, Virginia had all but forgotten the incident, until a tall Hungarian soldier came calling at the Florida, with a message that his commander, General Gal, regretted his rudeness and wished to invite her to lunch. An audience with a Soviet commander was beyond even Virginia's expectations and whatever qualms she might have felt about returning alone to the mill were soothed when she saw how festive it had been made in her honour. Roast partridges, fresh vegetables and wild strawberries were served at lunch; a large bowl of flowers was placed on the table; and the General's interpreter, an affable American Marxist named David, made sure that Virginia could follow the conversation. General Gal, however, struck her as remarkably boorish, and not at all inclined to make his promised apology. He was silent for most of the meal and, when Virginia ventured to ask, via David, if he would permit her to visit the Morata front, he looked at her with something like contempt. Gesturing towards her inappropriate footwear, he scoffed, "You are too soft. You would get tired and you would want someone to carry you."[19]

After lunch, though, the General had a change of heart, and proposed taking Virginia to the front himself. It was a dismal expedition. The day had turned grey, chilled by a thin, sharp rain, and the American volunteers to whom Virginia spoke were unable to give her the heart-warming, patriotic copy that Hearst required. Filthy, soaked to the skin and terribly young, these men looked completely ill-suited to soldiering, a motley collection of "idealists and down and outs," who seemed to know they were fighting for a doomed cause. By now, Virginia too was wet and cold, and very fatigued from her peculiar adventure, but when she asked her Hungarian driver if he could return her to Madrid, he informed her, with some embarrassment, that the General had other ideas. "He wants to convert you," he said, explaining that Gal had given orders for Virginia to be taken back to the mill and kept there as his guest while he tried to make a communist of her.[20]

Stupidly, Virginia had not told any of her colleagues where she was going; no one knew where to find her and she could only submit to the General's order with a reasonable grace. But she sensed that he meant her no harm. The room to which she was led was little more than a grubby cell, pungent with the smell of unwashed uniforms and old sweat, but Gal had allowed her some feminine necessities — a bottle of eau de cologne, some toothpaste and a comb — and, when she was invited to join him for dinner, he seemed to derive genuine pleasure from her company. He stared at her with frank interest while she ate, and, when it was time to begin their political tutorial, he ordered up three bottles of champagne, asking Virginia with artless enjoyment, "Did you ever imagine yourself drinking champagne with a Red Army general?"[21]

Her indoctrination was to last seventy-two hours. During the day, Virginia was permitted to mix with the Russian, Spanish and American soldiers who were camped around the mill; at night, she sat alone with David and the General to have the principles of Marxism explained to her. Gal seemed particularly concerned that she should have safely renounced her bourgeois ways by the time revolution came to America as, he earnestly promised, it must. Evidently, he'd half fallen in love with her, for, when he finally told Virginia she was free to leave, he handed her a single red rose. "It is stained with the blood of the revolution," he said. "I hope you will be faithful to it." Then, with a smile of unfathomable, ironic regret, he added that, while he hoped very much to see

Virginia again, he knew it would never happen. "You won't return, but you will boast to your friends that a Red Army General took a fancy to you."[22]

Gal's stiff, proud chivalry moved Virginia, and, two years later, when she learned of the military purge that had been ordered by Stalin, she was genuinely concerned for her General's welfare. Back in Madrid, however, she was in trouble. Journalists had to account for all of their movements to the military police, and when it was discovered that Virginia had not only gone missing for three days, but had managed to infiltrate a Soviet HQ, she became a target of intense suspicion. Tom Delmer said she was being investigated as a Nationalist spy and, urging her to leave Madrid immediately, warned that she must never travel in a car by herself, because "road accidents" were one of the Republicans' preferred methods "of settling accounts."[23]

Delmer was not exaggerating the danger. While Virginia was waiting for her plane in Valencia, a stranger approached and, with a twitch of a smile, asked why she was in such a hurry to leave. "We have a nice new jail in Albacete," he sneered, "you could write your articles from there."[24] Later, she was informed that she'd only avoided arrest because she was a U.S. citizen and the Loyalists were still hoping to secure America's support. But, even at the time, her nerves were starting to shred, and, once she was back in Paris, staying in a borrowed apartment near the Champs-Elysées, all her carefully suppressed fears came crashing in.

Virginia had agreed with Hearst that she would file her reports only when she'd left Madrid and was free of the censors. But, as she returned to the notes she'd made, she experienced chilling flashbacks to the bombardments, the bodies and the trenches. She jumped at every sudden noise; and it was only now she realized that she'd lived with her breath held in Spain, her mind in denial — and that she felt paralysed by the prospect of going back. Even worse than a return to danger was the knowledge that, once behind Nationalist lines, she would be among men whom she'd learned to regard as the enemy — that she would be "plunging into an atmosphere where triumph meant disaster for the people I had left."[25]

But Hearst was loving the piquancy of its flapper columnist turned combat reporter — "NY Society Girl Sees Americans Fighting in Trenches," ran the byline of her second report — and Virginia's own stubborn will required her to see the assignment through. Accompanied by her sister, Mary, who'd sailed over to Europe for a holiday, she travelled down to St. Jean de Luz, a pretty Basque resort just twelve miles from the border with Franco's Spain. It was also home to the temporary British embassy, and it took Virginia barely a day to "bump into" Anne Chilton, the ambassador's daughter, and get herself introduced to an elderly count who could arrange her onward visa. The Conde de Ramblas was a sufficiently old-fashioned National-ist to assume that all "ladies and gentlemen" would support his own side, and he nodded sympathetically when Virginia claimed that her assignment to Loyalist Madrid had been forced on her by her editor. The Count moved slowly, though, and Virginia was so impatient to get over the border that she tried to hitch an illicit plane ride with an Englishman named Rupert Belville. That attempt failed, but, in early August, her visa was issued and, with it, her train ticket to Salamanca, the capital of Nationalist Spain.

From there, the war looked shockingly different. Franco's forces were much better fed and equipped than the Loyalists, and, having already conquered swathes of north-western Spain, they were more arrogantly assured of victory. The military alliance with Mussolini and Hitler was also far more active than Virginia had realized — "German and Italian flags flew from one side of insurgent Spain to the other," she wrote. As she was driven through miles of ravaged farmland, passing bombed-out villages and columns of the homeless, she could see how viciously the alliance was fighting.[26] And when she visited a Nationalist base in the hills above Madrid, and looked down on the battered, besieged city, she realized for the first time how utterly vulnerable it was.*

Virginia had specifically asked to see Guernica, the ancient Basque town, which had been massacred by fascist bombs and bullets back on 26 April. Her escorting officer, Ignacio Rosalles, had tried to convince her it was the Loyalists themselves who'd attacked the town — a cheap trick to win sympathy for their cause. But, as Virginia walked around the ruins, she met one of Guernica's elderly survivors, who had a very different story to tell: "The sky was black with planes," the old man shouted agitatedly. *"Aviones, Italianos y Alemanas."*[27] Rosalles had ordered him to be quiet, but a few days later, Virginia interviewed a Nationalist staff officer who openly took credit for the carnage: "We bombed it and bombed it and bombed it," he boasted. "And, *bueno,* why not?"[28]

The scale of destruction seemed egregious, even for fascists, and it dawned on Virginia that Mussolini and Hitler were not simply helping Franco win a war, but were using Spain as a testing ground for their own weapons. Like Sigrid, in Berlin, she was

* Hitler sent in his new Stuka bombers and 3,000 troops, while Italy loaned planes and 80,000 troops.

bewildered that so blatant a violation of international neutrality was meriting so little attention in the world's press. The *Manchester Guardian* had been one of the few papers to report on Italian and German complicity in Guernica, and while the *New York Times* had also covered the story, it had opted to "balance" its condemnation with some blander, more sympathetic accounts of the Nationalists' agenda.

Virginia's own notion of balance was certainly shifting, for the more she saw of Franco's war, the more convinced she became that it was serving the corrupt interests of a powerful elite. The Loyalists could be ruthless, but they believed they were fighting for a higher cause, and they were amateurs in comparison to the brutality with which Franco's men were bulldozing through their conquered territories, making thousands homeless, and arresting, interrogating and slaughtering all those they suspected of Republican views. A careless remark could be fatal. When Virginia and Rosalles stopped for petrol, the man at the pump raised his fist cheerfully in the approved Loyalist style, then, realizing his error, blushed a terrified beetroot and hastily converted his fist to a fascist salute.

Nor was Virginia exempt from suspicion. When Rosalles was replaced by a new minder, she realized she was being placed under more aggressive scrutiny: Captain Aguilera was disturbingly quick to pounce on any questionable enquiry she made about displaced peasants or bombed-out villages, disturbingly quick to accuse her of being a "sob sister," "a Red." So marked was his hostility, Virginia feared he might do her real harm and, convinced that her time in insurgent Spain had run out, she put in a hasty request for an exit permit. Already, however, she was too late. Aguilera had filed his report on Virginia, and she was informed by a regretful official that, with no press car "available" to drive her back to France, she would have to remain in Salamanca until further notice.[29]

It was clear to Virginia that she was under investigation and that she might very well end up in a Nationalist jail, just like her hero Hubert Knickerbocker. But, in the memoir she published four years later, she would recount how her apparently inexhaustible network of contacts had facilitated her escape. Anxiously considering her options, she happened to "run into" the Duc de Montellano, a friend of Rupert Belville, whose wife happened to be driving from Salamanca up to Burgos that afternoon. Once in Burgos, she was able to locate a count whom she'd met during the course of her world tour, and who was so delighted to see her again that he offered to drive her to the border city of San Sebastian the following day.

Thus far, Virginia's invalid travel papers had not been a problem; every time the Count or the "amiable Duchess" had been stopped at a checkpoint, they'd simply been waved through by deferential guards. In San Sebastian, however, the bridge dividing Spain from France was patrolled by armed soldiers who were far too professional to be fobbed off by an aristocratic title and a charming smile. Her only hope of getting across that bridge was with a diplomatic escort, and the one person she could think to ask was Tommy Thompson, First Secretary to the British ambassador, who, back in St. Jean de Luz, had struck her as the sharpest and most sympathetic of the embassy staff.

It was impossible to cable Tommy with an explicit request for help, since the Nationalists were monitoring communications; all Virginia could do was send a breezy message, suggesting that the two of them "meet for lunch." Fortunately, rumours had already reached St. Jean de Luz that she was in trouble, and Tommy had guessed her predicament. Having spent a long, wakeful night imagining "footsteps in the corridor, a knock on the door and the sound of police voices," Virginia was relieved when Tommy appeared promptly at her hotel the next morning, much entertained by the idea of coming to her rescue.[30] Even now, however, escape wasn't certain. Virginia tried to look innocent,

144

unconcerned as the diplomatic car drove slowly across the bridge, but her heart flip-flopped with fear when the Spanish soldiers leaned in to inspect Tommy's *salvo conducto,* and she waited for "the terrible moment" when they would demand her own, non-existent permit. "It never came," she wrote dramatically. Tommy's diplomatic status had worked a charm, and the guards "nodded with a satisfied air, handed back the paper and saluted. The barriers rose slowly, Tommy stepped on the gas, and we dashed across the bridge to freedom."[31]

Although Virginia had developed a loathing for Franco and his coup, she had little doubt that it would succeed. For Martha, however, it was impossible to give up hope. The Loyalists had "an apparently unlimited supply of guts," she wrote, and she believed that the weeks she'd spent with them in Madrid had been "by far and away the best thing" she had ever "seen or lived through."[32] Once she'd left Madrid in early April, she'd stopped off in Paris and had been almost offended to find the French still engrossed in their usual pursuit of pleasure. She'd been unable to resist some of the city's seductions, and had gorged herself on unrationed food, luxuriated in freshly laundered sheets. But the familiar Parisian twittering over jazz bands and fashion, the gossip about Schiaparelli having gone surrealist with her collection of telephone-shaped handbags and lobster-decorated gowns, seemed to come at Martha from an alien world.

Surrealism was everywhere in Paris, its formerly radical spirit diffused over advertising, fashion and film. One of the most anticipated events of the social calendar, in May, was a surrealist costume ball at which guests would compete for the éclat of being the most bizarrely attired. Man Ray and Max Ernst would be among the artists in attendance, the latter dressed outlandishly as a beggar, with his thick white hair dyed a brilliant blue. Also present would be the American photographer Lee Miller, who'd once lived in Paris as Man Ray's lover and protégée. She'd returned there in flight from a failing marriage, to be reunited with her artist friends, and, at this point in her life, she would not yet pause to consider the irony of sophisticated Parisians impersonating beggars and tramps while, only a thousand kilometres away, innocent Spaniards were being bombed from their homes.

Those Spaniards were now lodged deep in Martha's conscience though, and before she returned to Madrid, she was planning to use her summer in America to drum up support for the Loyalist cause. In early June, she was at the Second Congress of American Writers, in New York's Carnegie Hall, overcoming her terror of public speaking to inform 3,500 writers that every one of them "must be a man of action now." In July, she arranged a White House screening for *The Spanish Earth,* hoping that its stark portrayal of Loyalist suffering would soften Roosevelt's heart and persuade him to reverse his government's renewal of the Neutrality Act.

But, back in Madrid, three months later, Martha was struggling to keep faith with her own call to arms. Two-thirds of Spain had now fallen to the Nationalists, the Loyalist army had been decimated and she was unable to ignore the "feeling of disaster that swung like a compass needle, aimlessly, over all the city."[33] So many had died in her absence: "I thought I knew everything about the war," she mourned, "but what I didn't know was that your friends got killed." As the gaiety and hopefulness of *La Causa* gave way to a creeping sense of futility, Martha was also tormenting herself with doubts about her relationship with Hemingway.[34] Although Ernest was adamant in his determination to marry, Martha was unsure if she could bear the guilt of breaking up his family, and even more unsure if she and Ernest were capable of sustaining a domestic relationship of their own. Once they'd left Spain behind, she suspected their love might not survive a more humdrum reality: "he and I will wear each other out, as millions have done so well before us, chipping a little each day," she wrote anxiously in her journal. "Oh God either make it work or make it end now."[35]

Their physical relationship still failed to inspire. As Martha later confided flatly to a friend: "my whole memory of sex with Ernest is the invention of excuses and failing that, the hope it would soon be over."[36] But, while she'd become accustomed to absenting herself emotionally from his lovemaking, she was finding it difficult to dismiss the professional tensions that were starting to niggle between them. Martha's reporting from Spain had brought her some modest celebrity: *Collier's* was now paying $1,000 per article, and other commissions were following. Yet, while Ernest could be generously proud of her success, he was also capable of turning it against her. Beneath his habitual swagger, he was as defensive and uncertain as any writer. If he was having a bad day at the typewriter, if Martha was succeeding a little too well, he had a tendency to punish her for it, belittling her talent, accusing her of being greedy for fame.

The ambivalence he felt towards Martha's journalism leaked into the new play he'd begun in Madrid. Its heroine, Dorothy Bridges — who was a war correspondent, and possessor of "the longest, straightest, smoothest legs in the world" — was obviously modelled on her.[37] But the portrait was far from flattering: Dorothy was described as "uneducated and lazy . . . a bored Vassar bitch, who . . . can write quite well [but is] enormously on the make," and while Martha tried to laugh the caricature off as a parody, it caught her where she was most vulnerable.[*]

She too had returned to fiction that autumn, starting work on a novel about Spain, but it was a painful exercise. Every sentence read to her like substandard Hemingway, and the more she edited, the "lousier and lousier" it became. By the end of December, she had become so entangled in private doubt and professional anxiety that she left Madrid for America, hoping to purify herself in one last-ditch effort for the Loyalist cause. She spent three weeks on a lecture tour, urging women's clubs and colleges to appreciate the international scale of the fascist threat, the necessity of combatting it in Spain. So vehemently did she throw herself into the tour, she lost almost a stone in weight and made herself ill with fatigue. Wretchedly, she admitted to Eleanor Roosevelt, "I don't believe anything that any of us does now is useful. We just have to do it."[38]

Still, Martha felt "angry to the bone" and,

[*] The hero of *The Fifth Column,* a hard-bitten but politically committed secret agent named Philip Rawlings, also bore some distinct resemblance to Ernest himself.

unable to abandon Spain, she returned with Ernest the following March. This time, they were in Barcelona, where thousands were now dying from slow starvation, as well as from the daily assault of bombs. When Martha walked through the children's ward of Barcelona's main hospital, she could hardly bear to look at the rows of small silent figures, their huge black eyes staring dully back at her, too scared and too hungry for tears. Travelling north to the Spanish–French border, she saw yet another tragedy unfolding, as the defeated and displaced were herded into squalidly makeshift camps. Martha cabled to *Collier's* that it was like "the last days of Pompeii," but her editor, Charles Colebaugh, had lost interest in this unravelling war. "Stale by the time we publish," he bluntly replied, and he told Martha that she was needed elsewhere in Europe, to cover events of a far more drastic immediacy.[39]

Exactly as Sigrid had predicted, Hitler had been impatient to embark on his own "eastwards push" once he'd successfully tested his weapons in Spain, and on 12 March 1938, he'd sent troops into Austria, annexing his neighbouring state in a coup of near-bloodless speed. So efficiently had this Anschluss been managed that Hitler had begun making belligerent threats towards the border territories of Czechoslovakia. It was early April, and as yet those threats were only vocal, but even Martha had to concede that Germany's unleashed aggression was a more imperative story than the end game in Spain. If Hitler's territorial greed was left unchecked, he could drag the rest of the world into war, and already Martha's political contacts were predicting that the resulting conflict could be a bonfire of the vanities, a toxic conflagration of ancient rivalries, imperial ambitions and vested interests. "The war in Spain was one kind of war," she observed hopelessly to Eleanor Roosevelt, "[but] the next world war will be the stupidest, lyingest, cruellest sell out in our time."[40]

CHAPTER FOUR:
THE LEAGUE OF NATIONS,
GENEVA, 1934–7

"Fighting the merchants of death"
HELEN KIRKPATRICK[1]

In the summer of 1934, a short article appeared in the British local press celebrating the achievements of a young peace activist, Clare Hollingworth. "Leicester Girl Honoured," ran the story, which boasted of Clare's rapid promotion to regional organizing secretary within the British League of Nations Union, a close affiliate of the international League. The piquancy of this titbit of news, at least for the press, was not that Clare was the first woman to rise so high in the LNU, but that at twenty-three, she appeared far too youthfully pretty for membership of the Union. With her hair elaborately waved beneath a close-fitting hat, and her large, brilliant eyes outlined with kohl, Clare glowed with the sweet, conscientious polish of an aspiring socialite, and she looked nothing like the earnest middle-aged cranks who were popularly assumed to dominate the peace movement.

The Union had in fact been very conscious of Clare's looks when they made her a poster girl for their cause, sending her out to lecture in schools and clubs, and to lobby Westminster MPs on their behalf. But, loyal though Clare was to the Union, she'd outgrown that photograph of herself and she was already becoming aware that her work offered limited prospects. The high point of her duties so far had been a visit to Geneva, where she'd represented the LNU at the League itself. Everything about that experience had felt momentous to her — wandering through the palatial rooms of the League's headquarters, listening to debates in the Council's chamber, hovering on the fringes of the press room, where some of the world's top reporters were gathered. Proximity to this level of power was dazzling, and Clare knew that she wanted her own share of it. Already, she was wondering how she could combine her loyalty to the LNU with some larger field of operation — parliamentary politics, academia or even journalism — and wondering how she could advance her own ambitions while remaining in the service of peace.

But the second half of the 1930s was a confusing and troubled period for pacifists like Clare. A catalogue of international crises — Japan's attack on Manchuria in 1931, followed by Mussolini's invasion of Abyssinia,

153

Franco's coup and Hitler's military incursions — would stall the League into an impotent dither. Resolutions were passed and sanctions threatened, yet, as the shadow of totalitarianism spread over Europe, a generation of idealists struggled to maintain a position that was not only an article of faith, but, for many, a way of life.

For Martha Gellhorn, the loss of her early pacifist beliefs had been more liberating than painful. They were interfering "with my principles to use my eyes," she wrote bluntly, and in Spain she'd embraced the view that anyone who believed in freedom and justice — "the decent words" — ought to be willing to defend them by force.[2] But Clare hesitated a long time before making that intellectual and emotional leap. She continued to oppose the use of arms right up until the end of 1938, and it would not be until September 1939, and almost by an accident of circumstance, that her life's vocation would shift from promoting the cause of peace to writing about war.

Nothing of the drama and the international reach of Clare's adult career could be predicted from the world of her childhood. Born on 10 October 1911 and raised in the pretty, tranquil Leicestershire village of Knighton, she was still a toddler when Britain went to war with Germany in August 1914. Her father, John Hollingworth, always called Albert, was a travelling salesman for his father-in-law's shoe business; when the war broke out, he was put in charge of the factory's rural branch and deemed to be engaged in essential war work. While other men were sent off to the front, Albert could remain at home with his wife, Daisy, and their two daughters — Clare, an attractive, energetic child with large round eyes and a tumble of dark hair, and Edith (always known as Peg), her more delicately blonde baby sister. When German Zeppelins flew over the house to bomb a nearby town, it was more of a novelty than a threat. "We children were awakened by the excitement," Clare recalled, "and were taken out into the garden to see those great silver flying machines slowly crossing the sky."[3] On 11 November 1918, when the church bells rang out for Armistice Day, the Hollingworth family had no dead to mourn and no reason to anticipate anything but a peacefully contented future — a future in which Albert would prosper in the shoe business and Clare and Edith would grow up to find decent, reliable husbands of their own.

This, at least, was the family's placid expectation, but Albert himself was to be partially responsible for setting his oldest daughter on a very different path. He had a keen interest in military history, much of it gleaned from a neighbour's extensive library, and lacking a son with whom to share his enthusiasm, he co-opted Clare. Some of her most vivid childhood memories were of accompanying her father to former battle-grounds, and being so proud of her chosen position that she would "memorize every thorn tree" on Bosworth Field and willingly walk every inch of ground at Naseby, Crécy and Agincourt.

By the time she was twelve and sent away to boarding school, Clare considered herself a history buff. A clever, confident child, she might well have been steered towards higher education, but, as she confided to Edith, the popular girls were all "mad about sports" and she was reluctant to be singled out as "a swot."[4] Years later, she would claim that she'd wanted to go on to university and had been denied the opportunity by her parents. Yet the more ordinary truth was that Clare was a conventional teenage girl, with conventional expectations, and she made no real protest when she was taken out of school at the age of sixteen and sent to a domestic-science college in nearby Leicester. She'd formed no independent plans of her own and, like almost every other girl of her acquaintance, she assumed that her next goal in life was simply to meet and marry a suitable man.

A year later, she thought she'd found him. Reg Burton was the son of a comfortably wealthy family and very good looking, in a sharp-featured way.[5] Decades afterwards, when Clare wrote her memoir, she would dismiss him in a single sentence — "a suitable young man in the county who was also active in the Territorials." But, at the time, he'd been fun, courting her with long drives in his expensive motor car, invitations to hunt balls and lessons in the newly fashionable sport of golf. After a proper interval, Reg proposed, and when the two of them sat for their engagement photograph — he a self-conscious dandy in a polka-dot bow tie; she with a large diamond ring sparkling ostentatiously on her hand — Clare gave every appearance of having settled for a happily married future.

Yet Clare hated that photograph. "It made me look like a jewellery advertisement," she commented dryly, and it was now that her curiosity and her restlessness began to quicken.[6] She was keen — far keener than most young women in provincial middle-class England — to have Reg make love to her. Sex had never been a mystery: the Hollingworths had lived on a farm for part of the war, and Clare had seen calves and lambs being bred and born; at boarding school, as she laconically recalled, "Lesbianism was not unknown."[7] Now that she was engaged, she saw no practical or moral reason why she should hang on to her virginity. And so pleasurable did she find the losing of it, she sent her little sister into a blush of embarrassment by suggesting that Edith and her boyfriend experiment with each other too.

Clare's adventurousness was presumably appreciated by Reg, but he was far less comfortable when she began to question other aspects of her life, to recognize that golf and motoring had only limited appeal and that she needed to fill her days with more useful employment. Had Clare volunteered for a local charity, Reg might have understood. But the job she found was managing a YWCA hostel in Worcester, seventy miles away, and not only would it involve her in the lives of potentially undesirable women, it would mean she was spending part of her week away from home.

Clare herself admitted she would have preferred some more intellectually challenging employment, but she had a small staff to manage at the hostel, a budget to command and, once she'd settled into the work, she discovered she had a talent for organization. She was also studying the newspapers, looking at world events with a more critical eye, and as she came to appreciate the gravity of America's economic crisis and the political chaos that was brewing in Germany, she realized it would be impossible to settle for a life with Reg. Later, she insisted the break had been initiated by her, but Edith's diary entries for July 1933 suggest that it was Reg himself, alarmed by the changes in Clare, who'd ended the engagement: "Reg ran away," Edith wrote. "Mummy is in an awful state . . . Poor Clare cried after lunch with tying Reg's letters up so we all cried."[8]

To be jilted at the age of twenty-one was mortifying, even for Clare, but she was temperamentally a realist and had little use for self-pity. Once she'd shed her tears over Reg, she was ready to embrace her freedom; that same summer, she enrolled for an intensive course on international relations, held at the Institut de Hautes Études, in Geneva. The Institut was housed in a large villa on the outskirts of the city, but its programme of lectures was affiliated with the League itself and the atmosphere was intoxicating. Clare was studying in the heart of world politics, she was being challenged to think rigorously for the first time in her life, she was mixing with students from all over Europe and she was half in love with one of them, an idealistic youth named James Avery. By the time she returned home to Knighton, she'd not only exorcised Reg from her life, but was ready to dedicate herself to the pacifist cause.

Conscious of her inadequate skills, Clare took a short secretarial course and then volunteered her services to the Worcestershire and South Gloucestershire branch of the LNU. As young as she was, no one expected very much of her. But Clare had a natural physical authority and a brisk, logical mind, and her promotion to lecturer, lobbyist and organizational secretary came in quick succession. Month by month, her world was expanding. In the summer of 1934, she spent her holiday in Zagreb, zealously keen to learn some Croatian and to get a grasp on Balkan politics. But the revelation of that trip turned out to be her friendship with a young German Jew named Otto, who had fled from the Nazis and was now lodging in the same pension. Clare had spent the last year denouncing the politics of fascism, but she'd never met one of its victims, and the story that Otto confided to her, of being hounded from his home during the first wave of Nazi anti-Semitism, of living in exile and in daily fear of arrest, was vividly, shockingly affecting. She drew close to Otto, and Patrick Garrett, Clare's great-nephew and biographer, suspects that the intimacy which sparked between them was probably sexual.

In Clare's own, subsequent recall of this summer, however, Otto barely featured. While she would always pride herself on having very modern relationships with men, she maintained an old-fashioned distaste for talking about them. She believed that a private life was precisely that — of no interest to anyone else, and of limited interest even to her. While many of her generation were fashionably obsessed with dreams and the subconscious,

160

Clare tended towards a sturdily pre-Freudian view of the world; while agony-aunt columns were all the rage in the popular press, she maintained her dislike of the confessional. Years later, when writing the story of her life, Clare not only edited out most of her three first loves — Otto, James and Reg — but gave very short shrift to her first husband, whom she met shortly after returning from Zagreb. Bluntly, she stated that Vandeleur Robinson had shared her own growing "interest in the politics of central and south-eastern Europe" and that, as a consequence, the two of them had "decided to marry."[9]

Vandeleur, always known as Van, was a fellow member of the LNU, an academic historian and radical socialist, and it's fair to assume that, when Clare first saw him in London, he wasn't an obviously romantic prospect. Ten years her senior, shabby, short-sighted and very frugal in his habits, Van was unhappily married and in the middle of a divorce suit. But he was also politically charismatic and very clever, and, because Clare was young and very hungry for knowledge, it did not take her long to believe herself in love. By the end of 1934, she'd moved down to London and, inflicting yet another blow to her parents' expectations, was living with Van in a modest rented flat on Ebury Street.

Everything felt possible now. While Clare

continued to work for the LNU, she was cramming her days with improving activities. She went to the House of Commons to follow parliamentary debates; she joined the Royal Institute of International Affairs; and, embarrassed by her limited education, she enrolled for a history course at the School of Slavonic and East European Studies. Her principal teacher, though, was always Van. During their first summer together, he took her on an ambitious tour of Eastern Europe and the Balkans, so that he could assess the region's political mood, its potential to become a flashpoint in a future war. For any other young woman, this holiday might have been an ordeal; Van had limited interest in sightseeing and was so rigidly parsimonious that they took overnight trains to save money on hotels and ate out in the very cheapest cafes. But the grainy little photographs which Clare saved from that holiday had a spirit of bohemian adventure: someone had captured the two of them sitting side by side in their sandals and shorts; Clare had been photographed, grinning and windswept, in her swimming costume by the side of the Sava River. However unsentimental she would become about Van himself, these images would obviously remain important to her, as markers of the distance her husband had helped her to travel from Knighton and from Reg.

Although Clare was intellectually in thrall to Van, she was very far from being his acolyte. When she agreed to marry him, in November 1935, it was only on condition that she retained her own surname. The following year, when he began to talk seriously of joining the Communist Party, Clare wasn't tempted to follow. She distrusted political dogma — even when she'd joined the Labour Party, she'd made it clear she disagreed with much of its manifesto. But she was wary, too, because Van's embrace of communism was driven by his growing disaffection with the League of Nations. Geneva's inability to deal with the war in Spain and the fascist alliance among Franco, Mussolini and Hitler had shaken Van badly, and, like many committed socialists, he was drawn to the idea of supplanting the League with a new international body — a group of left-leaning nations, led by Russia, which would have the collective muscle and will to tackle Europe's dictators.

Clare was not blind to the League's flaws, but she still maintained it was the world's best available option for maintaining a balance of power. Democracy, she believed, stood a far better chance when led by Geneva, rather than by Moscow; even when Hitler marched into Austria and threatened to make inroads into Czechoslovakia, she would try to keep faith with the basic principles of rational diplomacy. During the autumn of 1938, however, her certainties were shaken when she and Van went to Prague to help with the mass of refugees in flight from Hitler's eastward advance. Any one of those terrified, displaced people could have been an Otto, and, as Clare volunteered in the temporary refugee camps, trying to alleviate some of the misery, she was conscious, as never before, of the scale of human suffering that fascism could wreak.

Even now, she'd never visited Hitler's Germany; but, late in December, she and Van travelled to Kitzbühel, an Alpine resort in Austria which was popular with high-ranking Nazis. Scarlet and black swastikas hung from the town's Grand Hotel, uniformed SS officers shouldered their way through the streets; and it was plain from their grandstanding demeanour, from the insolent clip of their voices, that these men regarded themselves as the *Herrenrasse*, the master race of Europe. Their arrogance was so repellent that when Clare returned to London, she wrote in dramatically pessimistic terms about the menace they presented to the rest of the world. "There are many nations who, when they go to bed at night, can't be certain that their nationality will be the same when they wake up the next morning," she concluded. And now that she'd acknowledged the gravity of the danger, she was realist enough to let go of her pacifist faith.[10] All that she'd witnessed of the refugee crisis in Prague and the German occupation of Kitzbühel had fully convinced her that weapons, not words, were the only way to stop the Nazis and the only way to keep Europe free.

Helen Kirkpatrick had been no less devout a pacifist than Clare, but her faith in diplomacy and the moral case against war had foundered two years earlier, over the conflict in Spain. In 1936, she'd been working in Geneva as a freelance journalist and had been an unhappy witness to the League's ineffectual handling of Franco's coup and to the illicit alliance with Mussolini and Hitler. A Council debate on 17 November had disintegrated into an especially hapless display of hand-wringing, and Helen, sitting as usual in the press gallery, had noticed that one of her fellow journalists, a Czech, had been following the proceedings with peculiar agitation. When the session concluded and the delegates were preparing to leave, the young man rose suddenly to his feet. "Czechoslovakia is going to be next on the list!" he shouted, and then, in an anguished act of protest, he shot himself.[11]

The violent retort of the gun within the Council chamber, the mess of blood and the hopeless finality of the suicide felt shockingly symbolic to Helen, and reporting on the incident for the *New York Herald Tribune,* she prophesied that it must surely spell the end of the League. "Full realisation of [its power-lessness] to cope with the international situation dawned upon Geneva today," she wrote, and, accurate though that observation was, it had been horrible to write.[12] Ever since she'd been at college, ardently denouncing the "old men's regimes" and the "merchants of death" who'd sent the world to war in 1914, Helen had based her entire moral code on the League and its vision of global cooperation.[13] When she'd then had to watch that vision unravelling in late 1936, and experience the unravelling of her own convictions, it was very hard for her not to feel that some essential part of herself had been lost.

To Helen's parents, Lyman and Lyde Kirkpatrick, their daughter's identity had always been something of a puzzle. Both of them came from old family and old money, and, when Helen was born on 18 October 1909, they planned to raise her like any other little girl of their privileged tribe. She would be decently educated, of course, but would then be sent to a finishing school in Paris or Florence, where she would acquire the necessary polish to sparkle her way through a debutante's season and attract a suitably situated husband. As Helen commented, in dry retrospect, "This was the way one went at that time"; certainly it was the way it went in her family's own particular corner of Rochester, New York.

But, even at the age of six, she was deviating from the family plan. A tall, thin, sandy-haired child, she preferred stamp collecting to dolls and she greatly disliked being called Helen, answering only to derivations of her surname — "Pat" or "Kirk." Mostly, her parents were entertained by her independence. But, once she'd turned eighteen and had grown to her full height of five foot eleven inches, Helen became a more challenging prospect. "I was a late bloomer, a gawky awkward girl with no small talk," she remembered, and her coming-out summer was the most wretched of her life, as she fidgeted on the edge of the county's dance floors, hoping that a boy would offer to partner her, knowing that, if he did, he would probably "only come up to my chin."[14]

It was worth enduring the misery of that season, though, because it justified Helen's case that she be allowed to accept the place she'd gained to study history and philosophy at Smith. Her mother, Lyde Kirkpatrick, had always been opposed to the idea. Despite being clever and curious-minded herself, she'd always maintained that "college women were bluestockings, not very attractive."[15] Now, faced with Helen's gauche attempts to shoe-horn herself into society, Lyde could see that a degree from Smith might offer her daughter a much better future. But there was another, more painful reason why Helen went to college unopposed. During the last few years, her father, Lyman Kirkpatrick, had made a number of hapless property investments and was now on the verge of bankruptcy.* The family's finances were so fraught, and Lyde and Lyman were so bitterly divided over them, that the prospect of Helen becoming a bluestocking was the least of their concerns. Lyde was actually suing for a divorce and, while this period of discord would be temporary — she and Lyman would remarry just a few years later — Helen remembered her last year at home as frighteningly acrimonious. Mealtimes were "things to dread" and there were nights when her parents' rows would drive her little brother, Kirk, into Helen's own bed for comfort.[16†]

In September 1927, when she was driven up to Massachusetts to begin her freshman year, Helen felt a guilty relief that her own separate life was about to start. "It was wonderful. I loved it — loved every minute of

* Helen's grandmother had been paying the bulk of her tuition fees, but, when she died, Helen was forced to abandon Smith and attend the local college in Rochester. Her exile was only for one semester, though, as she was able to return to Smith on a scholarship.

† Kirk was christened Lyman Jr, but he too seems to have preferred to use a variant of his surname.

it." She no longer felt loomingly conspicuous among her peers — the unofficial uniform at Smith, a preppy tweed skirt, Brooks Brothers pullover, sports shoes and pearls, suited her very well; and her inadequate small talk was no longer an issue, now that she was in the company of clever, enlightened girls. "Everyone was very involved in things like disarmament and what was going on at the League of Nations," and during the long evenings in which Helen argued over the prospects for world peace, she found both her confidence and her voice. She was elected head of the college debating society, president of the international-relations club and, when she graduated in 1931, the glittering prize of her college career was a scholarship to Geneva, where, in very close contact with the League itself, she would be studying for a master's degree in international relations.[17]

It was, she wrote, simply a "dream come true." Great men like Léon Blum and Gandhi came to lecture, there was always some ongoing debate about the overthrow of capitalism or the possibility of a world government, and to Helen it seemed as though she'd arrived at the centre of everything that mattered, that Geneva was like a "seismograph . . . registering all the social and political upheavals of the world."[18] But what gave special lustre to all these new experiences was the discovery that she was attractive to men.

Ever since she'd turned eighteen, Helen had accepted that her sharp, candid features would never pass for prettiness, that her gawky height would make her tower over every room; now, in Geneva, however, where women students were a prized minority, she told her mother that men were lining up to give her "the swellest time in the world." There was Jean, the "most fascinating person . . . [who] has me at his feet"; a handsome Swede named Ivar, "very sophisticated, a very good dancer and lots of fun"; and an "earnest, tweedy, pipe smoking" Harvard graduate, with whom she had a brief and ill-judged engagement.

Lyde Kirkpatrick must have thrilled to the letters that Helen wrote home, letters that enthused in a most un-bluestocking way about the cut and colour of a new dress, about the giddiness of one end-of-term ball where she had "danced from ten until five and today have no skin on my feet."[19] Yet, even though Helen joked that she was spending more time in nightclubs than lecture halls, she was too sensible, too diligent to lose her head. In the autobiographical novel she'd begun drafting, she had her fictional alter ego reflect, with a mix of relief and regret, that despite the fact that she "danced extremely well and was as well dressed as any Smith girl is supposed to be" she would never become "one of those flighty girls" who abandoned their studies.[20] She was in fact working harder than she admitted. In May, she was one of just two students selected to give a paper at the League's disarmament conference; her tutor's reference was glowing: "of all the American students here in Geneva I think Miss Kirkpatrick by far the most promising;" and, when Helen graduated in the summer of 1932, she was very tempted to go on to a second, higher degree.[21]

But the family finances were still precarious, so precarious that Helen's mother had been forced to take a job in Macy's department store in New York and Helen was very conscious that she too ought to be earning some independent money. She'd had some success in Geneva with her student journalism, and had been encouraged by John Whitaker, diplomatic correspondent for the *New York Herald Tribune,* to try for a job on a foreign news desk — indeed, Whitaker had actually arranged for her to be interviewed by his own paper. However, it was in the office of the *Herald Tribune*'s managing editor that Helen first appreciated how protected she'd been within the rarefied ether of Smith and Geneva. Stanley Walker made it clear he was an old-school newspaperman with old-school views about women. As a courtesy to Whitaker, he could offer Helen some freelance work, but he was brutal about her chances of becoming a foreign correspondent — curtly dismissing her tentative enquiries with the assurance, "I would never send a woman abroad."[22]

Virginia Cowles, in late 1932, was still under the thumb of men like Walker as she tried to write her way to serious news. But Helen would not stoop to compromise. If journalism had no place for her Smith- and Geneva-educated mind, she would look for an alternative career; and, partly because she was now living with her mother and it seemed the most convenient option, she agreed to follow Lyde into Macy's, enrolling herself in the store's reputedly excellent course in shop-floor management.

For a few weeks, Helen congratulated herself on having made the sensible choice. The pay was good and, in early 1933, in the continuing economic slump, she knew she was lucky to have any kind of job. But, once the novelty faded, the prospect of spending day after day in the store's chinaware department filled her with a near-existential dread. "I'd wake up in the morning and say, 'You've got to get up.' Why? 'To go to Macy's.' Why? 'To earn enough money to pay the rent.' Why? 'So you can go back to work at Macy's.' "[23] So evident was Helen's misery in the checking of stock and the managing of staff rotas that, even though she was offered a permanent contract with the store, her supervisor begged her not to accept.

Meanwhile, there was a confusing, charming and very attractive man in her life. She'd met Victor Polacheck during her final weeks in Geneva and had fallen for his disarming mix of looks, brains and entrepreneurial gusto. Vic was fizzing with ideas about how to make his first million — he was determined to live up to his father, who was managing editor of Hearst — and Helen started seeing a great deal of him in New York. But while she acknowledged that she was "crazy about him," she grew wary when Vic started to talk about marriage. She'd always believed she would have a career before becoming anyone's wife, and, exhilarating though Vic's company was, she questioned whether the reckless vim and self-belief that made him so attractive as a lover would be quite so appealing in a husband.

Six months at Macy's, however, had started to make a future with Vic look more enticing. He'd recently moved to Chicago to launch a new business scheme, selling branded advertising to department stores, and he was putting pressure on Helen to join him as his wife. She knew in her gut it would be a mistake, but, faced with the alternatives of chinaware or unemployment, she couldn't resist and late in 1933 she accepted Vic's proposal. On 11 February 1934, Helen was walking up the aisle of the Church of the Ascension on New

York's Fifth Avenue, dressed in ivory satin and carrying a bouquet of calla lilies.

All her family had been against the marriage. It was evident to them that she couldn't be happy with Vic and, even at the church door, her brother, Kirk, had whispered that she should run while she had the chance. But Helen was too proud, too fastidious to create a fuss, and during her first six months of marriage, she and Vic were so busy with plans for their future, she had little time to examine her decision. Chicago turned out to be a dead end, Vic's advertising business flopped, but, once they moved back to New York, they were happily caught up in the novelties of life in Greenwich Village. Their house, rented from the poet Edna St. Vincent Millay, was in the middle of a gregarious community of writers, painters and communists; and, while Vic was intent on his next money-making scheme, Helen was occupied at the American Russian Institute, managing the publicity for an exhibition about Soviet education.

By the autumn, however, she had been married long enough to accept that her family's instincts had been correct and that Vic was "absolutely wrong as far as I was concerned." There was a streak of slyness and opportunism in his character, he lied a little too frequently, a little too well, and she could see that his business schemes were all a "bit close to the edge of being straight." When Helen discovered that she was pregnant, she knew, absolutely, that she had to terminate the pregnancy and, with it, the marriage.[24]

Her only thought was to get back to Geneva, where her life had once been so brimming with prospects and where she still had some friendly contacts. Paying for the abortion took most of her savings and she could only afford her boat passage to Europe by hiring herself out as a chaperone to a group of young women. She felt some bleak sense of liberation when she sent a cable from Geneva, informing Vic that she was "Not returning." But, otherwise, Helen had never felt lower or more vulnerable. She was debilitated by a bout of painful postoperative cystitis, Vic was "cutting up rough" about her request for a divorce and she had almost no money in her account.[25]* Too proud to ask for her parents' help, she rented a tiny room in a Salvation Army hostel and found some part-time work, interpreting for the French delegation at the League (her own excellent French acquired from a childhood governess). That first winter was very hard; weeks passed when Helen dined only on Brussels sprouts and cottage cheese, and she admitted

---

* Vic would continue to punish Helen in various ways, putting obstacles in the way of her proposed divorce and hounding her for forgiveness or even for money.

to her mother that she was "so damn sick of counting sous and being poor."[26] She felt very far from the hopeful girl who'd first arrived in Geneva, believing she had achieved her "dream." But, early in 1935, she managed to get herself a more substantial job, managing the Geneva office of the U.S. Foreign Policy Association.

The hours were still only part time, but the FPA was a worthwhile organization, its remit to educate the American public on international affairs, and the work was sufficiently interesting to lift Helen's confidence and re-engage her brain. Tentatively, she returned to the idea of journalism, and, encouraged by the success of some articles that she submitted to the League's in-house magazine, *Geneva,* she began asking around the press room if any of the correspondents could use her as a freelance stringer. Most of them had to cover news right across Europe, and Helen hoped that, during periods of high activity, they might find it convenient to have her gather information, check facts and even initiate her own stories. "If I can get my name on two publications then I am on the road I want," she wrote to her mother, and just three weeks later she was able to boast that she'd acquired "quite a clientele."[27] Diplomatic correspondents from the *Manchester Guardian,* the *Daily Telegraph,* the *Daily Express,* the *Paris Herald Tribune* and the *Montclair Times* all started to use Helen that autumn, and by early 1936 she'd become so well regarded that Léon Blum himself recommended her as a full-time stringer for the *New York Herald Tribune* — the same paper that, less than four years ago, had been so quick to dismiss her ambition.

The pay was meagre, just a hundred dollars a month, but it was enough for Helen to give up her job with the FPA and devote herself full time to news. She was modestly conscious of her youth and her sex; awed by men like Ed Mowrer, whom she revered as "perhaps the most interesting newspaper man yet," and wishing she could take advice from Sigrid Schultz, whose reporting from Berlin she greatly admired.[28] There were occasions when she doubted herself, especially when she had to interview a prominent public figure: "I used to die a thousand deaths before I'd go and see someone. I'd say, 'You have to do it, go ahead and do it.' "[29] Yet, even at these moments of uncertainty, Helen knew that journalism was her vocation. The challenges of meeting deadlines, mastering complex issues and shaping them into accurate prose were thrilling to Helen, and they were especially thrilling because she was writing in such extraordinary times.

■ ■ ■

One of the early successes she scored for the *Herald Tribune* was her coverage of Germany's reoccupation of the Rhineland. On 6 March 1936, she'd received a tip that Hitler was planning something momentous and, two days later, persuaded a friend to drive her from Geneva to Freiburg, near the head of the Rhine Valley. By the time they arrived, it appeared to Helen that the occupation was a fait accompli: Freiburg itself was in "gala attire with Nazi flags on every building and the streets filled with soldiers," while, along the western bank of the Rhine, the French seemed to be "lazing around," as though entirely indifferent to the Germans' presence.[30] At this point, Helen still considered herself a pacifist; yet, as she drove along the Rhine and stared at the disciplined ranks of Wehrmacht, at the unfurling swastikas, the symbolic display of tanks, she felt very afraid that this provocative show of force was merely a prologue for more aggressive incursions to come. She thought the French and their British allies had criminally misjudged the situation, guessing that if Hitler had been met in the Rhineland with a sharp military response, he would not only have been forced to retreat, but might even have been forced out of power.

Instead, he had triumphed, and Helen's fears of what might follow were heightened when she travelled from Freiburg to Berlin. She'd managed to arrange an exclusive interview with Carl von Ossietzky, the eminent German writer and Nobel Peace Prize winner, who'd been incarcerated back in 1933 for his opposition to the newly empowered Nazis. Ossietzky had suffered appallingly during the last three years. A Red Cross worker who'd visited him in his prison camp had found "a trembling, deadly pale creature, one eye swollen, teeth knocked out, dragging a broken, badly healed leg"; by the time Helen was able to meet him, he'd been transferred to a hospital and was dying from tuberculosis.[31]

She was incredulous that so distinguished a public figure could be abused with such impunity. Yet, the few days she spent in Hitler's Germany taught her that violence had become the norm. "The atmosphere . . . you could cut it with a knife. You had the feeling of being scared to death until you got out," she wrote, and she trembled for the friend with whom she was staying, a "very free spirit," who would happily tell a party official "to go to hell" if asked for a donation to Hitler's war machine.[32] By the time Helen left, she was so jumpy with nerves, she was terrified that the SS guards policing her train would discover some fault in her paperwork and drag her back to Berlin.

During that tense journey, Helen fell into conversation with an Englishman. He introduced himself as Dr. Simpson, director of the Imperial Chemical Industries at Mannheim, and at first Helen disliked him intensely. He appeared to be uncritically, even gushingly enthusiastic about the new Germany, praising Hitler's success in boosting the economy and in advancing technological research. But, once they'd reached the Dutch border and switched to another train, Dr. Simpson became a different man. He explained to Helen that he'd been subject to constant surveillance in Germany, that he feared his conversations were all overheard. Now that he was free to speak, however, he needed her to know that he had acquired crucial information about a chemical-weapons programme being developed in Germany, which he knew Hitler had every intention of deploying.

Simpson was going to pass this information on to London, but he begged Helen to use it too, in any way she could. During the summer, she would remember their conversation when she drove to the Spanish border and heard rumours of German poison gas being used against the Loyalists. She would remember it again, three months later, when she was sitting in the press gallery in Geneva and the young Czech journalist made his suicidal protest of despair. If a tyrannical state could harass a Nobel Prize winner to death, if a democratic nation could be bullied into submission with illegal chemical weapons, Helen had to concede, as Martha and Clare would do, that the League and its principles had been rendered useless.*

"In a year that has been filled with events of the most startling nature, there has possibly never been a month in which the European situation was so confused or so filled with the portents of war."[33] When Helen wrote that observation on 27 October 1936, she was already considering the merits of the radical notion, embraced by Vandeleur Robinson, that the work of the League could better be achieved by a new, Soviet-led organization. But she was temperamentally a moderate, and far more credible to her were the politics of a new pressure group which was gathering strength in London. Led by Winston Churchill, the maverick Tory MP, the group was united in its conviction that Britain could take the lead in creating an effective

* Although genuine reforms had been attempted, there was no collective will: France and Britain were refusing to commit to effective economic sanctions against Hitler or Mussolini for fear of damaging their own trade interests, while Russia, the other major power in Geneva, was no less obstructively in pursuit of its own agenda.

opposition to Europe's dictators, calling on the recently elected prime minister, Neville Chamberlain, both to position himself more aggressively as a champion of democracy and to build the British army back up to strength. To Helen, this Westminster cabal promised more hope of action than she'd sensed in months, and when an opportunity arose for her to go to London and work on a new magazine that would platform its views, she silenced her instinct for caution and jumped.

The *Whitehall Letter* was the brainchild of Victor Gordon-Lennox, diplomatic correspondent for the *Daily Telegraph* and one of Helen's closest friends in Geneva. He was a sentimental and generous man (while Helen and he were travelling to Paris for a story, Vic noticed that her winter coat was threadbare and tried to buy her a replacement). He was also fearless, and, with his collaborator Graham Hutton, he planned to shame the British press over its partial and inaccurate reporting of international affairs, and to shame the British government for its weak and complacent response to the fascist threat in Europe.

Chamberlain in particular seemed unable to believe that the civilized words and honeyed promises which came out of Berlin or Rome were fake. He was either too arrogant or too naive to believe that any fellow leader could lie to him, and Helen relished the story of how bemused the Prime Minister had been when warned that his correspondence with his sister-in-law in Rome was being monitored. "What a nasty mind you have," he had blustered. "Gentlemen don't do that."[34] Chamberlain's denial was fed by his belief that he could personally outwit the fascist alliance by forging closer diplomatic ties with Italy, putting a wedge between Mussolini and Hitler; and Helen, contemptuous of both the denial and the presumption, thought how magnificent it would be to be part of an enterprise that might expose the appeasers' folly. When she eventually flew to London, in October 1937 (the plane was "divine," she reported back to her family, "and the only way to travel"), she believed that she might be at the start of a brilliant new phase of her career. She had reached the point where she longed to have a regular news outlet of her own, where it was frustrating to stand in for other journalists, to pick up their slack. She wanted to investigate the issues she cared about, to have a voice that was powerful enough to call politicians to account. "Perhaps the start of another Dorothy Thompson," she crowed to her parents, and already she was imagining a future in which the *Whitehall Letter* might become known as one of the era's crusading publications, and in which she might make her name as its crusading reporter.[35]

CHAPTER FIVE:
SUDETENLAND, 1937–8

"The man who holds the
lightning in his hands"
MARTHA GELLHORN[1]

In mid-October 1937, Virginia Cowles was
also newly arrived in London and was being
driven out to the country to have lunch with
the former British Prime Minister, David
Lloyd George. The irascibly brilliant Welsh-
man, a ferocious opponent of Chamberlain's,
had been impressed by an article Virginia had
just published about her recent experiences
in Spain, and had asked a mutual acquaintance, Randolph Churchill, for an introduction to the author. Because no byline was attached to the piece, Lloyd George had
automatically assumed it was written by a
man, and there had been a moment of pained
confusion when he'd come out to greet his
guest and, instead of the military historian or
retired colonel he'd been led to expect, a
young American woman got out of the car,
wearing lipstick and high heels.

184

"The old man regarded me with a surprise that almost bordered on resentment," Virginia recalled, and she was cross with Randolph, who had deliberately and mischievously misled their host.[2] But, during the course of the afternoon, Lloyd George allowed himself to warm to Virginia. She stood her ground as he grilled her on the military situation in Spain; she nodded agreement when he lectured her on the likelihood of a wider war, stabbing at the map on his study wall to illustrate how many fronts the British would have to defend and how unprepared they were for the fight. By the end of the visit, he'd unbent sufficiently to honour Virginia with a tour of his farm — striding ahead, talking furiously and, to her fond American gaze, looking exactly "like an ancient prophet with his green cloak and his long white hair blowing in the wind."[3]

Virginia had grown up with an idealized view of Britain, derived largely from her childhood obsession with King Arthur and the stories of the Round Table. When she'd completed her assignment in Spain, her decision to spend a few months in London had been motivated as much by her desire to explore its "twisting crooked streets" as by the recognition that the city would be an ideal base from which to report on the gathering crisis in Europe.[4] It was Randolph, finally, who'd made up her mind. As the eldest son of Winston Churchill and a columnist for the *Evening Standard,* he'd not only promised to help Virginia find work, her contract with Hearst having ended with Spain, but to introduce her into his very large and influential circle of friends.

The two of them had met five years earlier, when Randolph had been touring the American lecture circuit. He'd been an opinionated twenty-one-year-old, very conscious of his status as Churchill's son, very free in his taste for women and drink, and when he'd appeared at Virginia's door one day, with a bouquet of flowers and a proposal of marriage, she'd told him he "was mad." Yet, while she could never entirely trust Randolph, she knew he enjoyed flexing his own power, and, true to his word, Virginia was commissioned to write a short series of articles on Spain for the *Sunday Times.*

She had good reason to hope that this could be her entrée into the world of British journalism. As far as she was aware, no UK correspondent had yet succeeded in reporting on the war from both sides, and most coverage had been skewed by the politics of individual papers — the Tory media embracing Franco as a crusader against communism; the left wing celebrating the Loyalist cause as a defence of democracy. Spain had become like "a crystal that held all the shades of rainbow," wrote Virginia. "You turned it to the light and chose the colours that suited you." In the current climate of bias and misinformation, there was no better moment for her to promote herself as a uniquely well-informed and disinterested commentator.[5]

Virginia's most detailed analytic report was published on 17 October and the following morning it was everywhere in Westminster and Whitehall. Her eye-witness account of German, Italian and Russian interference, her conviction that Spain had become a foreign-sponsored battle between communism and fascism, succeeded in ruffling the feathers of diplomats and politicians on all sides. Copies were placed on the desks of Chamberlain, Anthony Eden and Robert Vansittart; Lloyd George waved it vigorously in his hand as he addressed the House. Virginia could not have hoped for a better calling card in London, and within days it had opened the door to her ideal job, as roving correspondent for the *Sunday Times,* with a brief to cover political and social issues across Europe.*

This was the post towards which Virginia had been climbing, rung by rung, as she'd

---

* Virginia's father, who had begun following her career with pride, sent a copy to Eleanor Roosevelt, asking her to pass it on to the President in the hope of persuading him to reconsider American neutrality.

toured the world, interviewed Mussolini and braved the shells and interrogation cells of Spain. Yet, while she had worked hard for her luck, she'd also been fortunate in her friends — not least the man she'd just started seeing, whose father happened to be part-owner of the *Sunday Times.* Seymour Berry was a close friend of Randolph's, educated, like him, at Eton and Oxford, and with the same privileged assumption of social, intellectual and political status. (Seymour's father would shortly become Viscount Camrose, a title he would inherit.) Virginia was very susceptible to men with titles and brains, especially those who were British, and, on her first meeting with Seymour, she was disposed to fall very much in love.*

Those first few months in England were heady times, as, arm in arm with Seymour and Randolph, Virginia was welcomed into their interconnecting worlds. She took tea with the newspaper magnate Lord Beaverbrook, who evinced a "strange, almost feminine curiosity" as he probed her about the people she liked and didn't like in London. She gained privileged access to Robert Vansittart, the Undersecretary of State for For-

---

* Seymour would become a major player, appointed deputy chairman of the *Daily Telegraph* in 1939 and, three years later, vice chairman of a rival media group, the Amalgamated Press.

eign Affairs, who'd admitted that, on first hearing of Virginia as an expert on Spain, he'd imagined a "middle-aged frump" wearing "flat-heeled shoes and a man's tie."[6]

Most of these new acquaintances were from the anti-Chamberlain, anti-isolationist camp, and it was curious that Virginia did not record a meeting with Helen Kirkpatrick, since Helen, too, was being introduced to the same groups of people, including Beaverbrook (whom she thought "a real character and a rather sleazy one in many ways"), Robert Vansittart (who became one of her most valued sources for the *Whitehall Letter*) and Winston Churchill himself. Helen had been starstruck on her first encounter; the magnificent rolling certainties with which Churchill analysed the threats to European democracy and the strategies for countering them seemed to her both statesmanlike and agile: "He can produce a dozen [ideas] a day of which perhaps 5 or 6 are good," she wrote. "But they are so good he is invaluable."[7] She would, however, get nowhere near as close to him as Virginia, who, in her elevated position as Randolph's friend, was to become a regular guest at the family's home in Kent.

The first time she was invited to Chartwell, Virginia was unprepared for the amiable domesticity of her host. Dressed in a torn coat and battered hat, Churchill took her on a rambling tour of his house and grounds, showing off his paintings, his goldfish, and talking with sentimental pride about his wife, Clementine, and four children. He was nothing like the lofty politician and strict paterfamilias she'd imagined. But, over lunch, his mood turned and he'd silenced the table with a vehement diatribe against Chamberlain and his craven government. None of them had any true understanding of the fascist mentality, thundered Churchill. They might claim that the British were too psychologically and economically scarred by the previous war to accept the possibility of a second, but they had simply failed in their duty to explain the reality of the threat which the nation faced.

"We live in a very wicked world," he concluded. "English people want to be left alone [but] they can't escape"; and in February 1938, when Virginia was sent out to Barcelona, she would recall the pessimism of his words.[8] Like Martha, who would follow shortly afterwards, she was horrified to see the city staggering and starving under daily bombardment, and, now that the conflict in Spain was almost done, she also feared it would not be long before those fascist bombs would be directed elsewhere. This was the view of a Loyalist officer she met, who, resigned to the death of his own country, warned Virginia soberly, "We are only the first." Little more than a fortnight later, on 12 March, his prediction would be realized as Hitler sent his troops into Austria.

In London, the attack was initially viewed as an act of war. "Newsboys cried out to a cold grey world that Germany was on the march again," Virginia wrote, "and the tension was like a high-voltage wire."[9] An emergency debate was convened in Parliament, volunteers signed up for the territorial army and arms factories were put on high alert. Yet, bewilderingly to Virginia, that moment of crisis died away as powerful pro-German voices began reframing the terms of Hitler's Austrian Anschluss, presenting it as a necessary act of statesmanship rather than a violation of sovereign territory. Leading those voices was Sir Nevile Henderson, the British ambassador in Berlin. Henderson had long been in weaselly sympathy with the Nazi regime, approving most of its aims, if not all of its methods, and he now sent lengthy memos to Chamberlain arguing that Austria had been on the brink of anarchy, that it was infested with revolutionaries, and that Hitler's sole aim in dispatching his troops had been to restore order and protect the seven million ethnic Germans who were resident in the country.*

This was a perception that the Nazi regime

* When Henderson left Berlin to be treated for cancer, the dispatches written by his replacement were markedly more hostile towards the Nazis.

had been fabricating for months. They'd stage-managed street protests in cities across Austria, and they'd orchestrated attacks on businesses and properties, which were then catastrophized in the pro-Nazi press as signs of Bolshevik insurrection and social collapse. Although some of the crowds who'd cheered the arriving German troops had been under orders, Hitler was nonetheless able to boast that the people of Austria had welcomed his military intervention; if his Anschluss had been an act of war, it had, he claimed, been "a war of flowers."

As Virginia reported, the majority of the British establishment seemed ready to accept this convenient truth — including the Archbishop of Canterbury, who had "actually risen in the House of Lords to thank Hitler for preserving Austria from civil war."[10] She was disgusted by the muted official concern for the victims of this propaganda coup: the former Austrian Chancellor, Kurt Schuschnigg, who'd been thrown into a concentration camp despite his own fascist sympathies; the political dissidents who were beaten and jailed; the liberal-leaning lawyers and academics who were sacked from their posts; and the Jews who were being stripped of their dignity and rights with an implacable thoroughness and speed. Not only were thousands of them imprisoned and made homeless within days of the Anschluss, but community leaders were degraded with barbaric inventiveness — forced to scour out street gutters with their toothbrushes and to scrub public toilets with cloths made of their sacred tefillin prayer bands.

Of course, there were individual protests: on 24 March, Virginia was at the House of Commons to hear Churchill on his most coruscating form, pouring contempt on the lies being propagated by Berlin, begging the people of Britain to "rise up in their ancient vigour" and "save civilization." Yet, the pro-German faction had done its job; when Churchill finished speaking, the majority of the MPs simply "rattled their papers and shuffled their way to the lobby" — one of them, Harold Balfour, jovially assuring Virginia that, although "Winston likes to rattle the sabre and . . . does it jolly well, you always have to take it with a grain of salt."[11]

In May, though, Churchill and his sabre-rattling were vindicated, as Hitler began voicing his claim to the Sudetenland, the border areas of Czechoslovakia, which was home to three million ethnic Germans. There was a grain of legitimacy in Hitler's assertion that the latter regarded Germany as their natural home. Czechoslovakia itself was an awkward hybrid of a nation, constructed out of the dissolution of the Austro-Hungarian Empire in 1918, and within it the Sudeten Germans felt themselves to be an alienated, aggrieved minority. Ruled by a government that was dominated by Bohemian Czechs, the Sudetens believed they had been marginalized from recent economic reforms. When Hitler began making overtures to Konrad Henlein, leader of the Sudeten-German Party, it was a simple matter to foment active unrest. Using similar methods to those of the Anschluss, a string of protests and faked arson attacks had sent crowds of Sudetens out on the streets, not only demonstrating against the Prague government and its leader, Edvard Beneš, but demanding that Sudeten Germans be taken under the protection of the German Reich.

German troops were marshalled close to the border and Hitler seemed poised to annex yet another chunk of democratic Europe. But, unlike the Austrian Chancellor, Beneš was prepared to fight and when Virginia was sent out to report on the growing crisis, she saw a nation readying itself for war. In Prague, thousands of volunteers were responding to Beneš' call to arms, while, down in the Sudeten stronghold of Aussig, "a nightmare of flags, swastikas, banners . . . posters of Hitler and ear-splitting Heils" prepared a welcome for the Nazi troops.[12] Virginia was assured by one grinning official of the Sudeten-German Party that Hitler would not face much of a fight, because Beneš and his foreign allies had no real stomach for war. But she was unconvinced, and, when she returned to Prague to cable her report back to London, she discovered that half the world's press was apparently in agreement.

Within the space of twenty-four hours, her formerly deserted hotel had become crowded with foreign correspondents, all anticipating military action, all fiercely squabbling over the two international phone lines. And, in the centre of this raucous media circus, Virginia was pleased, but not entirely surprised, to find Martha Gellhorn. Martha had been typically quick to determine where her sympathies lay. Having walked around Prague, absorbing the "authentic, desperate, makeshift feeling of war," she'd already decided that Czechoslovakia was another Spain, another young democracy under threat from the fascist boot. When she witnessed the excited, angry crowds demonstrating their support for Beneš in Old Town Square, she believed that she'd seen the same "marvellous feeling of will" that had united Madrid.[13]

But there was to be no war, yet. Hitler had underestimated international concern about his latest show of force and, sensing that he'd pushed too far and too fast, he retreated with a show of self-righteous pique, declaring that he'd only been showing symbolic support for the Sudetens and that he harboured no "dishonourable intentions" towards the territorial integrity of Czechoslovakia. In France and

Britain, the retreat was hailed as a triumph of diplomacy, as proof that Hitler's grandstanding was mere bluster and noise. The new official motto was "standing firm," and the two Prime Ministers, Chamberlain and Daladier, actually tried to shift the blame onto Beneš, censuring him for the haste with which he'd mobilized his army, needlessly escalating the crisis.

None of this could be remotely reassuring to the Czechs. Now that their own closest allies had revealed their reluctance to fight, they were sure that Hitler would simply bide his time until the moment was ripe for another strike. They were equally sure that once he'd gained possession of Sudetenland, he would set his sights on the rest of Czechoslovakia. The country offered Hitler so much of what he required for the Reich's expansion — rich reserves of coal and timber, fertile pastureland and modern factories, as well as access routes to the Balkans, the Ukraine and the Black Sea. Yet, as starkly as the Czechs perceived their own peril, they had no friends left to assist in their defence and, as Martha miserably observed, their only option now was to wait — and to "watch the former house painter who . . . holds the lightning in his hands."[14]

While Czechoslovakia waited, Martha's next assignment was England, where her editor

Charles Colebaugh wanted her to canvass re-actions to this latest crisis. "Are the people alarmed?" he'd cabled. "What do they think of Fascism, or Aggression or the possibility of war?"[15] Her brief was to tour working-class communities in the Midlands and the North, a tranche of British life to which she was a complete stranger. And, according to Virginia, who volunteered herself as companion for the trip, Martha came away from the assign-ment convinced not only that the "people were not alarmed at all," but that the British were a nation of recalcitrant fools.

Perhaps it was Martha's appearance — her elegant clothes and her good American teeth — that made her subjects close ranks when she walked into a pub or factory canteen. Perhaps it was the directness with which she pitched her questions, the hint of imperious-ness with which she demanded to know what people felt about Spain, Czechoslovakia and the Nazi threat. Whatever the reason, Martha could find no one who wanted to engage with her on the subject of international affairs, no one prepared to venture more than a cosily stock response: "things were never as bad as the papers suggested," they said; "Chamber-lain was a fine man," and the government "always had an extra trick up its sleeve."[16] The apparent lack of curiosity, the smug insularity infuriated Martha: "They haven't any imagination at all," she fumed to Virginia, and so intense was her frustration, she forgot she was meant to be listening to the British and began lecturing them instead.

Virginia found the spectacle greatly entertaining — Martha on her soapbox, ranting about the evils of fascism, while her audience of farmers and factory workers gazed back in "mild surprise, as if she was a little queer in the head." She had formed a deep affectionate admiration for Martha, acknowledging that her "brilliant gift for writing," and her "passionate concern for the underdog" burned with a flame far hotter than Virginia's own. She would even unconsciously pay tribute to Martha's prose by adopting some of its characteristic phrasing and imagery.[17] Yet Virginia was also conscious that Martha could be too quick and too savage in her judgement. One elderly woman, who'd stoutly maintained that Britain "could never be defeated" whatever Hitler or any other fascist might do, had become the target of Martha's particular ire. Yet, as Virginia privately reflected, this was a woman who'd lived through three major wars and the "strange stubborn independence" with which she faced an uncertain future might not, she thought, be a reflection of ignorance, but an admirable form of courage.[18]

Her views had no traction with Martha. "The skulls of the British are so thick you can't crack them," she swore; all they cared about was "racing and weather"; worse, they had elected a Prime Minister who was a "kid-glove fascist," a craven hypocrite and the most "hateful figure in modern times."[19] But, if Martha was enraged by British inertia, the events of the summer gave her very good cause. Just as the Czechs had predicted, Hitler was quick to resume the attack, first issuing demands that Prague deliver political autonomy and financial recompense to the "abused" people of the Sudetenland, and then, on 15 August, reassembling his troops on the Czech border.

For the second time in three months, Europe was back on war alert: parliaments were recalled, diplomats were shuttled back and forth, and newspapers were scouting for every shred of news, opinion or conjecture. Virginia went to France, curious to know if there was any popular enthusiasm there for military intervention. But memories of the Great War still tormented the nation, like "an angry skeleton," and when she toured the desolate battlefields of Verdun and the Somme she understood why. Most of those she interviewed were desperate to avoid another conflict, and most took refuge in the certainty that Hitler would not be so rash as to provoke one. When she moved on to Berlin, however, to take a reading of the mood in Germany, she found the Nazis in a state of euphoric readiness for war. Uniformed soldiers and armoured cars patrolled the city and, even with her poor German, Virginia could sense a violent hysteria in the government's daily broadcasts and in the headlines blaring from newspaper billboards.

Every morning, a smiling official appeared at the Adlon Hotel to take charge of Virginia's day. He stuck implacably to his Party-approved script — that Hitler was a man of peace, that rumours to the contrary had been invented by the foreign press. Yet, as Virginia pointed out to her readers, these claims were belied by the "rumble of tanks" in the streets and by most of the other leading Nazis she met, who boasted openly that Germany would not only have control of the Sudeten-land by the end of the year, but would have the whole of south-eastern Europe in its grasp. If Chamberlain and his Cabinet still believed in the honourable intentions of Berlin, Virginia commented, "it was not due to Nazi discretion."[20]

The credulity of the British government was even more mystifying to Virginia when she travelled down to Nuremberg to witness the ceremonial opening of the Nazis' Tenth Party Congress. The event had been renamed "The Rally of the Greater Germany" in honour of the Austrian Anschluss, and as hundreds of thousands of Party faithful gathered in the city, their leaders were clearly preparing the way for an imminent attack on Czechoslovakia. Even before the congress had formally opened, Göring was whipping up the crowds with a speech that portrayed the Czechs as a "miserable pygmy race," and denounced their government as a bunch of racketeers in thrall to both the communists and "the eternal . . . Jew devil."[21] As Virginia walked around Nuremberg, amazed and repulsed by "the tramp of marching feet, the chanting of military Nazi hymns . . . the long red pennants fluttering from the turreted walls of the castle" it seemed to her that the entire city was participating in a fantasy of war, that the crowds were united by a rapt, religious blood-lust, like "some ancient crusade."[22]

The battle lines were drawn, even in the handling of foreign visitors. Journalists and diplomats from Italy, Spain and Japan were accommodated in the city's three central hotels, while those from less trusted nations were shunted into the sleeper carriages of parked trains. Access to top-ranking Nazis was also restricted to a privileged elite, and when it was announced that Hitler would be making only one informal appearance, at a teatime reception, Virginia considered herself lucky to be among the very few journalists who were allocated seats.

There were seventy other guests at that reception, and Virginia, seated near the back of the ornate banqueting hall, was expecting nothing from the event beyond her first glimpse of Hitler in the flesh. However, the rather ungainly young blonde woman who came and sat at her table turned out to be Unity Mitford, fourth daughter to Lord Redesdale and one of the Führer's more unlikely confidantes and friends. Unity had fallen under Hitler's spell when she'd attended her first Nuremberg rally, back in 1933, and he, flattered by her persistent courting, had admitted her into his inner circle. Now, at the reception, Virginia observed that it was Unity to whom Hitler directed his jerky flap of a salute when he acknowledged the room, Unity to whom "his glance wandered" even as he talked to the dignitaries at his own table. "I had the impression he was showing off to impress [her]," Virginia wrote. Shortly afterwards, an aide appeared, whispering to Unity that the Führer would like her to come to his suite as soon as the reception was over.

It was astonishing to Virginia that, on the brink of an international crisis, the "one person Hitler would condescend to see was a twenty-four-year-old English girl"; and she was determined to exploit this bizarre opportunity. Unity could prove to be one of the few people in Nuremberg to whom the Führer confided his private thoughts on Czechoslovakia, and, throughout the tea, Virginia worked hard to gain her trust, encouraging her effusive hero-worship of the Nazis, her inconsequential chatter about

London friends. Later that evening, when she "cornered" Unity in her hotel, the latter was more than ready to talk, but, while she claimed she had rarely seen Hitler in better spirits — "He says it is so exciting to have the world trembling before him" — Unity could not say precisely what his intentions were. When pressed by Virginia, she thought it unlikely that Hitler would actually go to war over Czechoslovakia, principally because he was too protective of the project he'd begun with the architect Albert Speer, to transform Berlin into a *Welthauptstadt,* a monumental world capital. Brightly deaf to the implications of her own remarks, Unity smiled: "He loves his new buildings too much to have them bombed."

As she babbled on, Virginia found it difficult to equate the Hitler of Unity's naive indiscretions with the warmongering dictator who "had people all over Europe tossing in their beds." Unity's Hitler much preferred gossip to politics, he disliked reading and he took great pride in impersonating his fellow fascists — Goebbels, Göring and Himmler, and most especially Mussolini. "If he were not the Führer of Germany, he could make a hundred thousand dollars a year on the vaudeville stage," Unity boasted. "But what he really likes," she added, "is excitement. Otherwise he gets bored."[23]

Virginia blanched to think that "world happiness hung on the *ennui* of one man." When she stood in the Nuremberg stadium, however, to watch Hitler address his Party faithful, it seemed to her that he was empowered by forces far greater than himself. Two hundred thousand Germans had gathered to hear their Führer speak and had greeted him with an ecstatic beating of drums, a roar of *Sieg Heil* chants and a "shimmering sea" of swastika flags. Objectively, Hitler had cut a drab, even meagre figure in his brown Nazi uniform, yet he appeared almost superhuman that night, his abrupt cartoonish gestures irradiated by vaulting columns of light, his words giving voice to a nation's collective fantasy of power.[24]

Disgusted and very much afraid, Virginia left Nuremberg before the rally was over, and she was back in Paris having a drink with Hubert Knickerbocker — "Knick," to her, now, as they were almost on equal terms — when the closing speech was broadcast on French radio. It came very close to a declaration of war, as Hitler, his fists pounding on the podium, his voice over-amplified to an operatic shriek, informed the world that, "if the poor tortured creatures of Sudetenland were not allowed to obtain rights and assistance by themselves," then Germany would come to their aid. So blatant was the threat that, early the next morning, Virginia and

Knick booked the next available flights to Prague.

When they reached the Czech capital, it was already on a military footing: martial law had been declared, air-raid shelters were being dug in the parks, children were being fitted with gas masks and volunteers were again lining up to enlist. Already there was talk of German troop activity in the Sudetenland, of German bombers in Czech airspace. Yet, still the crisis did not break. The British and French were still vacillating, and even though there was hopeful talk of military intervention, even though one rumour suggested they were working with a conspiracy of disaffected German officers to topple Hitler from power, everything that Virginia could learn from her own sources suggested that Chamberlain and Daladier were focusing all their efforts on the negotiating table.*

Days passed, and the stalemate continued. Daladier was no longer concealing his reluctance to fight, despite the defensive alliance between France and Czechoslovakia, and

* Helen, in London, was actually approached by a man claiming to be a "dissident officer of the German General staff" who wanted her to pass a letter on to the British Cabinet. She thought there was something fishy in his manner, though, and suspected he might have been a Gestapo agent, investigating British links with the conspiracy.

Chamberlain, too, was dragging his heels. Even though he'd finally accepted the necessity of military expansion, he maintained that Britain was far from battle-ready, its air force still only equipped with two dozen modern fighter planes. Meanwhile, in Berlin, the propaganda machine was in overdrive, issuing preposterous stories about Czech brutality, including the claim that Prague was sending armoured cars into Sudetenland "to mow down innocent women and children." Beneš no longer knew which way to turn and, on 21 September, he was forced to accept a proposal, formed in his absence, that, if he agreed to hand over all territories that were predominately ethnic German, Hitler would guarantee to leave the rest of Czechoslovakia alone.

"Absolutely forsaken," lamented the Prague media. However the situation was not yet resolved. Hitler had geared himself up for a war and he was outraged that the French and British had negotiated him out of one. Within twenty-four hours of signing the agreement, he issued a new round of threats, stating that, if the Sudetenland was not fully ceded within a week, he would send in tanks and bombers to take it by force. It was an impossible time frame and a ludicrous demand; Hitler himself had agreed that an international commission would be appointed to oversee the transition to German rule and, as Virginia reported, it seemed unlikely that even Britain and France would "have the face" to make the Czechs submit to this demand.[25]

Once again, the storm clouds gathered. When Virginia returned briefly to London to collect some warmer clothes, she saw slit trenches being dug in parks and precautionary gas masks being issued. As she travelled to the airport to catch the last remaining flight back to Czechoslovakia, she realized, with a sudden "queer feeling" in her stomach, that some of the buildings she passed might no longer be standing when she returned. When she landed at Prague, the airport manager, who'd only recently stamped her passport, was "torn with dismay" to see her again. He begged her to go back home, as did the worried desk clerk at the Hotel Ambassador, who told her that nearly all of the journalists had left and that the international phone lines were down. Virginia knew that Knick, at least, would still be in Prague, but when she found him, deep in discussion with his colleague John Whitaker, the two men seemed distinctly unenthused by her arrival. Whitaker, casting an irritated glance at Virginia's shoes, pointed out that there was likely to be "a hell of a lot of running to do" and that, if she wanted to stick around for the war, she should at least buy herself some more practical footwear.[26]

Early the next morning, 29 September,

Whitaker banged on Virginia's door. German planes were rumoured to be launching their first attack on the city at two o'clock, and, while he and Knick planned to go to the Czech war office to secure their formal accreditations, they needed Virginia to find a car and a supply of petrol. Two o'clock came, but still the skies remained clear, and, as the long afternoon dragged by, news came over the wires that Chamberlain and Daladier had been summoned to Munich. It appeared that Hitler had garnered insufficient support for his war, that several of his generals had joined with Mussolini in counselling prudence, and, having been urged back to the negotiating table he was obliged to put his signature to a new agreement, the terms of which were very similar to the one he'd just rejected.

On 30 September, Chamberlain was thus able to return to London with the triumphant announcement that "peace in our time" had been secured. Millions across Europe rejoiced — but, to the Czechs, the Munich Agreement spelled only betrayal and despair. For one glorious moment, they'd hoped that their allies would unite with them against Germany, but, as a violently distressed Beneš informed his people, that hope had been dashed. The Sudetenland was lost, the Czech borders had been compromised and it was clear that Hitler's guarantee to desist from any further land grabs was worth less than the paper on which it was written. Crowds surged onto the streets of Prague, chanting, "Let Czechoslovakia live! Long live Czechoslovakia!" and, to Virginia, the sound was "terrible to hear, like the cries of a wounded animal."[27]

All those who were rich enough or desperate enough were making plans to leave the city, and the foreign embassies in Prague were being mobbed with requests for emergency visas. Virginia, breakfasting in a pavement cafe with John Whitaker, was approached by an elderly German who begged openly for their help. He was a writer, whose dissident views had sentenced him to two years in a Nazi prison camp. "I couldn't stand it again," he said piteously. "I'm too old." Virginia and John tried to reassure him with reminders of the promises made at Munich, but, with an awful, tragic fatalism, the old man shook his head. "The Germans will be here soon. Everyone knows that."[28]

The doom that had descended on Czechoslovakia wrung Virginia's heart — and it half-killed Martha when she returned to write her final report for *Collier's*. She was convinced that Chamberlain and Daladier had always intended to make a sacrifice of the Sudetenland, that their temporary show of support had been a "vast comedy" designed to divert international censure.[29] Rage boiled in her as she drove around the region and learned that SS officers were already directing a purge of "anti-Nazi" elements, that children had been left alone, abandoned, because their dissident parents had been "disappeared." By the time she returned to Prague, Beneš had gone into exile and the crowds who gathered in the squares looked beaten and mute. They bowed their heads "as if for the dead," Martha wrote, and the article she filed for *Collier's* was titled, "Obituary of a Democracy."

CHAPTER SIX:
MUNICH, 1938–9

"Peace with dishonour"
DUFF COOPER TO VIRGINIA COWLES[1]

Helen Kirkpatrick had been at Heston airport, standing on the roof of a parked car to watch Chamberlain make his jubilant return from Munich. Crowds had gathered to cheer the Prime Minister as he'd stepped from the plane, his peace agreement waved aloft. But Helen, like Martha, felt only disgust. The world had entered "a state of godlessness," she wrote, and she despaired of the collective euphoria that swept through Britain, as newspapers heralded Chamberlain as a great man of peace and the public flocked to buy commemorative figurines in his image.[2] When Helen scoured the press for any dissenting views, it seemed that even the "ablest newspapermen" had been coerced to swell the applause for Munich — "to write things which they did not believe."[3]

Helen's own opinions on Hitler, Chamberlain and appeasement had been carefully positioned over the last year, principally within the pages of the *Whitehall Letter,* but in other publications as well. She'd fast acquired a reputation for clarity and insight, and if she wasn't quite the next Dorothy Thompson, a Gallup poll in July 1938 had listed her, alongside Thompson, as one of the world's top newswomen. That same year, the socialist and novelist Storm Jameson invited Helen for lunch at the Ivy and was impressed to find her as "well informed as anyone, as any foreign correspondent." So, when the *Sunday Times* commissioned Helen to write an opinion piece on Munich, she had every justification for assuming she would not be pressured to join the chorus of press endorsements, but would be free to express her own independent views.[4]

The article which appeared in print was barely recognizable, however, with every critical point either removed or rendered toothless. "I was mad," Helen recalled, almost as shocked by this violation of editorial principle as she was by Munich itself. With no other outlet, she vented her anger in a ferocious book, *This Terrible Peace,* whose one hundred and fifty pages gave her space to analyse all the ways in which she believed Chamberlain had not only cleared the way for Germany to become militarily invincible, but had diminished Britain's moral authority abroad.

The polemic took her just three weeks to

complete, but it had held Helen in such a white-hot rage of concentration that, afterwards, she collapsed. For several weeks she could barely eat or sleep, and eventually she had to admit herself to a private nursing home, where the staff took her condition so seriously, they put her under careful quarantine, forbidding her access to newspapers or radio and ordering her visitors to avoid all discussion of international affairs.

Later, Helen would acknowledge that she had written the book too fast and at too high a pitch. She'd been ignorant of key facts, like the telegram from President Roosevelt, which, far from condemning Chamberlain's stance at Munich, had simply read, "Good man." She'd downplayed the fine detail of the Agreement, which had warned that further German land grabs would be met with force.* But she was proud of it nevertheless. *This Terrible Peace* was respectfully reviewed in the British and American press — described as "required reading" in the *New York Sun* — and it so vexed Chamberlain that he attempted to get all copies removed from

---

* This would remain a contentious issue for decades to come; historians would argue that, if Chamberlain won time for Britain to rebuild its armed forces, he also allowed the Germans to expand their own war machine and to hone their strategies for invasion and occupation.

213

railway bookstalls.

It was, of course, popular among the Westminster anti-appeasers, whose attacks on the government were now doubly belligerent. Churchill's response to Munich had been typically magnificent, arguing that it had been a historic blunder, "a total unmitigated defeat for Britain"; but more damaging still was the resignation of Duff Cooper, First Lord of the Admiralty and a popular member of Chamberlain's Cabinet.[5] Afterwards, Cooper explained to Virginia Cowles that it had been Chamberlain's attempt to cast Munich as a moral triumph that had forced his decision: "it was 'peace with honour' that I couldn't stomach. If he'd come back from Munich saying, 'peace with terrible, unmitigated, unparalleled, dishonour' perhaps I would have stayed."[6]

Virginia and Duff had been dining together at the Ritz, where the post-Munich rapture was still casting its spell. A pair of giddy young lovers had taken over the dance floor, in a whirl of scarlet taffeta and black tails, and as Duff cast an ironic glance in their direction, he speculated grimly, "I wonder where that couple will be a year from today." He personally had little faith in the Munich Agreement holding, and everything Virginia had seen over the last two months convinced her, too, that Chamberlain's peace was merely a postponement of Hitler's war.

Just a few days later, however, Virginia was able to confront the Prime Minister face to face. She'd been invited to a small, politically gilt-edged supper party at which he was guest of honour, and had been seated beside him over coffee so that Chamberlain could quiz her about her recent trip to Prague. "I shall never forget [his] opening remark," Virginia wrote later. " 'Tell me,' he said smiling, 'did you find that the Czechs had any bitter feeling towards the English?' "[7] Startled into silence, unsure whether the question was grossly naive or grossly arrogant, Virginia reflected on the silent anguish of the Prague crowds, on the dignified fury with which a group of soldiers had warned her that France and Britain would surely come to regret the "two million Czechs," who would gladly have fought with them against Hitler but who would shortly "no longer exist" as a free people. When Virginia quietly described those scenes to Chamberlain, however, he showed no signs of remorse. He insisted that he could not have fought for the Czechs without Daladier, but he was also keen to impress on Virginia that military intervention would have been premature, because, in his view, Hitler was losing his grip. "A most difficult fellow," Chamberlain said ponderously, describing how irrational the Führer had appeared in recent meetings, and how out of touch with his own people. "The Germans are against war," added the Prime Minister, and, with a look of evident self-satisfaction, he described how he had been welcomed in Munich as a peace-making hero. "Even the S.S. men had cheered," he said, and he predicted that it would not be long before Hitler was removed from power by his own party.[8]

Virginia knew full well that those SS officers would have been cheering under orders, yet she preferred to let Chamberlain continue, unchallenged. This conversation was a professional gift, a blinding, if depressing confirmation of the gullibility, vanity and lack of imagination that had been muddling the Prime Minister's strategy, and as soon as she got back to her Mayfair lodgings, she typed up all she could remember of it, word for word.

Martha would have been incapable of such restraint. "Why don't you shoot Chamberlain?" she wrote indignantly to H. G. Wells. "What a man, with a face like a nutcracker and a soul like a weasel. How long are the English going to put up with these bastards who run the country?"[9] Europe had become a "stinking mess," Martha believed, and she'd developed a visceral hatred for all those "over medalled men" whom she deemed responsible. In November, she was in Paris, and on a mission to confront Sir Neill Malcolm, the elderly Englishman who was in charge of the League of Nations' Commission for Refugees. Back in Prague, Martha had grieved for the hundreds of thousands in flight from the Nazi advance, and she was infuriated by what she saw as the Commission's inadequate response to their plight. Banging on Malcolm's desk, she shouted that he himself had only "shown up in Prague for two days" and had failed to meet with "a single refugee."[10] But, while Martha needed villains to blame, Malcolm would not rise to her attack: the Nazis had imposed strict controls on foreign interference in Czechoslovakia, he said, and his sphere of influence was limited.

Faced with the implacable machinery of politics and power, Martha could only retreat — "I'll maybe lose my mind with the fury and helplessness," she wrote. In addition to the catastrophe of Czechoslovakia, she was struggling to bear the defeat of Loyalist Spain, and, almost worse, the realization that Russia had helped bring it about.[11] Ernest had just joined her in Paris, having spent most of the summer in America, and the two of them were given a detailed account of Russia's betrayal by Randolfo Pacciardi, the Italian officer who they'd met back in Madrid, and whose unwonted sexual advance had so insulted Martha. Pacciardi was no longer in uniform, though, no longer allowed to serve in Spain, and Martha instantly forgot his offence when she listened to his account of how the Soviets had effectively destroyed his brigade, the Garibaldi; first by replacing him as commander, then by rooting out all those below him who were suspected of holding anti-Stalinist views.

Ernest wept at Pacciardi's story. "They can't treat a brave man that way," he said, agonizing over the "carnival of treachery and rottenness" to which the Loyalist cause had been traduced.[12] Martha loved him for his tears, but Ernest was only in Paris for a few days before making one last visit of respect to Spain, and so she was alone, bereft of all support, when news broke of the fresh horror that was *Kristallnacht*. On 7 November, a young Polish Jew had walked into the German embassy in Paris, firing five shots at a mid-ranking diplomat and leaving him in a critical state. When he died of his wounds two days later, Nazi storm troopers across Germany had been let off the leash, and galvanized to an orgy of bloody revenge. During that long "Night of Broken Glass," over 7,000 Jewish businesses were smashed, 2,000 synagogues were torched, countless homes were ransacked and thousands of innocent men and women were dragged away to prisons, interrogation cells and camps.

The scale of the assault was shocking, even to many Germans. Although they had been groomed to despise and disregard their Jewish neighbours, the screams, the bloodstained pavements and the shattered buildings had been impossible to ignore. A small but significant number of Germans had actually tried to offer comfort and shelter to the victims. But their humanity had been offset by the vicious Party faithful who'd cheered the storm troopers on, even as they'd dragged children from their homes and clubbed their parents half to death. To Hugh Carleton Greene, Berlin correspondent for the *Daily Telegraph, Kristallnacht* was proof that some repellent force had corrupted the national psyche: "Racial hatred and hysteria seemed to have taken complete hold of otherwise decent people. I saw fashionably dressed women clapping their hands and screaming with glee, while respectable middle-class mothers held up their babies to see the 'fun.' "[13]★

Martha, reading the reports in Paris, could barely process this latest atrocity: it made her feel "tired in the head," unable to judge "what to believe in" or "whom to serve." A few months previously, she would have gone straight to Germany to write about *Kristallnacht* herself; now, she was so drained of hope in the world, so stripped of her belief that she could make any difference, she felt she would go mad if she didn't escape. Her

---

★ Outrageously, Jewish communities were charged with the expense of clearing up the broken glass and repairing the damage to properties.

only thought was to find some "beautiful desert island" where she and Ernest could live simply and happily together, where they could dedicate themselves to the writing of fiction, and shutter themselves away from the news.[14]

Martha always trusted her impulses, and after a valedictory visit to Spain and Christmas in St. Louis, she went south to Cuba, to bring her desert-island fantasy to life. Ernest was already there, at work on some short stories, and, once Martha had taken fastidious measure of the chaos in his Havana hotel rooms, she went in search of somewhere more permanent and beautiful to live. She found it in the Finca Vigía, a gracious colonial property just outside the city, and, channelling the impotent rage still churning inside her, she made the finca her passion and her project. Clearing the weeds from its magnificently rambling garden, painting its rooms an earthy pink and picking out traditional mahogany furniture, Martha believed she was creating a home where she and Ernest could be easy and productive together. During the spring and summer of 1939, the two of them settled into a domestic routine: writing in the morning, spending afternoons on the beach, getting "blotto drunk" in the evenings or simply sitting on the bougainvillea-covered terrace to watch the wide sea views. For the first time in her adult life, Martha believed she'd discovered the trick of being content, of feeling "serene and relaxed" in her own skin.[15]

Predictably, it wouldn't be long before the reporter's itch would drive her back into the real world, and, by 1943, Martha would reflect on her Cuban idyll with some shame. For Sigrid Schultz, in Berlin, however, even a fantasy of escape had been unthinkable. All through 1938, she'd reported as accurately as she dared on the Austrian Anschluss and the threats to Prague; in mid-September, at the height of the Sudetenland crisis, she'd attempted to rally international opposition to Hitler with the most inflammatory John Dickson piece of her career. It was a report on Buchfart, a recently opened prison camp near Weimar, and, under the cloak of her alias, she'd written in blunt, unmediated detail of the abuse to which the inmates were subjected: the twelve-hour days they were forced to work in the local stone quarries, and the barbarous punishments, tortures, even deaths, which they faced if they broke the camp rules. Several guards at the camp were begging for a transfer, because they could not stand to enforce this "sadistic and systematic torture."[16] Yet, even if the negotiators at Munich had happened to read Sigrid's article, it had clearly not affected their stance.

Sometime in the past year Sigrid had been hired by the American radio network, Mutual

Broadcasting System; and on 30 September, when she reported news of the Peace Agreement, the Nazi censors who checked her script were unable to edit the disgust from her voice, as she spoke of what an "overwhelming victory" Munich had been for Germany, and how shaming the "eagerness of the democracies to please."[17]

It was obvious to Sigrid that Britain and France had been played. Almost as soon as the ink was dry on the Agreement, Hitler revealed his disdain for Daladier and Chamberlain, publicly deriding the two leaders as "small worms." Within a fortnight, the German press were under orders to prepare their readers for further land grabs, reinforcing the Party's basic message, that Germany had a fundamental right to make itself strong and self-sufficient and, in doing so, reclaim all territories that had been "stolen" at Versailles. With the onset of winter, it was a message that became easier to sell; for as Hitler's war machine began shovelling up an even greedier share of the nation's resources, fuel prices rose, bread had to be bulked out with dry, tasteless bran, and the people's favourite *Kuchen* were filled with an ersatz froth that bore little resemblance to cream. To a cold, grumbling populace, Hitler's vow to reclaim lands that were abundant with wheat, dairy, timber and coal sounded insidiously seductive; by slow degrees, the German public were being persuaded that it was legitimate for them to oppose any state, any group who stood in their way.

Violence was being deliberately fermented in the nation's imagination and, for Sigrid, the twenty-four hours of *Kristallnacht* had been its hellish manifestation. The headline above her *Tribune* report had been graphic — "Hitler Seizes 20,000 Jews: Homes Burned, Stores Looted. Terror Reigns: Mobs Run Wild in German Streets" — and her account of that night detailed heart-rending examples of Jews who'd fled into the countryside, even committing suicide to escape the storm troopers. She had written, too, about the six Nazi bicyclists, who'd caught sight of a frail, elderly couple walking along Leipzigerstrasse and had given relentless chase. No one, she wrote, had "raised a hand or a voice in protest" as the old man and woman had been forced to run for their lives, not even when "the two elderly Jews [lay] crumpled on the street."[18]

As Nazi violence spiralled out of control, Sigrid's only relief was knowing that her mother was safe. Earlier in the year, as the situation for Jews had deteriorated and war seemed close to inevitable, she had persuaded Hedwig to leave for America, taking her own much-loved bulldog, Berbi, as companion. It had been a hard sacrifice, to give up both her mother and her dog, especially since the army had requisitioned her old apartment and most of the neighbours in her new building appeared to be spies. With no one to cook or to care for, Sigrid had only her work, and she felt the solitariness of her situation even more acutely because she was also having to renounce the other most important relationship in her life.

Contrary to *Tribune* gossip, Sigrid did in fact have a lover — a diplomat named Peter Ilcus, who was Press Attaché to the Romanian embassy in Berlin. Like everything else that was most personal to her, Sigrid kept the details of this relationship close, but it seems that by November 1938 she was having to place a careful distance between Peter and herself. The dangerously honed accuracy of her reporting had already put her name high on the Nazi blacklist and if ever her Jewish identity came to light, or her work with the Berlin underground, she would very probably be arrested. It was too dangerous now for Peter to be associated with her, and if their relationship had always been secretive, it now became close to impossible.

The pain of their enforced separation affected Sigrid badly enough for Bill Shirer, at least, to sense she was unhappy. Always inquisitive about his colleagues, he speculated that there might have been a man "she wanted to marry" and that "the luck of life" had turned against her.[19] That "luck," however, would prove far worse than Shirer could imagine. Sigrid would not only have to stay away from Peter during the winter of 1938–9, she would then lose all contact with him. Shortly after she herself was pressured to leave Berlin, in early 1941, Peter was arrested by the Nazis and, while he managed to survive the war, he was then incarcerated by the Russians. Sigrid and he would only be able to resume their relationship much later, by post, and while he would try to persuade her to come to him, presumably in Romania, too much time had passed.

The relationship was clearly precious to both of them, however, and the very last letter Peter wrote to Sigrid, dated 17 April 1980, was signed, as always, with his "heartfelt love."

Dearest Sig, your picture . . . lays in my room and has an honour place. It was for me, protection and a safeguard and hope during hard times and days.

What I should have done was impossible to do and now all too late and senseless.

It was a letter of devotion, loyalty and infinite regret, and, poignantly, Sigrid died just one month after receiving it.[20]

If Sigrid ever hoped for marriage with Peter,

it was not a happiness she could contemplate during the escalating crises of 1938–9. So certain was she that Hitler would be making an imminent move on Prague, she cabled a close friend, a Czechoslovakian diplomat, to "Drop everything move fast."[21] Camille Hoffman, however, remained obstinately unfazed. "Rumours, rumours," he'd replied. "Europe is filled with rumours," and it would be one of Sigrid's many private griefs that Camille was arrested by the Nazis the following March.

Virginia had been no less convinced of the convulsions ahead when she'd made a brief return to Berlin in December 1938. She'd noted with grimly ironic satisfaction that the press no longer wrote about Chamberlain as the "dear old man" who'd allowed Hitler to help himself to Sudetenland; he was now being cast as a treacherous turncoat, in league with "Jewish influences" and rearming his country against Germany. War was evidently anticipated: wrought-iron fences were being torn out of parks to be recycled for military use; armoured vehicles were massed outside the Ministry buildings along Wilhelmstrasse; and the shop assistant who asked Virginia for an obligatory "donation" to the Winter Relief Fund had grimaced cynically when admitting it was for guns.[22] Just before Virginia left Berlin, the government's traditional New Year message was posted up around the city and she noted, with a lurch of fear, that the usual sentiments of peace and good will had been replaced with the image of an Aryan soldier, wielding a fixed bayonet. Below it was the promise: "1939."

With Europe almost certainly on the brink of war, the question now occupying Virginia was the role that Russia might play. Her sources in London were speculating that Stalin would either choose to fight alongside the Western democracies or else sit on the sidelines, hoping that Europe would implode and become ripe for revolution. But her encounter with General Gal, back in Spain, had made Virginia curious to form her own views about Russia; she wanted to know what life was like under Communist rule, and she was hopeful, even, of interviewing the "bugbear Stalin" himself. She knew that it was currently very difficult to get into Russia, since Stalin's most recent bout of paranoia had resulted in 90 percent of the foreign press being expelled. Yet she still had strings to pull, and, on a frigid grey day in the middle of January, Virginia was at a dingy connecting station in Warsaw to catch the Moscow-bound train — a copy of George Bernard Shaw's *The Intelligent Woman's Guide to Socialism* packed prudently in her bag and a six-week visa stamped for Russia.

The train looked reassuringly comfortable, its silk and brass fittings distinctly un-Soviet in style; but there were very few passengers, and when Virginia asked one of the three men in her carriage why it was so empty he muttered ominously that no one travelled voluntarily to Russia these days: "when you cross the frontier you never know if you are going to come back." Virginia's contact in Moscow, a lively, independent-minded diplomat named Fitzroy Maclean, certainly claimed to be surprised and rather impressed that she'd made the journey: "People have a way of saying they're coming to Moscow," he said when he met her train, "but they don't always make it."[23] Virginia refused to be daunted, though; she'd come to Russia for an adventure, and as Maclean acknowledged, one of the first things he learned about Virginia was that once she'd set her mind to something, she usually saw it through. "She didn't miss a trick, she was ready to go anywhere and do anything . . . She was very ambitious, that was one of her great gifts — and she was unstoppable."[24]

But Moscow was much harder to crack than Virginia had imagined. Stalin himself was surrounded with near-impenetrable protocol and all of her formal requests for an interview were ignored. Her only option was to improvise, and she composed what she believed to be a winningly provocative cable, in which she pointed out that, while Stalin had done much to promote "equality of the sexes" in Russia, he'd never yet allowed himself to be interviewed by a woman. This "illogical precedent," she concluded, was one she was happy to help him correct. When Virginia asked her interpreter to translate the message, however, the woman's face turned ashen, and when an equally "awful silence" fell over the telegraph office, she guessed there was a very good chance the cable would never be sent.[25]

Certainly, it got no reply. But, even though Virginia had to concede defeat over Stalin, she was infuriated by the restrictions that were placed on every other aspect of her visit. At night, when Maclean took her to parties at the Metropol Hotel, to a movie or to a raucous concert of Russian "djaz," there were always a couple of watchful agents on their tail. During the day, she was never without a Party handler, one of a roster of enthusiastic young people who made her traipse around the showpiece sights of Moscow, the magnificent old Bolshoi Theatre, the latest model factory and school. The fervour with which they spoke of their city, as a pinnacle of culture and progress, struck Virginia as both touching and absurd, since all around her she saw decaying apartment blocks, broken-down cars, empty shop windows and pot-holed roads. Moscow seemed to her "a travesty of Western civilisation," a city where, for all the Party's fine slogans, most of the population lived in squalor and poverty. As for the way they dressed, Virginia could not begin to describe the winter wardrobe of the average Muscovite, who appeared to be wrapped against the cold in random fragments of cloth and fur.[26]

Little of this could be discussed with her handlers, of course. As Maclean was quick to see, Virginia's success as a journalist was predicated on her sociability — "by talking to a lot of people she could get a good grasp of her essentials in a very short time."[27] But this approach was all but useless in a state where everyone had learned to watch and weigh every word. Even when Virginia left Moscow, travelling west through Leningrad, Kiev and the Ukraine, she was still barely able to find a chink in the official wall of silence. Apart from one semi-illicit detour to a collective farm, horrifying in its rotting buildings and starved-looking peasants, she was given only curated snapshots of Russia. As for her mission to assess how it might position itself in a forthcoming war, that was as hopeless as Maclean had warned it would be. She was forbidden access to all military installations or military personnel and the one person who might have spoken to her, General Gal, was nowhere to be found. Virginia had been looking forward to seeing her gallant, romantic Marxist again, but his very name had apparently been excised from record, and she concluded, miserably, that he must, indeed, have fallen victim to the recent Red Army purge. By the time she completed her tour, frustrated by surveillance and browbeaten by propaganda, she concluded that there was very little to distinguish Stalin's Russia from Hitler's Germany.

There was the same "ruthless disregard of the individual," she wrote, the same "contempt for intellectual and moral values."[28] Yet, hatefully similar though the regimes appeared to Virginia, she knew how fundamentally divided they were in ideology and ambition, and she was unable to credit the rumour that she'd heard circulating through the Moscow embassies, suggesting that Hitler and Stalin might be moving towards some sort of pact. Six months later, when that Soviet-German pact was announced, she would regret her incredulity; but, back in Berlin, where she was catching the night express home, she could only regard it as fantasy.

The six weeks Virginia had spent in Russia had evidently triggered an alarm, and she had only just settled herself down to sleep in her wagon-lit, when three storm troopers burst in, looking for evidence that she was a Bolshevik spy. Even though she insisted, repeatedly, that she was a journalist and had been researching an innocent travel piece, the men ripped open her suitcases and threw around her clothes, books and papers with such violence, it looked as "though a tornado had hit." The leader of the trio — a brutally cocksure youth in his early twenties — lit a cigarette as Virginia attempted to gather up her ransacked belongings. "So you are on your way to England," he drawled. "Well, you can tell Mr. Chamberlain from us that if he tries to block our way in Europe any longer he'll have a war on his hands. We aren't going to sit back and take orders from anybody . . . Germany is too big to be strangled."[29]

If Chamberlain had any remaining faith in his Munich peace, it was dashed on 15 March, when Hitler made his move on Czechoslovakia. A "choice" was presented to Emil Hácha, the new Czech leader, between signing his country over voluntarily to the German Reich or having it taken by force. Later that day, when news was broadcast of the Nazi advance on Prague, Virginia observed that, even though the British were not yet ready to respond in kind, they were making themselves ready for war.* A limited form

---

* Hitler was disappointed not to have elicited an immediate military response from Britain and France. He actively wanted this war, as a means of claiming his desired spoils in Europe and the Balkans. "I am now fifty," he'd said. "I would rather have the war now than when I am fifty-five or sixty."

of military conscription was introduced and Chamberlain signed an agreement with three of his allies, Poland, Greece and Romania, promising that Britain would stand by them if Germany attacked.

While Virginia was reporting on the diplomatic and military consequences of Hitler's latest land grab, Clare Hollingworth's immediate concern was the 150,000 refugees who were now estimated to be in flight again. Having volunteered her services in Prague the previous autumn, she was quick to do so again, and this time her destination was Poland and the Baltic port of Gdynia, where workers for the recently formed (and cumbersomely named) British Committee for Refugees from Czechoslovakia (BCRC) were attempting to process the claims of all those seeking asylum. By the time she arrived there were 451 applicants, and as Jews, communists and political dissidents, all had genuine reason to beg visas from sympathetic countries like Belgium and Britain. So far, however, the BCRC had just 180 to distribute, and Clare's task in Gdynia was to prioritize those in greatest need. It was a life-and-death responsibility, an extraordinary burden, but Clare had a saving capacity for briskness. Rather than tormenting herself over those she had to reject, she focused on those she could save, and she performed her task with such efficiency that, in less than a week, she was reassigned to the far more chaotic situation that was developing in the south-western city of Katowice.

Lying very close to the border, this had become one of the main points of entry to Poland, and refugees were arriving at the rate of over a hundred a day. Every morning, the tiny British consulate was swamped with demands for visas — the two waiting rooms were overflowing and a long anxious line of people snaked down the staircase and onto the street. They would return day after day and, when Clare went to investigate how they were living, she was appalled to see families crammed together in vermin-ridden apartments or temporary camps. All were hungry, all were cold, yet all were valiantly clinging to dignity, and Clare was so moved by their uncomplaining misery, she was determined to override the visa system and rescue as many of them as she could.

Every day in Katowice, she too did the rounds of the foreign consulates, badgering staff to persuade their individual governments to improve on their asylum quotas. So tenacious was Clare, so morally persuasive, that, within a few weeks, she was able to secure visas for several thousand. It was extraordinarily gratifying work, to be doing this much good, to be wielding this much power. Yet the philanthropic satisfaction that Clare gained from her Katowice operations had also become laced with the thrill of low-level espionage.

The Germans were far from happy about the numbers escaping from Czechoslovakia. They were planning to use much of the population as a captive labour force, putting them to work in the farms and factories of the expanding Reich, even to serve in its army. And while they'd been willing to tolerate the presence of aid agencies like the BCRC — accepting that it was bad publicity to have a full-blown humanitarian crisis developing on their borders — they had not expected so many to escape their net. A network of Gestapo agents and SS officers had thus been posted across Poland and Czechoslovakia, to monitor the work of the agencies and to prevent the dispatch of their most high-value refugees. The harder the Nazis tightened their grip, the more ingenious Clare had to become in evading them, and she was soon adding basic spy craft to her operations, fashioning disguises for her escapees and devising codes for her communications with London. An urgent request for extra visas would be worded as an order for house furnishings ("300 feet of carpet is by no means long enough for the size of the houses out here"); information about the size of a refugee party in transit would be couched as a groceries delivery ("a consignment of 8

235

small and 22 large mixed pickles").[30]

This kind of undercover work was catnip to Clare, and during her four and a half months in Katowice she facilitated the escape of over 3,500 men, women and children. Like Sigrid, who kept modestly silent about her work with the Berlin underground, Clare spoke little of this achievement; it was only after her death that her family discovered a yellowing document, hidden in her trunk of mementos, on which was recorded the gratitude of those to whom she had given "a new homeland, new confidence, and new belief in the good and noble in humanity."[31] So exceptional were Clare's results that the League of Nations Refugee Commission proposed she should be made controller of all BCRC operations in Poland, while the British ambassador in Warsaw urged Chamberlain's government to offer her a full-time position.

Clare's fellow aid workers did not share this enthusiasm, though. She had become so focused on outwitting the Germans and beating the quota system that she'd dismissed the jeopardy into which she was placing the rest of the refugee mission. Several of her contacts were now under Nazi investigation, and the manager of the BCRC office in Prague had been hauled out of bed for interrogation; yet, when Clare had been ordered to show more caution and to moderate her operations, she'd simply shrugged and carried on.

Back in London, meanwhile, alarm was being raised at the highest levels. The British Passport Control Office and MI6 had both been alerted to the fact that a certain Miss Hollingworth, out in Poland, was exercising disproportionate power in the obtaining and distributing of British visas. It was of particular concern that many of these visas were going to German nationals, who would become enemy aliens if, or when, Britain went to war with Hitler. Although no complaint was made directly to Clare, moves were made to suspend the BCRC and to have the rogue Miss Hollingworth recalled.

It was early August when Clare reached home. Her family, relieved by her safe return, assumed she would simply settle back into her life with Van. But Katowice had been the adventure of her life. It had given her a taste for danger as well as for power; it had also involved her in an interesting romantic liaison with the British Consul General, John Thwaites. And, while she was still very fond of Van, Clare had discovered how much better suited she was to being a freebooting mistress, than to a wife. All she wanted was to find a way back to Poland, and she'd barely unpacked her luggage before she took herself up to Yorkshire, to tramp over the empty moors and consider her future options.

Aid work was now closed to her, but journalism might prove a satisfying alternative.

During her years at the LNU, Clare had written regularly for the union's magazine, *Headway,* and she'd published a few peace-related articles for the *News Chronicle* and the Fabian Society. She had also never been shy of selling herself. Confident that her working knowledge of Central and Eastern Europe might be as good as any correspondent's, exaggerating her command of languages and her familiarity with the Geneva press room, Clare telephoned everyone she knew in the newspaper world, asking for work as a free-lance stringer in Poland.

Her timing was excellent, for, on 24 August, news broke that Germany and Russia had formed an alliance, putting their signatures to a non-aggression pact. This was the rumoured accord that Virginia had dismissed as laughably improbable six months ago, and even now it had caught most of the world's press and politicians off guard. Its implications were chillingly obvious, however, for with Stalin as his ally, Hitler had removed any potential Russian opposition to his plans for Poland. Finally, a European war seemed inevitable, and, as every newspaper in Britain began looking to increase its foreign coverage, Clare's request for work reached the attention of Arthur Watson, editor of the *Daily Telegraph.* Despite her negligible qualifications, Watson called her in for an interview, assuming, at the very least, that her contacts in Katowice might prove useful. In the event, he was so impressed by Clare's unswerving confidence in herself, he was prepared to send her to Poland immediately; the issue of pay hadn't even been discussed before Clare was out of Watson's office and booking herself on the first available flight to Warsaw.

Meanwhile, news of the German–Soviet non-aggression pact was sending shockwaves through Berlin. According to Bill Shirer, negotiations had been so secretive that it was "as much of a bombshell for most of the big Nazis as it was for the rest of the world."[32] He was not, however, giving credit to Sigrid, who'd long suspected a deal was in motion and, eleven days earlier, had used her Dickson alias to make her prediction public. She'd been told by her military sources, back in May, that Poland was next on Hitler's list of acquisitions and she'd reasoned that some accommodation would have to be made with Stalin, who harboured his own designs on eastern Poland. She still needed confirmation, however, and early in August, her informant Johannes Schmitt suggested she should investigate whether Hitler had raised the issue of Russia with his private astrologer. Like many of his inner circle, Hitler was superstitious; he was convinced that he and his Party were instruments of a cosmic plan, and, before committing to any new policy, he would always try to ascertain if the planets were beneficially aligned. It was an astonishing weakness, ripe for exploitation, and when Sigrid booked a consultation with Hitler's astrologer, she could hardly believe her luck when the man proved so recklessly indiscreet that he not only boasted of his close relationship with the Führer, but freely admitted that his "client" had indeed consulted him about whether he should make his deal with Stalin.

On 13 August, when Sigrid went public with her story, the *Tribune* office was rocked by rebuttals and threats, and Goebbels denounced the report as one of Dickson's most egregious lies. Just eleven days later, though, the pact was announced, and an editorial in the *Völkischer Beobachter* was deployed to promote what was now the latest official line. A "long and traditional friendship" had always bound Germany to Russia, it stated and, in signing this new peace accord, Stalin was to be praised for helping Hitler in his mission to secure the "bloodless fulfilment of irreducible German demands."[33]

The Party's volte-face was so blatant that even the *Völkischer Beobachter* might have blushed. But years of official propaganda, of faked news stories and contradictory pronouncements, had reduced much of the German public to a state of collective apathy, and many found it simplest to accept, as truth, whatever they were told. The weather was also unusually hot during those last days of August and, in Berlin, the pleasures of picnicking in the Tiergarten, of drinking beer in pavement cafes, were more immediate than issues of foreign policy. Most people chose to ignore the anti-aircraft guns that were being installed on rooftops, the squads of soldiers marching through the streets. If the rumours were true that Hitler was about to invade Poland, it was of only mild concern. He'd been able to take both Austria and Czechoslovakia without German blood being shed, so why not Poland too?*

On 31 August, when Virginia flew into Berlin, it was as clear to her as it was to Sigrid that the German people were deluding themselves if they believed they could be left in peace. Even though British negotiators were still hoping to pull off another Munich, Hitler was, even now, preparing to take Poland. A dawn attack had been ordered on a German customs post in the west, which had been fabricated to look like the work of some Polish soldiers found dead at the scene. These soldiers were actually inmates from Sachsenhausen concentration camp who'd been

* Interestingly, McCormick didn't allow Sigrid to report on the confirmed announcement, fearing perhaps that she would be dangerously unable to control her contempt. Instead, the *Tribune* ran the news via a syndicated report from Associated Press.

dressed up in Polish uniform, and then casually butchered. But Hitler didn't even care if the evidence looked convincing; all he needed was an excuse to send troops into Poland, ostensibly to protect German interests, but, in reality, to provoke his long-desired war with Britain and France.

Every Nazi official to whom Virginia spoke in Berlin believed it was only a matter of days, even hours, before war began. "It was," she wrote, "like a death-bed vigil." Yet, even when Hitler broadcast to the nation, on 1 September, announcing that German infantry had been "returning" Polish fire since dawn, the waiting was not quite over. Britain and France had not yet shown their hands and, until they did, the Nazis were apparently keen to play the situation down. In Berlin, there were no parades, no flag-waving crowds, and Virginia noted that Hitler didn't even make his customary appearance on the Chancellery balcony. The few dozen people who'd gathered on the pavement below had been rewarded only by the sight of "three painters in white caps and overalls," who'd leaned out of the window to stare. Later, when Virginia canvassed the opinion of various waiters, taxi drivers and shop girls, they seemed to have no idea that an attack on Poland might embroil Germany in a far wider conflict. "What do you mean, a world war?" they asked, staring at her with genuine incredulity.[34]

That Friday stretched into a very long and very strange day. The Foreign Office spokesman was unable to comment at the afternoon press briefing, responding to every question on Poland with the same melancholy shake of the head. "*Ich weiss nicht* — I don't know, I don't know." It was only late in the afternoon, when some Party official ordered a safety drill and the unearthly wail of sirens rent the city, that Berliners showed their first real signs of panic. Some were packing up to leave and when Virginia went to catch the night express home, she and the friend who'd accompanied her to Berlin — a lively, inquisitive New Yorker called Jane Leslie — found their compartment already crammed.[35] At one point, SS officers made a sweep of the train, checking papers, ripping up cushions in search of smuggled currency, and eventually hauling off three or four "weeping, protesting" passengers. By the time they reached the Dutch border, Virginia felt as relieved as though she'd just "scaled the last walls of some terrible prison."

For one elderly Jewish couple, there was to be no safety.[36] They were heading for America, but, because their boat tickets were awaiting collection in Amsterdam, they had no clear proof of their onward travel, and, without it, the Dutch border guards refused to let them enter Holland. This was officialdom at its most stupidly and cruel, and, although Virginia tried to argue on the couple's behalf, the guards were obdurate. As the train left the station, the distressed couple were left sitting on a bench, their bags piled around them, their only option to go back into Germany.

This pitiful vignette coloured the story that Virginia jotted down as she travelled onwards to Rotterdam, to catch the boat for England. Everywhere was in darkness when she arrived, and she was just in time to make her deadline. The following morning, she was gratified by the sidebar that ran with her report, commending her courage for venturing into Germany after all of the "resident correspondents" had left town. But, within a few hours of publication, her Berlin article was old news. At eleven fifteen precisely, Chamberlain broadcast an emergency address to the nation. In a high, anxious voice, which bore no resemblance to the jubilant authority with which he'd returned from Munich, the Prime Minister announced that an ultimatum had been issued to Germany demanding that its troops be withdrawn from Poland by eleven o'clock. No such undertaking had been received, Chamberlain acknowledged, and it was his grave duty, now, to inform the British people that, as from today, 3 September, they were at war.

CHAPTER SEVEN:
POLAND, FINLAND AND
LONDON, AUTUMN 1939

"The relentless approach of the invader"
CLARE HOLLINGWORTH[1]

Chamberlain's announcement was still a week into the future when Clare flew off to Poland to start her new career. But, as her plane touched down in Berlin, she already sensed she was in enemy territory. The lines of Messerschmitts and Stukas that were parked along the runways of Tempelhof airport looked to her like a swarm of malign "black insects," and no less sinister were the uniformed officials who ordered her to wait in a wire-mesh pen while checks were made on her and the two other journalists who'd been on board her flight. "After our bags, books and papers had been taken, we sat like three fowls on a perch, wondering whose necks would be wrung," Clare wrote, very scared that her rogue operations in Katowice might make her a particular target.[2] It was two long hours before she was finally allowed to board her connecting flight to Warsaw, but, by early evening, she was in the Hotel Europejski, drinking cocktails with the *Telegraph*'s Central European correspondent, Hugh Carleton Greene.

Greene had been reassigned to Poland after his incautious rage over *Kristallnacht* had got him expelled from Berlin, and Clare liked him immediately — an amiably lanky man, with enormous feet, a "grin like a half moon" and an absolute seriousness of mission.[3] The previous day, Chamberlain had issued a warning to Hitler, reiterating his resolve to assist Poland in case of attack, and, when Hugh took Clare on a drinking tour of Warsaw, the Poles seemed almost hysterical in their conviction that they "would give the hated Germans a good hiding." In the mirrored, smoky bar of the Hotel Bristol, the collective mood of intoxication seemed only partly due to the excellence of the vodka: "journalists, diplomats, spies and call girls" all stood crammed together, Clare wrote, "jostling, laughing, whispering and hugging" as they waited to see whether the scales would tip them towards peace or war.[4]

The following morning Clare travelled straight down to Katowice, where Hugh needed her to monitor activity around the German border, and the mood here was surprisingly phlegmatic. Soldiers might be crowding the streets and mobilization notices might be plastered on the buildings, yet most of the people to whom Clare spoke seemed to believe that Hitler would not make his move. She was unconvinced, however, which was why she resolved to cross into Germany and look for evidence of military activity. She knew she was taking a risk and she was very careful with the truth when she begged her lover, John Thwaites, for the loan of his consular car. But, while the guards on the German border looked surprised to see Clare, they waved her through, and, buoyant with the success of crossing her first hurdle, she was determined to make the most of her adventure. She dined on an excellent lunch of roast German partridge, she went shopping for goods like camera film and torches, which had become scarce in Poland, and it was while she was driving along the frontier road from Hindenburg to Gleiwitz that she lucked into the evidence she'd been hoping for. As the wind had blown aside the camouflage screens that flanked the route, Clare saw the battle-ready tanks, armoured cars and field guns that were parked in the valley below.

John Thwaites had assumed Clare was joking when she returned with her news. "Now, come on, old girl," he'd chaffed. "Stop pulling my leg. You could not have got into Germany."[5] His tone had changed, though, when she'd flourished her German shopping bags, and he'd instantly retreated into his office to prepare a coded message for London. Clare, meanwhile, telephoned Hugh, and it was on the basis of her startling dispatch that the next morning's *Telegraph* boasted its first exclusive of the war. "1000 tanks massed on Polish border. Ten divisions reported ready for swift stroke," ran the, slightly exaggerated, headline; and while the report was published anonymously — attributed only to "Our Own Correspondent," as was the *Telegraph*'s way — Clare knew, and her bosses knew, that she'd made her reporting debut in remarkable style.

Even with this new information in play, the British were hoping to keep Germany at the negotiating table. But Hitler had his own agenda. Early on 1 September, Clare was awoken by an apocalyptic sound, "like the slamming of giant doors." It was German bombers, delivering the first of their payload, and, in the pale dawn sky, Clare could see them circling close to the border, haloed by the smoke of anti-aircraft fire. Somewhere in the distance, she could also hear the bark of artillery, the rumbling of Polish tanks. Guessing this must be the start of the invasion, she immediately telephoned Hugh.

It was, he acknowledged, "the most dramatic call of my life," and he had no hesitation in passing news on to London that the war had begun. When Clare tried to alert Robin Hankey, First Secretary at the British embassy, however, he was sceptical. Even when she held the telephone receiver out of her window so that he could hear the sounds of gunfire, Hankey doubted it was a German attack, and when hopeful rumours began flying around Katowice that it was merely a practice drill, she began to question herself, and to panic that she had "made the gaffe of my life by reporting a non-existent war."[7] Later that morning, however, German tanks were reported on the Polish side of the border, and Clare understood that she was now, by default, an active war correspondent. It was a heady realization — as far as she could tell, she was the only British reporter on the scene — but it was also daunting; unlike Martha, in Madrid, she had no one to mentor her and she would have to work out for herself what kind of stories she was meant to relay back to London, and what level of danger she was meant to face.

Hugh had asked Clare to remain close to the border for as long as possible, but, having driven around the region during the afternoon, she learned that the Germans were blitzing their way through Poland's defences, and that Katowice must soon become a target. John Thwaites urged her to retreat with him to Krakow overnight, where he reckoned they would be safer from German bombs, and by the time they embarked on the seventy-kilometre drive east, there were hundreds, maybe thousands of men, women and children already travelling in the same direction. "The road for miles was a jostle of peasant wagons," Clare wrote, "and the blue lights of my car brought out the humped figures, the carts over-piled and everywhere the white discs of children's faces . . . I felt inhumane then, passing in my car, but I should have felt infinitely worse had I known what sad days awaited these folks."[8]

She and John had to return to Katowice the following morning to evacuate the consulate. All sensitive documents had to be destroyed and transport organized for the staff, and by the time the little convoy of diplomatic cars set off for Krakow, the route had become even more jammed. Military vehicles were competing with columns of civilian refugees, and the slow-moving traffic had become a target for German fighter planes, which circled overhead, strafing the roads with machine-gun fire. Eventually the consulate party was forced to bump its way east down tiny lanes and farm tracks, and when they eventually reached Krakow they were not surprised to learn that the invasion was progressing faster than anyone had previously thought possible. German bombers were crippling the Polish air force by targeting its bases and fuel depots; German tanks were rolling effortlessly across the dry, flat, and recently harvested fields; German guns were mowing down regiments of Polish infantry before they'd even mustered their positions of defence. Everyone wanted to know where the British were, given their guarantee of support. As things stood, it seemed to Clare that the helplessly out-classed Poles were fighting "like a second-rate boxer being beaten to the punch."[9]

She and John Thwaites had booked themselves into the Hotel Francuski, in Krakow, while John awaited his next orders, and they were still there on 3 September, when Chamberlain finally committed Britain to the war. Clare would always remember how she'd felt when, walking down the Francuski's grand circular staircase, she heard the Prime Minister's speech being broadcast in the lobby. The Poles in the hotel had been exuberant, joining in the singing of "God Save the King," but Clare had to stop and steady herself. "It was the worst moment of the war for me and I felt slightly sick . . . I thought of my years on the staff of the League of Nations Union and all that we had worked for seemed lost. London would be bombed and the friends and the buildings I loved would be destroyed."[10]

There was little time for mourning, though. The Germans were closing on Krakow and, as the British contingent prepared to retreat further east, there were now six of them squeezed into John's car — Clare had to transfer all her belongings into a pillowcase, which she could sit on to make extra room. The war was spiking in all directions: they had to drive through air raids and machine-gun fire, to cross bridges that might be booby-trapped with explosives. But at least they were in cars, unlike most of the refugees, who were having to camp along the roadside at night and beg the passing traffic for food. "I felt the loneliness and hopelessness of a nation awaiting the relentless approach of the invader," Clare wrote, and it was with a melancholy stab of guilt that she observed a group of peasants stoically gathering in the last of the harvest.[11] The scene appeared almost pastoral, the men rhythmically bending and scything as the early September sun glowed low on the horizon. But then a squadron of German bombers emerged, high and leisurely, from a bank of cloud, and Clare braced herself for the now familiar "puff of shells" and "tremor of bombs." A cylinder of smoke, pushing upwards from the nearby city of Łuck, told her the Luftwaffe were hitting their mark; and, as the last of the day's sun illuminated the scene, it seemed to Clare that the sun was setting on Poland itself.[12]

But still the British were doing nothing. Despite Chamberlain's declaration of war, there was no sign of his promised troops and arms, and now, when Clare and her party needed to buy petrol and food, they were met with increasingly marked hostility. It's unclear why Clare, in such difficult circumstances, made the decision to finish the journey alone, in a separate car. Perhaps John's over-burdened vehicle was struggling, more prob-ably she wanted the freedom to follow her own reporter's itinerary. But she'd made herself vulnerable, and she was badly shaken by one particular incident, when two terri-fied, wounded horses came charging at her from nowhere and almost wrecked her car: "They galloped with a hideous high action of the forequarters and below, blood and intes-tines came away" Clare wrote, and it was with this image still horrible in her mind that she continued her solitary way east, to the hillside city of Krzemieniec.[13]

Krzemieniec had become the temporary refuge of the Polish government and the foreign embassies, now that Warsaw was uninhabitable, and Clare was delighted to find Robin Hankey and the rest of the British embassy already settling into a small hotel and toasting their safe arrival with sherry. Gratefully, she accepted a glass, but she'd barely sat herself down on one of the wooden crates that crowded the floor when she was accosted by the British ambassador, Sir Howard Kennard, who seemed irascibly put out by her presence. "Hmm, you're a peculiar woman, Miss Hollingworth," he huffed. "What are you doing running about in the middle of all this? Love of excitement, I suppose." When Clare politely responded that she was a reporter for the *Daily Telegraph,* Sir Howard had been rudely unimpressed. "Pfff, journalist! What's the trouble? No family?" he'd asked, clearly unable to comprehend why any woman should choose to get involved in so unreasonable a profession.[14]

In fact, Clare was pretty much the only British journalist left in Poland; that evening, over a meagre dinner of eggs and rice, she learned that even Hugh Carleton Greene had retreated to the safety of Romania. He was expecting her to follow, but the fact that she now had near-exclusive access to the war made Clare reckless. She learned from Hankey that Warsaw, encircled by German tanks and planes, was now battling for its life and she believed that, if she could only find a way to report on that battle, she'd be back on the *Telegraph*'s front page. "I was not being brave," she insisted, "my overriding feeling was enthusiasm for a good story." The next morning, after begging the loan of a diplomatic car, she filled a hip flask with whisky, tucked a revolver in the glove compartment and set off on the 500-kilometre drive.[15]

She was heading right back into the heart of the fighting. Lublin, still intact when she'd passed through two days earlier, was now an unrecognizable shambles of rubble, corpses and free-running sewage. A young man whom she met wandering through the ruins stared at her uncomprehendingly when she asked for the best route on to Warsaw. Undeterred, Clare continued, keeping to the safety of cart tracks, dry river courses and bridle paths; when night fell, she curled up on the back seat of the car, congratulating herself on evading bombs and machine-gun fire, and dosing herself to sleep with whisky. The following morning, however, she hadn't driven far when she spotted a division of soldiers marching in her direction. They were wearing the field-grey uniform of the Wehrmacht, and she saw, "with a hollow feeling under my heart," that they were "striding with a precision that had nothing to do with defeat."[16]

For an instant, she was paralysed, "so scared that instead of turning the car I actually shut off the engine and gazed at the green uniforms approaching." But, once the adrenalin began to course through her body, she realized how powerful this fear could be. It was one of the defining moments in Clare's war, for, as she gunned her car into action, "bumping across maize-stubble, rolling into rutted tracks," she felt preternaturally alive, high on a cocktail of euphoric hormones.[17] Trying, rather inadequately, to compare the sensation to the "glow" that she got from "a very cold bath," Clare understood that this was the reason why people became war reporters. Although she never made it to

Warsaw, her near-encounter with German troops had been more exhilarating than anything she'd known and, over the next few years, she would seek to replicate that exhilaration again and again.[18]

Whatever remained of the pretty Knighton girl, with her marcelled hair and hopeful ideals, was being whittled away during these last days in Poland. A future colleague would describe Clare as "wiry as a tennis player in training," as mentally alert as "a bundle of tightly wound springs," and, if she was acquiring a new physical toughness, she was also disciplining herself to a new level of detachment.[19]

On 17 September, Poland's last hope of resistance was crushed, as Russian troops crossed into the north and east to claim their own chunk of the beleaguered nation.* By now, Clare had joined Hugh in the Romanian border town of Cernăuți, and, with him, she was watching the rump of the Polish air force fly overhead for the safety of Bucharest airport. The narrow, muddy streets were choked with the cars, wagons and bicycles of fleeing Poles; the cafes and bars were crowded

* It was the most cynical of manoeuvres, facilitated by the Russians' pretence that they were helping the Poles to fight back against Germany — a pretence that led to many Polish divisions obediently surrendering themselves to the Red Army.

with dazed, distraught people, searching out news of their families and friends. But, while Clare could acknowledge the tragedy of Poland's defeat, her principal concern was where the war would take her next. While journalists like Martha would focus on the human tragedies of this conflict, Clare would always follow the hard news. "The three-weeks war was almost over," she wrote, "but for Britain and the rest of the world it had hardly begun."[20]

Just a day or two after Clare had moved on from Cernăuți, Virginia Cowles arrived. She'd badly wanted to cover the invasion, but had been delayed by visa regulations and by the newly tortuous complications of wartime travel; when her train had finally steamed into Bucharest station on 18 September, she was told that Poland was no longer accessible. "I had never imagined," she wrote, "that a nation could be destroyed so quickly there wouldn't even be time to get to it."[21] Germany and Russia had sealed all the borders, and the only stories that were left for Virginia to write were of the Poles who'd managed to escape. At Bucharest airport, she interviewed some of the dozens of Polish pilots who were now sleeping rough in the terminal, their planes parked on the runways outside. Dishevelled and exhausted though they were, most seemed unable to accept the collapse of their country and determined to continue the fight: "They can't shut us up," one young officer repeated again and again. "We must go on." But, when Virginia arrived in Cernăuți, and walked among the crowds of refugees, she could see no signs of hope or resistance, only defeat and despair.

The small town had become a theatre of tragedy: "Every now and then an incident caught your eye like a fragment of broken picture and your imagination flared up as you wondered what story lay behind the scene." Virginia was transfixed by one very young woman, with "a fine head and long slender hands," who was sitting alone and silently weeping. Her heart broke for the three tiny children whom she saw perched obediently on their suitcases, apparently expecting to be met by their mother and father, still innocently unaware that their parents were almost certainly dead, or else trapped on the wrong side of the border.[22]

Images of these poor smashed lives would stay with Virginia as she travelled back to London. An American woman was interrogated at the French border because she'd been unable to produce the correct travel papers. "I only wanted to buy a dress at Schiaparelli's," the woman had shrilled indignantly at the police, and, to Virginia, it already seemed impossible that a world had existed where anyone cared so much about clothes. Once home, she wished desperately to be assigned to some serious war news, yet the strategy on which Chamberlain and his war cabinet had decided was one of attrition. Rather than engaging directly with the enemy they planned to blockade the northern sea routes to Germany, impeding the import of its fuel and food and starving it into submission. The air-raid wardens and firefighters of Britain might be manning their posts, the hospitals might be geared to a state of readiness, yet the most significant casualties during the autumn of 1939 would be the 1,300 civilians who were injured or killed during the blackout.[23]

"The period of inactivity seemed interminable," Virginia reflected, as Britain languished in what newspaper wits were already calling the "Bore War" or "Phoney War." She wrote about the charities being set up to assist families deprived of their breadwinners, about the women signing up for work in munitions factories, but she felt like a war correspondent without a war. And there was a very personal twist to her frustration, too, because the man with whom she'd recently fallen in love had been sent away to a Sussex air base for training, and, since neither the RAF nor the Luftwaffe had been ordered to engage, it was hard to accept the necessity of his absence.

Aidan Crawley, in peace-time, had been a political journalist. Committed to his work, unaffectedly handsome, with his broad shoulders and open smile, he had been very attractive to Virginia when Randolph Churchill had introduced them two years earlier. At the time, however, she'd been too much in love with Seymour to take more than a friendly interest and had not been aware that Aidan's own curiosity had gone deeper. He'd actually recognized Virginia straight away, as the party girl he'd seen in Long Island in 1933, being "rushed" by admiring young men. Half-dazzled, half-disapproving, he hadn't asked for an introduction back then, but, meeting her properly in London, he realized that Virginia was both more serious and more complicated than he'd imagined. As he wrote, decades later: "She was not so much pretty as fascinating to look at, with large brown eyes, far apart, which held one's own steadily, a broad forehead, wide mouth, tapering chin and a slender figure. She was neither flirtatious nor coy, but had a talent for entering swiftly and sensitively into one's thoughts."[24] She was also a woman whose upbringing and experience made Aidan acutely aware of his own quintessential Englishness.

As the second son of Reverend Stafford Crawley, Canon of Windsor, and just one or two removes from aristocracy, Aidan had progressed easily from Harrow and Oxford to a brief but distinguished outing in first-class cricket. He'd then drifted into journalism, where an assignment to cover impoverished mining communities in Wales had turned him from moderate liberal to socialist. In 1936, he'd resigned from the *Daily Mail* in protest at the paper's whitewashing coverage of Hitler and Mussolini, and afterwards had travelled to Palestine to make a documentary about gathering tensions between native Arabs and incoming Jewish refugees.

The political sensitivity of that project made Aidan doubly impressed by the "scrupulously honest" balance to which Virginia had aspired in her reporting from Spain.[25] He found himself admiring her very much, but, attracted though he was, there was an older married woman in his life with whom he was making himself romantically miserable; for the time being, he was happy to settle into a platonic routine with Virginia, breakfasting in her Mayfair lodgings or lunching with her in a local pub.

By the early summer of 1939, though, Aidan had accepted the futility of his own affair, and Virginia was ready to move on from Seymour, who, always a heavy drinker, was showing signs of becoming a drunk. Friendship progressed naturally to love, and when Britain went to war on 3 September, Aidan thought very seriously of proposing marriage, gripped by the same romantic fatalism that was prompting a rash of wartime weddings across Britain. A mixture of good sense and superstition held him back, however. Aidan had long been predicting this war and three years earlier had signed up for the British Auxiliary Air Force, a government-sponsored network of civilian pilots which could be drawn on in times of crisis. Guessing that the conflict could be professionally dangerous for both Virginia and himself, he felt it might jinx their chances of survival if they were to marry, and, sensing that Virginia would agree, he remained silent.*

Yet, separation was hard on them both when Aidan's mobilization papers came through and he had to leave London to begin training. Virginia managed to wangle a visit to his camp, on the pretext of writing a story about pilot morale, and when Aidan emerged from his barracks he looked reassuringly himself, despite his stiff blue uniform. He had a thick economics textbook under his arm, using the empty hours between training sessions to study for what he hoped would be his post-war career in Parliament. But he told Virginia that most of the other men were wretched with boredom. They'd signed up to

* Aidan had joined the 601 squadron, whose membership, rather contrary to his politics, was dominated by rich young men who owned their own planes.

fight the Germans but the only missions to which they could currently look forward were reconnaissance or patrol.

Autumn turned to winter and still everyone waited. In northern France, the troops who'd been stationed to defend the Maginot Line were becoming drunk and mutinous from the tedium of their *drôle de guerre.* The Germans' term for this Phoney War, *der sitz krieg,* "sitting war," was no less telling. Keyed up from their success in Poland, they found it ignoble as well as frustrating to be doing nothing. And, in Britain, where most of the civilian population had willingly blacked out their homes, where women had hidden their tears as they'd sent their men off to fight and their children away to safety, the mood was similarly souring to one of sullen rebellion.[26]★

Helen Kirkpatrick, however, had much to keep her busy and buoyant. Her career was still on the rise: she was broadcasting for the BBC, she was working on a new book† and

★ Helen Kirkpatrick believed that, even though few of the British had actually "cared two hoots about Poland," they had become so "sick to death" of international crises that they wanted Hitler to be dealt with once and for all.

† It was titled *Under the British Umbrella: What the English Are and How They Go to War,* and it was essentially an American's guide to the social and

263

she was, most important, writing for one of the great American publications, the *Chicago Daily News*. The paper's London bureau chief, Bill Stoneman, had come to rate Helen's work highly, over the last two years, and, although he could only offer her a stringer's contract, he was giving her responsibilities far above her pay grade. During the summer and early autumn, as the news cycle accelerated, Helen was assigned a number of key pieces, including an analysis of German and Russian interests in the Balkans; and, at the beginning of September, when Bill had to go to France to investigate rumours of military action, he entrusted her with running the office. "How will I know when I'm really covering the main story?" Helen had asked in an attack of stage fright. But she had good instincts and, even in the media doldrums of the Phoney War, she'd been able to provide her paper with one remarkable, front-page exclusive.[27]

The exiled Duke of Windsor — formerly King Edward VIII — had just returned to

---

political hierarchies of Britain. Helen's editor was the legendary Max Perkins. "I didn't fully understand at the time how lucky I was," she admitted, conscious of Perkins' long-standing association with Hemingway and F. Scott Fitzgerald. (Helen Kirkpatrick interview, Session 1, p. 55.)

England in the hope of securing some kind of official war role. A friend of Helen's had learned that he and his wife were staying in Sussex, at the home of the Duke's aide-de-camp, Edward Metcalfe, and, because this friend was a close neighbour of Metcalfe's, she thought she could help Helen organize an interview. Bill Stoneman's response had been withering when she pitched the idea — the former King had attracted so much scandal when he'd abdicated the throne, he had vowed to have nothing more to do with the press. Even if the Duke and Duchess had been disposed to make an exception for Helen, Bill pointed out they were under orders from the government to give no interviews during their visit home.

Disobedience did not come easily to Helen but she knew that Bill was wrong to order her to drop the idea. Quietly, she asked her friend to contact "Fruity" Metcalfe, and, within a day or two, she was told that the Duke had agreed to an informal conversation. Helen's hands were shaking as she drove up to Metcalfe's house. She believed that she'd finally got the measure of the British upper classes. Victor Gordon-Lennox had secured her invitations to the London salons of Sibyl Colefax and Margot Asquith, where, as she'd reported back to her family, "the conversation was fascinating and I sat flapping my ears."[28] She'd been taken to country house parties, where she'd familiarized herself with the inbred oddities of English etiquette and pronunciation, and where she'd learned to understand that two politicians of ragingly opposed views could still remain clannishly united because they'd attended the same public school, or ridden with the same hunt.

But royalty, even ex-royalty, was a different matter, and as Helen tried to rehearse her line of questioning, she was fretting over the correct form of address and wondering whether she was obliged to curtsey. Mercifully, when the Duke and Duchess came sauntering out to meet her, they were far less intimidating than she'd feared. While the Duchess merely proffered a formal handshake before returning to the house, the Duke seemed positively eager to talk — so eager that he claimed to have had an amusing idea about how to circumvent his own media ban. "I didn't say that *I* wouldn't interview anybody," he said, with his boyishly charming smile. "Why don't I interview you?"[29]

Helen could already see the headlines dancing. Even though the Duke's notion of an interview didn't go much beyond gossip about American politics and a few of their mutual acquaintances, and even though a large part of her finished article had to be padded out with descriptions of his "Riviera tan" and the "smart knitted black suit" worn by his wife, their conversation had opened a window onto the Duke's character and situation. She could sense the urgency of his desire for rehabilitation, his hunger to be back in uniform or to do "something with the war cabinet" which would liberate him from the banality of his exile's life.[30] Several years later, when Helen learned about the treacherous links which the Duke had formed with the Nazi regime, she was surprisingly lenient in her judgement. He was "a weak character," she thought, who'd been flattered into the belief that he was serving his country's best interests. She also felt she owed the Duke a certain retrospective gratitude, since it was the fluky success of their interview which would eventually give her the nerve to lobby her bosses for promotion.[31]

In the meantime, as the war news remained sluggish, Helen was also having to accept less starry assignments. As the only woman in the office, it was left to her to cover the female angles on the Phoney War — the trend for military-influenced tailoring, the shocking rise in hosiery prices and the prejudices surrounding wives and girlfriends who were replacing their men at work. "Mrs. John Bull may soon run the land, Englishmen fear," ran the headline of one piece, which Helen had clearly written through gritted teeth.

But, if a touch of humiliation rankled through her reporting that autumn, by the end of November, she was back on hard news. For months, Stalin had been issuing threats to Finland, pressuring for the return of territories that had been taken from Russia back in 1917. He'd been particularly hungry for the Karelian Isthmus, a wide stretch of land that was the Finns' main link to Europe and central Asia, and, now that he had Hitler's backing, he was ready to take it by force.

When the "Winter War" began on 30 November, everyone assumed that it would be even shorter than the Three-Week War in Poland. The Russians were fighting the Finns with three times the number of soldiers and planes, and with hundreds more tanks and armoured vehicles. So massively disproportionate was their display of military strength that Helen had speculated whether Hitler himself had requested it, hoping that his new ally might help cow the French and British into suing for a negotiated peace. Yet, against all the odds, against all the predictions, the 300,000 men of the Finnish armed forces were magnificently holding their own. In the south of their country, they fought with what traditional arms they possessed, doggedly maintaining their defence of the Mannerheim Line. Up in the frozen north, however, they were waging their own ingenious and deadly form of guerrilla warfare. Finland's dense, snowbound forests were difficult for the cumbersomely armoured Russians to navigate, yet the Finns were in their natural element. Travelling swiftly and silently on skis, they had all the advantage of surprise, disabling enemy tanks with flaming bottles of petrol (the original "Molotov cocktails") and forcing armoured convoys off-road with hidden mines. So effective were the Finns at disabling their enemy's supply and communication lines that entire Soviet divisions were left stranded in the forests, their men freezing and starving to death, or picked off by sniper fire.

When the world awoke to the fascination of this David and Goliath battle, over a hundred correspondents began converging on Finland. Helen was hoping to be among them, but, because she was not yet on staff and had no previous combat experience, she was left to process the incoming war reports from her desk. Virginia, though, had better luck. As a veteran of Spain, she was able to persuade the *Sunday Times* to send her to Finland, and, early in January, with an uncharacteristically practical wardrobe packed in her bags, she embarked on the long journey for Helsinki.

The first leg of that journey took her to neutral Stockholm, and Virginia was so disorientated by its brightness and bustle, she could almost imagine that the war in Europe was a bad dream. But, twenty-four hours

269

later, when she was flying over Finland, everywhere was in darkness and she could sense violence in the blackness below. On the way to Helsinki, the train passed through air-raid territory, and an attack forced the passengers to take cover in the snowy forests. It was thus two in the morning when Virginia, exhausted and shivering, arrived at the Hotel Kämp, where she and all the other foreign correspondents were based. She'd been assured that Helsinki itself was not especially dangerous, even though Moscow Radio had recently announced that a "special bomb" was awaiting the Hotel Kämp and all "the Lying Journalists of the Capitalist Press."[32] The following day, when Virginia was driven on a tour of the region, she learned that the Russians were currently focusing their bombs on the ports and factories, and on the smaller towns and villages, whose traditional wooden houses could burn like tinder from a single incendiary raid.

It actually seemed incredible to her that so frozen a country could still be so flammable. On her first morning she'd been shocked by the cold, a cold so cutting it had bored through her fur-lined boots, her woollen underwear and her padded ski suit. Yet when she stopped at a cafe for a meal, she discovered that the upper half of the premises was still alight from a recent attack, that she was actually "sipping coffee in a burning building . . . trying to get warm in a house that was on fire."[33]

No one but she was alarmed, however. The proprietor stoically assured Virginia that his sons were putting out the flames, and, in the following days, she formed a wondering respect for the Finns, "a quiet, reserved people who made no show of bravado." One night, when her press car got stuck in a snowdrift, she and her driver were given shelter by a middle-aged woman who assured them of her absolute faith in the Russians' defeat: "God will not let us perish beneath so terrible a foe," she said serenely. "All will be well."[34]

Virginia was reminded of the Loyalists in Spain, who'd shown similar fortitude against impossible odds. But privately she doubted the Finns' chances, for, while Britain, France and America had promised to send out planes and anti-aircraft guns, Sweden and Norway were refusing them transit, for fear of German reprisals. On the other hand, Virginia had yet to visit the northern fronts on which the Finns were pinning their best hopes of a military miracle, and, in the second week of January, she requested permission to go up to Rovaniemi, capital of Lapland, where the northern press centre was based.

Until this point, she had been allowed to travel wherever she wanted. There were an unusual number of female correspondents in this war* — the majority from Sweden, according to Virginia, who was greatly entertained by their uniform prettiness: "all had blonde hair, big blue eyes, and wore dainty white fur coats and little white hats that tied under their chins. They looked like the front row of a Cochran chorus."[35] The Finnish military had seemed happy to accord all women the same treatment as men. However, the day before Virginia filed her application to go north, one of the Swedes had complained of an "inappropriate advance" made by the public-relations officer who'd been escorting her to the south-eastern front at Viirpuri. In their rush to limit the scandal, the authorities had slapped out an order requiring all female journalists to remain close to the Hotel Kämp, where their "safety" could be guaranteed; and Virginia, aghast, saw her assignment slipping away: "My heart sank, and I wondered if I had come all the way from England merely to sit in Helsinki."[36]

Back in Madrid, she would have been able to find a biddable or bribable officer to get her to the front, but here in Finland the protocol was far more centralized and strictly enforced. Experience, however, had taught Virginia that there was always someone,

---

* Including the photographer Thérèse Bonney, who won accolades for her coverage of the Winter War.

272

higher up the chain of command, who had the power to waive the rulebook; after furiously cabling her best contacts, she was able to reach the Finnish Minister in London, who was willing to grant her a special pass to Rovaniemi. The twenty-four-hour drive north was long and arduous — the remote icebound city was just a mile and a half from the Arctic Circle — and Virginia shivered under coarse military blankets as the car jolted along ice-rutted roads. Once in Rovaniemi, the cold felt even more inhuman than it had in Helsinki. But the landscape was exquisite — mile after mile of "white forests and glassy lakes." Every morning, when Virginia rose early to catch the brief hours of daylight, she was captivated by the pristine beauty of her surroundings — the air still frozen in an unearthly calm, the ice-frosted trees etched to "lace valentines" by the glow of the rising sun.[37]

It was on a particularly beautiful morning that she was driven out to investigate the scene of a recent battle at Suomussalmi, but, on this occasion, the magic of the landscape felt suddenly malign. The Finns had won a stupendous victory, annihilating two Russian divisions, and the sub-zero temperatures had left the battle scene freakishly intact. "It was the most ghastly spectacle I have ever seen," Virginia admitted. "For four miles the road and forests were strewn with the bodies of men and horses, with wrecked tanks, field kitchens, trucks, gun-carriages, maps, books and articles of clothing." Some of the dead Russians had been covered with a merciful blanket of snow, but others, she wrote, had been frozen hard, "like petrified statues, sprawled against the trees in grotesque attitudes."[38] A small group of boys was playing with one of the corpses, burying it head down, so that its desiccated legs stuck up stupidly from the snow, and this childish act of desecration was too much for Virginia. It was all she could do not to vomit.

She imagined what terrors those 30,000 Russians had endured at Suomussalmi — ambushed by an invisible enemy, trapped in a wasteland of whiteness and cold — and when she was permitted to speak with some of the luckier men, who'd been taken prisoner, she felt nothing but pity. They were very young, uneducated and raw, and they'd clearly been sent out to Finland with little understanding of who they were fighting or why. They'd even been told that the Finnish people would welcome them as liberators. When they'd been confronted by an army of white-camouflaged fighters, gliding out of the trees, they'd believed they were fighting against demons or ghosts.

But it wasn't just the ignorant Russian conscripts who struggled with reality out here, in the snowy remoteness, on the edge of the world. Virginia noticed that she and the rest of the Rovaniemi press corps were also losing their bearings. One day, they'd been moved to a nearby ski resort, to escape a Russian raid, and they'd whiled away the hours at the rifle range. Virginia — a terrible shot — had earned a crashing defeat when she and her fellow Americans had competed against the others in the group. But the one German present, Herbert Uxkull, for United Press, had joked in a melancholy way that he and the BBC correspondent, Eddie Ward, ought to have been firing at each other. Virginia had been baffled by this remark, and it was only after a moment or two that she remembered "the other war" in Europe and was reminded that Uxkull and Ward were officially each other's enemy.

Otherwise, there had been an unusual camaraderie within the northern press corps. The sheer strangeness of this Winter War, with its freezing logistical challenges, had bound them all together, and the intensity of the fighting precluded any rivalry over stories. During the month that Virginia was based in Rovaniemi, she crawled across a frozen lake to find shelter from Russian planes, she dodged Russian shells, just 300 metres from the border, and she narrowly escaped the inferno of a burning building.

Despite the Finns' heroic defence of the north, however, they were running out of time. Down in the south, the Russians were conquering swathes of territory, and by the time Virginia returned to Helsinki in late February, they had breached the Mannerheim Line and were closing in on Viipuri.

Here there was no more possibility of romance or hope. So fierce was the fighting that none of the journalists, male or female, was allowed anywhere close, and they had to get their information from official briefings and second-hand rumours. The Finnish telegraph and phone services, meanwhile, were so badly disrupted that most of the stories they managed to file were too old or too mangled to be fit for publication. Virginia was livid when she learned that United Press had bribed the authorities for priority use of the phone lines, but her frustration would be short-lived. With the approaching spring thaw, the Finns were losing their only military advantage, and, faced with the collapse of their army, the Helsinki government was pressing for a negotiated peace. It was the only viable option, but to the people it felt like a betrayal: "We've had a lot of bombs fall . . . but the worst bomb of all has been this peace," mourned one elderly factory worker.[39] And on 12 March, when Virginia watched the flags of Helsinki being lowered to half mast, she despaired that Finland had joined Czechoslovakia and Poland in the roll call of valiant nations, thrown under the wheels of tyranny and greed.*

Martha, too, had despaired. Back in October, a cable had come from Charles Colebaugh suggesting that she travel to Helsinki to report on the then-deteriorating relationship between Russia and Finland. So deeply ensconced had she become in her Cuban idyll, she'd all but cut herself loose from international news, and she admitted that she could not even identify Finland on a map. Yet, she was glad of a chance to pick up her reporting career. The writing of her Spanish novel had been going badly: "What I have is patience, care, honor, detail, endurance and subject matter," Martha grieved. "And what I do not have is magic."[40] She couldn't understand how Ernest was able to get roisteringly drunk every night, yet still wake up the next morning to produce pages of magnificently concentrated prose, while she, with all her discipline, was left with characters and dialogue of dismaying flatness. When the assignment came from *Collier's,* it felt like a

* The Finns were not to be left in peace: between 1941 and 1944, they were drafted into the Axis alliance against Russia, changing sides in 1944 to join the Allies in hostilities against the Nazis. By 1945, they'd regained their independence, but had to cede nearly 10 percent of their territory to Russia, in addition to financial reparations.

reprieve, allowing her to escape from the frustrations of fiction to the writing she knew she did best.

This time, however, Martha was resolved not to feel the pity and the fury that had crushed her in Czechoslovakia and Spain. During her fourteen-day crossing to Europe, she schooled herself to a state of near-anaesthetized calm. "For the purposes of mental hygiene, I gave up trying to think or judge," she recalled, "and turned myself into a walking tape recorder with eyes."[41] Even when her ship passed through a flotilla of bloated corpses, victims of a recent U-boat attack, she strove to keep her terror in neutral gear.[42] But, in Helsinki, all of Martha's instinctive partisanship came flooding back. Like Virginia, she was deeply moved by the courage of the Finns as they withstood the first of the Russian air strikes: "the people are marvellous, with a kind of pale frozen fortitude," she wrote to Ernest. "They watch with loathing but without fear this nasty hidden business which they did nothing to bring on themselves."[43]

But, however unhesitatingly Martha drove out to the battle zones to watch the Finns wage their Winter War, she had no intention of lingering longer than was necessary. The cold was intolerable, she missed Ernest, and, by the time Virginia arrived, the only news she had of Martha was an anecdote told her by the American military attaché, Frank Haye. He recounted how he'd spotted a "beautiful blonde" drinking in the bar of the Hotel Kämp one night, and how, having warned her that the press were being bussed out of town to escape the night's raids, he'd been impressed by the speed with which she'd run up to her room and returned, almost immediately, with a pair of pyjamas and a bottle of whisky. Admiringly, Haye had whistled: "I knew that girl had been evacuated before."[44]

Once back in Cuba, Martha had been happy to put Finland behind her. Warmed by the colours of her garden and the exuberance of Ernest's welcome, she told *Collier's* that she was resolved to accept no more assignments for the present. "I have grown wondrously fat," she wrote to Charles Colebaugh. "It is perhaps wrong to be so happy in this present world but, my God how I love this place and how happy I am."[45] But, even in her desert-island refuge, Martha could no longer ignore the war. Now that Stalin had defeated Finland, Hitler was ready to take his own piece of Scandinavia, and, on 9 April, he launched a dual attack on Denmark and Norway. Ernest, under pressure from Martha, had bought a small radio so that they could "get [their] disasters shrieked fresh and on the minute" and, by early May, the two of them were grimly transfixed by the news as

German forces, having smashed their way into Denmark and Norway, began turning their firepower on Holland, Belgium and France.[46]

The response in Britain was cataclysmic. On 2 May, Helen was in the House of Commons to witness the jeers that erupted from both sides as Chamberlain announced that Norway was lost. Grey faced and shaking, the Prime Minister looked disturbingly frail, and it was clear to Helen that he was slipping from power. She herself had long been campaigning for a change of leadership, and the authority with which she was now able to argue her case, within the pages of the *Chicago Daily News,* was due to her finally getting the promotion she'd sought, to the paper's elite cadre of foreign correspondents.

That promotion had not come without a fight. Early in 1940 Helen had been invited on a lecture tour of America, to promote her new book, and speak about the British war effort, and she'd taken the opportunity to meet with her paper's publisher, Colonel Frank Knox, and her Chicago editor-in-chief, Paul Scott Mower. Bill Stoneman's high regard for Helen, coupled with the Duke of Windsor scoop, had raised her hopes of gaining a place on the foreign news team, but her two Chicago bosses had been unmoved, informing her that it went against their policy to promote a woman above the level of stringer, however impressive her work. This was exactly the line that Helen had been spun a decade earlier, when she'd sought work at the *New York Herald Tribune,* and impatience now made her uncharacteristically rude: "Well, you know you can change your policy," she'd snapped at the two men, "but I can't change my sex."[47] She feared, afterwards, she might have argued her way out of a job, but she had an admiring ally in Chicago — the foreign editor, Caroll Binder — and he went to Knox with a trumped-up story about United Press making moves to poach Helen for their London office. Suddenly, it seemed the "policy" could be changed. "We can't have that," Knox had briskly responded, and the following week, when the *Chicago Daily News* ran a full-page promotion of its international news team, Helen's name and photograph were prominently displayed. Even though there were complaints, from a conservative core of readers, who did not want to get their war news from a woman, Knox and Binder would continue to promote Helen as one of the paper's stars.[48]

It was spring when she returned to take up her new staff position, and she could discern the "undercurrent of desperate tension" in London, as the British war cabinet floundered to keep abreast of events.[49] Plots were being hatched to get Churchill installed in Chamberlain's place, and, when Helen went to stay at Ditchley Park, the Oxfordshire home of Ronald and Nancy Tree, she found herself in the midst of a political conspiracy. "There's much fascinating [*sic*] that can't be written about," she confided to her parents,[50] but she was taking careful notes, and, later, she would have an exact recall of the moment when Nancy Tree came in from the garden and, "dancing through the room," had urged the assembled plotters to call for an immediate vote of no confidence in Parliament. "Listen, all you people, talk is cheap. Why don't you make up your minds?"[51]

As the political crisis unfolded in London and the war began to escalate, Helen was writing up to twenty or thirty articles per week. To her family, she complained she was "going grey" from the strain, but the knowledge that she was writing history, fresh each day, was exhilarating.[52] On 3 May, she was able to send an explosive dispatch to Chicago, with news that the Belgian army had been placed on high alert in anticipation of a German attack. The information had to be published anonymously to protect Helen's source, but there was no question of its accuracy. A week later, Hitler sent his troops into Belgium.

Virginia was in Rome when she learned that the battle for Europe had begun, but, unlike Helen, she'd been taken off guard. Although she too had sensed a nervousness in London, although Aidan had been sent on his first serious mission, assisting the Balkan intelligence service in Istanbul, it seemed to her that the Phoney War still had months to run. The grass in St. James's Park was a reassuring spring green, the middle-aged businessmen were going to work in their pinstriped suits and, when she was sent out to Rome in early May, to assess the mood of the Italians, the prospect of fighting seemed equally remote to them. None of the civilians to whom she spoke were enthused by Hitler's war, and Italo Balbo, "as lively and gutsy as ever," was only interested in persuading Virginia to fly back to Libya with him. Typing up her article on the evening of 9 May, she concluded that, while Mussolini might have an appetite for battle, his people didn't, and he would only risk committing himself once he was certain of being on the winning side. Virginia was uneasy about the piece she'd written, fearing that she hadn't canvassed a sufficiently wide range of opinion. But in the end, it didn't matter. The following morning, she was telephoned by John Whitaker, who told her that speculation about Mussolini's intentions had become irrelevant. "Tear up your article, honey," he brightly announced. "No one wants to read about the Wops. Hitler's invaded Holland and Belgium."[53]

CHAPTER EIGHT:
THE FALL OF FRANCE,
SPRING/SUMMER 1940

"It was like watching
someone you loved dying"
VIRGINIA COWLES[1]

There was elation and relief, as well as a raw
kind of terror, now that the uncertainty was
over. When Virginia and John turned on the
radio to learn that Churchill had been instructed to form a new coalition government,
John whooped out loud at the news. "Oh boy,
oh boy. Now everyone will start going places,"
he roared. Like so many, he'd pinned his
hopes on the "British Bulldog," and when
Virginia flew to Paris on 12 May, she found
the French in a similarly ebullient mood. So
firm was their faith in the strength of the Allied armies and in the unbreachable defences
of the Maginot Line, they appeared almost
relieved the Germans had attacked. Now that
the war in Europe had properly begun, it was
possible, at least, to anticipate the end.[2]

Only twenty-four hours later, that confidence had disintegrated into panic, as the

Germans advanced and rumours jumped through Paris that Holland was in flames; that thousands of enemy parachutists were being dropped into France, disguised as nuns, priests and, improbably, as ballet dancers. Virginia had hoped to get news of the fighting from Fruity Metcalfe, the Duke of Windsor's aide, but Metcalfe's habitual hearty grin was frozen to a grimace. The Germans had crossed the River Meuse in three separate places and they were bulldozing south through France at incredible speeds. "You can't even tack a map up on the wall, much less put the pins in before it's all over," he lamented, and his despair would have been even greater had he known what Bill Shirer and some of his colleagues were observing, when Goebbels sent them on a press tour of the Belgian front.[3]

Sigrid had not been part of that tour, since Hitler had banned women from all aspects of the fighting, but she would hear from Shirer how hard it had been not to marvel at the formidable military juggernaut the Nazis had created. He'd watched the progress of one apparently endless convoy as it rolled through the flat Belgium landscape — the infantry leading the advance in armoured trucks and firing on Allied ground troops; the heavy artillery and the Stuka bombers bringing up the rear and between them laying waste to buildings, factories, railways and bridges.

Shirer had no knowledge, then, of the methamphetamine-laced chocolate, *Panzers-chokolade,* which was fuelling this apparently superhuman army; all he could see was the paralysis it spread among the Allied forces, who, in contrast with their enemy, struck him as pallid, ill fed and fighting with antiquated weaponry.

The Allied command, meanwhile, were hoping that the sheer speed of the German advance must prove counterproductive — that their supply lines would eventually become overextended and their troops made vulnerable to counter-attack. Virginia was also working on this same assumption when she went to the British embassy in Paris, hoping to expedite a travel permit to the front. She knew, of course, about the War Office ban prohibiting women from British war zones. But, now that the fighting was spreading through Europe, she was hopeful that the regulations might be eased, and that the contacts who'd helped her in the past might work their influence again, to secure her some form of accreditation.

Her friend at the embassy, Charles Mendl, could do nothing, however. As head of the press office, he had no power against military protocol, and he advised Virginia that her best plan was to return to London and go through official channels. But time was against her, for it took the Germans just eighteen days to occupy Holland, force the Belgians to surrender, and effectively isolate the French and British armies from each other. On 28 May, Virginia was sitting in the House of Commons to hear Churchill admit the "grievous peril" Britain faced, and to note the alarming decline of his confidence as he battled to retain control of his Cabinet.

There was intense pressure, now, for Churchill to sue for a negotiated peace. But he and his army would be saved that week by a near-impossible combination of heroism, strategy and luck. A temporary lull in the German advance had allowed the bulk of the British Expeditionary Force to fight its way to the wide, flat beaches around Dunkirk, and, on 27 May, the British navy had sent out ships to start bringing the men back home. The rescue, code-named Operation Dynamo, had begun slowly, and Virginia, who was staying with friends near the English coast, had little confidence in its success. She could hear, and feel "the distant explosion of bombs" on the other side of the Channel, and imagined it must spell disaster for the British. But the Admiralty had put out a call for civilian boats to assist in the rescue and, after hundreds of fishing smacks, pleasure boats and trawlers began plying across the sea to France, the British were, extraordinarily, able to turn defeat into what the press was now calling the "Miracle of Dunkirk."[4]

Virginia was in tears when she went down to Dover on 1 June to watch some of the tired and filthy troops disembark. Emotional crowds had gathered, eliciting self-conscious grins from the British soldiers, jauntily blown kisses from the rescued French and Poles. There were similar scenes along the railway line that took the men back to London — houses were draped with Union Jacks, and waving families crowded the platforms of every station. The success of Operation Dynamo had helped to unite a jittery nation, for even though many had been killed in its execution and up to 40,000 taken prisoner, the bulk of the British Expeditionary Force, nearly 338,000 men, had been brought home. When Virginia was back in the Commons on 4 June, the atmosphere could not have been more different from the previous week, and nor could Churchill have been more magnificently in charge. The House was silent as he launched into what was to become one of the defining speeches of his career, assuring the British that, whatever might happen to the rest of Europe, they, as a nation, would never "flag or fail."

"We shall fight on the beaches, we shall fight on the landing grounds, we shall fight in the fields and in the streets, we shall fight in the hills; we shall never surrender." This was perhaps the moment when Churchill mobilized his oratory into a weapon of war. But, even while the British were hailing Dunkirk as "the greatest rear-guard battle in history," the Germans were gloating over their own victory, and in Berlin, it was confidently predicted that the swastika would shortly be flying over Trafalgar Square.[5] "Catastrophe Before the Doors of Paris and London — five armies cut off and destroyed," ran the headline of *B.Z. am Mittag*,[6] and, for Sigrid, who had tried, and failed, to alert the French to the danger they'd faced, these were awful times. The Nazi propagandists were working overtime to claim that Germany had always been the innocent party in this conflict, that it had been forced to defend itself against "Jewish reactionary warmongers," and other corrupt elements within the "Capitalist democracies." Every news report of military success came freighted with a repellent mix of triumph and piety; and Goebbels had conceived a specially refined punishment for the foreign press who were now summoned, once a week, to sit in the small screening room at the Propaganda Ministry to watch detailed film footage of the German advance.

So certain had Hitler been of winning this war, he'd ordered camera crews to record every stage of it, co-opting some of the Reich's most skilled directors and cinematographers. Edited versions of the footage — with long tracking shots of heroic helmeted Aryan soldiers, gleaming Panzer divisions and exploding shells — were shown to the public. But the press got the films uncensored, and as Sigrid and her colleagues were subjected to scenes of fleeing refugees, slain animals, flaming buildings and captured soldiers, they also had to endure the malicious grins of all the Germans in the room, as they nodded along approvingly to the film's commentary. "Thus do we deal death and destruction on our enemies," intoned the narrator, as the camera lingered sadistically over the corpse of a British pilot, slumped inside his burnt-out cockpit.[7]

Within this foully intimidating climate, Sigrid was struggling to publish her own small acts of truth and correction. The outbreak of war had inevitably brought new levels of threat and obstructions and, as early as October 1939, she was despairing to McCormick that "the whole of my carefully built-up organization has gone to pieces."[8] It had become far more difficult to travel outside Germany to file her most sensitive material and she'd begun to experience malicious glitches in the Nazi-run telegraph service which disrupted the transmission of her articles and dispatches. Using her own money, Sigrid set up a private telephone line to Copenhagen, paying a contact there a hundred dollars a month to forward her copy on to Chicago, but she could only make sparing use of it, for fear it would be detected by the authorities.

A far greater problem, though, was retaining the confidence of her sources. A new law had been passed, making it a capital offence to do or say anything deemed detrimental to state security, and it was so rigorously enforced that three teenage boys were executed simply for robbing a soldier's house. Passing inside information to a foreign journalist was riskier than ever and only very few brave individuals, like Johannes Schmitt, were still willing to work on Sigrid's behalf.*

Meantime, everything she did publish was subjected to even tougher scrutiny. Newspapers remained officially exempt from censorship, but foreign journalists had to monitor themselves continually because Goebbels and the Foreign Ministry now regarded the most trivial offences as treasonous. When Sigrid had reported on the invasion of Norway, her use of the phrase "big Germany" and "little Norway" was considered potential grounds for expulsion, and, however obediently she accepted each new ruling, she was aware that the regime was closing in on her.[9] There were renewed at-

* Unable to cover news from the front, Sigrid hired a young, male stringer. But John Raleigh spoke little German, and was far too easily fooled by the propaganda fed him during military briefings and press tours of the front.

tempts to frame her for espionage: a danger-ously controversial story was filed to the *Tri-bune* under her byline, and aggressive investigations were being made into her finances. "We run up against things that are so incredible," she told McCormick, "that it seems useless to write about them, because the casual reader far away will think they are inspired by prejudice or hate and simply won't believe them."[10]★

The Colonel, partly out of genuine concern for Sigrid's welfare, partly to protect his own political interests, chose not to publish some of her more hard-hitting articles; yet, accord-ing to Bill Shirer, she was still able to use "her independence and her knowledge of things behind the scenes" to impressive ef-fect.[11] Under her Dickson alias, she wrote about the rising numbers of concentration camps in Greater Germany, about the mass deportation of Jews to the eastern territories. She was still reporting for the Mutual Broad-casting System, and, even though her radio scripts were rigorously censored in advance, she was able to smuggle in some hint of the truth, through the style of her delivery.

"Oh, I worked so hard to write the text so that, if I put the intonation in, it would show

★ A list had been compiled of words considered politically out of bounds — a list that even came to include the word "Nazi."

what I was thinking, without my saying anything I had no business to be saying."[12] Sigrid enjoyed her radio work, too, because it took her into a different professional world from her own office. She broadcast late at night to accommodate the time difference with America and, while the censors at Haus des Rundfunks were checking her script, she was able to eavesdrop on Lord Haw-Haw, the Irish journalist turned Nazi propagandist, as he practised the delivery of his sneering, quisling rants; and she was able to enjoy a bracing gossip with Bill Shirer, whose studio slot was just before hers.

Bill was always excellent company. His hatred for the Nazis ran deep, but he had a darkly enjoyable gallows humour and he was always at his funniest when dissecting the characters of Goebbels and von Ribbentrop, who, as Minister of Propaganda and Foreign Minister respectively, were locked in a vicious rivalry for control of the foreign press. The two men had taken to scheduling their press briefings at clashing times; they'd even built two rival press clubs, each one fitted out with listening devices and staffed with spies, who kept tabs on the journalists' conversations. Von Ribbentrop's club was sumptuously furnished, but Goebbels', on Leipziger Platz, did better business, largely because its restaurant served steaks, pastries and the now-indescribable luxury of real coffee. And, realizing that the journalists' stomachs might be the best way to their hearts and minds, Goebbels also took to handing out ration coupons at the end of his own press briefings, allocating foreign correspondents twice the allowance that was usually given to office workers.

But the ranks of the foreign press were much depleted. The British were long gone, and there was a rapid turnover among the Americans. Beach Conger, correspondent for the *Herald Tribune,* had barely lasted a month before his refusal to retract a mildly controversial comment had got him deported, while one of Sigrid's own young stringers had got kicked out on his very first day, because he'd commented too incautiously on Hitler's failed attempt to get Churchill to beg for peace. On 14 June when German forces entered Paris it was thus a small, muted group of journalists who gathered in Berlin to mourn the very first images of Nazi soldiers marching up the Champs Elysées, and of the Nazi swastika now flying from the Eiffel Tower.

For Sigrid, personally, these were the darkest of days. She still had good friends in the French capital, some of her happiest, most hopeful years had been spent there, and it was terrible to read the exultant gloating of the *Völkischer Beobachter* which promised that the Paris "of frivolity and corruption," where "Jews had entry to the court and niggers to the salons," would never rise again.[13]

In Britain, meanwhile, the gravity of the situation was not fully reported, until just before Paris fell. Journalists were genuinely unsure of the facts on the ground, but they were also under pressure to maintain morale. Even on 10 June, when Panzer tanks were within fifty miles of the city gates and the French government was in flight, the *Daily Telegraph* assured its readers that the capital must stand. "French Hold German Onslaught: Heaviest Defence in History" ran the headline; and Virginia, no less determinedly optimistic, was at that very same moment preparing to fly out to Paris to report on the defence.

The fact that the British no longer had an active military presence in France meant that she no longer had to work her way around the War Office ban. The French Ministry of Information, far more amenable to women, had been willing to grant her a temporary pass to the front, and the only issue in her way was transport. Civilian planes were reportedly no longer flying to France, but, on the morning of 11 June, Virginia got a call from Cook's Travel Bureau informing her that one very last-minute flight had been scheduled from Croydon airport, and that she had just about time to catch it.

Reading the day's papers en route, Virginia

could not help but be disconcerted by their abrupt change of tone. Overnight, the "heaviest defence in history" had been demoted to "a back-to-the-wall stand" — and the formerly defiant Parisians were now said to be abandoning their city in droves. Yet, perilous though her assignment was starting to look, Virginia never considered abandoning it. She'd been the last journalist to go into Berlin in 1939, she could be the last into Paris — and her resolve didn't waver, even when her plane was diverted to a bomb-pitted aerodrome near Tours, 230 kilometres south of Paris, nor when she was taken aside by angry French officials and interrogated for a full five hours.

Initially it seemed that the French would not allow Virginia anywhere near Paris: "[It] is out of the question," they snapped. "No one is going . . . *C'est très dangereux.*" Eventually, however, one of the officials conceded that an evening train might still be running, and they allowed Virginia and one fellow passenger, a tearfully agitated Egyptian, to leave the airport and take their chances at Tours station. By now, the whole of the city appeared to be on the move, and the station was in chaos. "Everyone had dozens of bags and bundles, they were jostling, pushing, sleeping and even eating on the platform." There was no apparent timetable, and, whenever a train did appear, there was such violent competition to board that Virginia's companion, alarmed by the "wild scramble of the crowds" and desperate to get to Paris, refused to wait in the station cafe, insisting instead that the two of them sit on the platform, as close to the tracks as they could get.[14]

During the six hours they waited on that hard platform, the Egyptian man explained to Virginia that he'd had to leave his children in Paris while doing business in London, and that he was naturally now terrified for their safety. When the Paris train finally arrived, it was after midnight, and it filled up with so many people and bags that Virginia doubted they could survive the journey. Twenty or thirty kilometres outside Tours, however, the train emptied with another "scramble"; everybody, it seemed, was catching a connecting service for Bordeaux, and, as their own train rumbled northwards, through "the terrible stillness of the blackened countryside," there were just three passengers left — Virginia, her Egyptian friend, and one other man.[15]

Earnestly, Virginia tried to maintain her companions' spirits. Every war she'd ever covered, she said, had taught her that "the closer you get to the front, the calmer it is," and she assured them that Paris must be far "more normal" than Tours. Five hours later, though, when they arrived at the Gare d'Austerlitz, Virginia's confidence faltered. The station itself was eerily deserted, but outside its locked gates a riot was brewing, as crowds of frightened, angry Parisians threatened violence against the gendarmes who were trying to convince them that no more trains were running. Hundreds, maybe thousands were besieging the station — so many that Virginia, exhausted and starving after her long and difficult journey, thought she might be hallucinating. She knew that she needed a bed, some sleep. But when, by a miracle, she succeeded in hailing a taxi, she found that every hotel in the city, even the Ritz, had shut its doors; and when she tried to call her trusted mentor, Knick, for advice, she was told that he'd abandoned Paris four days earlier.

"If Knickerbocker had left, things must be bad."[16] Virginia was starting to panic, but, as she fought to stay focused, her driver paused outside yet another hotel, the Lancaster, and she was suddenly reminded of a conversation she'd had with the *Herald Tribune* correspondent Walter Kerr, about a poker game he used to run from its premises. Incredibly, the hotel was still open, and, even more incredibly, when Virginia asked the concierge if any journalists were in residence, she was informed that Monsieur Kerr was asleep in his room.

Walter was no less astonished than Virginia

when he heard her voice on the lobby telephone. But he was also unable to hide his dismay, for the Germans were now just fifteen miles from Paris, and the retreating French government had ordered a cessation of all resistance. Occupation, within a day or two, was inevitable; and, while Walter had decided to run the risk of staying on, he was tersely insistent that he could not be responsible for Virginia's safety. All he could do was help her get out.

Virginia was too stunned and remorseful to argue. Walter suggested they should drive around the city while they planned her escape route, and now, at mid-morning, she could see clearly that Paris was lost. "It was like watching someone you loved dying," she wrote. The boulevards were silent, the cafes were locked, the fountains had stopped playing and the only people in sight were knots of last-minute escapees, trudging along the pavements with their suitcases, and the occasional straggle of soldiers, limping, bandaged and caked in mud.[17]

Aware that she was one of very few journalists to witness these bleakly historic scenes, Virginia scribbled in her notebook while Walter remained focused on her departure. His first idea was to hire a car, but the proprietor of the single garage they'd found had all but spat at them in frustration and disgust: "Listen, if there was one car in Paris, *one* car, I would have it. In fact, if it were possible to steal a car, I would have it. I would even kill someone to get a car. Instead I must stay here and watch the filthy Boches come into Paris."[18] Moving on to the harassed American embassy, they were greeted with little more grace — but they did at least learn that a British journalist, Tom Healy, was still in Paris and was planning to drive to Bordeaux that afternoon.* It took over an hour to track him down — an hour that seemed "endless" to both Virginia and Walter. But, finally, word came back that Healy had a spare seat in his car; by five o'clock, having typed up her notes at Walter's office, Virginia was packed into his impractically sporty Chrysler and was driving west along the bank of the Seine. As she gazed at the river and at the reflections of Paris "shimmering . . . blue black . . . in the water," she felt almost guilty to be leaving the city to its fate. Yet she and Tom had barely reached the outskirts before it looked as though escaping the French capital might be very much harder than they imagined.[19]

"Try to think in terms of millions. Try to

* Healy, correspondent for the *Daily Mirror*, had been driving around eastern France to look for Italian troop movement near the border. Knowing nothing of the latest developments, he had "drifted [into Paris] by accident."

300

think of noise and confusion, of the thick smell of petrol, of the scraping of automobile gears, of shouts, wails, curses and tears."[20] Every vehicle in Paris, every car, truck, lorry, cab and hearse, seemed to be caught in the giant traffic jam that had formed on the road leading south; and, although Virginia had seen refugees in Romania, Prague and Spain, she'd never witnessed anything approaching the scale of this exodus, nor anything so bleakly callous. Dotted along the roadside were broken-down cars, their occupants left to trudge on, forlornly, by foot; yet, as the traffic ground slowly forwards, no one was sparing them a glance. The single thought on everyone's minds was escape, not only from the advancing German tanks, but also from the planes which, even now, had begun circling overhead and strafing the traffic with machine-gun fire. At one point, Virginia and Tom passed a woman and her four children, who were standing by their van in the middle of the road, begging for a can of petrol. No one was stopping, though, apart from a group of angry men, whose only concern was to shove the van aside and keep the traffic moving. They acted with brutal efficiency, and as the vehicles resumed their grinding progress, the woman was left weeping helplessly on her knees — the rear axle of her van broken and her family's possessions scattered over the verge.

This was one of a thousand small tragedies that Virginia glimpsed, but she and Healy were fortunate in being able to divert, eventually, onto a quieter route. As an accredited war journalist, Tom was allowed onto roads that were reserved for military use, and, navigating along small country lanes, they were able to reach Tours by lunchtime the following day. It was Friday 14 June, and when Virginia bumped into Knick, coming out of his hotel, he told her that the Germans had already entered Paris and that it was a miracle she'd got out in time. "My God, how did you get here?" he enquired, and Virginia, who was nearly dead from fatigue, acerbically replied, "You're always asking me that."[21]

Tours was "bedlam," every vacant hotel room was occupied, but Eddie Ward, the BBC journalist whom she'd met in Finland, told her she could find a bed in the large, outlying villa which had been commandeered by Reuters news agency. While the rest of the world "was turning upside down," Virginia found it very strange, that night, to be dining on turtle soup, steak Béarnaise and cherry pie, to be sleeping in a ritzily mirrored bedroom. It was even more disconcerting, the following morning, to hear the voice of her Egyptian friend calling out to her from the teeming crowds. He looked filthily dishevelled, and even more distraught, for by the time he'd reached Paris, his children had already fled their apartment, and while he'd been scouring the city for news of them, the first cavalcade of German motorcycles had come roaring though the Porte d'Auber-villiers. He told Virginia he had witnessed scenes of unbelievable despair: "Some of [the people] went crazy. I saw one woman pull out a revolver and shoot her dog, then set fire to her house."[22]*

Virginia, always the journalist, had pressed for more details, but the poor man was frantic to renew the search for his family, and, in any case, she had a boat to catch from Bordeaux. Tom could no longer drive her, because his car had sprung a leak after he'd swerved into a ditch the previous night, but she'd been offered a lift by Eddie, who was driving to the port with four other colleagues. They travelled in two cars, and, keeping to the back roads of rural France, it was briefly possible to imagine that the war was behind them — the vines were still being tended, the *boulangeries* were baking bread, and some of the people to whom they spoke had not actually heard that Paris had fallen.

But, when they reached Bordeaux, late on

* Such was the chaos in Tours that there were no military censors to vet Virginia's copy, and those back in London were so alarmed by the negative content of her report that they held it up for several hours until they were certain it could be published.

16 June, new crises were unfolding. All that day, the French government had been debating their next strategy — whether to regroup their army in North Africa and continue the war from there, or whether to trust the Germans to offer a civilized armistice. The eighty-four-year-old war veteran Marshal Pétain was arguing a powerful case for surrender, and, by the time the journalists arrived in Bordeaux, he'd won a majority agreement. As news spread throughout the city, the consulates and shipping offices were mobbed with demands for exit visas and tickets, and Virginia's party were lucky to secure places on the SS *Madura,* a cargo boat that was due to sail for England the following day. At midday on 17 June, they were lunching in a cafe, waiting for the tender to ferry them aboard, when Pétain made his broadcast to the nation. Even though capitulation had been expected, Pétain's announcement broke on the cafe like a death sentence, and the waitress who was serving them broke into violent sobs. "We can't live under the Boches," she wept. "We can't. It's not possible." Virginia, ever susceptible to guilt, felt wretched to be sailing away while this stricken young woman was left to face her country's as yet unimaginable future.[23]

Even now, her own safety was not guaranteed. One thousand six hundred passengers were to sail on the *Madura* — a ship designed only for a tenth of that number — and, during the twenty-four hours which it took them to board, the harbour was periodically strafed and bombed. German attacks were likely to continue even when they were at sea, but, because Virginia and her party feared U-boats more than they feared planes, they opted to spend the thirty-six-hour voyage up on deck, taking it in turns to keep watch for the enemy, and eking out the last of the champagne and foie gras pâté on which they'd squandered the last of their francs.

They were preoccupied, too, by the chances of Britain continuing the war on its own. Although soldiers from the Commonwealth and the Empire were serving with the British army, along with valiant support from the Polish air force (and the soon-to-be-formed Free French), Britain was essentially without allies. Its situation had become even more dire since Mussolini, assured of German victory, had at last entered the war, and was predicted to focus his fire on British interests in North Africa and the Mediterranean. Virginia fully expected to find the nation in grief and turmoil when she reached shore. Yet, when the SS *Madura* docked at Falmouth harbour, it was to a strikingly cheerful welcome. A line of stout-bosomed women were handing out sandwiches and lemonade, and when Virginia asked one of them what she thought of Britain's current situation, she was taken aback by the woman's bright and pleasant answer: "Improving, on the whole. At least, there's no one left to let us down."[24]

This was the spirit that Churchill was hoping to stir when he urged the British people to gird themselves for the battle ahead, to fight for a future when the world "may move forward into broad sunlit uplands." But, to Helen Kirkpatrick, those words had sounded like hollow theatrics. She'd been haunted by images of Nazi tanks and jackboots, desecrating the streets of Paris, and with the French capital lost, it seemed to her that everyone's future was doomed. "One's own life and plans fade so completely into the background and seem so insignificant," she wrote to her friend Amy Lois. "Security, a home, children, are finished, done, out of reach for me and for millions of women." Always vulnerable to depression, Helen believed that, even if the Germans were eventually beaten and "right" prevailed, she might not be alive to see it.[25]

Clare Hollingworth was in Bucharest when the French surrendered, and, while she was no less conscious of the shadow that now stretched all the way from Paris to Eastern Europe, she was far less prone to existential despair. Her principal concern was how to get her own reporting career back on track, for, once she'd completed her assignment in Poland the previous September, she'd been brusquely informed that the *Telegraph* no longer had need of her services.

It was an unfair, unexpected blow — a poor return for her services — but Clare had had other concerns to distract her then. The refugees who'd been pouring into Romania and Hungary needed urgent care, and she'd enlisted with one of the charities in the region, Save the Children, to monitor aid provision across a network of camps. She'd been appalled by what she found, especially the lack of coordination among the different agencies, who, as she reported, "bickered and obstructed and wrangled, while food and supplies remained in the capital and the refugees in the camps half starved and more than half froze."[26] Typically impatient, typically impulsive, she'd decided to take charge of the situation — hiring two lorries and organizing her own rogue system of distribution.

The charities were furious when they realized. But it was on the orders of a higher authority that Clare's welfare work was brought to an end. Back in London, alarms had again been sounded about the British visas she'd distributed to refugees before the war. A significant number had gone to communists, and, now that Russia and Britain were effectively enemies, it was feared that these same communists might be working against British interests. A report by MI5 officers had speculated that the securing of asylum for certain high-profile Bolsheviks might have been part of a "dangerous experiment, creating favourable circumstances for propaganda and subversive activity," and questions were asked about whether Clare might have been unwittingly or even wittingly involved. No proof of conspiracy could be found, but the questions themselves were damning. Clare was judged to be a dangerously loose cannon, her file at the Foreign Office was reopened and it was advised that no British relief agencies should accept her services again.

Banned from Save the Children, and with no other justification for remaining in Eastern Europe, Clare's only option was to return to England. A friendly diplomat, possibly Robin Hankey, sorted out her travel papers and booked her a berth on the Simplon Orient Express, and, to her parents' joy and relief, she was home in time for Christmas. Her husband's reaction was more ambivalent, however. Although Van had supported Clare in her initial decision to go to Poland, he had, as she chose to phrase it, been "growing a little restive about the time I was spending abroad."[27] Furthermore, although she did not choose to admit it, he'd been seeing another woman during her absence, and Clare was thrown into an uncharacteristic turmoil, as she wondered whether to stay in

London and mend her marriage, or whether to try and find her way back into journalism and the war.

Little of this pain would be acknowledged, however, when Clare came to write the story of this period. She claimed to have spent the following two months in discussions with a "number of publications"; she signed a book contract, for a study of the Balkans; and in February 1940 she made a failed attempt to get to the Maginot Line to report on the British presence there. The sole explanation she gave for why that trip had to be aborted was that northern France was "already crawling with journalists"; in truth Clare hadn't yet been hired by a new paper, and, even if she had, the War Office ban on women was still forcibly in place. Always keen to skate over any professional obstacle, her own account simply jumped forwards to late February, when, as she commented, she "found" herself in Paris.[28]

A feverish gaiety animated the city, which reminded Clare of Warsaw during its last hours of peace. Restaurants and bars were crowded, shop windows were bright with the new season's fashions, and Clare, staying in the Ritz, gave herself over to an enjoyable routine of drafting her new book by day and partying with friends and acquaintances by night. Paris was living on borrowed time, though, and, when Hitler sent his forces to

Scandinavia, it was obvious to Clare that northern Europe must be next. Rather than remaining in France, however, she was curious about how events might develop in the Balkans, and especially in Romania. Now that Germany was fighting on several fronts, its war machine was becoming ravenous for fuel, and Clare guessed that the rich Romanian oil fields must soon be in Hitler's sights. "Never had my instinct said so firmly, 'Go East,' " she recalled — and, early in May, she packed up her "T and T" (her "toothbrush and typewriter") to begin the journey to Bucharest.

There was a good chance she might not make it: German bombers flew over her train as it approached Switzerland and, at the border, Clare had to argue her way past jumpy custom guards, who were under orders to vet every foreigner. By the time she got to Yugoslavia, the Germans had begun their assault on Belgium and there were rumours that another front might be opening up further east. Everyone was tense, and as Clare nervously boarded the Lufthansa flight that was to take her on the final leg of her journey, she found herself staring at every Aryan-looking individual who might be a Nazi agent.

Once in Bucharest, however, she could discern little evidence of war nerves. The beggars and landless peasants who scratched a living in the sprawl of shanty towns around the city could barely see beyond the daily task of feeding themselves. Yet, the Bucharest elite, and its community of rich East European exiles, seemed equally oblivious, apparently taking their cue from the narcissistic lifestyle of the Romanian monarch, King Carol. In Clare's opinion the King was an idle, corrupt playboy; that summer, when she briefly rented a penthouse flat which had been used to house Carol's mistresses, she was revolted by its expensive vulgarity, by the rooftop pool and cocktail bar, by the collection of gaudy nude portraits, which had all been paid for from the national purse.

Clare also regarded the King as a military disaster. He'd made no decisive response to the developing war in Europe, and when Russia, Bulgaria and Hungary began taking advantage of the volatile international situation to make aggressive claims on Romanian border territories, he did not know how to act. Clare was meant to be completing her Balkans book, but as the mood in Bucharest darkened, she longed to be reporting the daily news, especially since she had two female rivals in the city — Dorothy Thompson and Sonia Tamora, the latter a Russian-American writing for the *New York Herald Tribune*. At some point during the last six months, Clare had rejected the offer of a stringer's contract with the *Daily Express* because she had so disliked its right-wing, populist politics; now, for the sake of a press pass and a platform, she was willing to stomach the paper's stance.

Initially, the material she filed tended to languish in the middle pages; analysis of the military and diplomatic skirmishes affecting Romania's territorial integrity was hardly headline material for the *Express*. She strove, manfully, to keep her editor's interest; while reporting on negotiations for the disputed province of Transylvania, she managed to file her copy far ahead of the other journalists present, simply by crawling between the legs of her rivals, grabbing hold of the one available telephone and retaining possession while she dictated her hastily assembled dispatch. Very soon, however, the *Express* would be actively hounding Clare for news.

King Carol's ineffectual response to his neighbours' attacks had prompted a wave of anti-monarchist sentiment throughout Romania, and, on 4 September, the extreme, hard-right general Ion Antonescu launched a coup against the throne. Antonescu not only carried the disaffected army with him, he also had the support of the Iron Guard. Rabidly nationalist, rabidly anti-Semitic, this paramilitary organization had briefly been banned from Romania in the late 1930s, but its members had found a welcome in Germany, where they'd been schooled in the Nazi arts of propaganda and political agitation. On their return, they'd joined with Antonescu to form the National Legionary State, and so formidable was their combined force that the King yielded his throne with only a symbolic show of resistance. His nineteen-year-old son, Prince Michael, was installed as puppet ruler and, when Clare saw the new teenage King making his first awkward appearance on the palace balcony, she pitied the future that awaited him: "He looked lonely and unhappy . . . king of a country with neither government nor constitution."[29]

Now that Antonescu and the Iron Guard were in control, Bucharest became a very different city. SS officers and Gestapo agents appeared on the streets to reinforce army patrols; curfew restrictions were imposed, phone lines were tapped and there was a rigid clampdown on the media. Under this new, Nazi-style regime, Clare had to submit all of her copy to censors. She soon found ways around the system, using the unmonitored phone line at the British Legation to dictate her more urgent dispatches to a contact in Geneva, but in doing so she was putting herself at risk. Antonescu's officials were learning to scan the foreign press for hostile comment, and, while Clare was not the only journalist to criticize, she'd made herself particularly vulnerable to the regime because she'd foolishly allowed her visa to lapse and was now in Romania as an illegal alien.

Just a month after the coup, they came for

her. Clare was preparing her early-morning coffee when four men pounded on her door, demanding that she accompany them to the Prefecture of Police. The one thing Clare knew, in that moment of alarm, was the necessity of staying put, for those who were taken for questioning at the Prefecture rarely emerged unhurt. Only days earlier, three foreign oil engineers had been accused of plotting to disrupt Romanian pipelines, and their interrogation had been so brutal, they'd been unable to speak or stand by the time they were released. Clare had just seconds to act, but, instinctively calculating that even the Iron Guard would balk at dragging a naked Englishwoman to jail, she stripped off her clothes and, slamming her door on the momentarily discomfited men, was able to make some urgent phone calls for help.

The first person to come to her aid was Robert St. John, an American journalist with whom she'd become very friendly in Bucharest. By the time he arrived, the Guardists had retreated, leaving two militia men to guard the flat, and Clare herself was in a dressing gown, drinking her coffee and glaring at her guards. Robert tried to deflate the tension with a feeble joke: "You are the first woman in years who has invited me to have breakfast," he grinned at Clare, "but is it really necessary for these friends of yours to act as chaperones?" The danger was still real, though, and Clare was very lucky that Robin Hankey (now head of the British Legation in Bucharest) appeared shortly afterwards, brandishing his diplomatic credentials and tersely informing the guards that Miss Hollingworth was a British citizen and would be under his protection until they could bring an official charge.[30]

The story that Robert St. John filed for the Associated Press was picked up by the BBC, and Daisy and Albert Hollingworth had the alarming experience of hearing about their daughter's ordeal on the radio. Even though Clare was theoretically under the protection of the British Legation, the rule of law was counting for less and less in Romania. Shortly after her near-arrest, the *Times* correspondent Archie Gibbons was beaten up and carted off to jail, and by the end of October, there were only four members of the foreign press corps left in the city. Day-to-day survival was everyone's paramount concern; after Clare was paid a second visit by the Iron Guard, she was careful never to sleep at her flat again, either staying with friends or camping out in her car, a pearl-handled revolver by her side.

Every day she remained in Bucharest, the danger increased, but Clare was determined to hang on because she had a theory that Hitler's greed for Romanian fuel must soon reveal itself, and that he would either invade the country or send in a "protective" force.

When he did so, she predicted that his first aim would be securing the oil fields of Ploeşti and she wanted to be the first to cover the story. Robert St. John was exasperated when Clare announced her intention to scout the area. Ploeşti was heavily guarded and just about the most "dangerous spot in the world"; if she were discovered, she would surely be arrested for spying or sabotage.[31] Yet the lure of the headline was too strong. Clare had scooped the invasion of Poland and it would be a remarkable feat if she could repeat her success in Romania. "I do know what fear is," she would later admit. "But I don't experience fear in war; I just know it won't happen to me and I'll come through all right."[32]

On this occasion, Clare did come through. Having borrowed a diplomatic car from Hankey, she managed to drive in and out of Ploeşti without being caught. Her mission had been worse than fruitless, though, for, while she'd been correct in predicting the imminent arrival of German troops, she'd been wrong about their destination. When she returned to Bucharest, she learned that a large contingent of SS officers had just arrived at the Athénée Palace Hotel, that more troops were to follow — and her colleagues had already filed the news.

For the moment, there was nothing further to investigate — Antonescu was a willing ally;

he had no intention of disputing Germany's right to oil — and finally Clare accepted it was time to move on. Fresh war news was brewing on the Greek–Albanian border, where Mussolini was rumoured to be massing an invasion force, and, because the British army were not yet actively engaged in the region, Clare was free to try to cover it. She had to wait for five anxious days while the regime debated whether or not to grant her an exit permit, but, by the end of October, she was on the way to Greece, hoping to catch the start of its defence against the Italian invaders.*

But Britain, too, was now fighting for survival. Once Hitler had control of France — his own forces occupying the northern half of the country, with Pétain's puppet Vichy government in charge of the rest — his ambition was focused on bringing Churchill to heel. The plan was to invade by sea, and in July, the Luftwaffe began bombing the southern coast of England, aiming to disable its ports and industrial facilities, and establish aerial supremacy ahead of the amphibious assault. Throughout the summer, the mild blue skies

* Mussolini had invaded Albania in the spring of 1939, angering Hitler, who feared that it would destabilize the Balkans, disrupting his access to the region's natural resources.

were transformed into an aerial battleground, as Messerschmitts, Junkers, Heinkels and Dorniers swarmed over the Channel, and RAF Spitfires and Hawker Hurricanes rose up to intercept them. The journalists based in London finally had a war on their doorstep, and small groups of them would regularly take the train down to Dover, booking rooms in the Grand Hotel and climbing up to the nearby Shakespeare Cliff, from where there was a clear view of the fighting.

Helen, recovering from her despair over Paris, was often among them. The War Office regulations had no power over what was now being called the Battle of Britain, for, as Helen informed her readers, it bore no resemblance to a conventional combat zone. "You have no feeling of carnage. Walking about on the cliff . . . under the warm summer sun and the bright blue sea beyond and the butterflies fluttering about . . . it is impossible to feel that this is actually bitter war going on overhead."[33] Observers on the ground were often unable to distinguish between British and German planes, which spiralled and swooped far above, like a choreography of swifts. The distant sound of an explosion, carried on the wind, or a trail of smoke that suddenly erupted from a burning wing were the only signs that these planes were being piloted by vulnerable young men, squinting through their goggles, pitched between life and death.

One afternoon, though, the war came unnervingly close, as a couple of enemy fighters flew straight towards the cliff and began strafing it with machine-gun fire. The buccaneering American reporter Vincent "Jimmy" Sheean was present that day, and he admitted that "all hell" had broken loose as "every man in sight took cover." His emphasis on "man" was significant, too, because the only two journalists who'd kept their cool in the group had been women. One was Helen, the other was Virginia Cowles, and, even as the bullets had zinged overhead, the two of them had remained where they were, "lying out in a meadow," according to Sheean, "flat on their backs and counting aeroplanes."

Both women were operating on the unspoken but obvious principle that, as the only female correspondents in Dover, it was imperative to betray no signs of weakness. Even Sheean, who liked and admired the two of them, had unconsciously enforced the prejudices of his profession, by focusing on the women's appearance rather than their professional background. Virginia was "a rather helpless-looking very feminine girl," he wrote; Helen, "a tall slender girl with a humorous glint." And, if Sheean could not be blamed for describing them as "girls" — this was the currency of the 1940s — he'd still written as though their presence, among a group of male war correspondents, was an entertaining novelty.[34]*

As the Battle of Britain extended into late summer, the RAF continued to stave off the enemy invasion. It was the duty of the press to maintain national morale, and newspaper and radio reports were dominated by stories of the pilots' heroism as they fought to defend the English coast. Virginia, revisiting Aidan's camp and very conscious of her lover's absence, was struck by how young these airmen appeared: "boys with blonde hair and pink cheeks who looked as though they ought to be in school." She went out with them on one of their reconnaissance missions, but, when she complimented their courage, they claimed that the risks they ran were nothing compared to those faced by the bomber crews. Flying over Germany every night to disable communication links, oil refineries and industrial facilities, the latter had to run the gamut of anti-aircraft fire as well as enemy fighter planes, and the casualty numbers were atrocious.[35]

"Those boys are really tough," they said,

* The incident was picked up by *The Sketch,* which ran portrait photos of Helen and Virginia and declared, "We take off our hat to U.S.A. newspaper girls for calmly watching a tremendous air battle over Dover at close range so Americans may know the truth." (*The Sketch,* 4.9.40.)

and, on their advice, Virginia went to observe a bomber squadron at work on a remote Lincolnshire air base. She was accompanied by Knick, and the two of them were permitted to sit in the operations room to watch six enormous Wellingtons take off for a night mission over the Ruhr Valley. It was an awesome spectacle — "plane after plane swept down the runway and disappeared into the uncertain light" — and as Virginia and Knick awaited their return, through the small hours of the morning, they became acutely aware of the tension that thickened in the operations room when one of the planes failed to come back on time.[36] Eventually, it landed safely, the crew explaining that they'd overshot their mark and lost their bearings, but others would not be so fortunate; out of the thirty men who flew with that squadron, only three would survive the war. Virginia's job was not to dwell on the doomed odds these young men faced, however, nor the nerve-lacerating strain of their missions. The story she filed for the *Sunday Times* was all about the gallantry of the bomber crews, the modesty with which these "brave and handsome men" had discounted the risks they ran, the schoolboy jokes they'd cracked to give each other the courage to fly.[37]

If British airmen had to be framed as heroes, so did British civilians. The Luftwaffe was inflicting far more damage on lives and homes that summer than the press was allowed to acknowledge, and the BBC reporter Iris Carpenter was only free to describe the raid that decimated her own Kent village when she came to write her war memoir, six years later. Parachute mines had been dropped, and, although Iris's home had been spared, she'd had to try to comfort others whose world had been destroyed: the traumatized young mother, still cradling her baby, even though its face had been "mashed" to a bloody pulp; and the weeping woman who stood by the ruins of her home, as auxiliary workers battled to extricate the broken body of her husband, and her dead, suffocated daughter.

Although the British press were less aggressively censored than their German counterparts, and although they were still held to a notional benchmark of the truth, these were details that could not be published. When Helen reported the bombing of a residential district of Southampton, she was cautiously vague about the number of casualties and carefully upbeat in her conclusion that "the British are fully prepared to take it no matter what form it takes."[38] Virginia assumed a similarly optimistic tone when she described the aftermath of an air attack on Dover. The residents, she reported, had been admirably sanguine and the town had recovered so fast that, within the hour, "the roller-skating pavilion in the small square next to the hotel was crowded with customers" and music was once again bowling out gaily across the sea front.[39]

These hopeful sentiments would shape the narrative through which the Battle of Britain was reported — the RAF cast as heroic underdog, besting the might of the bullying Luftwaffe. They even permeated Berlin, where Sigrid was able to report that a "smokescreen of patriotic silence" had replaced the usual triumphalist gloating. Clearly, the "British flier" was far braver and better trained than the Germans had anticipated, and she guessed that Göring, as newly appointed *Reichsmarschall,* must be under ferocious pressure to explain himself.[40] Yet, despite the Luftwaffe's failure to penetrate and destroy the RAF, Hitler was not to be deflected from his invasion. On 7 September, Virginia was having afternoon tea with some friends in Kent when 150 German planes roared up from the coast, heading north, to London. She could see every one of the planes' insignia as they flew deafeningly low over the garden, "the bombers flying in an even formation with the fighters swarming protectively around." A couple of hours later, when a lurid glow appeared over the horizon, she knew they must have reached their target; and during the long night that followed, she forced herself to listen to German radio, as it broadcast hourly updates on how the very "heart of the British Empire" was being "delivered up to the attack of the German air force."[41] It had been relatively straightforward for her and her colleagues in the press to portray the Battle of Britain as a form of victory, but now, as German bombs exploded over London and the raids spread out to other towns and cities, Virginia could not see how any kind of hope or moral high ground could be salvaged from the ensuing destruction.

CHAPTER NINE:
BRITAIN UNDER FIRE, LONDON, AUTUMN 1940

Grim Glory

LEE MILLER[1]

"Fright becomes so mingled with a deep almost uncontrollable anger that it is hard to know when one stops and the other begins." When Helen filed her first report from the Blitz, she chose to abandon her usual professional neutrality and acknowledge the depth of her terror. Taking shelter in a friend's basement, she'd felt assaulted, invaded by the Armageddon of noise outside, by the whomp of falling bombs, the banshee screams of German Stukas, the roar of falling buildings, and she'd been convinced "the entire center of the city [must be] blasted out of existence." Yet, the following morning, when the all-clear sounded and she was cycling back to her lodgings, Helen was astounded by how little damage she could see. "London still stood," she wrote, the traffic was venturing back onto the streets and, in the weak early sunshine, she rejoiced that her own little house in

325

Mayfair had escaped intact.[2]

For the next two months, the city was pounded night after night, and, like all Londoners, Helen had to acclimatize to the new Blitz conditions: the choking yellow dust that mingled with the acrid aftertaste of cordite; the cratered roads, burst water pipes, smashed buildings and eviscerated family homes. At the height of the raids, the paper booked her a room at the Dorchester, but, while she reassured her parents that its concrete-lined basement made it the "sturdiest hotel" in London, she rarely bothered to seek refuge underground. Like most of the other journalists who'd decamped to the Dorchester, Helen was usually at an upstairs window, making notes on the frequency and location of the bombs, and flattening herself against the floor if one exploded too close.*

She'd begun to feel that mix of exhilaration, resignation and dread which distinguished those who preferred to take their chances each night, rather than opt for the fetid, cramped conditions of the public shelters. The casualty figures were grim — officially estimated at 2,100 dead and 8,000 injured for the first month alone, and, ac-

---

* Helen would have to move several times during the war — an irksome waste of time, made additionally challenging because she had to report each change of address to the police.

cording to Helen, probably double that number. As for the rescue squads, digging bodies out of rubble, and the firemen risking their lives in collapsing buildings, this was a winter of gruelling exhaustion. Yet Helen also observed that an admirable "toughness and realism" was emerging in the British spirit, and she acknowledged that Churchill, in his Sunday-night broadcasts to the nation, knew exactly how to inspire it.[3] "He restored their faith in things [with his] blood sweat and tears talks. The worse he painted it, the better they felt," she commented, and she described the case of her secretary, Dorothy, who lived in one of the worst-affected areas of East London, yet would arrive at work on a Monday morning chipper with enthusiasm from Churchill's speech the night before. "Well, the old boy, he certainly gives it to 'em," she'd say, "and he makes you feel good, you know."[4]

During the very first weeks of the Blitz, Helen was mostly writing about air-raid shelters and the heroics of plucky civilians. Even though several of her English colleagues — Iris Carpenter, Hilde Marchant and Audrey Russell among them — were out reporting on the nightly bombings, some combination of gallantry and unexamined prejudice had prompted Caroll Binder and Bill Stoneman to keep Helen from danger. It took several weeks of quiet campaigning before she, too, was assigned to the raids, riding out with fire crews and ambulance drivers, or standing alongside the men and women who manned the city's defences, the ack-ack guns and searchlights.

Much of what she witnessed was too gruesome to report, and Helen would privately admit to her parents that the bodies she'd seen "spilled out" across the London pavements came to haunt her dreams. However, Ben Robertson Jr., correspondent for the New York paper *PM,* reported that she betrayed no signs of distress, that she became famous, in fact, for cruising through the Blitz with a professional calm, her only indication of fear a "mild compressing of her lips" if the ground was shaken by a nearby explosion or an incendiary bomb fizzed too close.[5] Once, she was blown, bodily, out of a building, but, according to Robertson, she merely shrugged off her cuts and bruises and carried on scribbling her notes. Helen Kirkpatrick was "one of the six bravest women in London," he claimed, and, not to be outdone, the *Chicago Daily News* ran a half-page profile on their star female reporter, boasting that this "slender and stately woman, barely out of her twenties is hourly writing flaming chapters in newspaper history — unparalleled, perhaps, by any woman foreign correspondent before or during her time."[6]*

During the second half of November 1940, the Luftwaffe focused their most murderous sights on the Midlands city of Coventry. People emerged from their shelters to scenes of soul-destroying horror — an entire neighbourhood blasted, a dog running by with a child's arm clamped in its mouth. Helen, assigned to the story, was only able to write in general terms about "the smoking mass of rubble" and the miserable clusters of homeless, who hung around the streets "clutching the pitifully few possessions they were able to salvage from the destruction."[7] But she was even less free to report on the damage that had been done to the city's morale.

Valour, not despair, was the message required from the media, and like the rest of her colleagues, Helen rarely commented on the reverse side of the Blitz spirit, on the freshly bombed houses that were burgled each night, the rifling and looting of dead bodies. Nor did she dwell on the furious bitterness building up among the country's poorer communities, who, living for the most part in densely populated industrial areas,

* Queen Mary was also a fan, informing Helen that she made a point of reading her articles "every day." (Letter, Helen Paull Kirkpatrick Papers, box 13, Smith College.)

were bearing the brunt of the raids. When Churchill went to meet a group of East End dockers and their wives, his assurances that the country could "take it" were met with contemptuous jeers. "You can fucking take it," shouted one woman. "We've had enough."

Journalists and editors exercised their own internal vigilance, but they were also subject to military censors who, in addition to scouring their copy for negative comment, were also checking for detail that might provide useful intelligence for the enemy. Helen understood the necessity of this, but she was often frustrated. As a reporter who valued high standards of accuracy, this continual accommodation between truth and expediency was hard, and the irony wasn't lost on her that, in a war fought to defend liberty and democracy, one of the very first victims was the freedom of the press.*

In Germany, the notion of a free and honest press had long been bastardized out of recognition. While the British could still go

---

* Helen couldn't understand, at first, why she was banned from mentioning the actual times and locations of raids, since the enemy presumably had that information already; but she was told that the most innocuous-seeming fact might assist the Germans in fine-tuning their bombers to achieve a more accurate aim.

some way towards admitting their military losses, the German media were allowed nothing but sycophantic euphoria, their coverage rarely acknowledging that a single plane had been shot down or a single life lost. In the summer of 1940, however, this collective bluff was becoming harder to maintain because British bombers had started to attack Berlin, and were now striking at the very heart of the Nazi regime.

The first of the bombs had struck on 25 August, and, even though relatively little damage had been caused, Berliners were stunned. Göring had always boasted that the city's air defences were impregnable, and nobody had been prepared for the nightly shrilling of sirens, the manic bursts of flak and the hours of broken sleep. Nor had it escaped the public's notice that, while the press were still serving up the London Blitz as Hitler's stupendous revenge against Churchill and his "apostles of hate," all promises of an early victory had faded, and the painted grandstands, erected in anticipation of a September parade, had been quietly removed from the streets. More and more Germans were starting to question the point of this war, and a frankly treasonous joke was now doing the rounds: An aeroplane carrying Hitler, Göring and Goebbels crashes. All three are killed. Who is saved? Answer — the German people.

Sigrid had rejoiced when the first of the RAF Wellingtons and Hampdens flew over Berlin, and she had stood on a balcony with her colleagues to cheer them on. The second raid occurred on the night of her scheduled broadcast for MBS, though, and, while no bombs were falling close to Haus des Rundfunks, the flak from the anti-aircraft guns was clattering down from the sky in a hot metallic rain. The broadcasting studio was not in the main building, but in a small wooden construction out in the grounds. Late at night, with only a weak torch to light her way, Sigrid had never relished the two-hundred-yard walk to the studio: even without the bombs she'd had to navigate a dark and rickety flight of stairs, and run the gauntlet of SS guards, their guns pointing threateningly while she fumbled to find her pass. With the onset of the raids, however, that walk had become actively dangerous. When Bill Shirer returned from making his own broadcast, he begged Sigrid to abandon hers. No one, he urged, would blame her for a few minutes of empty airtime. But Sigrid was adamant, and it was while she was making a blind dash for the studio that she stumbled and caught a burning fragment of shrapnel in her knee.

Shocked and in considerable pain, Sigrid still refused to turn back. But, while she managed to read through her script, the broadcast never went out, because the Haus des Rundfunks' radio transmitter had been damaged during the raid. Not only had her act of heroism been futile, the wound to her knee had been serious and, in her weakened state, Sigrid then fell ill with a bronchial infection and had to book herself into a clinic near Zurich to be treated for a mild case of pneumonia.

The illness was almost certainly genuine — she'd inherited her father's weak chest — but there's also good reason to suspect that Sigrid exaggerated its severity in order to evade Nazi surveillance, for just before leaving for Zurich, she had written a five-page letter to McCormick, containing information so dangerous that she could only dare post it outside Germany. She'd recently learned from her two loyal sources — Johannes Schmitt and Kurt von Hammerstein — that Hitler was considering two alternative strategies, once he had beaten Britain. He would either go west, attacking American trade interests and forcing Roosevelt to declare war, or he would go east, consolidating his control of the Balkans and then, tearing up his pact with Stalin, turn his guns on Russia. Sigrid suspected, rightly, that he would take the second route, and she assured McCormick that she would soon have the evidence to back up her hunch. Once she was discharged from the clinic, she was planning an investigatory tour of the Balkan region, additionally taking in parts of Central Europe and Greece.

Sigrid didn't explain how she persuaded the Nazi authorities to sanction this 3,000-mile trip, a trip that would give her damning information about the numbers of German troops entering Romania that autumn. It's actually possible they had wanted her out of Berlin, for it was during Sigrid's absence that an attempt was made on the lives of Schmitt and von Hammerstein. The method had been identifiably Gestapo — armoured vans with blacked-out windows had tried to force the cars which the two men were driving off the road — and Sigrid's distress when learning of their narrow escape was compounded by the terror that she herself had endangered them. Out in Zurich, suspecting she might be being watched, she'd given her incendiary letter to McCormick to one of the doctors to post. Several weeks later, however, she learned that this same doctor was rumoured to be a Nazi agent and she was tormented by the possibility that he might have delivered her letter into Party hands. Even though she hadn't named her two sources, there was enough information to point in their direction. The dread she now felt, surrounded by spies and unable to move without incriminating either herself or her friends, made Sigrid finally accept that she needed to get out of Berlin.

She'd been approaching that point, even in early October: "I do hope you realise I have . . . never been a shirker," she wrote to McCormick, "but from everything I have seen and experienced I think I should be coming home for a while this winter to recover." Even before the attempt on her informants' lives, she'd begun to doubt her ability to continue battling the regime. The latest round of "high-treason legislation" had left her so "thoroughly muzzled" she believed she might actually do "a better job" reporting on the Nazis from home. But she also admitted to McCormick that she was personally at her lowest ebb: "I have violated no laws, but this constant attempt to trap me at times seemed more than I could cope with. I have even been denounced as being Jewish etc." And, while Sigrid was careful to underplay that final threat, suggesting that the Colonel might even find it "funny at a distance," in reality, of course, it was the most terrifying of all.[8]

Sigrid planned her departure carefully, plotting a route through Switzerland, Vichy France and Spain, then on to Lisbon, where she would catch her boat for New York. But, during the weeks before she left Berlin, she knew the regime was closing in on her. She was hauled off the streets to be questioned at the Gestapo HQ, a sinister barracks of a building on Prinz Albrecht Strasse, whose warren of white-tiled cells was known to house unspeakable violence. Even though her interrogators did not harm her, physically, they knew exactly how to intimidate, warning Sigrid that her John Dickson ruse had been penetrated and that, if any more stories appeared in his name, the Party "would know where they had come from." The implied threat was made all the more chilling, too, by the obstructions that were being placed in the way of her departure. Sigrid had anticipated delays in the granting of her exit visa, which had to be approved by three different bodies — the Foreign Office, the state police and the secret police. But Goebbels, fearful of what she might publish once she was free of Berlin, was also holding up her application. By the time the American embassy had pressured for her departure, it was early February and Sigrid's nerves were shot. She had stood up to the state's bullying for close to a decade; yet, now, with freedom so close, she cowered from every knock on her door, from every accelerating car on the street. Even when she was on the train to Switzerland, she was unable to relax. Escape routes out of Germany were aborted all the time; trains were mysteriously cancelled, papers refused, and Sigrid feared that SS guards might enter her compartment at any moment and march her back to Berlin.

When she eventually caught her boat, in

mid-February, she was exhausted and ill: in one interview, she described her sickness as "war typhus"; in another, she said she'd been bitten "by the wrong kind of bug." Once in America, it took her months to recover, and she never stopped looking over her shoulder. A minor traffic accident in which she was involved in New York convinced her that Nazi agents were on her tail, and for a while she refused to travel anywhere by car. Yet, despite all she'd gone through, Sigrid was still determined to resume her post in Berlin, and she was bitterly angry with McCormick when he refused to support her return. The Colonel had good reason to fear she would no longer be safe in Germany: later, it would transpire that she'd been put on the blacklist of U.S. journalists who would not be repatriated if or when their two countries went to war. But he also had his own political motives for keeping her out of Berlin. As a still-implacable isolationist, he was troubled by a change in American attitudes: President Roosevelt had recently passed a new Lend-Lease Act, by which U.S. arms could be supplied to Britain at a deferred cost; meanwhile, the American public, 77 percent of whom had initially been against the war, were starting to accept it was their nation's duty to fight. In such a climate, McCormick was unwilling to have Sigrid back in Berlin, writing more anti-German stories, ferreting out more dangerous facts, to undermine U.S. neutrality.

Deprived of Berlin, Sigrid begged for a posting elsewhere — to a neutral county, like Portugal or Switzerland, where she could at least exploit her knowledge of European politics. But McCormick refused and, while she was able to continue her crusade against the Nazis, lecturing to clubs and colleges around America and, under great secrecy, feeding information to the Office of Strategic Services (precursor to the CIA), she was essentially sidelined from her reporting career for three and a half years. She would not be able to return to it until January 1945, when the Allied forces began pushing into Germany, and when McCormick had no arguments left to prevent her return.*

If Sigrid had been effectively silenced from the start of 1941, there were other American voices who were arguing for their government to join the war, and one of the most impassioned was that of Virginia Cowles. She'd arrived back in London for the second day of

* Dorothy Thompson thought it disgraceful that Sigrid was not treated as a national wartime asset. "She has uncountable German and other European contacts . . . why she is not in Sweden collecting data on Germany from the many Germans who come and go is beyond me." (*Ladies' Home Journal,* March 1944.)

the Blitz, and had reported on the raids regularly for the next three months. They were, she acknowledged, unlike anything she'd experienced in Finland or Spain — "the blinding flashes of gunfire and the long hiss of the bombs" more relentless than any previous attack she'd known.[9] Like almost everyone in London, she'd been undone by her first night of the Blitz, her knees buckling at the sound of sirens, her only thought to pray for a clean "instantaneous" death.[10] The unusually golden weather had struck her as additionally cruel — every day, the sun shone down on the devastation with a "Mona Lisa smile." Yet she'd learned to acclimatize, had gone out in the blazing streets to write her own reports; had even managed a smile of thanks when, dining out one night, a waiter had passed on the message that her lodgings had been hit in an incendiary attack.

By December, however, Virginia had reached her limit. She believed she'd exhausted everything she had to say about the Blitz for the *Sunday Times,* and was convinced that her typewriter could be put to far more valuable service. She moved out of London and, for the next six months, free from the distraction of deadlines and bombs, she hammered out a book through which she hoped to entertain and shame her American readers into a more active support of the war.

Looking for Trouble was ostensibly a memoir

about Virginia's formative experiences as a war journalist; yet, even as she wrote vividly, self-mockingly about her early adventures and misadventures, she was laying down her argument that the fight against Hitler was not a distant foreign quarrel, but a battle for freedom and justice that concerned the world. She wrote eloquently of the many different groups who'd already fallen victim to tyranny: "the ragged soldiers fighting in the mountains near Madrid; the weeping women in the streets of Prague; the tragic refugees streaming across the Polish frontiers; the Finnish patrols slipping through the icebound forests of the Arctic; the terrified flow of humanity choking the roads from Paris to Tours."[11] And she excoriated the U.S. government for failing to come to these people's defence. In her final chapter, "Only United Will We Stand," she pitched her rhetoric to near-Churchillian levels of emotion as she called on her country "to rise up now in all our splendour and fight side by side with Great Britain until we reach a victory so complete that freedom will ring through the ages to come."[12]

While Virginia was down in the countryside, shaping the cadences of her polemic, the American photographer Lee Miller was being drawn into the war effort almost by chance. Her photographic career had always been rooted in fashion and the surrealist avant-garde, and, while she'd been as morally contemptuous of fascism as she had of all forms of bullying, she'd never been drawn to any kind of public engagement. To her mind, politics was a game played by governments, far outside her control, and her life had always revolved around her own very personal concerns — her quest for the next lover, the next adventure, the next creative high.

But Lee happened to be in London at the start of the war, living with her English lover, Roland Penrose, and, during the first months of the Blitz, she had seen a brutal and profoundly photogenic poetry emerging from the shattered city. A mangled typewriter blasted from an office desk; a marble statue, lying scarred and filthy among rubble; the doorway of a Camden chapel, crowded not with a congregation of worshippers, but a heap of broken bricks. When these images had caught Lee's eye, she'd seen them not merely as snapshots of London's physical devastation, but as metaphors of the violence being inflicted on culture, community and civilization.

The eerie, arrested beauty of Lee's Blitz photographs came to the attention of Ernestine Carter, a stylishly influential recruit to the Ministry of Information. They struck Carter as far more effective, interesting visual propaganda than the increasingly clichéd images of grinning air-raid wardens, gutted streets and burning docks which dominated the press, and she persuaded Lee to let her include them in a new book of photographs she was editing. Titled *Grim Glory: Pictures of Britain Under Fire,* with a rousing introduction by the American broadcaster Ed Murrow, and an even more rousing dedication to Winston Churchill, the collection was rushed out to American bookstores by May 1941.

It was a beautifully produced piece of work, a highly sophisticated weapon in the campaign to persuade America into the war. But, for Lee, the significance of the book was far more personal. In photographing the Blitz and committing herself to the war effort, she believed that she'd finally discovered a subject and a cause which could "concentrate" her eye, her brain and her craft to their best potential: "I had thought and burned with ideas for years," she wrote, "and suddenly found a peg on which to hang them."[13]

Lee always liked to claim that she'd "practically been born and brought up in a darkroom."[14] Her father, Theodore Miller, was a mechanical engineer by profession, but he was also a natural tinkerer, an enthusiast for progressive ideas, and his interest in photography was one that involved his entire family. Most of the images which Theodore developed in his amateur "photo lab" were portraits of his wife Florence, his sons John and Erik, and his daughter Elizabeth ("Li Li," then eventually plain "Lee"), who was born on 23 April 1907: and many of them were taken in the rambling grounds of Cedar Hill Farm, the rural property on the edge of Poughkeepsie to which the family moved in 1912.

As a father, Theodore had egalitarian views, and little Lee was raised with the same freedom as her brothers, dressed in overalls and gumboots, encouraged to play with the same toy soldiers and cars. As the most inquisitive of the children, however, it was she who was most drawn to Theodore's photography, and, when she was given a box camera of her own, she liked to work alongside her father, taking photographs with him and sitting in his darkroom while he magically transformed their tiny opaque negatives into pictures of her family and home.

Despite Lee's claims to a lifelong vocation in photography, however, there was a long period during which she could take no interest in it at all. At the age of seven, she was raped, and the trauma of that experience had a fracturing effect on her personality, violating her self-confidence and scattering her focus.

The assault occurred when her mother, Florence, fell ill and Lee was sent to stay with family friends in Brooklyn. It should have been a happy arrangement — Lee felt "quite at home" with Mr. and Mrs. Kajderdt — but, one afternoon, the couple went out and she was left in the care of a young man, either a relative or a lodger.[15] The specific details of what took place remain unclear, since afterwards the Millers could barely speak of it. But there had definitely been a rape, and, if that had not been a sufficiently hideous ordeal, Lee's attacker also infected her with gonorrhoea. During the next twelve months, the little girl had to suffer an excruciating regime of treatment — a daily vaginal douching and twice-weekly swabbings of her cervix. Florence, who'd been trained as a nurse, took it upon herself to administer the treatment, but it was an agony for both mother and daughter, and inevitably it made Lee relive her rape, over and over again.

Florence and Theodore, to their credit, consulted a psychiatrist, but he was out of his depth; while he tried to reassure Lee that the assault on her body was nothing like the consensual married love which she could one day enjoy, this was impossible knowledge for a seven-year-old to assimilate. Lee knew only that she felt dirty and damaged — years later, she would allude to the "swollen awkward feeling which has followed me from childhood" — and the only way she could deal with her secret shame was by acting out a public version of it, becoming rude, manipulative and wild at home, and playing the class clown at school.[16]

By the time Lee graduated, she'd been expelled so many times that her education was patchy at best. But she was a clever, creative child, and the very last school she'd attended, run by Quakers, had helped to channel her wildness into a belief that she could do something with her life. She was also desperate, however, to get out of Poughkeepsie, and her chance came unexpectedly when a former teacher offered to take her to the South of France, where she and a companion had been hired to teach at a finishing school. Theodore and Florence, exhausted from the worry of managing their daughter, and persuaded that Madame Kohoszynska would be a suitable chaperone, accepted the offer. On 29 May 1925, a triumphant Lee was boarding the SS *Minnehaha* for France, eighteen years old and dressed in the most fashionable cloche hat and paisley frock that Poughkeepsie could supply.

Perhaps the Millers should have foreseen that their daughter would not remain long in the company of two middle-aged women. Once the trio had arrived in Paris and booked into a budget hotel (which, to Lee's delight and Madame Kohoszynska's confusion, turned out to be a brothel), she announced that she would be staying put in the city, rather than travelling onwards to Nice. Wiring Theodore for extra money (a request to which he helplessly agreed), she found a tiny *chambre de bonne* for rent and set about reinventing herself as a Parisian *garçonne.*

Lee's expectations of Paris were very different from Martha's. She was drawn to the artists and the performers, rather than the writers, and, once she'd discovered an art school with classes in stage design, she fell in with a group of experimental theatre makers who welcomed her collaboration on costumes and sets. Lee had also come to the city with far fewer moral scruples than Martha, and, having allowed herself to be seduced by her college tutor, she embarked on a determined period of sexual self-discovery. She was growing into her adult beauty, now — tall and slender, with a creamy blonde radiance that even turned heads in Paris. Yet, she was still very naive, and, in her anxiety not to appear a provincial prude, she couldn't see that she was subjecting herself to what she later admitted were some "nasty affairs."[17] Living by herself in the City of Lights, Lee simply felt electric with possibility, elated by the power of her own desirability, and by the conviction that "everything [was] opening up in front of me."[18]

Florence and Theodore were understandably less enchanted by Lee's Parisian adventure, and, when they eventually blocked her allowance, insisting she return home, Lee believed she had been robbed of her future. Throughout her adult life, she would suffer from periodic depressions — her brain and body so silted up with misery she could barely get out of bed — and those first weeks back in Poughkeepsie, as she crashed into a deep, paralysing despair, were among the worst. It wasn't simply that she missed the rush and colour of Paris — she also began to doubt everything she'd tried to achieve. Her diary entries turned bleakly self-flagellating as she looked back over her experimental affairs and tormented herself with the belief that, rather than liberating herself into bohemian adulthood, she'd simply been acting like "an animal with unhealthy desires." She had, she wrote, set herself up for a pattern of "sordidly experienced life" and she feared, very much, that she would never know what it was like to be loved "purely and chastely" for herself.[19]

Those weeks, she acknowledged, were "the nearest to suicide I have ever been," but Lee was too young and too energetic to suffer for long.[20] She was still drawn to the idea of theatre design, and, when her strength returned, she enrolled in a course of stage production at nearby Vassar College. For several months, she was engrossed in her new studies and in the projects she was planning with a small drama group in New York. But she was restless, self-critical, and, abruptly

347

convincing herself that her designs lacked "genius," she decided that her talents were better suited to a career in dance. She'd taken classes as a child and, largely on the strength of her looks and her height, was hired for the chorus line in the Broadway revue *Scandals.* Renting a small room in a Manhattan hotel, immersed in the greasepaint and gossip of showgirl life, Lee was momentarily certain that her body was to be her new creative medium and that dancing was to be her route out of Poughkeepsie.

It took barely two months for that notion to lose its appeal. "My fingers feel empty with the longing to create," she scribbled moodily in her diary, and, after briefly earning her keep as a lingerie model, she enrolled in a painting course at the Art Students League in New York.[21] Here, she made some very close friends. Lee was magnificent fun, when she wanted to be — worldly, inquisitive, reckless and generous — and she loved the company of other women. But she could never break free of the fidgeting discontent that sent her rebounding between headstrong enthusiasm and listless disillusion. After a few months, she decided she had neither the talent nor the vision of a true artist. "All the paintings had already been painted," she concluded, and it was now, with a defiant sense of yielding to her own worst instincts, that Lee abandoned her creative ambitions and drifted into a life of parties and love affairs among the Manhattan rich.[22]

"I looked like an angel but . . . was a fiend inside," she commented later, and she might have lost her way entirely had she not been thrust, almost literally, into a new career.[23] One afternoon in early 1927, Lee was absent-mindedly crossing the road when she was grabbed by a tall, theatrically expensive man who'd seen her stepping into the path of an oncoming car. Her rescuer was the publishing mogul Condé Nast, and, when he took a second look at the woman in his arms, he saw that she was not only exceptionally lovely, but, even in her state of shock, possessed a natural elegance and flair.

Nast was convinced Lee had a future in front of the camera, and so promptly did he act on his hunch that by March he'd put her face on the cover of *Vogue,* and by the summer he promoted her to his top team of fashion models. The rangy length of Lee's limbs made her a natural fit for the decade's streamlined couture, and her strongly modelled features read with an exceptional legibility on film. But the other reason why photographers at *Vogue* and *Vanity Fair* all wanted to work with Lee, was her unusually professional composure. Years of posing for her father, coupled with her brief apprenticeships as dancer and lingerie model, had freed her from the awkwardness of the novice model, and any lingering inhibitions she might have had in her new career had been dispelled by a series of nude photographic studies on which she and Theodore had recently been at work.*

Lee had approached these studies as though they were art. She'd rehearsed her poses with the seriousness of a dancer, working with a mirror so that she could see how a twist of the waist, an arch of the back lent a flattering line to her body. So certain was she of the project's artistic value, she'd also encouraged several of her friends to take part. Yet, even though Lee herself felt no coercion in modelling nude for her father, even though Florence was present at most of their sessions, it is hard to look at those images now without a certain retrospective queasiness. There's a complicity to some of Lee's poses which barely falls short of the erotic, and they beg the question of whether Theodore, in encouraging his daughter to strip naked for his camera, had ever troubled to think back to the tiny, terrified little girl whose innocence had been so cruelly violated, and whether he ever entertained a moment's doubt over the appropriateness of what he was doing.†

* The March cover was not in fact a photograph of Lee, but, in keeping with the magazine's tradition, was a stylized drawing of her face.

† One of Lee's friends did admit that she'd only

At the time, however, it was generally agreed that Mr. Miller's nude portraits were tastefully and artistically modern, and they were clearly of professional benefit to Lee. She thrived on the knowledge that she excelled at her new métier and she was excited by the photographers with whom she worked — men like Edward Steichen, whose mastery of light and composition opened up possibilities far beyond Theodore's amateur efforts. These two years were formative also because Condé Nast knew almost everyone who mattered in New York, and, when Lee was invited to his parties and was introduced to figures like Dorothy Parker, Edmund Wilson, even Charlie Chaplin, she was challenged to sharpen her own wits and to acquire her own gilding of Manhattan sophistication.

As Lee matured, it was almost inevitable she would want to make the transition from model to photographer, to step out of the camera's gaze and take control of it herself. Most of the professional photographers she knew about were men, but, when she discussed her aspirations with Edward Steichen, he suggested she might follow the example of the young Berenice Abbott, who'd begun her

---

agreed to pose for Theodore because it felt prudish to refuse, but insisted, nonetheless, that she'd never felt threatened.

own career in Paris, as darkroom assistant to Man Ray. The idea of returning to Paris, of apprenticing herself to one of the world's most notoriously avant-garde photographers was irresistible to Lee, and, in the spring of 1929, she gratefully seized on Steichen's offer to write a letter of introduction on her behalf.

Years later, reflecting on the role that chance had played in her life, Lee would describe how she'd very nearly missed her moment with Man Ray. When she presented herself at the photographer's Montparnasse studio, the concierge informed her that Monsieur Ray had just finished work for the summer and was about to depart for Biarritz. Unprepared for such a setback, unsure what to do next, Lee wandered into a nearby bar for a consoling glass of Pernod, and, had she chosen a different bar, had she been half an hour later, her trip to Paris might have been fruitless. However, a figure appeared in the bar shortly afterwards, whose "extraordinary torso, very dark brows and dark hair" she recognized instantly. It was Man Ray himself and, determined not to let him escape, Lee not only introduced herself as "his new student" but blithely persuaded him to take her to Biarritz.[24]

"I guess he fell for me," she wrote, and that would be the most flippant of understatements, for while Man, as a good surrealist, had always dismissed romantic love as a bourgeois myth, a trap for the unwary, in Lee he met his nemesis. He saw in her a perfection which he longed, obsessively, to own; according to one of his friends, she was "fatal" for him, and "he loved her without restriction."[25] During their first summer together, he photographed her again and again, a series of inspired, inventive portraits, in which he strove to capture not only the elusive quality of Lee's beauty, but the peculiar charisma of her personality — that combination of elegance, wit and raw energy, against which other women now struck him as vapid or shrill.

Yet while Lee was excited to be Man's acolyte, collaborator and muse, she would not commit to being his faithful mistress. As a man, as a lover, he was captivating — "if he took your hand or touched you, you felt an almost magnetic heat" — and she was grateful for the generosity with which he took her out to "wonderful restaurants" and introduced her to Jean Cocteau, James Joyce, André Breton and Marcel Duchamp — stars of the city's cultural firmament.[26] But she saw no reason why gratitude and affection should require her to be submissive — in fact she was under no illusion that, even had she been willing to make a promise of fidelity to Man, she would actually be capable of keeping it.

Lee knew that there was a compulsive pattern to her affairs. She enjoyed sex with lovers who were gifted or generous, and, like most of her professional and social circle, she believed that a woman should be as free as any man to explore her own desires. But she also recognized that there were other less rational, less benign impulses which kept her in flight from one man to the next, and, while she had no interest in being analysed by a therapist, she did intuit a probable connection between the promiscuity of her adult behaviour and the "swollen awkward feeling," which had been coiled in her since childhood.

Everything we know today about the long-term effects of rape would suggest that Lee's sexuality was tangled in the roots of her early assault. It's possible she had come to use sex as a form of control, as a way of taking charge of her own body and of the men who desired it or threatened it. But, whatever Lee may or may not have understood about her sexuality, she still embraced it as a badge of freedom and she was not prepared to moderate her behaviour for Man, however much he suffered.

"You are so young so beautiful so free, and I hate myself for trying to cramp in you what I admire most" wrote Man. He despised his own jealousy, but was helpless to control the accusations and recriminations which were wrung from him, with each of Lee's infidelities.[27] She, in turn, was frustrated and humiliated by his rages, but she admired Man too much to abandon him yet. None of the photographers with whom she'd worked at *Vogue* had approached his level of genius, his technical inventiveness, and his ability to re-frame and reimagine the world. When Lee walked with Man through the streets of Paris, she learned how to spot poetry in an odd juxtaposition of objects, a serendipitous trick of perspective and light. Some of her own early photographs were lucky finds — four rats perched on an iron rafter, their tails hanging down in exactly parallel lines — but she also learned from Man how to manipulate her imagery, and one of her most shocking apprenticeship images was a close-up of two (medically) amputated breasts, which she'd placed on a dish to look like a macabre ver-sion of *îles flottantes.**

So fast did she progress that, within nine months, Lee was acquiring a prestigious cli-ent list of her own, her wittily off-kilter im-ages appearing in magazines like French

* It was with Man, too, that Lee came to see how the best art could arise from mistakes. She thought she had ruined a set of photographs that were being developed, by accidentally switching on a light, but Man was intrigued by the ghostly luminescence the images had acquired and, insisting that they explore it further, developed a new technique, solarization, which both of them began to use.

Vogue. Yet Man's possessive tantrums eventually became too high a price to pay for the privilege of being his protégée and collaborator, and, by the summer of 1932, Lee was ready to break free. She'd received a proposal of marriage from a rich, cultivated and very tolerant Egyptian named Aziz Eloui Bey, but she saw a better chance of escape in the offer made by Julien Levy, a rising star in the gallery business, who wanted to help her establish a studio back home in New York.

Man was wretched when he discovered Lee's plans, venting his rage in theatrically vindictive works of art — one of them a suicidal self-portrait in which he posed with a noose around his neck, and a gun pointed dramatically at his temple. Yet, although she fled from Man's theatrics with relief, Lee was not above exploiting his name; indeed, when she got to New York and opened her own modest studio, she shamelessly advertised herself as "the American branch of the Man Ray School of Photography." Her opportunism wounded him almost as much as her leaving, and briefly he considered taking legal action. But Lee was unrepentant. To one of the several journalists who interviewed her on her arrival, she airily claimed that she'd only absorbed "the personality of the man," not his "technical genius"; and, if there were a small number of critics who disagreed, who considered that Man's signature style was all over Lee's work, their opinions were easily disregarded.[28]

Riding high on her success, and taking on her younger brother, Erik, as darkroom assistant, Lee and her East 48th Street studio began to do brisk business. Despite the aftershocks of the Wall Street Crash, there were still plenty of New Yorkers rich enough to commission portraits of themselves, plenty of fashion houses with money to spend on advertising campaigns. Lee, with her cachet of Parisian chic, was soon in such demand that she'd silenced every voice who tried to dismiss her as a mere novelty, a fashion model who'd moved to the other side of the camera. By May 1934, her reputation was such that when *Vanity Fair* published a list of the seven most distinguished living photographers, Lee Miller's name was among them.

To be ranked alongside luminaries like Cecil Beaton was a fabulous accolade, especially for a woman with less than five years' experience. But restlessness and perversity — Lee's worst demons — made it impossible for her to build steadily on success, and, just as photography was starting to yield money and acclaim, she suddenly began to sicken of it. Her commercial assignments bored her (New York was less responsive to avant-garde photography than Paris), but Lee's dissatisfactions were essentially with herself. Even when she was experimenting with her

357

own creative projects, she found herself missing the acuity of Man's eye and the stimulus of his imagination; however hard she tried to stifle her doubts, she began to fear that she'd only ever been tagging on the coat tails of her former lover's brilliance.

There were days, even weeks, when she felt such a loathing of photography, she could barely pick up her camera. Erik loyally shouldered as much of the work as he could, expecting that his sister's mood would turn. But, early in July, Lee confounded him with a bombshell piece of news: she was shutting down the studio, she was leaving New York and, most improbably of all, she was getting married.

Her former suitor Aziz Eloui Bey, had suddenly appeared in New York, officially to do business on behalf of the Egyptian State Railway, but actually to look for Lee and repeat his proposal of marriage. When he'd fallen in love with her, in Paris, he'd sensed the vulnerability beneath her transgressive glamour and had felt it was his own special calling to take care of her and "bring peace to her heart."[29] And while Lee's family and friends were bemused when she accepted his proposal, incredulous that she could give up her work and her independence and sail to Cairo, a world away from everything she'd ever known, Lee herself had been more desperate than they knew, to let someone else take charge of her troubled life.

Aziz was a beautiful man, handsome and saintly; he was also very rich and, if Lee believed he could rescue her from the exhausting uncertainties of maintaining her public career, she also hoped he might save her from the private demons and doubts — "the jitters" she called them — which continued to blight almost every project and every relationship she undertook. Even though she was technically unfaithful to Aziz just days after their wedding (seducing a nineteen-year-old boy on the boat out to Egypt), she genuinely wanted to be a good wife to him. And, when she first arrived in Cairo, she genuinely believed she could create a good new life. From the start, she revelled in the pungent hustling streets, in the shadowed souks, the smells of cooking and spice. She especially loved the desert, and early on formed the habit of going on extended treks, so that she could learn the changing colours of its landscape — the quiet blue of early morning, the flat glare of noon, the fiery glow of sunset and the plummeting blackness of night.

But, sensual, exotic though this Egyptian life was for Lee, its novelties inevitably faded. Aziz, for all his kindness, was no intellectual, and the people with whom they socialized were no substitute for Paris or Manhattan. The wealthy Cairo elite tended to fritter away their afternoons in gossip and cards at Groppi's cafe, they spent their evenings drinking and dancing at Shepheard's Hotel, and it was partly out of sheer boredom that Lee willed herself to take up her camera again. Some of her photographs bore signs of her old invention, but the most powerful of them all was, significantly, the bleakest. *Portrait of Space* was technically a landscape — a view of bleached desert sands, shot through a gap in a torn, tattered flysheet — yet it carried such an emotional depth charge of loneliness, claustrophobia and ennui that Lee might just as well have titled it *Portrait of a Marriage*.

Aziz was slowly killing her with his kindness and, in May 1937, she begged him to let her go alone to Paris, for what she called "a bachelor holiday." Just as she arrived, Virginia Cowles was sitting in her borrowed apartment off the Champs-Elysées, reliving the violence of Madrid and dreading what awaited her in Franco's Spain. Lee hadn't come back to Europe to worry about its politics, however; she was there to recover her old life, to surround herself with cultured creative people and, above all, to find herself a lover who could challenge and amuse her in ways that were beyond Aziz.

It was on her very first night, attending the season's surrealist ball, that she found him. Roland Penrose was a painter and collector of modern art, with a long, clever face, a quick, authoritative mind, and an elegantly delinquent view of the world that Lee found compellingly attractive. Although she had only planned on a bachelor fling in Paris, the affair felt serious, and Lee barely hesitated when Roland invited her to join the artists' house party he was planning to host in Cornwall, south-west England. There was to be a mingling of surrealist royalty — Paul and Nusch Éluard, Leonora Carrington and Max Ernst, and Man Ray and his current mistress, Ady Fidelin (Lee and Man had, by now, achieved a wary reconciliation) — and the four weeks they spent together were to be filled with characteristically performative fun — the staging of avant-garde theatricals and of experimental communal sex (Roland apparently keen "to turn the slightest encounter into an orgy").[30]

Lee's enjoyment of the party radiated through the photographs she took, one of which was her restaging of Manet's painting *Le Déjeuner sur l'herbe,* in which Roland, Man and Paul, fully clothed, were posed alongside Ady and Nusch, both women stark naked from the waist up, their bodies stretched out carelessly, for the men's delectation. Leonora Carrington was not in that photograph, and later she would express scorn for the surrealists' much-vaunted principles of sexual freedom, claiming that they'd only ever been designed to gratify men. Yet, if Lee had intended an ironic slant to her Manet homage, it was lightly done; when the group moved on to the South of France and Roland "offered" her up to his friend Picasso, she was helplessly flattered. To be fucked by the world's greatest artist was considered a privilege in their circle, and Lee's pleasure was sealed by the portrait that Picasso painted, her face an exuberant sunny yellow, singing out against a bright pink background.

That portrait was alight with energy, colour and sexual joy — and, when Lee had to return to Cairo, the wrench of leaving Roland's world was compounded by the certainty that she was now in love with him. She scribbled to him constantly during the following months, love letters in which she confessed to the "agony of ecstasy" of missing him, and to her desire to be with him "always" — even if, she joked, "my always don't always mean that much."[31] The following summer, she pressured Aziz to grant her a second holiday, so that she could travel with Roland on a hedonistic tour of Greece, Bulgaria and Romania. But she was no longer capable of dissembling, and, once she'd blurted out the truth of her affair to Aziz, she knew she'd boxed herself into a situation where she would eventually have to commit to one or the other of the two men.

Still, it felt like an impossible choice. Lee

cared deeply for Aziz and had become very dependent on the kindness he so beautifully lavished, however stifling it might be. So lost did she feel in her "sick muddle of indecision" she took refuge in yet another affair, travelling to Beirut in the company of a young diplomat named Bernard Burrows and using her distance from Aziz to try to rationalize her emotions. "I frankly don't know what I want unless it is to have my cake and eat it," she wrote guiltily to him. "I want to have the utopian combination of security and freedom and emotionally need to be completely absorbed in some work or in a man I love."[32] But, candid though Lee tried to be, she was confused and cruel enough to let Aziz believe that the crisis was temporary and that her affair with Roland would soon run its course. In the summer of 1939, Aziz gave his blessing to yet another holiday, trusting once again that Lee would return. But events beyond their control would force the matter, because, when Lee and Roland were in the South of France, Hitler invaded Poland and, faced with the threat of closed borders and chaotic travel, Lee had to make a snap decision. She could either go back to the safety of Cairo and marriage, or she could accompany Roland to London. In the heat of the moment, she chose London.

The headlong drive through France and the

dash for the ferry back to England had galvanized Lee with the certainty that she'd done the right thing. Roland was independently wealthy, if not quite as rich as Aziz, and when they arrived in London, on 3 September 1939, Lee was entranced by the spaciousness of his Hampstead house and by his astonishing collection of Picassos, Magrittes, Brâncuşis and Ernsts. There were parties too, and, while most of London would soon be wilting under the uncertainties of the Phoney War, Roland could even turn these to fun, building an air-raid shelter in the garden of 21 Downshire Hill, but painting it a ridiculous, flaunting pink and blue.

While Lee had still been trying to convince Aziz of her need for escape, she'd explained that she had to "become concentrated again" to feel "awake and alive" — and, above all, to find a renewed focus on work.[33] In London, at the start of the war, she was eager to use her camera again, and when she asked for an interview at British *Vogue,* she assumed that her former connection to Condé Nast would smooth her way into a job. Dismayingly, however, the studio head informed Lee there was nothing for her; and while she softened the blow, explaining that the magazine had to reduce its photographic content to accommodate wartime restrictions, it was clear from her tone that the five years Lee had spent away from the profession had stripped most of the lustre from her name.

The rejection posed a practical problem, too, because American citizens who lacked a solid reason for remaining in Britain — a British spouse or a regular job — were now under pressure to return home. Lee's familiar prickles of anxiety — her "jitters" — threatened to spook her new-found contentment, and she began writing long letters to Aziz, seeking his comfort and advice. In his infinite sweetness, Aziz had gifted her shares in his company so that she could always rely on an independent income, and these letters rekindled his hopes of her return. In January, however, Lee begged another interview with *Vogue,* and on this occasion her timing was fortuitous. Several of the magazine's staff had been conscripted to military duties, and, as long as Lee could get a permit from the Home Office Aliens Department, a position was now open to her as a full-time photographer, with a weekly wage of eight pounds a week and the far more valuable right to remain in London.*

Lee also discovered that a third and very precious advantage of the job was working with the young ambitious woman who was shortly to be appointed *Vogue*'s editor. Au-

* Some Americans were actually having their passports withdrawn by the U.S. State Department in order to force their return home.

drey Withers was an Oxford-educated feminist and socialist, with a droll sense of humour and a fierce commitment to her staff, and she'd worked her way up the magazine with an ambitious agenda for change. She believed it was "simply not modern to be unaware of or uninterested in what is going on all around you" and, even though she respected *Vogue*'s historic status as a bible of fashion, she wanted to expand its cultural and political coverage, to acknowledge rather than escape the war. With a sure instinct for turning deprivation into style, Audrey would shortly be commissioning expensive-looking photo-spreads of utility clothing, she would run features that made even the growing of vegetables, the organizing of factory canteens sound chic, and in this new spirit of practicality — and subversion — Lee herself would be freed to produce some of her most imaginative magazine work.

Inspired by Audrey, she searched for a new semantics of wartime glamour, and her early shoots for *Vogue* were alive with a spirit of collaboration and fun. One of her models — exquisitely tailored in a leopard-trimmed suit — was posed against a map of Europe, with a clutter of military boots, bags and helmets at her feet; two others were photographed at the entrance of Roland's air-raid shelter, their beautifully made-up faces half obscured by wardens' helmets and protective eye-shields.

Had these fashion assignments formed the limits of Lee's work, she might well have grown fractious and bored, but, in September 1940, the Luftwaffe began bombing London, and she and her camera were presented with a dramatically altered world.

During the first week of the Blitz, Lee had been as frightened as anyone, feeling as defenceless against the bombs as "a soft-shell crab," but, once she acclimatized to the raids, she became entranced by their visual spectacle.[34] Secure in Downshire Hill, she spent hours at her bedroom window, from where she could look out over London, watching the traceries of light that shot upwards from anti-aircraft guns, the arcing searchlights, the boiling crimson glow from the distant docks. When London was taking a particularly heavy pounding one night, she accompanied Roland on his fire-watching duties, and, as fallout from the ack-ack guns drummed down on the rooftops, she gripped hold of his arm and gasped, "Oh darling, aren't you excited?"[35]

Hampstead itself was a relatively safe distance from the Luftwaffe's main targets, and Roland's house became the scene of nightly Blitz parties, as friends turned up to play Scrabble or cards, to drink, joke and argue until the all-clear sounded. Valentine Penrose, Roland's estranged wife, also sought refuge when her own home was bombed, and

Lee, conscious of the laws of wartime hospitality, felt obliged to welcome her.

It was a novelty for her, this Blitz spirit, and, when the *Vogue* offices were struck by incendiary bombs, she was proud to tell her parents that she'd mucked in with everyone to help: "it became a matter of pride that work went on . . . [despite the] horrid smell of wet charred wood — the stink of cordite — the fire hoses still up the staircase," and despite the fact that everyone had to wade barefoot to get to their desks.[36] Because the gas, electricity and water supplies had also been disrupted, Lee was forced to develop her prints at home, and it was the photographs she took of the gutted *Vogue* building and of the staff's dedicated efforts to return to their desks which Audrey used to illustrate that month's rallying editorial — "Still Smart Despite All Difficulties."

Those photographs also became the starting point of Lee's *Grim Glory* collection. As London was ripped apart by the Luftwaffe bombs, she began carrying her camera everywhere, marvelling at the daily transformation of the city's streets. There was a surreal quirk of comedy in some of the images she took — one of a line of shop dummies left out on a pavement — stark naked save for the top hats still perched on their heads; there was a heroic kind of beauty too, exemplified in her shot of University College London, its shattered roof reflected in a gleaming puddle of rainwater. Photographing the Blitz, Lee was drawing on all that she'd learned from Man Ray about the poetics of light, perspective and visual juxtaposition; with war as her subject, though, she finally felt the burden of his influence lift. She was learning to trust her own internal viewfinder now, and, in the months that followed, when the *Grim Glory* photographs were published to gratifying acclaim, she began to look for other ways in which she could put herself and her camera in the service of the war effort.

CHAPTER TEN:
ATHENS AND CAIRO, 1940–41

"I'll have no women correspondents
with my army"

BERNARD MONTGOMERY[1]

Clare Hollingworth, stumbling alone through the mountains of southern Albania, was on the verge of questioning where her own war ambitions were leading. She thought she'd developed a sound instinct, later claiming, "It has got me into tight corners at times but I have never regretted giving it its head" — but this particular battlefield was making her doubt her judgement.[2] The rocky scree beneath her feet was treacherously unstable, she could hear the bark of rifle fire ricocheting over nearby slopes, and, in places, the sullen, rain-drenched clouds were so dense she could barely see the track ahead. It was almost impossible for Clare to know if she was navigating a safe path, yet the most perilous aspect of this Albanian front line was the absence of any discernible command structure. While she knew that the Greeks were pushing hard against their Italian invaders, she could see no evidence of any organized fighting, nothing like the choreography of "blazing guns [and] well-uniformed marching men" that she'd witnessed in Poland, the previous year. Up here in the mountains, Clare feared she was as likely to be killed by a stray Greek bullet as by a knife in the back from an Italian deserter.

She had arrived in Albania in November 1940, almost a month after leaving Bucharest, and after a journey that had almost cost her job. Driving through Bulgaria, she'd stumbled across information that the Germans were constructing a military aerodrome in the country, a project that sounded to her like the harbinger of a Nazi-Bulgarian alliance, and as soon as she reached Sofia, she'd passed the information on to the British Legation. They, nervous of doing anything to push the still-vacillating Bulgarians into Hitler's arms, ordered Clare not to go public with the news. Yet while she would protest that she'd complied with those orders, she seems to have been recklessly cavalier in interpreting them. Her report for the *Express* was headlined "Germany rebuilding Bulgaria's roads. Engineers speed work on Balkan battlefield" — and, even if the British censors had been culpable in letting it past, she herself became the target of official fire. A volley of outraged telegrams was sent, threatening cancelled travel permits and a recall to London, and an additional warning was flagged on her Foreign Office file. Although Clare did not know it yet, everything she now published would be scrutinized with extra vigilance, and her future at the *Express* was hanging by a thread.

Unrepentant and typically unperturbed, she pressed onwards to Greece and, in early November, arrived at the "god-forsaken" border town of Pythion, from where she was to catch the first of several trains to Athens. Clare was seething with impatience, now. The Greeks were already driving Mussolini's army back into Albania and, with the Axis alliance facing its first significant defeat of the war, the journey felt like an agony of slowness. As Clare's filthy little train chugged through the Greek countryside, she despised herself for not having argued her way onto one of the military transports that regularly overtook her. "I lacked the guts," she wrote — and, by the time she reached Athens, three days later, she was dismayed to find the city already crawling with correspondents.[3]

At the Greeks' military press bureau, the situation was chaotic. Unprepared for the deluge of interest in their war, officials hadn't yet formulated a policy on accreditation and were locked into angry negotiations with frustrated journalists. Clare spent days trying to secure a travel permit up to the Albanian border, batting off her editor's complaints about the money and time she was wasting. But at least the Greeks had no specific protocol against women, and, when the first group of journalists were issued with permits, she was among them. There were two other passengers sharing her press car for the long drive north: Henry Stokes, a correspondent for Reuters, who struck her as a foolish, dandified man, who'd dressed for the mountains "as though . . . for a walk in Hyde Park," and an Athenian stringer, who was known by everyone to be an informant for the Greek secret police.[4]

Conversation was awkward at best, but Clare took little interest in her companions as the car drove through air-raid territory, and finally approached Mount Morava, where the fighting was at its most intense. Barbed-wire barricades were scored across the landscape, burnt-out vehicles littered the roadside, and the air had become tainted with the sickly smell of mutilated horses and mules, their flesh hacked to the bone by hungry troops, their entrails left as food for the flies. As the road wound higher, the evidence of battle became distressingly human. The Greeks were apparently taking no prisoners in the defence of their country, and Clare saw lines of dead Italians, not only shot in the back, but stripped of their clothes and valuables. She had witnessed war casualties in Poland, and had seen what burning hot metal could do to young men's flesh, yet these particular violations made her recoil. Only when she and her companions caught up with a regiment of Greeks did she realize that their callousness had been motivated as much by necessity, as revenge. Mobilized in haste, they'd been sent into the mountains with cheap boots, cotton jackets and inadequate arms, and they'd had to loot whatever they could find from their better-provisioned enemy.

For Clare at least, the Greeks' poor organization proved fortuitous. She should, by this point, have secured an additional permit for the forward area of battle, and the one she'd acquired en route, begged from a tobacco-starved colonel in exchange for a few dozen cigarettes, was almost certainly dubious. But when she arrived at the abandoned farmstead which served as the Greeks' Advance HQ, no one seemed interested in her credentials. Nor, when she asked for a car to take her to the front, did anyone try to make her go with an escort. The Greeks probably did not expect her to get very far, because she'd barely driven a kilometre before the narrow road became so boggy she had to abandon the car and continue by foot, picking her way over discarded weapon cases and empty ration cans. The higher she trudged, the more clearly it also dawned on Clare that there might not be an actual front to reach. The Greeks were fighting an old-fashioned form of mountain combat, rounding up pockets of Italian resistance as they moved rapidly from one rocky spur to another; most of the time, she could only sense where the action was from the exchanging rattle of rifle fire. Once or twice, the cloud lifted to reveal a group of soldiers fanning out over a distant slope, a river running rust-coloured with blood at the bottom of a ravine. So eerie, so intangible was this combat zone, that even the sound of a dislodged stone had Clare feeling for the revolver in her pocket. She'd thought herself almost invincible but this battlefield struck her as thoroughly "unprofitable," and, once she'd seen enough to report, she was uncharacteristically keen to retreat.[5]

Scrambling her way down to safety, Clare was greeted by Arthur Merton, veteran correspondent with the *Daily Telegraph.* "I decided not to get my boots dirty," he genially admitted, but he was concerned that Clare herself "must be cold," and he urged her to sit down and share the picnic he'd brought with him, an impressively stocked hamper of brandy, chocolate and foie gras sandwiches.[6] Merton, an old hand at war campaigns, was famous for attending to his own well-being, yet, for a moment, Clare hesitated. Competitive with herself as well as with her male colleagues, she was proud of her ability to travel light and sleep rough. At the border station of Pythion, when told to expect a fourteen-hour wait for the train, she'd simply settled down to doze on the platform, inspiring the admiration of the one other journalist present. Merton's view, however, was that anyone could make themselves miserable in a war, that the canny reporter would always prioritize their comfort. And, when Clare returned to Athens (forcing her driver to race through air raids so that she could file her story ahead of her rivals), she was sufficiently impressed by Merton's example to permit herself a few days' holiday.

"Even with a war on, Athens was delightful. The climate was enchanting, warm and sunny. In the square in front of the hotel, oranges were ripening on the trees."[7] With news of fresh victories each day, Clare was swept up in the city's rejoicing, as church bells pealed and young women bestowed kisses and flowers on enlisting troops. The mere fact that she was British and fighting the same enemy was sufficient for complete strangers to embrace her and offer drinks. However, the main attraction in Athens, the main reason for Clare's untypical idleness, was the officer in charge of the British military mission.

General Gambier-Parry was a very handsome man, very vigorous in his gleaming boots and uniform, and, while Clare herself was poorly kitted out for flirtation — her sturdy winter clothes much stained by travel, her hair cropped short and slicked back with brilliantine — she was always drawn to the company of powerful men. She'd lost almost all contact with Van, who'd been drafted for secret intelligence training in Cambridge, and she was discovering that wartime affairs were not only a release from the slog, fatigue and anxiety of work, they had the advantage of being simple and short. She and Gambier-Parry owed each other nothing but a good time, and they spent a few mutually happy days together before he left Athens to take command of British forces in Crete, and she made plans for her return to Bucharest.

Clare had developed a very proprietorial interest in Romania and, when she heard rumours of a new crisis brewing, she was determined to report on it, despite the perils she might face. General Antonescu had created a monster when he'd rewarded the Iron Guard for their assistance in his September coup, and, within four months, the Guardists were out of control. Wildly abusing their new positions of office, they'd appointed themselves masters of Romania's "Jewish problem" and were committing atrocities of which even the Nazis disapproved. In one night alone, they'd dragged 500 Jews to a slaughterhouse, slit their throats and labelled their corpses "Kosher meat." Even though Antonescu was no friend to the Jews, this was a massacre he couldn't let pass. He stripped 10,000 Guardists of their official powers and ordered his army to keep the organization in check.

The Guardists, however, had no intention of being leashed, and, on 21 January, just after Clare reached Bucharest, they mounted their own coup against Antonescu. The fighting was bitter and bloody, and although Antonescu's forces prevailed, they'd been unable to prevent the Iron Guard from making one last assault against the Jewish community. Clare was keeping a detailed diary of her time in Romania, and her entry for 27 January was a stark itemization of rebel atrocities: "Jews were strangled in public places outside the burning synagogue, Jewish children were killed by Guardists while their houses were being looted, elderly bearded Jews were slain in the streets, and I have seen their bodies lying naked in a yard after the Guardists had stolen their possessions."[8]

The aftershocks from the coup continued for days. Rebel snipers remained on the loose and government forces were licensed to shoot any suspicious individual on sight. Nazi reinforcements appeared, jamming the squares of Bucharest with their armoured vehicles, taking possession of the hotels and bars, and creating a "tense atmosphere of . . .

antagonism" for the few remaining British. Clare and her compatriots had to retreat into their apartments, where, in a heightened state of siege, they held almost nightly parties for each other — a curious huddle of English people, "drinking, dancing, singing Russian songs, and being very light-hearted" in defiance of the dangers outside.[9]

Precarious though her situation was, however, Clare was not yet ready to leave. She'd been the only British correspondent to cover the coup and her reputation was riding high. Banner headlines flagged up her stories in the *Express* and sidebars rehashed the history of how this "Woman Scarlet Pimpernel . . . dark, handsome and apparently without fear," had not only scooped the start of the war, but helped thousands of Nazi victims escape. Now she believed she was on the tail of yet another exclusive, for, early in February, she was given good information that lorryloads of German troops and equipment had been seen crossing the border into Bulgaria. This was surely proof that Hitler planned to force an alliance with the latter, even if he stopped short of full invasion; and while Clare knew the British would want this information suppressed for as long as there was hope of Bulgarian neutrality, she was too impatient to consider caution.

During the past eighteen months, Clare had escaped from Poland, witnessed two armed coups and dodged several arrests, and she presumably felt that a diplomatic ruckus was a comparatively trivial concern. Her only anxiety was how to get her story past the Romanian censors, and she'd organized a plan for getting her copy hand-delivered to a colleague in Sofia, who could then telephone it on to the contact she'd been using in Geneva. She'd assumed the scheme was watertight, but somehow an official at the British Legation in Sofia had intercepted her article and, alarmed by its "irresponsible" contents, had pressed Whitehall to intervene. Their response was swift and merciless: "Miss Hollingworth" was judged to be a "menace," her reporting was condemned as "sensational and inaccurate" and the editor of the *Express* was instructed to fire her.[10]

"It is wearisome to be a Cassandra, destined always to prophesy truly and always to be disbelieved," Clare wrote with melodramatic outrage.[11] At the beginning of March, the Bulgarians would be dragooned into the Axis alliance, exactly as she'd predicted, and while she refused to doubt the correctness of her actions, she was now stuck in the Balkans without a job. Momentarily, she considered going back to London, either to "take her turn" with the auxiliary services or to serve in a munitions factory. Yet, while she piously opined that "everyone should do some hard work," she was too much the reporter now and, instead, she hitched a ride with the British Legation when it was evacuated to the safety of Istanbul, and spent the next three months sifting through her options.[12]

One possibility was a return to Greece. Hitler had been profoundly frustrated by Mussolini's botched invasion and, on 6 April 1941, had sent in his own, more lethally disciplined force to do the job. Clare mourned for the brave and festive Greeks and wondered about the fate of her handsome General, but before she was able to find employment with a new paper, the country was overrun. By 25 April, swastikas were draped from the Acropolis, and by mid-May only Crete remained unoccupied. Nation after nation was now losing the struggle against Germany, and, as Clare studied her map of the war, the only theatre of operation that seemed left to her was North Africa.

Fighting between the Axis and the Allies had been rumbling since the previous summer. As soon as France had fallen and Britain was under threat, Mussolini had judged that the moment was ripe for him to launch an attack on North Africa, as well as on Greece. If the British could be ousted from their colonial base in Egypt, he calculated that other key assets — the Suez Canal, the south-western Mediterranean ports and the Middle Eastern oil supply routes — would simply fall into his hands. Back in June, Italo Balbo had shown unusual mettle in advising Mussolini to defer his desert campaign, to wait until Hitler had Britain on its knees. But Balbo and his plane were shot down in accidental friendly fire, and there was no one to oppose Mussolini when, on 9 September, he ordered four divisions from the Italian Tenth Army to begin fighting their way towards Egypt.

Operazione E was as lacklustre in its planning as it was in its execution, and by December 1940, one Allied soldier was reporting that "several acres" of Italian troops were milling around the desert, simply waiting to be taken prisoner. For a brief and dangerous period of complacency, the British assumed that victory was theirs. But Hitler, stung by Mussolini's failure, took over the offensive and, early in 1941, sent his most brilliant commander, General Lieutenant Erwin Rommel, to take charge of the Desert War.

Rommel was fortunate that the Allied defence would shortly be weakened, as Churchill made the controversial decision to divert 58,000 men from North Africa to assist with the defence of Greece. But the German General was also a strategic genius, mapping out the vastness of the terrain as though it were a chess board, and by spring, the "Desert Fox" had reversed nearly all Allied gains in North Africa. Even so, his Afrika Korps was still a long way from Egypt, and, as he battled the Allies for control of the intervening desert, Clare was confident that there would still be months of action for her to report.

Her journey to Cairo, hub of the British military presence, would prove to be expensive and hard. German occupation forces now blocked access by land and few civilian ships were risking the sea. But, towards the end of May, Clare made a tour of the southeastern ports of Turkey and found a Palestinian captain who was sailing to Alexandria, in pursuit of what she guessed was some "dodgy enterprise." He'd already accepted four passengers on board his simple wooden caïque, and, for a price that Clare could just about afford, he was prepared to take her as well. There were no cabins, of course, and, when Clare wasn't being scorched by sun or soaked by choppy seas, she was under siege from evilly stinging insects, which came crawling out from the sacks of nuts that were stored on deck. The five-day voyage was miserable, "among the worst I have ever endured." She attempted some conversation with her fellow passengers, among them two Belgians and a British officer, but the former were too miserably seasick for company, and the latter only wanted to fantasize about the pub crawl he planned for his next home leave.[13]

Bored, itching, damp, Clare found it hard to remember exactly why she was seeking out yet another "god-forsaken" corner of the war. Her gloom lifted, though, as the boat reached Alexandria at last, the sun-flecked harbour busy with merchant ships and brightly painted pleasure craft which were ferrying rescued Allied troops back from Crete. She felt "dirty but cheerful" as she booked herself into the Cecil Hotel, and was much amused by the vagabond she saw reflected in the mirrored lobby, her clothes stained with water, her hair rimed with salt. She was also looking forward to some good conversation when she went to the British consulate to beg twenty pounds for her hotel bill.

But the lift to her spirits was only temporary. At the consulate she learned that the last Allied forces had been beaten in Crete, while in North Africa Rommel's advance appeared unstoppable. "Victory looked further away than ever," Clare reflected, for not only did it seem that the Allied command "could never hold any position in the face of a German attack, much less carry out an offensive," but they were also losing control of their men.[14] Outside on the streets of Alexandria, fights were breaking out among those who'd been recently evacuated from Crete, ground troops blaming pilots for providing inadequate air cover.* The entire war looked

* Failures of intelligence had allowed German planes and paratroopers to conquer Crete with such

to Clare like a grotesque shambles, and, the following day, when she caught her train for Cairo, she could summon little interest in the landscape she passed. The drab mud villages along the banks of the Nile, the buffalos, the water wheels, the flamboyantly blossomed flame trees made her long for the gentle green of an English summer. It seemed to her that decades had passed since she'd last been at home, and decades since she'd so innocently believed that the world could be run along sane and decent lines.

Cairo, however, was impossible to resist. Emerging from the railway station, Clare's depression was routed by a blast of heat, dust and noise, by a sensory assault of spices, incense, exhaust fumes and shit. The city was much as Lee had known it, except that over 35,000 Allied troops were now stationed there, and large groups of tanned, purposeful, uniformed men were striding among the filthy, flyblown beggars, the sway-haunched camels and the pedlars hawking falafel and fake antiquities. With rising energy, Clare realized she had arrived at the "rumbustious centre of it all," and, having caught a ride in one of the dilapidated vehicles that passed for a taxi in Cairo, she found a vacant room

devastating speed that only 18,000 of the Allies' 30,000 men could be evacuated.

in the luxuriously modernized Continental Hotel.[15] Its crisp linen sheets and fan-cooled air came at a price far higher than she could afford, but she needed to be rested for the following day, when, dressed in a new safari suit, she was to present herself at "Grey Pillars," the imposingly columned British HQ, and request that its director of press relations, Lieutenant Colonel Philip Astley, give her special permission to report from the desert front.

By this point, Clare had managed to get work with the Kemsley newspaper group, and was now a North African stringer for two of its publications, the *Sunday Times* and the *Daily Sketch*. Years later, she would imply that, armed with her new contract, she had only suffered minor obstructions from Astley, and that she had managed to make her way to the desert action almost from the start. But she was, as so often, being free with the truth, for Astley's communications with the War Office in London make it clear that he took the continuing ban on women very seriously; he was zealously committed to keeping battle zones under his jurisdiction safe from female correspondents, and he certainly had no intention of making an exception for Clare.

We can only guess at the conversation, as each argued their case. Astley was not an ungenerous man. He could acknowledge, from Clare's account of herself, that she was a reporter of guts and initiative. But, as he would emphasize in one of his War Office memos, the courage of female correspondents was not his real concern; the overriding issue was the "embarrassment and worry" that their presence could create. He believed that in the thick of an active battle zone, the soldiers' "natural chivalry" would always make them prioritize a woman's safety ahead of their own military duties. More troubling still was the "unacceptable embarrassment" the men would suffer if forced to relieve themselves in mixed company. This "convenience question" was especially delicate, Astley argued, "out in the open conditions of the desert," and he would cite as dire proof the collective bout of constipation that was suffered by one British battalion when they were visited by a rogue female journalist.[16]

"At least three hundred men were unmoved for three days," Astley quipped discreetly, and for him this was the end of the matter. Clare, like every woman who managed to write her way to the front, considered this position absurd and felt nothing but contempt for the military bureaucrats, who, from the safety of their desks, knew very little of the facts on the ground. In reality, troops and journalists simply learned how to accommodate each other, and the "convenience question" was routinely solved by what would become known as blanket parties — the women relieving themselves behind one temporary screen, the men behind the other, effectively rendering Astley's concerns redundant. And, while there was one very material issue on which female correspondents might have welcomed some official intervention, it was one that Astley and his War Office colleagues were far too squeamish to address.

Menstruation was still barely acknowledged in polite society. Lee Miller herself had been "horrified" when her photograph had been used to advertise Kotex sanitary towels, back in 1928; and even now, for an officer and a gentleman like Astley, the subject remained a fathomless taboo.[17] For a woman in the chaos of a war zone, however, the onset of her period could be a very real and raw anxiety. Even if she didn't suffer from pain or cramps, she still had to contend with the practical logistics, making sure she had an adequate supply of sanitary protection, and a discreet way of disposing of it. The patenting of the Tampax tampon, just three years before the war, should have simplified the issue — tampons were both more portable and more comfortable than regular pads, and far superior to the crudely traditional method of folded linen rags. But supplies of Tampax had become erratic during the war, and, in 1944, when Lee was reporting on the Allied liberation of France, she considered herself fortunate to procure several boxes in advance. Most of the women who made their way to the battle zones either had to improvise their protection or beg their supplies from nurses close to the front.

Clare, in Cairo, must surely have glowered as Astley skirted pompously around the convenience question and hinted at the unruliness she might spark among the troops; she must have insisted again and again that no one had bothered about such matters when she'd been reporting from Poland or Greece. But the only point which Astley was prepared to concede was to allow Clare into the army's twice-daily press briefings. She was banned from contact with soldiers on active duty, and any war reports she might choose to file would have to be based on official communiqués or on information she'd gained from her male colleagues.

The only live news available to her would be political developments in Cairo; yet, galling though this situation might be for Clare, it wasn't without interest. Rommel's rapid advance through the desert had sent waves of agitation through the Egyptian government, and advisors to King Farouk were pressing him to switch his allegiance from Britain to Germany. Nazi agents, meanwhile, were infiltrating the smaller towns and villages, persuading the more credulous Egyptians to believe that Hitler's sole concern was to liberate them from their British oppressors and restore the authority of Islamic religious law.* Clare had a lot of complex history and culture to master, very fast, and, where she'd once had Van to tutor her on the Balkans, she now found a generous mentor in Christopher Buckley, Merton's junior colleague at the *Daily Telegraph* and a specialist in the geopolitics of North Africa.

Later, Clare would pay tribute to Christopher Buckley's professionalism, singling him out as one of the "greatest" correspondents she'd known. But in Cairo he also became her tour guide, introducing her to the "colourful melange of smart hotels . . . night clubs, belly dancers and tarts, noisy trams and faded monuments, spies and intrigue," which made the Egyptian capital "a city for fun" as well as for war.[18] He secured her a room in "the Chummery," a ramshackle five-bedroomed apartment whose rent was cheap and whose fast-changing population of journalists, officers and diplomats was an excellent source of gossip. Most importantly, he helped her acclimatize to the very particular rhythms of a Cairo day: the early-morning work rush of press briefing, copy writing and wrangling with censors; the mid-morning

* One propaganda leaflet distributed by the Nazis actually claimed that Hitler was a secret convert to Islam.

game of tennis at the Gezira Club; the extended lunch, the late-afternoon briefing; and, finally, the long, velvety nights, when journalists would gather with diplomats, officers, expatriates and spies, to drink and dance into the cool early hours.

Even for Clare, it was seductively easy to sink into this lazy and, for her, sybaritic routine. Dressed in one of the two startlingly cheap but fashionable gowns that she'd ordered from an Egyptian tailor, half-cut on gin cocktails and swaying to the records of Vera Lynn (whose recording of "A Nightingale Sang in Berkeley Square" would become the theme tune of her Desert War), Clare could almost accept her confinement to civilian life. But idleness was unnatural to her and, once the exoticism of Cairo began to pall, she hankered for a return to the war. Sitting through briefings on tank manoeuvres and defensive positions was, for her, a form of torture, and she despised all the men who, while lucky enough to report from the front, seemed grouchily unaware of their privileges, and did little but complain about the heat, the sandflies, the near-inedible bully-beef rations.

In the end, it was Christopher Buckley who found an outlet for Clare's frustrated energies. He and two other colleagues had formed an unofficial scouting team, trekking deep into the desert to look for signs of German activity, and he suggested that Clare might like to accompany them. Even though these desert treks fell short of an actual war assignment, they soothed her craving for action, and they taught her to love the desert. On first arrival, Clare had seen it as a baked, arid wasteland, but now she became attuned to its subtle variations — the way it was shape-shifted by winds, and changed colour with the light. Among her most treasured memories of this period were the nights she camped out with Christopher and his companions, staring up at the high, bright canopy of stars, and discussing what their lives might be like once the war was over.*

So much time did Clare spend with Christopher that most of the Cairo press corps assumed they were lovers. They held hands as they walked together in the gardens of the Gezira Club and they were rarely out of each other's company. Yet Clare, who wrote so sketchily about most of her relationships, would make a point of insisting that she and Christopher had never had "an *affaire* in the accepted sense of the word."[19] He was "basi-

* Christopher Buckley also helped Clare resume work on her abandoned Balkans book. It was eventually published under the title *There's a German Just Behind Me,* and it contained such a blunt account of Clare's clashes with the British war bureaucracy that there was talk of legal action.

cally good looking," she acknowledged, but her observation that "few women noticed him" implied that his lanky stoop and bespectacled face held no sexual appeal for her.[20] In mid-August, when Clare was assigned a new story in Iran, over 2,500 kilometres from Cairo, she seems to have left Christopher behind with barely a pang.

Iran had long been one of the potential flashpoints in this war. While its ruler, Reza Shah, had declared himself neutral, he'd been wavering towards an alliance with Hitler, and was giving the Allies increasing cause for concern about their access to Iranian oil supplies. Negotiated threats had failed to impress, so, in the summer of 1941, forces were sent in to depose the Shah and to root out any covert Nazi presence. So swiftly efficient was Operation Countenance that, by the time Clare arrived in late August, the fighting was almost done and the Shah's more compliant son was preparing to take the throne. On this occasion, however, Clare was not bothered about missing the action, for the story to which she'd been assigned was not Operation Countenance itself, but the fact that the British had secured their victory with the help of the Russians.

It was back in June that this startling new alliance had been made, and as Sigrid had predicted the previous year, it had been precipitated by a stunning act of German betrayal. Stalin had never had any long-term illusions about the pact he'd forged with Hitler — their enmity was too profound — but he had calculated that it would remain in their mutual interests for several months to come. On 22 June 1941, he was thus desperately ill-prepared when four million Wehrmacht soldiers began pouring over Russia's borders and Luftwaffe planes began pounding its communications and air bases.

The timing of Operation Barbarossa had been no less confounding to the British, but with German weapons now turned on Russia, it had also brought a wave of relief. There was a rush to get journalists out to Moscow, and Helen Kirkpatrick, driving through the British countryside, was actually stopped by the police, with urgent instructions to get herself to the airport, where her housekeeper would be waiting with her luggage and passport. Helen was very hopeful of seeing combat at last, but, on arrival at the airport, she learned her visa had been denied. The American ambassador in Moscow was unwilling to take responsibility for a large influx of journalists, and the Kremlin, too, was creating difficulties, permitting entrance only to correspondents who were able to supply proof of allegiance to the Communist Party, or the far-Left.

One of the very few Westerners to escape

those strictures was the American photographer Margaret Bourke-White, who already happened to be in Russia with her husband, Erskine Caldwell, at the start of the German attack. Margaret's war career would intersect with several of the women in this book, yet with Operation Barbarossa, she had the field almost to herself, and the exclusive images that she sent back to *Life* magazine would make her famous. One series was shot from the roof of the American embassy in Moscow during a raid, and it almost cost Margaret her life. Mesmerized by the light show, she'd somehow intuited that "the bomb of the evening" was hurtling her way, and had barely had time to scramble inside before it exploded. "It was not sound and it was not light," she recalled, "but a kind of contraction in the atmosphere which told me I must move quickly."[21]

By the beginning of October, it was too dangerous for Margaret to remain. Germany had taken most of Ukraine and western Russia, Leningrad was under siege and ground troops had got to within striking distance of Moscow. All expectations that Hitler would overreach himself in tackling the might of the Red Army had faded; and as Russia struggled for its life, Helen reported that London was gripped by a sense of "impending crisis such as has not existed here since Dunkirk." The once-unimaginable question of what would happen "If Moscow Falls" was now being headlined across every British paper.[22]

Moscow did not fall. While German ground forces got to within twenty-seven kilometres of the city, the harsh Russian winter was taking its toll and the inadequately uniformed Wehrmacht began to freeze and starve. In the territories they conquered, however, the Nazis established a merciless grip. Russian civilians were rounded up to work in German factories and in military brothels; intellectuals, community leaders and high-ranking officers were summarily executed; and over three million captured soldiers were worked, tortured or starved to death. In 1942, when Hitler sent his troops into Stalingrad, the city that bore his enemy's name, he ordered every male citizen to be killed and every woman and child deported.

As always, though, the most cold-blooded atrocities were reserved for Jews. "Shoah by bullets" had become the Nazis' preferred method for purging their newly acquired territories, and mass shootings — overseen by dedicated killing units, *Einsatzgruppen* — were taking place across the Eastern Front. Between 29 and 30 September 1941, an estimated 33,700 men, women and children were lined up at Babi Yar, a ravine on the outskirts of Kiev, and shot by a detail of increasingly drunk and sickened conscripts.

■ ■ ■

By the end of the war, the total number of Russian deaths, civilian and military, would rise to around twenty-seven million, and Stalin would hold Britain to account for having left him to fight this Eastern Front alone, and for so long. Back in August 1941, however, when Clare was sent out to Tehran, the friendship between Stalin and Churchill was still new-minted and the British public were curious to know more about their Soviet allies.*

For decades, Russia had exerted a fearful hold over Western imaginations; it was a country vast and unknowable in its fraught history of regicide and revolution. Now, it was a friend, and Clare's first assignment in Iran was to go to the Soviet-controlled zone of Tabriz, where she'd been offered an exclusive interview with their Commanding General. She had high hopes of getting an international syndication for the interview, since, as far as she knew, she was one of the first Western journalists in Tabriz, and her encounter with the General had started in promising style. With an eccentric disregard of military etiquette, he'd received Clare in his hotel

* Iran's long-standing enmity towards the Soviet Union was one reason why the Shah had turned against Britain in the early summer.

bedroom, his pyjamas clearly visible beneath his "heavily decorated jacket," and, given the unusual casualness of his approach, she hoped for some interesting confidences.[23]

The conversation that followed was disappointingly formulaic, however. Speaking through his translator, the General refused to disclose anything beyond "a cautious briefing on the military situation." And while the mere fact of having spoken to him was enough to guarantee Clare the syndication for which she'd hoped, she had only one small outlet for her second, and far more interesting, Russian story, about the women who were now serving with the Red Army.*

It was fascinating to Clare that, when Russia had begun mobilizing for its Great Patriotic War, it had accepted women volunteers, as trainee fighter pilots, anti-aircraft gunners, tank drivers and snipers. The Soviets' military egalitarianism was a world away from the British, and Clare was gratified to observe how the Russian women in Tabriz appeared to nullify every one of Astley's fuddy-duddy concerns. "They share in the same discomforts as the men," she reported, "living in the same quarters, eating the same rations and doing the same tough jobs." They were also promoted to positions of genuine authority

---

* It was published only in the Allied forces magazine, *Parade.*

and one female commissar particularly impressed Clare with the professional manner in which she "fingered the trigger of her revolver with unmanicured hands," while checking the soldiers' mess for any infringements of the rules. When Clare enquired if any sexual problems arose from having men and women serve alongside each other, she was met with an emphatic denial: "NO, never. There is no room in the Red Army for troublesome women or men. There is plenty of room in Siberia."[24]

To Clare, the Russian army looked like a utopia of progressive good sense, but, had she been allowed to question these women more closely, she would have learned that many paid a brutal price for their "equality." Among the 800,000 women who ended up serving, there were many who had to barter their bodies for the privilege of fighting near the front. The prettiest and the most fortunate were commandeered as "campaign wives" for senior officers; the unlucky ones had to fend for themselves against assault and abuse from the lower ranks.

These facts, like many of the war's darkest aspects, would only later become public, and, during the eight months that Clare spent in Iran, she saw nothing to temper her admiration for Soviet policy. She was greatly enjoying her new posting. Tehran was an easier city than Cairo, its spacious boulevards and scented bazaars more European in feel, and she was happy to meet up once again with Robin Hankey, who was now in charge of the British consulate. With the help of his press secretary, she secured another exclusive interview, this one with Mohammed Reza Pahlavi, the newly enthroned Shah, and Clare got on with him so well that she was invited to have lunch with him and his wife. It was not, however, an easy encounter. Princess Fawzia appeared "somewhat overdressed," with her "long, heavily jewelled earrings," and Clare felt awkwardly wrong footed when asked if her hostess might pass for a European.[25] Kitted out, as usual, in her battered safari suit, Clare thought she could "hardly offer a comment on fashion." And certainly she felt herself to be on far more solid, professional ground when a friendly intelligence officer, Colonel Ralph Neville, took her up to the Darband Mountains to report on his mission to find stockpiled German weapons, some of which were being hidden by Iranian tribesman.

So absorbed was Clare in the complex war politics of Iran, she could almost forget about the conflicts waged elsewhere. Early in December, however, news came over the wires of a momentous twist in the war — a twist that would not only change the course of the fighting, but would also bring significant changes to Clare's own career.

■ ■ ■ ■

On 7 December 1942, when Japan bombed the U.S. naval base at Pearl Harbor, the loss of four battleships, two hundred aircraft and over two thousand men was calamitous enough to persuade all but the most hardened isolationists to accept the inevitability of war. Hirohito's motive for the attack on Pearl Harbor had been to provoke America into battle for possession of the Philippines, which had been a U.S. colony since 1898. But the Emperor had also been serving the interests of his German ally, for, as Sigrid had warned McCormick, Hitler had always planned to target U.S. interests once he'd subdued Russia and Europe, and, on 11 December, four days after Roosevelt declared war on Japan, Hitler had the excuse he needed to declare war in return.

In Britain, there was jubilation. Now that they had the full military and economic support of America, they must surely be able to defeat Germany. However, they would still have to wait another year for American troops to be mobilized and for a command structure to be negotiated with their own generals. And in the summer of 1942, when Clare was recalled to Cairo, the British Eighth Army were still fighting their Desert War alone against Rommel and were staring at a very stark defeat.

The worst of their losses was the Libyan port of Tobruk, a key base for Allied ships and transport; and coming just a few months after the British had lost Singapore to Japan, it had a crushing effect on morale. Back in London a vote of no confidence was mooted against Churchill, whose whole war strategy was now in doubt. Rommel, by contrast, appeared unstoppable, and at the end of June he'd reached El Alamein — just 250 kilometres north-west of Cairo and within striking distance of the heart of the British military. Panic flared throughout the Egyptian capital as wealthy refugees fought over tickets for the last outbound flights, and every sensitive document at the British HQ was burned. Journalists, too, were encouraged to leave. But Clare recalled that, even though the Gezira Club was deserted and "the cooks at Groppi's were icing cakes with the German and Italian colours," a determined core of the British press remained.[26]

For the next two months, Rommel and the Allies battled for control of those crucial kilometres of desert. In Cairo, a siege mentality developed that felt very familiar to Clare, as every night she met up with her colleagues to pick gloomily over the day's news and get fatalistically drunk on rum daiquiris. But, on 13 August, a new general was assigned to the British Eighth Army, and, tentatively, the city allowed itself to hope. Clare would find much to dislike in Bernard Montgomery, who she considered a "bustling little commander" and "something of a woman-hater" in his disdain for female journalists.[27] But she acknowledged that he brought with him an undeniable charisma and strategic confidence, and, on 23 October, when the reinvigorated Eighth Army launched a counter-attack at El Alamein, the momentum of the Desert War was turned. Although the fighting was long and bloody, with massive casualties on both sides, by the middle of November, Rommel and his Afrika Korps were on the run.*

Although Clare was still banned from frontline reporting, she was slowly gaining traction in her war coverage. She'd recently been promoted from stringer to special correspondent and her reporting privileges had expanded accordingly, to include the occasional interview with pre-vetted soldiers. More significantly, she was also receiving inside battle information from Colonel Ralph Neville, the intelligence officer with whom she'd worked in Iran, and who was now, in Cairo,

* One significant factor in Montgomery's success was his willingness to defy Churchill. Rather than pressing forward with the second battle of El Alamein, as the Prime Minister had ordered, he insisted on waiting until his men were fully rested and re-equipped.

her lover.

It's possible Clare had turned to Ralph Neville for support when she received a letter from Van's lawyers with news that her husband was suing for divorce. Even though she would later insist "there was nothing really dramatic in the failure of my first marriage," it was a sad and grubby ending to her first fully adult relationship and she must have been grateful for the consoling attentions of another man.[28] More restorative than Neville's companionship, though, was his willingness to assist her defiance of Astley, not only giving her illicit intelligence about the Allies' progress and brokering introductions with fellow officers but, as in Iran, allowing her to join him on searches for enemy weapons.

These scouting expeditions came with a lively degree of risk, because Axis troops were still embedded in the desert around Cairo. One night, after Clare had hollowed herself out a bed in the sand, she was jerked from her sleep by the sound of German voices. "They were quite clear . . . a German recce party, which had stopped awhile among the huge sand dunes," and she acknowledged that the courage on which she'd always prided herself had momentarily deserted her: "I literally sweated with fear. I had never been so frightened. I could feel the sand sticking with perspiration to every pore all over my body. I hardly dared breathe: a sneeze would have brought death to us all." It could certainly have brought death to Clare, since without military accreditation, she did not fall under the protection of the Geneva Convention — and it felt like an "eternity" to her before "the sound of an engine . . . the crunch of a gear" signalled that the "unseen Nazi threat [was] moving further and further away."[29]

Terrifying though that escapade had been, it inevitably left Clare hankering for more, and she was doubly frustrated by Astley's continuing obstructiveness. Since her return to Cairo, the Lieutenant Colonel had become even more defensive about his protocol, and he was scape-goating Clare for the behaviour of a small but very well-connected number of American women journalists who'd started to appear in the desert. Pearl Harbor had prompted a surge of American media interest in all aspects of the war, and one of the first correspondents to reach Cairo had been Ève Curie, daughter of the scientist Marie Curie, and a reporter for the *Herald Tribune* group. Astley had made it clear that Curie was not to visit the front, but she'd simply gone to Randolph Churchill, now a major and in overall command of Army Information, to get the order overruled. Ever susceptible to a glamorous woman (Curie had made time to have her nails manicured and her hair styled during her first day in town), Randolph had personally driven her out to the desert, where she'd been able to observe a tank battle in progress and interview a number of top-ranking officers at the Advanced HQ, to whom even the male press corps had been barred access.

It had been Curie, according to Astley, who'd also been responsible for the outbreak of desert constipation. But, even after he'd fired his angry memo off to the War Office, other women had followed. One was the writer Clare Boothe Luce, who came to Cairo as a "distinguished guest" of the British; another was Dixie Tighe, a correspondent for the International News Service. "It is no part of a woman's function to usurp the prerogatives of a war correspondent in desert warfare," fumed Astley, smarting from the wounds to his authority and pride. And Clare was smarting too, for she was convinced that these Americans had only beaten her out to the combat zones by virtue of their connections and their glamour. At least one of them — she named no names — had treated the desert as her own publicity exercise, swanning around "the fringes of the battlefields in a sort of Dior creation for woman war correspondents in pale beige silk and trimmings!"[30]

Late in February 1943, she made one more effort to get close to the British front. The Eighth Army had just seized control of

Tripoli, and, having hitched a ride with a sympathetic pilot, Clare had high hopes of reporting on the last stages of the fighting. When she arrived at the Libyan capital, she spotted a group of soldiers from the Highland Division wandering the streets in search of some off-duty fun, and she was able to dash off a lively piece for the *Sketch* — topped by the excruciating headline, "Scots wha' ha'e a fling." However, her hopes of covering more serious military issues were thwarted by Montgomery. When he heard that Clare had shown up in Tripoli, he was livid: "I'll have no women correspondents with my army," he bellowed, and ordered his chief of staff to personally track her down and return her to Cairo.[31] She was discovered fast asleep in the back of a truck at Tripoli airport, and, faced with a direct order, she had no choice but to obey. Yet, humiliating though it was to be hustled back to Cairo, this moment was also decisive for Clare. She had tried, and exhausted, every option for reporting on British action, and the only alternative now was to switch her affiliation to the Americans.

The newly formed U.S. Department of Public Relations had come into the war with a far more positive attitude towards the press. While the British War Office chose to tolerate front-line journalists as a necessary evil, the Americans actively welcomed them, believing they could play a significant role in disseminating information from the front and in boosting morale — most soldiers had a morbid terror of dying anonymously in war, and they welcomed any reporter who could send news of them back home. But the U.S. Public Relations Department also had a specific idea of how women correspondents could be deployed. In November 1942, when the U.S. Expeditionary Force first landed in North Africa (its mission to liberate Tunisia, Morocco and Algiers from the Vichy French and consolidate Allied control of the Mediterranean), it had brought a small but significant cadre of drivers, secretaries and signallers from the Women's Army Auxiliary Corps. To much of conservative America, however, the very notion of this "skirted army" was an abhorrence, so decisions were made to accredit a few female journalists who, in writing about the WAAC and the essential service they performed, could help to convince the U.S. public that women had a necessary role in this war.* None of these journalists were meant to go anywhere near the fighting, nor be permitted contact with serving troops, but,

* In Britain, where the ATS was formed in 1938, and where the conscription of women to non-combat duties with the army, navy and air force was enforced in December 1941, the patronage of Queen Elizabeth and the Princess Royal went a long way to garnering public support.

in the fast-changing realities of the desert war zones, it soon proved possible for the most determined and ingenious of them to bypass official protocol.

If Clare was to get her own U.S. accreditation, however, she would need to work for an American publication, and by April she managed to get herself two stringer's contracts, one with the *Chicago Daily News* and the other with *Time*. Astley had been furious when he discovered what she was doing, and had contacted the American HQ in Algiers with a request that "nothing would be done to embarrass us." But Clare's application was already being processed and, in May 1943, she was issued with her AGO licence (named after the issuing Attorney General Office) and her army-issue uniform — an olive drab jacket with a war correspondent's insignia stitched onto its pocket and a yellow "C," for "Correspondent,"* emblazoned on its sleeve.

Finally, she was free of Astley and his War Office rules. As the last of the conflict rumbled around North Africa and the Middle East, Clare became expert in working every loophole available to her. She taught herself to parachute and flew on bombing missions with the U.S. air force, she interviewed lead-

---

* Eventually the "C" was replaced with a rectangular insignia "War Correspondent" sewn over the left jacket pocket, and a round insignia on the cap.

ers of the rebel Druze army in Beirut, and, later, travelled back to the Balkans and Greece to report on anti-German guerrillas. None of these experiences would ever quite match the drama of her early rogue reporting, none would equal the magnificent luck of her first Polish scoops. But Clare had wasted so much time and energy in arguing her rights with Astley that it was a triumph simply to be wearing her war correspondent's uniform and to be treated with the respect of a card-carrying combat journalist.

CHAPTER ELEVEN:
LONDON, ALGIERS AND
MONTE CASSINO, 1941–3

"You ought to see me in my soldier suit"

LEE MILLER[1]

For Helen Kirkpatrick, it had been a professional and personal relief when Roosevelt finally committed to the war. She'd been ashamed of her country's long delay, and, like many Americans in London, had felt herself a target of growing resentment. To the war-wearied British, abandoned by their U.S. cousins, the mere sound of an American accent had become a provocation and, during the last year or two, Helen had had to steel herself against hard glances and muttered insults.

But, on 11 December 1942, the insults had turned to smiles, and the smiles grew more welcoming still when Helen was put into uniform. Along with Mary Welsh, who'd been working in London for *Time* magazine since the previous year, she was the first American woman to be granted accreditation. Her seniority within the press corps had been

411

recognized and, once she'd filled in a security questionnaire and sworn to "truthfully convey the facts of the war without jeopardising military engagement," she was issued with her AGO card and sent to a tailor in Savile Row to be measured for the jacket and two skirts that would comprise her new military dress.*

Helen was proud to wear that uniform when she was sent to Northern Ireland in January 1942 to report on the first batch of GIs to arrive in Britain, and later when she covered a royal visit to a U.S. army base — a novel entertainment for the King and Queen, who watched American servicemen parading to Sousa marches and were served with "pint-sized mugs" of coffee, which, Helen reported, had greatly "amused the Queen."[2] But, at this stage in Helen's war, her accreditation felt largely symbolic. Pleased though she was by her military khaki, she was far more excited by the new silk dress she'd acquired off-ration, and by the blue Schiaparelli coat that had been given her by Nancy Tree. While her AGO gained her privileged access to U.S. army briefings and use of its London mess, her duties remained largely desk-bound. It

---

* The two skirts, one khaki and one pinkish-grey for evening wear, were clearly impractical for war conditions, and, at the women's request, would eventually be changed for trousers.

was only eighteen months later, when Helen became impatient for combat action, that she started to appreciate both the obstacles that had been placed between women and front-line reporting, and the pioneering efforts it had taken for the few who'd been able to overcome them.

One of those was Margaret Bourke-White, who'd been given her own accreditation when she came to Britain to photograph the U.S. 97th Air Bombardment Group. It was the summer of 1942, and the crews were preparing their B-17 "Flying Fortresses" for daytime missions over Europe. Margaret's request to fly in one of the big, high-altitude bombers was refused on predictable grounds. But, later that year, when the 97th Group was sent to North Africa, she followed, and the dangers she braved en route from violent sea storms and torpedo attacks so impressed the group's commander that he agreed to let her go up on a bombing raid over enemy desert lines.

Conditions on board the Flying Fortresses were gruelling, and Margaret had to prepare for freezing temperatures, altitude dizziness and the cumbersome weight of an oxygen bottle strapped to her chest. But the mission, on 22 January, went smoothly, and, when the plane was heading back to base, diving and ducking through a hail of German bullets, Margaret could be heard gasping joyfully through the plane's intercom, "that's a beautiful angle . . . Hold me this way so that I can shoot straight down."[3] The photographs she took for *Life* were another landmark in her war career, and "Maggie the indestructible," as she became known to the troops, was featured prominently among them, jaunty and laughing in her flying suit.

Margaret's celebrity eased the path of several other women who were trying to bend the rules, and it was especially useful to Virginia Cowles, who arrived that same month to report on British troop action in Tunisia. She'd taken a circuitous route back into combat reporting, having devoted all of 1941 to the writing of her memoir, *Looking for Trouble,* and to a six-month promotional tour of the States. By the time she returned to London, America had joined the war and she was being acclaimed for her contribution to the propaganda effort. She was, however, unemployed, and the first job that became available was not in journalism, but in the office of the American ambassador, John Gilbert Winant.

Winant was "a gaunt awkward Lincolnesque sort of a man," according to Bill Shirer, a natural philosopher as much as diplomat, and he'd immediately grasped that the alliance between Britain and America would require careful engineering.[4] The British had naturally been delighted to welcome the first wave of the American Expeditionary

Force to arrive on their soil. These vigorous young men, with their squadrons of factory-fresh aircraft, weapons and tanks, had brought with them a sugar rush of energy and hope. But, over the next three years, more than two million American servicemen would pass through Britain, half a million pilots would be permanently stationed there, and — to some, at least — the huge "Yank Army" would come to feel something like an invasion force. Valuable family farmland had to be sacrificed for its camps and air bases, and the habitual reticence of British life was overturned as brash, crew-cut GIs appeared in pubs and on street corners, offering their easy gifts of nylons and scent to the local girls, flaunting their privileged access to whisky and cigarettes.

Most of these servicemen had never been abroad and, despite being provided with educational pamphlets, they struggled to understand the sensitivities of this drab, chilly island, thousands of miles from home. They didn't see why it was considered rude to chew gum in the street or shout compliments at passing women, and they didn't see why the British had any right to complain, since it was the Americans, now, who were paying for their miserable war.

Winant was very conscious of this cultural and social divide, and also conscious that many Americans still needed persuading that

Britain actually deserved their help. Back in the summer of 1941, a survey had revealed that nearly 50 percent of the U.S. public were dubious about Britain's moral and military record in the war, and believed that many of the thousands of British fatalities had been victims of incompetent leadership.

American journalists in London had immediately been annexed to Winant's mission to foster close links between the new allies, and Helen, as the only female staff writer on the *Chicago Daily News,* was obliged to write upbeat articles about all that American women could learn from the ingenious and plucky British housewife — the "fun" that could be had with utility fashions, the delicious meals that could be cooked on rations. Meanwhile, Virginia's role at the embassy was largely to research and write a series of briefing papers that would assist Winant and his staff in a more detailed grasp of British institutions and etiquette.

Some of Virginia's papers focused on the military, while others concerned domestic issues — British laws on drinking and prostitution, the gulf in manners that led American familiarity to be so readily interpreted as "effrontery." She found the work absorbing, a congenial alternative to journalism. She relied on it too, as a distraction from her anxieties about Aidan, who, back in July 1941, had been shot down over the Libyan desert and was now incarcerated in a German POW camp. Yet, glad though Virginia was of company and occupation, the routines of the office grated. Travel and news had been her life for over a decade — and, in January 1943, when the ambassador proposed that she take a two-month leave of absence to write about British troops in North Africa, she was more than ready to see combat again.

What Winant wanted from Virginia was a series of sympathetic valorizing reports that would help him in the battle for American hearts and minds. An agreement was reached with the *Sunday Times* and the *Sketch* to publish those reports, and a guarantee elicited from the War Office that she could travel to the front as a "distinguished visitor." With the combined weight of the American embassy and the British War Office behind her, Virginia was naturally expecting a helpful response when she reached Cairo, and put in a request for travel papers and a driver to take her onwards to Tunisia. But she hadn't been warned about Philip Astley, and the Lieutenant Colonel was so affronted by yet another female challenge to his authority that he curtly denied her access to any zone where the British were engaged.

Astley, equally, had not been warned about Virginia, though. She'd got wind of Margaret Bourke-White's proposed mission with the 97th Group and, fully prepared to use it to her advantage, she wrote a letter of appeal to the Commander of the Allied Armies in North Africa, General Eisenhower. As she carefully informed the General, it had been the U.S. ambassador's idea for her to "collect material . . . that would promote Anglo-American friendship in this, the first great Allied undertaking," and she pointed out that Astley's obstructive attitude was not only a direct contravention of her War Office guarantee, but was made "even more embarrassing" by the fact that another woman had been operating in "the forward area for a considerable time." Adroitly hinting that "Miss Burke-White" [*sic*] would surely hear of her own "unfortunate situation" and would surely make it known when she returned to America for a much-publicized lecture tour, Virginia suggested that Eisenhower might want to take action on her behalf.[5]

Eisenhower did not care for "Maggie the indestructible," whom he considered pushy and reckless, but he did not want her making trouble. More crucially, he understood the propaganda power of the press and he supported Winant's desire to promote American sympathy for the British troops. A terse cable was thus sent to Cairo requesting that Miss Cowles be allowed to "go where she liked" and receive "every possible assistance" — and Astley had to accept he was overruled.[6]

It was mid-February by the time Virginia

was authorized to begin the long drive west. She was heading for the Atlas Mountains, where the British were fighting for control of the Kasserine Pass, and on the way she could see where the fighting had already been and gone. Unburied corpses lay rotting on the open ground, their flesh half eaten by carrion birds; miles of pristine desert had been turned into a rubbish dump, littered with burnt-out vehicles, stinking latrines and piles of trash. When she eventually reached Sbiba, on the north-eastern edge of the pass, she was met by Nigel Nicolson, an intelligence officer with the 6th Armoured Division, whose parents were the diplomat Harold Nicolson and the writer Vita Sackville-West. Nicolson claimed to be astounded by Virginia's arrival. To his knowledge, no journalist, male or female, had ever been allowed so deep into the Desert War and at so critical a moment. But he was game to escort her wherever she wanted to go, and straightaway led her up to a ridge from where she could observe the 6th Armoured Division engaging with the enemy.

The battle was spectacular, but curiously brief. After the British and German tanks had been manoeuvred, tortoise-like, into position, the heavy artillery followed with a blazing eruption of smoke, flames and dust. Then, as if by an agreed sign, both sides abruptly withdrew, leaving behind a detritus of fallen bodies and incinerated vehicles. At this distance, the battle had looked more like a ritual dance, and had there been time, Virginia would have pressed Nicolson to let her go down and examine the scene. But orders had just come through that the 6th were to move on, deeper into the pass, where there were warnings of an imminent German attack. A long convoy was formed and, as it rumbled onwards through the desert, Virginia began to appreciate the very real danger she was in. Rommel was fighting for every inch of terrain; there were German planes circling overhead, German mines had been laid alongside the stony track and the driver of her vehicle was visibly sweating as he tried to steer a steady path.

Once the convoy reached the village of Thala, the situation became graver still, for enemy tanks were just four miles away and Stuka bombers were approaching fast. When the first explosion came, Virginia was grabbed by a young British captain and bundled into a nearby house, but, while she suffered nothing worse than a smothering of plaster dust, others had been killed, and Nicolson begged her to leave, while he and the division fought on. She, however, had moved into the same state of dissociated calm she'd experienced on the Dover Cliffs, insisting first that she must take some photographs of Thala and, only then, agreeing to hitch her way back to the British camp. All the while, German fighter planes were strafing the road and Virginia, at that moment, seemed to Nicolson an unfeasible combination of courage and glamour. Later he wrote that the men in his division had lost their hearts to her. "She was the first Anglo-Saxon woman, literally, that we had seen for months," he wrote, "an unbelievably lovely vision on the battlefield."[7] They loved Virginia, too, because they knew she'd be writing about them in the British press. Some of the men had been in the desert for so long, they'd come to doubt how well they were being remembered, and it meant everything, Nicolson recalled, that Virginia would be taking home news of them, "telling our people . . . something of what we were doing and suffering."[8]

When Virginia's North African reports were published in the *Sketch* and the *Sunday Times,* much was made of the risks she'd run in acquiring them. Clare, still working for those papers herself, felt understandably overshadowed, and it was now that she redoubled her efforts to get closer to the action. But Virginia, too, had been energized by this North African tour. It had reminded her of all that she'd been missing — the thrill of chasing a story under fire, the camaraderie of being among troops — and, once she was back in London, she began to investigate her chances of returning to the war, if and when a second front was opened up in Europe.

■ ■ ■ ■

Meanwhile, there were others coming to London with the same ambition, and a photograph that had been taken in January that year showed the two old hands, Helen Kirkpatrick and Mary Welsh, lined up in uniform with four other fully accredited American women — Kathleen Harriman, Tania Long, Dixie Tighe and Lee Miller.

Lee had only recently applied for her own AGO, and had done so only under pressure from a fellow photographer, Dave Scherman, who, for the last twelve months, had also been her lover. The two of them had met in December 1941, a few weeks after Dave, a young and inexperienced twenty-five-year-old, had come to London as a photojournalist for *Life.* Lee had struck him, quite simply, as the most extraordinary woman he'd ever met: a woman who'd been mistress and muse to Man Ray, a friend of Picasso, yet was also a gifted artist in her own right. It was barely credible to him that this beautiful, funny and complicated creature, who could flip on a dime from "cosmopolitan *grande dame*" to "upstate hick and consummate clown," should take an interest in "a brash and bumptious squirt" like himself.[9] But it was no less astonishing to Dave that Roland, far from objecting to the affair, had actually invited

422

him to come and live at Downshire Hill. The notion of a ménage à trois seemed very European, very sophisticated to Dave, although the arrangement was very much to Roland's own advantage. He'd been called up to serve as a camouflage consultant, advising on techniques for disguising military bases and equipment, and he would have to be absent for frequent periods. He didn't want Lee to be alone in the house, in case it was bombed, and he preferred her to be in one, dependable relationship with Dave, rather than chasing after other, more fugitive affairs.

If Lee herself was conscious of Roland's calculations, she didn't object. Dave's corny jokes and unselfconscious enthusiasms reminded her of the boys at home — the two of them spoke the same slang. And, as a fellow professional, Dave interested her even more. In contrast to her own, highly stylized approach, his job was to turn photography into a narrative art, and the techniques that he used in devising his stories for *Life* — planning, sequencing and captioning his images so that they carried a simple message or theme — struck Lee as fascinatingly appropriate for war.

She wanted to learn Dave's craft — fundamentally, she had "the soul of a tinker," he thought. And so intently did she study with him, and so enthusiastically accompany him on shoots, that within weeks he was urging her to go to *Vogue* with some photo stories of her own. Lee demurred, however. She'd had such high expectations of herself after the *Grim Glory* collection, yet afterwards had been unable to sustain her creative momentum; and the fact that she was still essentially photographing models and celebrities had sent her confidence into a slump. When she visited Dave at his *Time-Life* office in Soho she barely noticed the frisson she created — according to Mary Welsh, the combination of Lee's beauty, her "crusty cool intelligence" and fabulous past would always make "hearts beat quicker." Lee herself was conscious only that these tough young news journalists were busy with "the biggest story of the decade," and that she was still frittering away the war in a women's magazine.[10]

She felt more inadequate still when *Vogue* sent her to photograph Margaret Bourke-White during the latter's summer assignment with the 97th Air Bombardment Group. Lee had become quite friendly with Margaret back in New York; she'd received one of her photographs as a wedding present and considered her, then, as a professional equal. Now, though, Margaret had established herself as one of the war's top photographers, and when Lee travelled to the 97th Group's air base, it was very galling to have to follow her around as she fraternized with pilots and clambered in and out of B-17 bombers.

Margaret was engaged in the kind of serious reportage that Lee wanted for herself, yet it seemed to her, then, that even if she possessed more experience as a photojournalist, *Vogue* would be unlikely to send her out on any military-themed stories. Lee had, however, seriously underestimated Audrey Withers. Believing, as she did, that all magazines had a responsibility to "the here and now," Audrey had already been wondering if she could push *Vogue*'s war coverage even harder; and when Lee eventually yielded to Dave's pressure and tentatively pitched some ideas, Audrey's response was immediate.[11] Once the New York office had been persuaded to sponsor Lee for accreditation, an AGO licence bearing her photograph, signature and fingerprints was issued; and early in January 1943, she was sent to have her "soldier suit" fitted in Savile Row. "You ought to see me," Lee wrote triumphantly to her parents, "all done up and very serious like in olive drab and flat-heeled shoes."[12]

Lee's first batch of war stories were all about women: she photographed a contingent of American nurses, newly arrived in England; an all-female group of ATS workers, operating a searchlight battery in North London; and a squad of trainee recruits to the Women's Royal Naval Service. For this last assignment, she travelled to a secret loca-

425

tion in Scotland, where, she proudly reported, she "almost drowned" in her enthusiasm to photograph the Wrens as they scrambled down the ship's ladders and precariously traversed a narrow boom.

Excited and absorbed though Lee was by her new métier, it came with frustrations of its own. Early in 1944, she spent five days collaborating with Dave on a story about British war artists, and she was proud of the results. The centrepiece was a photograph she'd taken of Henry Moore sketching in Holborn Underground station, back in the Blitz. It was a magisterially composed image, almost biblical, with the artist appearing to stand sentinel over a huddle of vulnerable, exhausted Londoners, their bodies illuminated by a faltering glow, the rest of the shot receding into a yawning blackness. The month it was scheduled to run, however, Audrey was unusually short of page capacity, and, to Lee's fury, the entire story, her Moore portrait included, was compacted into a mean and unflattering space.

More distressing still was the flimsy, ill-informed text which accompanied the images. Up until now, Lee hadn't had the courage to attempt her own words, but this botched piece of journalism made her determined to try. She had a particularly personal investment in her next assignment — a profile of Ed Murrow, the CBS broadcaster who'd written the introduction to her *Grim Glory* collection — and she wanted her story to capture the physical brio, the dazzling spontaneity with which Murrow delivered his reports on wartime London. Photographing him was easy, but when Lee sat down to describe Murrow, she was appalled by the feebleness of her prose. "I am cutting my own throat," she agonized, as she discarded one draft after another and begged Audrey to make her stick to photography, "you know, the thing that is worth ten thousand words."[13]

But Audrey actually thought the final text very fine. Lee's account of the beetle-browed Ed, crouched over his microphone like a Spitfire pilot, had all the trademark acuity and wit of her photographs, and Audrey was keen to push her harder. Even as she hoped to make a writer of Lee, however, she still needed her visual input on the fashion and society pages. And, back in November 1943, one of the tasks she entrusted to Lee was a photo-shoot with Martha Gellhorn, who'd arrived in London to begin a three-month assignment in Europe.

Lee had never met Martha, but she knew something of her reputation both as a war correspondent and as Hemingway's wife. According to Dave and the rest of the *Time-Life* crowd, Martha had come to London with a rather inflated awareness of her own status, and with rather too many opinions about the current state of combat reporting, which she was prone to dismiss as a toothless affair compared to the glory days of Spain. Martha was admired by her younger colleagues, but also regarded as something of a diva, and when Lee went to photograph her at the Dorchester Hotel, she may well have been influenced by this later view. Out of the dozens of portraits she shot, the image she highlighted for *Vogue* showed Martha seated at her dressing table, her back to the camera and her face reflected in the mirror, as though she were a celebrity actor in her dressing room.

Years later, Martha would claim there had been so many photographers in London, she had no recollection of this session with Lee. She'd looked very much the professional, her expression carefully composed, her hair recently permed and dyed. But, in some of the photographs, Lee had captured a fleetingly hunted look, which was, in fact, a far truer register of Martha's feelings. A pile of social invitations had been awaiting Martha at the Dorchester, and, while she'd made herself accept some of them, she'd felt cranky and shy, anxious that most of the fuss being made of her was only on account of Ernest, and very concerned that her arrival in London, alone and without her husband, would give rise to unfriendly gossip.

Martha was surprised, at first, by the pleasure

she got from becoming Mrs. Hemingway. The wedding had taken place on 21 November 1940 — a modest event, held in the dining room of the Union Pacific Railroad at Cheyenne — and afterwards she'd written confidently to Eleanor Roosevelt, "Ernest and I belong tightly together. We are a good pair." She believed she had gone into the marriage with open eyes, that she had fully got the measure of her husband, and that marrying did not have to spell the end of her independence, nor her ability to live "simple and straight."[14]

There had been difficult times, of course: Martha had felt both guilty and resentful when forced to resist Ernest's hopes of a baby daughter; she'd suffered a shaming degree of bitterness when their respective war novels were published, and her own thin reviews for *The Heart of Another* were eclipsed by the tidal wave that had greeted *For Whom the Bell Tolls*. Marriage to a man whom the world regarded as a genius was evidently going to be hard. Ernest could be touchingly generous — "I have no greater joy than seeing your book develop so amazingly and beautifully," he would tell her in 1943 — and he could be devastatingly tender. "I love you," he wrote, "because your feet are so long and because I can take care of you when you are sick, also because you are the most beautiful woman I have ever known." But there were periods, too, when his volcanic brilliance was alarming to Martha, when she feared that he would eventually suck the oxygen from her own writing, her own ideas, and when she dared to wonder if she'd made the mistake of her life in marrying him.[15]

She'd been especially ambivalent when, shortly after their marriage, Ernest declared his intention to travel with her on an assignment to the Far East. Two years had passed since her last major piece of reporting and, as she admitted to a friend, she was longing to "be a journalist again," to have "that life of rushing and asking questions" and being in the places "where it is all blowing up." Early in 1941, she arranged with *Collier's* to write about Japan's imperialist ambitions, its invasion of China and its threats to other countries in the region. Ernest, however, was worried that Martha was exposing herself to danger, undertaking "a son of a bitching dangerous assignment in a shit filled country," and, without informing her, he got himself a contract with *PM* to cover the same story. It would be a "crazy honeymoon," he'd said cheerfully when telling Martha of his plan, and she had not known whether to be touched by his concern or infuriated by the arrogance with which he'd muscled in on her trip.[16]

In fact, Ernest did little reporting when they arrived at their first destination, Hong Kong. He fell in with a group of local boxers and policemen, who kept him busy with drinking and pheasant shoots, and Martha was left to follow her own instincts as she explored the city. She ventured into a brothel and an opium den, where she watched a fourteen-year-old girl, with a pet tortoise, expertly filling the clients' pipes; she got herself lost in alleyways and street markets, and she took detailed notes about the families who squatted in derelict buildings, the children put to work in sweatshops. The poverty of Hong Kong appalled her, but she was entranced by the otherness of this "rich and rare and startling and complicated city." "I go about dazed and open mouthed," she wrote. "Everything smells terrific. I have never been happier, only a little weary."[17]

But Martha had come east for a war story and, while in Hong Kong, she was offered a freezing sixteen-hour flight over mainland China to get an aerial view of its battle-ravaged landscape. In 1931, when the first Japanese raids had begun on Chinese soil, Martha had paid no more attention than the majority of the Western world. Now, with Emperor Hirohito in alliance with Hitler, and making open threats on American and British colonies, she understood that the Far East could no longer be safely or decently ignored.* Indeed, when she and Ernest sailed

* Japan was not only planning to take the Philip-

to mainland China in early March, Martha had already framed the conflict with Japan as a re-run of the Spanish war, a free and innocent nation invaded by a barbarous, bullying dictator.

Her sympathies were severely tested, though, as she and Ernest made the arduous journey up to the Seventh War Zone, sailing part of the way in a rickety, crowded boat whose noxious fumes made her retch, then switching to a pair of "obstinate, iron mouthed and mean natured ponies."[18] The Zone turned out to be huge, the size of Belgium, and with the fighting having stalled in intractable mountainous terrain, the only action Martha saw was a simulated attack, executed by very young Chinese soldiers, who looked to her like "sad orphanage boys" in their skimpy uniforms.

Their tour of the region started to feel interminable, as every stop they made, every barracks they visited, came with a seemingly endless banquet, and Martha had to force down dishes of sea slugs and drink the local delicacy of "cuckoo"-infused wine. Her hands had become virulent with a peeling fungal infection which she had to treat with an evil-

pines from America, but to oust the British from their historic colonies, including Burma, Singapore and Hong Kong.

smelling ointment. Lying on the wooden board that passed for her bed in one guest house, and feebly swatting away mosquitoes, she swore to a heartlessly amused Ernest that she wanted to die.

"Too late," he grinned. "Who wanted to come to China?"[19] But more dispiriting than the physical discomfort was the corruption they discovered at the heart of this war. China's weak showing against Japan was not solely the result of poor equipment and bungled strategy, for its leader and war general, Chiang Kai-shek, was deliberately undermining his own army. As an official ally of America, Chiang had benefited from generous U.S. aid, but, rather than using it for the good of his country, he'd been pocketing some for himself and using the rest to fund his own personal war on Chinese Communist insurgents.

Martha and Ernest were invited to lunch with the General and his impeccably groomed wife, and found the opulence of their Chungking residence in grotesque contrast to the poverty outside, and when Martha dared to enquire about the community of lepers who were begging nearby, she was met with a frigid stare. The Chiangs revolted her — "Their will to power was a thing of stone," she decided — and she despised their callous sense of entitlement even more when, in great secrecy, she and Ernest were taken to meet

Zhou Enlai, international representative of the Chinese Communist Party.[20] Despite his filthy tattered uniform, Zhou was a compelling figure, a very handsome man, with "brilliant amused eyes" and an irresistible aura of mission. Martha thought him "the one really good man" she'd met in China, yet she knew it was impossible for her to promote his cause.[21] America had invested too much in Chiang for *Collier's* ever to consider publishing the "straight truth," and just as she could not write about the corruption of Chiang's regime, so she could not comment on the righteousness of those who rebelled against it.

Ernest, meanwhile, had proved his worth as a travel companion. Although he too had complained viciously about the food and the bed bugs in mainland China, he'd laughed Martha out of her misery and had given her wise, sympathetic counsel about how to write her compromised report. At moments, the trip had actually felt like the "crazy honeymoon" he'd promised, and, after he'd left Martha to complete her tour of Burma, Singapore and the Dutch East Indies, he'd written to remind her of how good they'd been together: "I am lost without you . . . just straight aching miss you all the time. And with you I have so much fun, even on such a lousy trip."[22]

Martha had missed Ernest too, but her

pleasure in their reunion was diluted by the shame of her China article. "You have to be very young, very cynical and very ignorant to enjoy writing journalism these days," she wrote to her friend and one-time lover, Allen Grover. She knew that her integrity, her writing had been tainted, and her despondency over China began to leak into her perceptions of the European war. She felt, as she had in the horrible autumn of 1938, that she was unable to judge confidently between right and wrong, and she feared now that, even if Hitler were eventually defeated, the evil he'd unleashed would remain in the world, "like an infection of the blood."[23] On 7 December, Pearl Harbor was bombed, and at Christmas Virginia came to stay in Cuba, celebrating the end of her American book tour. But a "cosmic indifference" had settled over Martha, and she believed she was finally done with journalism, and finally done with wars.*

In the end, it was Ernest — or, rather, her frustrations with Ernest — that changed her mind. On their return from China, he'd drifted — squandering days at a time with

---

* She would fret over the piece, too, because she'd wrongly predicted that Japan would never risk attacking the U.S. Few could equal Martha in capturing the human detail of war, but military analysis was not her strength.

his boating buddies, barely touching his typewriter, and unable to access the white-hot focus with which he'd written *For Whom the Bell Tolls.* Yet, if Martha ever dared ask if he had a new project in mind, he reacted with disproportionate viciousness. She was a "conceited bitch," he raged, for presuming to question his work and, hatefully, he reminded her of the disparity in their literary reputations — "they'll be reading my stuff long after the worms have finished with you."[24] If Martha had been a very different kind of woman — more saintly, more gentle and without a talent of her own to defend — she might have coaxed Ernest into admitting the fears that needled him to so violent an overreaction. She might have realized that beneath his bluster lay a terror of failure, a terror that he would wake up one day and find that his gift had deserted him and all his words had gone. She might have realized, too, that he was equally afraid of his own nature. His father, cursed with depression, had killed himself, and Ernest sensed that the darkness was inside himself as well. But weakness was difficult to admit, especially when Martha was at her most impatiently judgemental. Instead, Ernest turned away from her, and when America went to war, in December 1941, he furnished himself with the perfect excuse for both ignoring her and neglecting his writing.

Cuba and its surrounding waters had suddenly become targets for German attack and, inspired by rumoured sightings of Nazi agents and lurking U-boats, Ernest had formed a sea patrol unit, using his own boat *Pilar* and enlisting the help of eight other crew. He thrilled to the idea of being a man of action again, especially since a $500 monthly stipend from Central American Naval Intelligence allowed him to furnish his self-styled "Crook Shop" with an armoury of bazookas, grenades and machine guns. Martha, however, was sceptical. Early in January 1942, she'd been commissioned by *Collier's* to do some submarine hunting of her own, but had been rewarded with nothing but a dose of dengue fever. Ernest and his Crook Shop fared no better, and, as the months passed, Martha could not help but dismiss his activities as a machismo fantasy. She'd tried to suppress her doubts, concentrating on the completion of her latest novel, about a young French Caribbean woman, torn between money and love. But once the manuscript was with her publishers, she had nothing to think about except Ernest, and the barbs of distrust and disillusionment between them. It seemed to Martha a long time since she'd been able to feel or think "straight," and, in September 1943, when *Collier's* suggested a prolonged assignment in Europe, she was happy to immerse herself back in events which were so much larger, and more important, than her marriage.

Initially, she'd hoped to make Ernest come with her, and had even suggested he might write one or two of the pieces *Collier's* had proposed. It would be a way for them to rekindle the crazed hilarity of China, the purposefulness of Spain. But Ernest was angry. He was offended, first, by Martha's assumption that he could so readily abandon his spy-hunting, yet he minded even more that she would consider going to Europe without him. The barbed resentments became a thicket of spite: Martha accused Ernest of being drunk and deluded, he retaliated by calling her a selfish, unnatural wife, and, most woundingly of all, a moral hypocrite, who only went chasing after war because she was greedy for fame.

By the time Martha left for New York to catch her Pan Am Clipper flight, she'd re-established peace. "We have a good wide life ahead of us," she promised, "we will write books and see the autumns together and walk around the cornfield waiting for pheasants and we will be very cosy." Yet, it was impossible for her to disguise the lift of excitement in the letters she wrote to Ernest during her journey. The two of them had agreed on a code that would tell him where she might travel after London — a reference to Herbert Matthews meant Italy, one to the photographer Robert Capa meant North Africa — and

Martha longed to see both. "I am happy as a firehorse, feeling ahead already the strange places," she admitted, and even now the distance between her and Ernest was threatening to stretch longer than the promised three months.[25]

Martha had last been in London in 1938, and when she arrived in early November 1943 she was shocked by its battered alteration. The worst of the Blitz damage had been cleared away — the larger bomb sites had been screened behind hoardings and the craters had been filled — but she could still see how much life had been blasted from the city. Glassless windows stared from abandoned buildings, and sheared-off walls bore the ghostly lineaments of stairways, fireplaces and lintels, traces of families dead or departed. After the bright, clear air of Cuba, London seemed shrouded in a permanent gloom: smog-bound by day and blacked-out by night, when the only sources of light were the wavering beams of torches or the blue phantom glow of dimmed headlamps.

As a creature of warmth, Martha also suffered from the relentless chill of under-heated rooms, from bath water that was never quite hot. Yet, these small deprivations aroused in her a new admiration for the British. "Nothing becomes them like a catastrophe. Slowness, understatement, complacency change into endurance, a refusal to panic, and pride, the begetter of self-discipline."[26] It seemed to her that their detestable native phlegm had been elevated to heroic resistance, and, with the "weasel" Chamberlain long gone from office, she was ready to applaud them as champions in the fight against fascism.

On arrival, Martha's first instinct had been to telephone Virginia and invite her to breakfast. If she felt wary of the American press corps in London, she now regarded Ginny as her "good close pal," one of the most loyal of her female friends.[27] It was on her instructions that Martha went to Savile Row to be fitted for her uniform (Virginia having secured her own military accreditation via a freelance contract with the *Chicago Sun*). And it was through her that Martha acquired a rather grand and agreeable circle of London friends. She was particularly taken by Duff and Diana Cooper: "a little guy in an absurd high collar with a fine honest head," his wife, "so beautiful you wouldn't believe." Warmed by the novelty of her new London set, she realized how very isolated she'd allowed herself to become in Cuba: "I am in love with the human race again and thank God for that," Martha wrote to Ernest, unconscious perhaps of the wounds she was inflicting. "It was getting sort of dry inside my head, but the dryness has gone."[28]

Over the next three months, she channelled

that love into her prose. She celebrated the British in their war effort: the teenage cockney boys who worked long cheerful days in munitions factories; the teams of doctors and therapists patiently intent on rehabilitating burned, disfigured soldiers; and, above all, the bomber pilots who risked their lives over Germany each night. There was little new in the story that Martha wrote about her visit to a Lincolnshire air base, but she saw her material through a novelist's eye. Sitting with the men as they awaited their evening's orders, she thought they had the air of "good tidy children," drinking "the shaving mugs of sweetened, lukewarm tea" that seemed so comforting to them all, and they seemed to her far too young to be undertaking such perilous missions. When they took off for Germany — their Lancaster planes like "enormous deadly black birds going off into the night" — Martha tried to imagine the physical and emotional toll of what lay ahead.[29] Sacrifice and heroism — words that she feared had been lost with the Loyalist cause — had returned to her professional lexicon, and she concluded her *Collier's* article with the plea that all those airmen who survived this war should be rewarded with whatever "lovely life they want. Let those of us, who have never been where they have been, see to it."[30]

The "cosmic indifference" that had clouded

441

Martha's faith in journalism had lifted; she was convinced once more of her power to influence and inform, and the most urgent piece she wrote from London was about the prison that Poland had become under Nazi occupation. She interviewed three Polish men who'd managed to escape, and was stricken to hear their accounts of how blonde, blue-eyed Polish girls were being sent to Nazi breeding farms to produce Aryan babies for the Greater Reich; to hear about the seizure of Polish farms and businesses, the murdering of community leaders and the ruthlessness with which the nation's Jews had been dispatched. One of the three men was a Jew from Warsaw, who had been corralled into the city's ghetto along with the rest of his community; he described in agonized detail how those who hadn't perished from hunger or disease had been left to the mercy of bored German guards, who amused themselves with "rabbit-hunting" competitions.

As Martha renewed her commitment to speak for the "silenced millions," she realized that she'd always been a journalist at heart, that even her fiction was driven by a need to know and understand the world.[31] "I'll never see enough as long as I live," she wrote to Ernest, and she begged him to come to London. "I think it is so vital for you to see everything. You would be the darling of all and as you are so much smarter than me I would not have to work so hard because you could do my thinking for me."[32] Ernest might have been tempted, but, despite her flattery, Martha could never suppress the tough-corded honesty that was both her gift and her curse. With a monumental lack of tact, she concluded that it had been wrong of them both to retreat to the finca, adding that, when she looked back at their life together in Cuba, it seemed to her like "being strangled by . . . tropical flowers."

Ernest, stung, did not come to London and he felt doubly wounded when Martha wrote in late January to say that she was delaying her promised return. There had been too much to write about in London and she had yet to report from Italy, where, in another twist of the war's narrative, the Allies were now fighting against a German assault.

Mussolini's war had not gone well: his failed campaigns had earned the contempt of his people and, on 25 July 1943, he'd been arrested and stripped of his powers. The King and Prime Minister had then moved into negotiations with the Allies, signing an armistice on 3 September. But Hitler had not been prepared to cede Italy without a fight. As German troops were sent in to reinstate Mussolini, the Allies had launched their own invasion, Operation Avalanche, and, on 9 September, had landed an armada of men and arms at the southern port of Salerno.

The battle for Italy would be among the bloodiest of the war. By early 1944, the Allied troops (an international mix of American, British, Polish, Canadian and Free French) had become stalled at Monte Cassino, and it was here that Martha was heading. She was to travel via Algiers — now under Allied control — where she'd been invited to stay with Diana and Duff Cooper, the latter having just been appointed to the FCNL, a committee tasked with planning the postwar future of France. It was a delicious diversion. After the smoggy greys of London, she was dazzled by the colours of North Africa, the canary yellow of the mimosa, the morning glory that covered everything in a purpling riot; she was equally captivated by Diana, who'd immediately created a festive hubbub around herself, hosting long gregarious dinners, where the whisky made up for the terrible food, and stringing "red, blue and green fairy harem lights" in the rooms of their dusty Algiers palace. "She is lovable . . . odd . . . rum," Martha wrote to Ernest with admiration, and she was enjoyably conscious of being admired in return: "a packet of fun," wrote Diana of Martha, "yellow hair en brosse, cool slim lines and the most amusing patter imaginable."[33]

Pleasurable though Algiers was, the Italian war awaited, and, more specifically, the question of how Martha would be able to cover it. She'd only been given permission to write about the work of medical teams, not to go near any front, and her travel orders required her to report to the American Press Relations Officer, in Naples, who would arrange her transport to a military evacuation hospital, safely behind Allied lines. Obviously, this didn't suit Martha at all, but she was fortunate that the Free French forces engaged in southern Italy were far more casual about protocol. They didn't care if a journalist was male or female, and, when Martha's plane landed in Naples, it was relatively easy for her to find a French transport officer who was willing to drive her the one hundred kilometres north to the Cassino front.

The journey itself was filthy. Wind and rain whipped through their open jeep and Italy looked to Martha like a "land of snakes," blasted by bombs and shells, and infested with randomly detonating mines. But, seven kilometres south of Cassino, the weather cleared, and, as Martha lifted her face to snow-covered mountain peaks and a piercingly clear blue sky, she felt the sudden, flooding exhilaration of being a survivor. That night, she found shelter in an abandoned cellar, where an American major and a French doctor had already laid out their bedrolls and had just tuned their forces radio to a concert of cello music. The yearning sweetness of that music cut Martha to the quick, and it was all the more poignant because it was being broadcast from Berlin, transporting her back to an ideal of Europe, a Europe which had been civilized by art, not ripped apart by guns.

But, in Cassino, in February 1943, Germany was the enemy, and, dug into high, fortified positions on top of the mountains, they were mercilessly raining down shells on the French below. It was perilous for Martha to report on this section of the front, but she was told that, as long as she didn't obstruct the soldiers, she was free to take responsibility for her own movements. During the next few days, she came to revere the French for the heroism with which they fought to dislodge the Germans. At a mobile medical unit, she watched a very young doctor, half-blinded himself, using a clasp knife to perform an emergency amputation on a comrade's half-severed leg. Back in Cuba, Martha had despaired that all "the faith and the glory" had gone from the world, but, faced with these extraordinary acts of courage, she saw how facile that assumption had been. Inspired, and humbled, she vowed to "blast" Ernest loose from his Crook Shop so that he might experience this war for himself.

Before Martha left Cassino, she felt obliged to scout for some more specifically American stories for *Collier's,* so, late in February, she crossed into the U.S. zone, making her presence known to the commanding PRO. She'd resigned herself to a dreary few days of regulation and harassment, of being sidelined from any interesting action. Instead, however, she found Ginny Cowles.

Virginia had persuaded the *Daily Telegraph* to send her out to Italy, ostensibly to interview some of the desk-chair officers in strategic command of Operation Avalanche. Like Martha, she'd broken her journey with the Coopers, Diana cheering her arrival, "cold from the clouds in [her] battle dress," and, although she'd had to spend a dull few days in the Caserta HQ, studying diagrams and maps, she'd then been able to pursue her true objectives: locating Martha, and seeing some more interesting action.

Once near Cassino, Virginia had hitched a lift to the press camp in the American zone and had sweet-talked its commanding officer into providing accommodation for both Martha and herself. This was a coup, for under U.S. protocol women were prohibited from all press camps, the assumption being that an awkward, frat house rowdiness was likely to prevail, with male journalists walking around naked after showers, and even pinning pictures of half-naked girls on their walls. At the Cassino camp, however, high in the mountain village of Sessa Aurunca, there was no such rowdy behaviour. Four very bored men were in residence, and they'd been stuck at Cassino for too long to have any taste for offensive high jinks. As for the "darling, loopy British officer" who'd been entrusted with running the camp after being invalided out of action, he could not have been more delighted to welcome a couple of lively women into his care.[34]

The camp's accommodation was primitive, "a beat-up brick house" divided into squalid little cubicles, and predictably the women were not allowed near any American-run combat zone. But they were too pleased with each other to care. Virginia occupied her spare time cadging scraps from the camp kitchen to feed the half-starved children who came begging at the door. And, while Martha did try to hitch an illicit lift to the front, it was largely for form's sake. Ironically, some of her strongest writing from Cassino was inspired by her tour of an American military hospital, where she'd reflected on the fact that the men who lay broken and scarred in the wards had become, even more than weapons, the "basic material" from which this war was fought. It had seemed to her then, that the only decent response to their suffering was to honour the professionalism and dignity with which they'd served: "You speak to the wounded who look at you, assuming that they may want your company. You try not to let your own health shout down at them; and you try to keep your face and your voice clean of pity, which nobody wants."[35]

Martha's hospital report was one of six that she wrote from Europe, and *Collier's,* very pleased with her coverage, chose to honour her with a short profile. "Blonde, tall, dashing — she comes pretty close to living up to Hollywood's idea of what a big-league woman reporter should be," ran the piece.[36] Even though Martha huffed a little — resenting the attention being paid to her sex and appearance, and particularly disliking the glossy photograph that accompanied the profile — she was pleased by the accolade and touched by the quote that *Collier's* had got from Ernest: "She gets to the place, gets the stories, writes and comes home. That last is the best part."[37]

The enthusiasm of that quote was reassuring, for it was very unlike the tone of her husband's recent cables — a spate of recriminations, which had pointed out that Martha's absence was lasting for months longer than promised, and which had concluded with the stark ultimatum, "Are you a war correspondent or wife in my bed?" She hoped, now, that the sweetness of their reunion, coupled with the excitement of her war stories, would bring her forgiveness. But, when she finally returned to the finca in mid-March, Martha realized how dangerously she had underestimated Ernest's anger.[38]

The reunion was, in fact, horrible. During

her absence, Ernest had convinced himself that Martha had become "mentally imbalanced" in her hunger for war and for fame, that she was no longer capable of love. And the contempt with which he greeted her attempts to persuade him otherwise was so cold, so vicious, that Martha feared their marriage was irreparably broken.

Yet the Hemingways' troubles were far from unique. Clare Hollingworth had already lost her husband, Van, because she'd been too much the war correspondent and not the wife; Margaret Bourke-White's marriage had also collapsed, despite a prenuptial promise made by Erskine Caldwell never to try to separate her from her career. Most of the women who reported on this war would end up separated, divorced, or deliberately unattached; and back in the spring of 1943, when Helen Kirkpatrick was given her own first assignment abroad, she'd been gratefully conscious of having no husband or lover to accommodate as she shut the door on her London flat.

Helen had hardly been chaste over the last few years. She'd been courted by several men, the most serious of whom was Richard Keane, diplomatic correspondent for the *Times.* When she'd held a dinner for the visiting American theatre critic Alexander Woollcott (a wild dinner that had ended with quantities of brandy and music from a band of street musicians), it was noted that at least "half a dozen" bachelors had been in attendance. But Helen had made no commitment to any of them, and, when the *Chicago Daily News* had assigned her to Algiers, the fact that she might be gone from London for an indefinite period was of no consequence to anyone but herself.

One of the issues she'd been sent to cover was the emerging power struggle between Henri Giraud and Charles De Gaulle, the two French generals most likely to lead their country, once it had been freed from German occupation. De Gaulle was not popular with the Americans, and Helen, who'd met him in London when he was first trying to marshal the Free French army, could understand why: "a man of no small talk at all," she reported, adding that he was rarely able to break a smile and was far too impatient for diplomacy.[39] But Giraud lacked support among the French, principally due to the period he'd served as commander of the hated Vichy army, and Helen was fascinated to observe the "tangled political situation" that was now being played out on the sidelines of the war, and the power grabs already underway for the ensuing peace.[40]*

Most of all, however, she adored her new

* Both generals were sitting on the committee to

life in North Africa. Even though there was hot water for only an hour each day and her billet was "a terrible room on the edge of the Casbah," Helen was awed by the "incredible beauty" of the landscape, and exhilarated by the dances, bathing parties and sightseeing trips that were possible now the worst of the fighting was over. "I haven't felt so happy in years," she told her parents. "I don't mind the discomfort, which really isn't discomfort but merely lack of luxury. I feel so terrifically well and full of energy."[41]

Then, in July 1943, came the scent of fresh war news. Although Mussolini had yet to fall, Churchill was impatient to launch an attack on the southern coast of Italy, which he considered the "soft underbelly" of Axis-held Europe. His first target was Sicily, and, because this was a relatively easy distance from Algiers, Helen put in an immediate request to go there. It was now, however, that she came up against the limitations of her own accreditation, for, while her request was approved by U.S. military command, the local PRO had other views. He insisted that it was impossible for her to go to Sicily because no "provision" had been made for any women. And, while Helen refused to let him

---

which Duff Cooper had been appointed British representative.

get away with that smug euphemism — "If you mean the latrine business," she'd snapped, "there aren't any latrines at the front, it is exactly like camping in the woods" — the PRO was immovable, and the closest she got to the action in Sicily was flying over the island in a military plane.[42]

Throughout her career, Helen had tried to stay clear of sexual politics, hoping to be judged neutrally, for her work alone. She'd always been at pains to avoid special treatment — arriving in Algiers, she'd been offered a comfortable hotel but had insisted on a regular army billet, along with the men — and if ever she'd been confronted with professional prejudice, she'd preferred to fight her battles alone, without turning for support to other women. Like many of her generation, Helen regarded the organized, militant feminism of the early twentieth century as a closed chapter. The vote had been won, the professions had been opened up and, by 1943, the very word "feminist" had become associated with an outmoded politics of stridency and suffering. But the complacent idiocy of the Algiers PRO had roused Helen to a more combative anger, and when Margaret Bourke-White had appeared in Algiers, and was also being refused a permit for Sicily, Helen was pleased to have another woman with whom to vent her frustration. The two of them formed an immediate kinship, saluting each other as fellow professionals and uniting in a cheerfully satirical alliance against the pettiness of the army bureaucrats. When their PRO enquired patronizingly what Margaret and Helen "found to talk about," the brilliant war photographer and the equally distinguished journalist rolled their eyes at each other and replied, sarcastically, "Clothes."*

Eventually, Helen got her combat posting, her path smoothed by Eisenhower's chief of staff, and, in early October, she boarded a French destroyer for Corsica, where the Allies were in the final stages of ousting the occupying Germans. At first sight, the island looked idyllic, "completely unspoiled, the most beautiful I have ever seen." But, hitching a lift with three American officers, she found that the port city of Bastia was still a raging war zone; entire neighbourhoods had been razed to the ground and German marksmen were battling with rogue groups of Corsicans. This was a far more visceral kind of war reporting than the Blitz; Helen and her companions had to crawl across the main square under fire, and they had to sleep that

* Helen was still far better placed than her British counterparts, and this was the year that sixty-two of them formed their own press club in London to lobby the British War Office for women's accreditation.

454

night in an abandoned nightclub, covering themselves with filthy velvet drapes. The following morning, when conditions were safe, Helen went down to watch Allied troops securing the port, where she learned that they were being hampered by booby-trapped corpses — young Axis soldiers, killed in action, whose bodies had been piled together and stuffed with explosives. To her, this seemed the most barbarous revelation of German cruelty: "What a people," she raged in a letter home. "I never want to have to listen to anyone talking about the decent ones." And, while she knew that she'd signed herself up for horrors, in becoming a war correspondent, she also knew herself well enough to respect her own limits. Driving away from Bastia, her American companions had stopped to inspect a burned Italian tank. Helen had refused to join them, however, for, as she carefully explained to her parents, she knew the sight of the incinerated crew would remain with her: "I've seen enough of the human body spilled over pavements in this war to wish to see no more than is absolutely necessary. I find I dream of it afterwards and I see no point in looking at that kind of thing unless it cannot be avoided."[43]

But there would be more blood and trauma for Helen to face when, on 31 October, she flew to Naples to join the British 10th Armoured Division on its northward advance.

It was a difficult journey: the autumn rains had set in, cold and hard, turning sections of the road into perilous mudslides. Enemy planes were also patrolling the route, strafing the British convoy at their leisure. And although Helen was being sent to the supposed safety of an American mobile surgical unit, close to the mountain town of Venafro, the four days she spent with that unit were among the most dangerous of her war.

The unit gave emergency treatment to soldiers whose injuries were too grave for them to be transported to more distant evacuation camps, and it was pitched on a rough piece of ground, barely a mile from the front. The barrage of noise was constant, as was the risk from a passing shell or bomb. Whenever Helen used the one available latrine — essentially a hole in the ground — she was acutely conscious of the German reconnaissance planes within whose sights she was in "chilling" view.[44] But her fears for herself were overshadowed by her concern for the medical staff, who worked under atrocious conditions. The unit itself was little more than a huddle of tents, which provided inadequate shelter from the driving rain, and doctors were performing up to twenty operations a day under sodden canvas and on ground that was slick with mud and gore. Helen tried to offer what assistance she could, fetching pails of water, swabbing away the blood, performing very minor nursing duties. Often, she had to brace herself against the more serious casualties: men who were delivered to the camp with bashed-in skulls, with flayed or flapping flesh, with bones sticking out from shattered limbs. "I found I could tolerate anything as long as I didn't see the face," she wrote. "When they were operating on the head, that I couldn't watch — I didn't care for that because the casualty became a person."[45]

The doctors and nurses who worked on those men were among the "unsung heroes" of the Allied campaign, Helen wrote, possessed of the same awe-inspiring yet modest courage as the radio operators, engineers, and the ordinary ranks: "There isn't much glory and there isn't any glamour in mud, C rations, sleeping in foxholes and crawling up the sides of mountains on your hands and knees," she reminded her readers, yet it was by these small daily feats of endurance that the war was being won.[46] She wanted to see more of Italy, and she was dreading a recall to London, even though her own exposure to the mud and rain had got her hospitalized with a chest infection. In early December, when Helen was summoned to Algiers by her publisher, Colonel Knox, she was hoping against hope that all he wanted from her was an informal update on ground conditions in

Italy, and that he would then sign off on her return.

Since she last saw the Colonel, he'd been appointed secretary of the U.S. navy, and, in keeping with his status, he'd been allocated a luxuriously appointed villa in Algiers. Helen, who'd barely had time to change out of her muddy boots and filthy uniform, was dazed by the polish of her surroundings and by the army of "Filipino stewards in white jackets running around with cocktails." She was also caught badly off guard when she was ushered into Knox's office and informed by her boss that, far from being allowed to continue her coverage of Italy, she was required to return immediately to her desk. Wreathed in pipe smoke and official protocol, the Colonel had intimated that the order had come from above, that it was top secret and Helen was not to question it. He did, however, hint that any disappointment she might currently be feeling would shortly be compensated. She was needed in London, he said, to assist with an organizational shake-up of the press, itself necessitated by a major Allied initiative. And given that Helen had already predicted so much of the war so accurately, the Colonel must have known she would guess that the initiative to which he was referring was the liberation of France.

Like everyone, Helen had yearned for this — if the Germans could be ousted from

France, it would be a body blow for Hitler, a symbolic and military defeat from which even he might fail to recover. But she also knew how challenging were the odds. The Germans had erected a solid line of defence along the western coast of France, which only a massive force could breach; she herself had written how, until the Allies had built up their armies to sufficient strength, it would be "suicidal" for them to make the attempt. Yet, from everything Knox had hinted, the assault would be set in motion the following year. And, while Helen had no option but to return to London and await further orders, she'd already decided that the liberation of France was a story she would not miss; she'd already promised herself that, as soon as Allied soldiers had been landed on French soil, she would find a way of getting there too.

CHAPTER TWELVE:
D-DAY, 1944

"The invasion feels like something
we have always had"
MARTHA GELLHORN[1]

Helen had to endure six months of delay, frustration and, most dangerously, of hope before Operation Overlord was launched, and, by early May, she was writing to her parents, "I'm just about ready to start chewing rugs." Before the Allied armada could sail, a smokescreen of fake intelligence had to be fabricated to conceal both its timing and destination from the enemy. Weather conditions also had to be calm. And, if Helen fought against impatience during those long months of waiting, she was additionally burdened with the managerial task to which Knox had elected her — preparing for the media storm which would certainly erupt once the liberation campaign was underway.

Given the number of journalists who would require access to the campaign story, the Allied command, now designated SHAEF

(Supreme Headquarters of the Allied Expeditionary Force), had called for a committee of four to manage the logistics of the situation. They would determine which of the visiting journalists could be admitted into London briefings and which would receive the military communiqués second hand; they would also decide how many reporters and photographers could feasibly be permitted to travel to France with the first wave of troops and what measures were needed to ensure their copy could be filed. Helen — the only woman on the committee — was tasked with issues relating to newspaper coverage, while Ed Murrow dealt with radio, and the two other members divided the magazine and wire services between them.

It was a tribute to Helen's knowledge, to her steadiness and powers of organization, that she'd been given this appointment, but the work was dull and it would not, as she'd hoped, be rewarded with a permit for France. A total of 558 writers, photographers and radio journalists were being allowed to cross the Channel on D-Day, the first day of the invasion, and, with SHAEF having tightened its accreditation protocol to ensure stricter controls of the press, the regulations concerning women were now punitively specific, and none were to be allowed anywhere near the fighting. Helen had protested, pointing out that she'd already spent days within range of enemy shells and that, as a reporter in France, she would face no more danger than the nurses in surgical units. But, while voices had been raised in her support, including one Texan colonel who'd offered to bet five pounds on Helen Kirkpatrick being able "to dig a latrine faster than any man in this room," the prohibition was to remain absolute.[2]*

Towards the end of May, as the men of the press began disappearing from London, Helen had to bite down on her disappointment. Operation Overlord was being orchestrated in such secrecy that she could not even go down to the coastal areas where the invasion force was being marshalled — and there was just one woman, Iris Carpenter, who would glimpse something of the giant army camp into which much of southern England had been transformed. Iris had been given special dispensation to travel down to Kent, because her children were still living there with relatives. Her reporter's antennae had prickled as she'd spotted flowering hedgerows that were "spikey with guns and jammed tight

---

* Had Helen known about the female agents in S.O.E., the Special Operations Executive, who were being sent out to France to assist the resistance in advance of Operation Overlord, and whose life expectancy would be just six weeks, she would surely have used them to strengthen her case.

with vehicles," and sleepy villages that "bristled with men, armour and equipment."[3] While she was under strict orders not to report on anything she saw, there was no way she could ignore the story unfolding around her, and, hoping to make informal contact with some of the soldiers, she volunteered her services to a Red Cross group who were delivering coffee and doughnuts to an American camp nearby.

Iris was a very attractive woman, a porcelain blonde, with a tough streak of humour and subversion. At the camp, she found a group of bored young GIs who were lonely for female company and eager to talk, and, while they could say nothing about the approaching operation, they were very forthcoming in their views on England, especially the beer (tepid) and the local girls, who they claimed were always ready for "a pretty good time" if bribed with sufficient chocolate and sweet talk. The men snickered that they would kill their sweethearts back home if they "put out" that way, but, if Iris was offended by their callowness, she didn't judge. Some of these GIs were barely out of their teens, and she could only guess what strain they must be under as they waited, day after day, for their orders to embark.

She was back at the camp when those orders came through, and close to tears as she heard the men trying to joke away their nerves. It was 2 June 1944, and these American servicemen were to be among the 2.5 million troops setting sail for five targeted beaches — respectively code-named Omaha, Utah, Gold, Juno and Sword — which lay on the Normandy peninsula in north-west France. Miserably, for these overwound men, their departure was delayed by storms over the English Channel. But, on 6 June, the weather had cleared, and, in London, Helen was woken by an immense weight of sound as British fighters and bombers flew over the city, wave after wave of planes en route for France, to provide air cover for the Allied armada.

Buzzing with anticipation, she went directly to SHAEF headquarters to receive the first of the morning's briefings, and for the next sixteen hours she was travelling between there and her office, processing news of the invasion. As she herself reported, there were cautious grounds for optimism: "The first landings today were made on the Normandy coast of France at six a.m. Landing craft continued to disembark initial assault troops through eight a.m. First reports indicate that minesweepers had effectively cleared long lanes for the convoys to go in and for bombardment ships to get into position for naval shelling of the beach and enemy artillery . . ." However, as the hours wore on, that optimism faltered under reports of the Germans' implacable defence. And on day two of the invasion, when Martha Gellhorn managed to bypass SHAEF and actually set foot on Omaha Beach, she would witness scenes of carnage beyond even her powers of description.

Martha had returned to London fully keyed up for Operation Overlord, and had been appalled to learn that she was to be kept in quarantine with "a good percentage of the world press." She'd telephoned Helen with a breezy overture of friendliness — her suggestion that "it's time we met" almost certainly an attempt to gain some inside traction.[4] But Helen was powerless to help, and, on 6 June, Martha had to wait in the "great guarded room" where the briefings were held and where she was to be spoon-fed the news like everyone else.[5] By the end of the day, she'd already lost patience, and, even though she risked being court-martialled and losing her accreditation, she was resolved to find some way of reaching France.

She had no clear plan in her mind, but, under the cover of her uniform, she was able to hitch a ride to one of the English ports (she never identified which) and, once there, to persuade the military policeman on guard that she had permission to interview some American nurses before they set sail. The policeman nodded her through and, forcing herself to look purposeful, Martha headed towards a large vessel moored nearby, with a Red Cross sign painted clearly on its hull. Walking up the gangway, hardly knowing what she was doing, she searched the corridors for an empty bathroom and locked herself in to wait.

Martha had been luckier than she knew in getting this far. Reporting restrictions were very jittery around the docks, and, the following day, when Ruth Cowan was sent by Associated Press to watch the first injured soldiers returning home, she was accosted by an agitated PRO who told her that she'd be shot if she tried to speak to any of them. But, even if Martha had fully understood the risks she was running, she was not in a mood for caution. She was firing on cylinders of pure rage — rage against the military bureaucrats who persisted in treating women like "lepers," but also against Ernest, who had finally agreed to go back to war journalism, but, in an act of pure malevolence, had done so by ousting Martha from her position with *Collier's*.

When she'd returned to Cuba in March, Martha had tried to believe that she and Ernest would still find a way back to each other. She'd known that neither of them was entirely innocent, neither entirely guilty, as they'd battled over what he dismissed as her "war craziness." Ernest could be monstrous

466

— a coercive bully and a supreme egotist — but she accepted that there was a commensurate ruthlessness in herself, a "little empty space" of selfish independence which she had to "keep free or die." She'd turned against Bertrand when he'd encroached on that space, and now she was kicking against Ernest.[6] What she failed to understand, however, was that her long absence in Europe had crossed a line. Ernest had loved Martha with a greedy, needy wholeheartedness, but, once he felt betrayed by her, he was capable of withdrawing himself entirely and punishing her in the cruellest possible way. After a fortnight of snarling rows and sullen silences, he suddenly announced that he was going to Europe after all. And with a viciousness that winded Martha, he added that he would not be going there as her companion, but her replacement — as the newly appointed *Collier's* "Special Correspondent for the Allied Invasion."

Martha's world caved. Only a month ago, the magazine had been feting her as their prized "gal" reporter, and she could not believe that Charles Colebaugh would so readily abandon her for the cachet of the Hemingway name. In fairness to Colebaugh, he may well have predicted that Martha's movements would be restricted by the new SHAEF protocol, and that his budget was better spent on a man. But he'd made a sacrifice of her, nevertheless, and, bereft and floundering, she wrote to Eleanor Roosevelt, "I have lost out on the thing I most care about seeing or writing of in the world and maybe in my whole life. I was a fool to come back from Europe and I knew it."[7]

Still, Martha refused to be beaten. At the beginning of May, while Ernest was preparing to catch an RAF flight to England (a flight she herself had negotiated), she was pressuring *Collier's* to let her work freelance. She had to fund and organize her own travel, but, with the help of Allen Grover, she managed to get a berth on a Norwegian freighter which was transporting military equipment to Liverpool. The voyage was long — twenty days — and at first Martha wondered how she could endure it. Fog shrouded the Atlantic and, with no other passengers on board, she had little to do but pace through the ruins of her marriage. She wanted to believe that Ernest was a good man — a great man, even — and that the two of them had simply been wrong for each other. Yet, the very thought of him frightened her, and she longed "most violently" to be out of the marriage and to be rid of the Hemingway name.[8]

As the days passed, however, the weight of failure, humiliation and misery began to lift. Martha could sense that her mind was shifting back into gear, ideas for new stories were forming, and, by the time the Liverpool skyline appeared on the horizon, she was startled by a sudden "wild happiness." She was back in the war, back in the game, and, for the first time in years, she felt close to being her own woman again — "free to breathe, live, look upon the world and find it however it is."[9] So resolute was she to embrace her independence that she wanted to confront Ernest as soon as she reached London and to insist on the clean "amputating pain" of a divorce. He, however, had been injured in a drunken car accident and, when she visited him in hospital, he was holding court among an unruly crowd of friends.[10] That same crowd hovered around him even after he was discharged, and, picking up on the fact that Ernest was circulating vindictive stories at her expense, Martha chose to retreat and focus only on her work and the war.

Nevertheless, her thoughts had flown automatically to Ernest when, on 6 June, she was awoken at dawn by the "giant factory of bombers." "Now getting scared. Worried for E," she jotted in her diary.[11] She tried to imagine what he'd be facing as he sailed towards Normandy on one of the Allied assault crafts. But her anxiety turned to rage when she remembered how Ernest had got his place on that assault craft, and that rage helped propel her down to the docks and up the gangway of the hospital ship.

Once she'd locked herself inside the bathroom, however, she had hours of empty anxious time to wait until a groaning clank of metal signalled that the ship had weighed anchor, and was heading out to open sea. Crouching in her hiding place, Martha expected any moment to hear a rattle of the door handle, a challenging shout. But her presence remained undetected, and, when she finally dared to leave the bathroom, her uniform seemed to forestall any awkward questions. She was lucky that the ship she'd chosen to ride stowaway was crewed by merchant seamen, not American navy, and they seemed happy to leave Martha alone, as she spent the rest of the voyage up on deck, drinking whisky and trying to picture what lay ahead in the squally darkness.

When dawn broke over Omaha Red, the American sector of Omaha Beach, the scene that revealed itself was unlike anything she could have imagined. "It was the greatest naval traffic jam in history," she wrote, "so enormous, so awesome, that it felt more like an act of nature than anything man made."[12] Ships were crowding the limits of her vision — assault crafts delivering men and machines to the beach, hospital ships taking on board the wounded, battleships firing shells at the enemy defence — and, for a few moments, Martha could only gape, transfixed by the immensity of the scene.

The scale of the Allied armada had been

no less stunning to the Germans, when they'd awoken on 6 June to see a giant wall of ships looming out of the sea mist. Even though they'd been warned of a possible assault, they'd never pictured something so colossal, and their first response had been one of panic. Yet, as the first Allied soldiers had clambered down from their landing craft, wading through the shallow sea with their heavy load of equipment, the Germans were shocked to be handed such easy targets. "I felt pity for them," recalled one gunner. "They kept arriving . . . and we fired on them . . . My loader shook his head, saying that the Americans should not sacrifice their men in this way."[13]*

By the time Martha reached Omaha Red the following morning, the shore was a slaughterhouse. Once she'd stopped marvelling at the size of the armada, she could see that the waters around her were churned up with oil, mud and blood, and bobbing on the surface was the nightmarish flotsam of the dead — sodden and barely human, "like swollen greyish sacks."[14]

It was the living who demanded Martha's

---

* Although historians have acknowledged the detailed accuracy of the information given in Eckhertz's collection of interviews, *D Day Through German Eyes,* some have queried the provenance of the interviews themselves.

attention, though. During the last twenty-four hours, the Americans had secured a small but critical strip of beach, and the wounded were now laid out on the sand, awaiting rescue and treatment. Small landing craft were launched from Martha's ship to collect the casualties, and, as the onboard medical teams swung into action, she pitched in too, fetching water, organizing corned-beef sandwiches for those who could eat, and acting as interpreter for the non-American casualties — some of them French, some of them captured Germans.

When darkness fell, Martha was permitted to go ashore to assist with the recovery of more bodies. Even though the fighting had moved beyond the cliffs, the noise on the beach was overwhelming — shrieking metal, staccato gunfire and anguished cries of pain. Every time a shell burst, Martha could see the wreckage of trucks and tanks illuminated with a ghastly clarity, and it was astonishing to her that, even in the midst of this inferno, she could still smell, somewhere, the sweetness of summer grass. During that long night, she and her colleagues moved beyond fear or fatigue as they located the injured and got them lifted onto stretchers and ferried back to the ship. "There is a point where you feel yourself so small and helpless in such an enormous insane nightmare of a world that you cease to give a hoot about anything,"

Martha observed. "Day merges into night and the invasion . . . [feels like] something we have always had, so that no other condition of life seems imaginable."[15]

At last, the ship could take no more bodies, and, as it turned back towards England, Martha continued to do what she could. The GIs inspired her to helpless, tender admiration: "Men smiled who were in such pain that all they can really have wanted to do was turn their faces away and cry, and men made jokes when they needed their strength just to survive."[16] But, for the wounded Germans, she had only a fascinated revulsion. Under the rules of the Geneva Convention, she was forbidden to question them, but she stared at them openly, surprised that they were not the blond Aryan giants of her imagination. She assumed they must have been either opportunists or dupes to have fought for the Nazi regime, men who "either take advantage or take orders, there is nothing in between." And, secure in that condemnation, she sympathized with the "gentle-faced" U.S. lieutenant she was attending, who, on hearing that the patient in the bunk below him was German, had whispered in disgust, "I'd kill him if I could move."[17]★

The two articles that Martha wrote on her

★ The fittest German troops had actually been posted to fight the Russians, or to defend the more return were among her best, written with an exact observation, a simple human register that communicated the immensity of the invasion without melodrama or cliché. She knew they were good and she might have minded that Ernest's name was emblazoned above hers on the *Collier's* masthead, had it not been for the trouble she now faced. Her presence on board the hospital ship had been discovered by an American PRO, and, given the doubly egregious nature of her offence — riding stowaway and entering a prohibited combat zone — she could not possibly appeal the punishment that had been determined by SHAEF. As soon as Martha was back in London, her AGO was to be rescinded and she was to be escorted to a nurses' training camp, and remain there until further notice.

From SHAEF's perspective, the punishment was reasonable. Once a sufficiently large beachhead had been secured in Normandy, they were planning to grant limited day trips to women, and, at that point, Martha's accreditation would be restored. But this concession was meaningless to her. "I had been sent to Europe to do my job," she wrote, "which was not to report the rear areas

southern coastline of France, where the Allied invasion had been most expected.

or the women's angle."[18] The suffering and the heroism that she'd witnessed on Omaha Red had redoubled her determination to write everything she could about this war. She believed it was her duty to become the eyes, ears and heart of all the "millions of people in America who are desperately in need of seeing but cannot see for themselves"; as soon as she realized that no one was actually guarding her at the camp, Martha searched for a gap in the perimeter fence, rolled under it and hitched her way back to the Dorchester.[19]

By now, she'd decided that it made little difference whether her AGO was returned or not. Although she went to the trouble of writing a formal letter of complaint, protesting at the "curiously condescending treatment of women correspondents," she was ready to wash her hands of SHAEF. The success of her stowaway adventure convinced her she was far more likely to get the stories that mattered if she improvised her way through the war. And she was resolved, now, to operate by one simple rule: "if they don't want to accredit you, you just do it, any little lie will do."[20]

France was still too heavily regulated for her, though, so Martha opted for Italy, where it was easier to sneak a way around the rules. She hitched a plane ride to Naples, fooling its pilot into believing she was searching for a missing fiancé, and from there she joined a convoy of Poles, the Carpathian Lancers, who were monitoring the Germans' retreat from the rear. As they headed north, towards Rome, the convoy came under regular aerial attack — "it was a game of roulette and you had to hope that if you were hit, you crawled out before being burned alive" — but, for Martha, the dangers were nothing to what she'd witnessed in Normandy. The Italian summer was golden, and camping out with the Poles was "like being gypsies or a small-town circus," as the men drank wine every night and sang rowdy, melancholic, complicated songs about the battles they'd fought.[21]

By late July, Martha had reached Florence, where the Allies were still battling for control of the city. Enemy shells were blasting from German positions, there was fighting in some of the outlying streets, yet, here, in the confusion of this urban battle zone, Martha again met up with Ginny. It had been four months since Virginia was last near combat, during which time she'd been set the driest of tasks, writing a primer on the U.S. constitution for British readers. Yet, when Martha had returned with her stories from Omaha Red, Virginia had felt the call of the battlefield and had persuaded the *Daily Telegraph* — to whom she was still contributing the occasional piece — to send her back to Italy. It's probable the two women had estimated a date for their reunion and that they'd planned to stick together, for just before Virginia had left London, she'd contacted General de Lattre de Tassigny, commander of what was then known as French Army B, and obtained signed permission for both herself and Martha to travel with the Free French through Italy as *correspondantes de guerre.*

Typically, there was a fuss from the British and Americans, who clung defensively to their own rules, and Virginia was forced to send a message of complaint to General Sir Maitland Wilson, Supreme Commander of the Mediterranean operations, demanding that her permit be respected. But she made her way unhindered to Florence, and, once there, was not only reunited with Martha, but also with Nigel Nicolson her intelligence officer from Tunisia. "It was always wonderful to see Virginia, with her glad smile, her lovely voice, her adventurousness, her style," Nicolson later recalled; but she was no less pleased to see him. The middle of Florence was still an active battle zone, still prohibited to journalists without military escort, and, in Nigel, Virginia knew she had a willing volunteer.

Together, the two of them spent an extraordinary day touring around the historic monuments of the city, and concurring that it felt both miraculous and wrong to be art tourists in the middle of a war. An agreement had been reached between the Axis and the Allies that the cultural treasures of Florence should be preserved, as should those of Venice and Rome. But the fighting had still made devastating encroachments: the Ponte Vecchio was in ruins, a hole had been blasted in the Uffizi Gallery, and the dead lay in open pits in the Boboli Gardens. When Virginia and Nigel clambered over piles of rubble to inspect the magnificent cathedral, it seemed fantastically improbable that the Duomo's Gothic carvings, its magnificent dome and campanile had survived the shelling; and it was stranger still to see Benozzo Gozzoli's masterpiece, *The Journey of the Magi,* undamaged, in the chapel of the Medici Palace. These were the kinds of details around which Virginia always liked to peg her war reports, yet her tour of Florence was abruptly cut short when, walking around the Uffizi, she was bent double by what Nigel later described as "some awful cramp or internal pain."[22]

So excruciating was the pain, Virginia could barely walk, and Nigel had to drive her to the nearest British medical station, where the doctors considered her condition sufficiently serious to order her back to London. There's no record of an actual diagnosis — it's possible the British were simply looking to get a troublesome female removed from the field. But, whatever the nature of her illness, it would lose Virginia her Italian adventure, and it would also mark the end of her combat career. Once she was back in London, she had her book on the American constitution to finish, yet she was also wondering if she'd exhausted her appetite for war. The following year, she and Martha would write an autobiographical comedy about their experiences as correspondents, and Virginia's character, Jane, would list all the reasons why she was falling out of love with the job: the obstructive PROs and the egotistical male journalists, the grind of sleeping rough and the ghastliness of military rations. "I'm even getting tired of being shot at," shrugged Virginia's fictive self — and, for a woman who'd prided herself on braving enemy fire in Spain, Finland, Dover and the North African desert, this was the most revealing admission of all.

Martha may have momentarily regretted the loss of Ginny's jokes, her shrewdness and her balance, but she also knew that, while she was travelling solo, she was far more open to the serendipitous encounters, the fleeting relationships that were, for her, the essence of war reportage. During her remaining time in Florence, she shared her lodgings with a British captain, a talented pianist who played Chopin études while Allied shells "whistled over the house like insane freight engines." She spent two days and nights with a "tall and beautiful and funny" American major, with whom she fancied herself half in love.[23] Then, when she'd seen enough of the city, she found a Canadian regiment willing to let her ride with them to the Apennine Mountains, where they were planning a major assault on the Germans' Gothic Line.

The Canadians were travelling in a vast armoured convoy, which threw up a tunnel of dust several miles long on the dry Italian roads. The men's faces were coated with a "greenish white" film of grit, and, to Martha, their dusty pallor looked like the colour of fear. She knew that the battle awaiting these soldiers would be terrible: the Gothic Line was a formidably solid wall of pill boxes, tank traps and machine-gun nests, and its breaching would cost thousands of lives. Martha had tried to communicate to her readers how difficult it was to describe the overall feel of a battle, to capture the "jigsaw puzzle of fighting men, bewildered terrified civilians, noise, smells, jokes, pain, fear, unfinished conversations and high explosives." But, when she came to document this particular attack, she felt she owed it to the men to be unflinchingly exact.[24] She described what it was like to peer inside the turret of a crippled Sherman tank, and see its Canadian crew spattered across the interior in "pieces of flesh and much blood"; she described the body of an incinerated German who'd been thrown free of his own exploding tank — a half-

480

human thing, with "two black, claw-like hands . . . swollen blood-caked head and . . . twisted feet." It shamed her, she wrote, to use the easy jargon of war reporting, to suggest that the Canadians had found some "soft place" through which to breach the enemy defence. Tersely, she informed her readers that "there can be no soft place where there are mines and no soft place where there are Spandaus and no soft place where there are long 88 mm guns."[25]

Over the next two weeks, Martha zigzagged around north-east Italy, observing the slow, steady rout of the Germans. No one bothered her, for, as long as she steered clear of the British and Americans, the rest of the Allied forces were too much a "hodgepodge of nationalities" to consider her their responsibility. Later, she would admit that her blonde hair and long legs had eased her way. Some of these fighting soldiers had not seen a woman in months and, for the sake of Martha's company, they were willing to let her come and go as she pleased. Perhaps she was bothered by a coarse joke or muttered innuendo, perhaps she sensed the occasional sexual threat, but, in her diaries and articles, Martha wrote only about the rare and privileged camaraderie she had felt with the men. She jeeped with them through enemy fire; she led them across a mine-strewn beach to go swimming in the sea; she discussed the technical details of warfare; and, with some of them, she developed a rapport so close that they confided intimate details of their lives, their hopes, their fears, their memories of family, which they would never have revealed to a man.*

Now that the war was turning in the Allies' favour, Martha was haunted by all those soldiers who had yet to be sacrificed: "It is awful to die at the end of summer," she mused, "when you are young and have fought a long time and when you remember with all your heart your home and your love, and when you know the war is won anyhow."[26] Just before she left Italy, she went to a beach, hoping to savour a few hours alone with a book and a bottle of sweet Italian rum, but her tranquillity was invaded by a dogfight overhead, and the sight of a pilot bailing out of his burning plane. The image of that parachute, billowing white against a clear blue sky, had a dreamlike beauty, yet Martha knew that the pilot himself must be feeling catastrophic terror, and she could not bear to see another young life being lost: "one would have to be a liar or a fool not to see this and feel it like a misery," she wrote, "because the

* As well as the Canadians, Poles and Free French fighting in Italy, there were soldiers from New Zealand, South Africa and South-East Asia.

end of all this tragic dying seems so near."[27]

Back in June, when the Allies were still fighting on the Normandy beaches, there had
seemed no end to the dying. Capturing the
peninsula had been harder than anticipated:
the port city of Caen, which Montgomery
had hoped to conquer on D-Day itself, had
taken six weeks to secure, and over the next
two months pockets of enemy resistance
continued to stall the Allies' progress as they
fought their way towards the centre of France,
village by village, town by town.

Helen was still following the invasion from
London and was complaining to her parents
that she was "doing the job of six men" —
attending press briefings, distributing news
among the other print journalists, organizing
the London office and writing her own
stories. On 21 June, permission was granted
for her and nine other women to go on the
first of their promised day trips to Normandy.
But, while Helen had been eager to see the
D-Day locations, the trip itself was an insult.
The women were confined to a small back
corner of the Allied beachhead, where they
were herded around by a particularly patron-
izing PRO, who, even during their tour of an
evacuation hospital, allowed them to speak
only to nurses and patients whom he'd
personally vetted. Helen wrote with quiet
compassion about one badly wounded boy,

"his head buried in a blanket," as he grieved for his brother, "who was killed beside him last night"; yet, like all the other women on the trip, she was fully conscious that most of her readers had lost interest in hospitals now that the fighting was approaching its climax.[28]

So offended was Helen by the pointlessness of this excursion, she refused to apply for another. But Iris Carpenter, who'd recently joined the *Boston Globe* for the sake of a U.S. accreditation, was one of several who maintained a steady pressure of complaint and eventually got their Normandy visits extended to three days. It was a victory, but it was a partial one. Not only were the women restricted to the rear fringe of the beachhead, they were now obliged to organize their own transport, and this, according to Iris, was a humiliating and time-wasting business, for a shameless number of officers were exploiting the women's situation and demanding sexual favours in return for their assistance. "No holds and no tactics, including wolfing, were barred," Iris claimed, citing the experience of one colleague who'd been promised a berth on a Channel crossing, only to discover that she was expected to share it with the ship's captain.[29]

Once in France, the women were denied all the facilities their male colleagues took for granted. They had to manage their own sleeping arrangements, finding a bunk in a moored transport ship, or a cot in a military hospital. They also had to organize their own filing arrangements; while men in the press camps had on-site censors, teletypists and radio transmitters, women had to beg one of the overworked field messengers to bike their copy to the nearest airstrip, from where it had to be flown to London, then biked to the censors at the Ministry of Information. By the time an article reached its editor's desk, it was often days, even weeks out of date. But an even more unfair and distressing consequence of this sexual apartheid was the level of risk to which women were exposed.

Sleeping in tented hospitals or on board transport ships, they were far more likely to get caught up in an enemy attack than if they'd been billeted in a press camp.* The greatest dangers of all were in London, however, where the women were required to return every three days. In the middle of June, Hitler had unleashed his new secret weapon, a V-1 radar-guided bomb that required no planes or pilots to deliver its payload — and the streets of London were once again strewn with rubble and broken glass. Even though Hitler's buzz bombs were

* The Germans, believing the Allies had adopted their own strategy of painting Red Cross signs onto military convoys and encampments, had become notorious for targeting medical facilities.

not nearly as deadly as they first appeared —
a design flaw meant they often fell short of
their intended targets — they were lethally
effective as a terror weapon. They came at
random hours of the day and night, flying in
too fast for any effective warning; but more
terrible still was the macabre buzzing of the
bomb's engine and the awful suspense for
those on the ground, who knew that, as soon
as the buzzing stopped, it meant the engine
had cut out and the bomb was about to
explode.

That moment of silence could mean death,
and, to Helen, these raids felt sinisterly
personal: "It seemed to me that every time I
took a stocking off there was a buzz bomb
overhead and I'd be sure it was looking down
at me."[30] She dreaded a return of the frayed
nerves and broken nights of the 1940 Blitz,
and it was now that she focused her efforts
on getting an official posting to France. Going straight to General Eisenhower, hinting
that SHAEF was surely in her debt for her
long months of managing the press pool, she
joked wryly that no one could be worried
about her going off to a war zone, when
London itself was one.

Eisenhower had come to admire Helen —
out in Algiers, he'd been fully aware of her
professional diligence — and, even though he
knew he was stirring a nest of bureaucratic
hornets, he ordered a permit to be issued,

which would give her unique privileges in France. On 12 July, when Helen flew out to Normandy, it seemed she'd finally been granted her place with the boys. She hadn't had to barter for her seat on the transport plane; she'd been automatically allocated a room in the pretty hotel where the other journalists were housed; and, when the first of the press tours was arranged to the freshly liberated port of Cherbourg, there was no question of her being held back.

It was 14 July and the city was celebrating its first free Bastille Day in five years. Helen's euphoria — for herself, for the victorious troops, for the people of Cherbourg — lit up the story she filed, as she described American and British soldiers marching shoulder to shoulder with French resistance fighters to join the 3,000-strong crowd who were cheering and singing in Cherbourg's main square. "There is nothing to drink in Cherbourg but we are all intoxicated," she wrote. "American soldiers started dancing with French girls and soon the circle of dancers grew larger with French and British sailors and soon civilians joining in."[31]

That intoxication kept Helen flying through the next fortnight. She'd been assigned to a division of British troops, with whom she had almost unfettered access to the war: "We used to set out in the mornings to find out where things were happening. And if there was a good tank battle going on down near Caen, we'd go down there and watch it. You know, it was rather like choosing which theatre to go to today."[32] Now that the Allied advance was gaining ground, she dared to believe the end of the war must be close. "The Boche is licked and fighting with the desperation of a beaten man just before he goes down," she wrote jubilantly to her parents. There were unexpected joys, too: a rich beef stew cooked for her by a grateful farmer and his wife, and a chance encounter with her brother.[33] Kirk, as a newly appointed intelligence officer, had been sent out to Normandy with the second wave of troops, and Helen discovered him in a restaurant, celebrating his birthday with fellow officers. "I'm completely happy," she wrote home. "This is the life I love, including the dirt, which seems to be a necessary accessory of war. The dust [is] inches thick on my face. Sicily-dust, Italy-mud and France-dust. I get to bed by ten and get up at seven, eat like a horse and feel marvellous."

But, inevitably, a reaction set in. The Allied liberation campaign was inflicting deep collateral damage on Normandy's towns, villages and farms, and rendering thousands homeless. On 24 July, Helen visited a warren of caves just outside Caen which had become home to 3,000 refugees. Sleeping on straw pallets, breathing air that was rank from the smoke of multiple cooking fires, these stranded French families looked to her like figures from Dante's purgatory. "I sometimes wonder if this liberation can really be so much of a gift," she reflected, fully conscious that, even though the Germans had been enemy occupiers in Normandy, they had at least left the fabric of the region intact.[34]

Helen struggled to keep her emotional bearings, but prolonged combat reporting was more stressful than she'd imagined. Her nerves had grown jumpy from days spent diving into ditches when a bomber flew overhead, flinching from a shell that whined too close. Yet, it was the "perpetual and infernal noise" that got to her, as day and night she was assaulted by a cacophony of planes, artillery fire and military convoys, which made it difficult to sleep and impossible, sometimes, to think.

She was bothered, too, by small, accumulating slights to her own status. The male journalists in Normandy had been welcoming — Helen had long earned their respect and friendship — but Montgomery's stubborn misogyny had set the tone for the British PROs and it seemed to her that, when interviews were being handed out, she was always the last in line, and that the few soldiers to whom she was allowed to speak had been coached "to be on their best manners," and were stiffly unforthcoming.

Since Eisenhower's guarantee of equal access was not being respected by the British, Helen requested a transfer to the U.S. Fourth Army, who, late in July, were moving south towards Rennes. It was a timely move, for the story of Rennes' liberation turned out to be the most thrilling yet of Helen's war. The Americans allowed her a clear view of the final battle, as the Germans were forced from the city, dynamiting bridges as they fled; and they allowed her to march with them the following morning into the Place de la Mairie, where the entire city appeared to have gathered. Never in her life had Helen seen so many "radiant faces," and, when a man climbed out onto a window ledge to play "La Marseillaise" and the weeping crowd sang their national anthem for the first time in years, she admitted to her readers that she wept along with them. "These are days not to be missed and never to be forgotten. My face has not been washed for three days and is covered with the smears of many kisses."[35]

But, even as Rennes rejoiced in its freedom, the city was poised for revenge. There were many who were known to have collaborated with the enemy, many more suspected of doing so, and people wanted to see them punished. Women who'd slept with the Germans were paraded in public, their cruelly shaved heads exposed to missiles and jeers; individuals accused of graver crimes were rounded up in the Place de la Mairie and Helen reported that the atmosphere turned so ugly that it was only the "resistance men, tough and dirty, with their Sten guns slung from their shoulders [who] prevented the crowds from tearing them to shreds."[36] Similar scenes were occurring elsewhere, and the Civil Affairs Units, which the Allies were sending into all newly liberated towns, were struggling to maintain public order. Four years of occupation had created bitter divisions in France; communities, even families, were turning against each other, and one GI confessed to Helen that he'd seen vigilante groups committing acts of rough justice far more distressing than anything he'd witnessed in battle.

Shaken though she was by the violence, Helen hesitated to judge. Back in February, she'd interviewed an escaped French deputy who'd told her that "the reign of terror in France is beyond anything the outside world can imagine," and, towards the end of her stay in Rennes, she was given her first physical proof of that terror.[37] A press tour had been arranged of the dank, bloodstained cells where the Gestapo had imprisoned resistance fighters, and when Helen saw the crudely brutal instruments which had been used to punish and interrogate, she could only sympathize with the hatred that was exploding against anyone accused of complicity.

Her icily indignant report was headlined

"Gestapo Torture Method, Vestige of Middle Ages," but, obedient to her paper's editorial policy, she had only been able to hint at the "methods" deployed, alluding to a truncheon, which had been designed to inflict maximum damage on bones and internal organs, while leaving only minimal outward marks.[38] No such reticence limited Iris Carpenter, however, when she came to write her post-war memoir. She'd gone to Cherbourg two weeks after Helen, and there had been no Bastille Day celebrations to distract her from what she witnessed during a tour of the Nazis' former HQ. The building still contained storerooms of plundered food and liquor, wardrobes crammed with expensive women's clothes, but most disgusting of all to Iris was the dining room, where an orgy had evidently taken place — a flagellation whip left abandoned on the floor and bloodstains still visible on the wine-splattered tablecloth.

She shuddered to imagine what the people of Cherbourg had endured during the Nazi occupation, but the Germans were no less brutal to their own. When they'd retreated, they had left behind 300 wounded soldiers, abandoned without clean water or adequate food. They lay, Iris wrote, in "misery and filth beyond description," and this inhumanity seemed indicative to her of a profound evil.[39] She was aware, even then, that only a fraction of what she'd seen could be published in the *Boston Globe,* that she would have to wait until after the war to do justice to it all. However, when she returned to London, she was faced with a far more immediate threat to her freedom of speech than the strictures of editors and censors.

Iris's trip to Cherbourg had been in clear violation of SHAEF rules. Desperate to report on something other than hospital stories, she had hitched a ride to the port, travelling far beyond her permitted boundaries and outstaying her designated date of return. She knew she was committing a crime, but she was hopeful that one of the American commanders with whom she'd formed a mutually respectful relationship would shield her from its repercussions. The American and British chiefs of Public Relations, however, were not inclined to be lenient, and, when they learned of Iris's transgression, they summoned her for a court martial.

"I was dry in the mouth from nerves," she admitted. But the American chief, Colonel Dupuy, turned out to be both an admirer and an ally. When the British demanded to know who had allowed Iris out to Normandy, he'd grinned: "Nobody lets Carpenter do anything. All we can do is try to stop her" — and he urged the British to accept the logic of her carefully prepared defence.[40] As Iris reminded the court, she had been issued, like every correspondent, with a travel order that specified where she was permitted to go and for how long. That order, worded according to a formula that had been agreed back in June, had simply stated that her movements were restricted to the Allied beachhead; and as Iris was able to respectfully point out, the fact that the Allies had now conquered an area stretching from Omaha to Cherbourg had surely justified her in interpreting "beachhead" as the entire region.

Forced to acknowledge the ambiguity of their own orders, the authorities dropped their charges. In fact, Iris's court martial became a significant test case, forcing SHAEF to accept that improved conditions in Normandy justified a relaxation of their rules. From the end of July, women were allowed into north-west France for periods of up to a month, and the British War Office, already under pressure from a newly formed women's press club in London, was shamed into granting its own first cautious accreditations to female correspondents. The situation remained grossly unequal; none of the women, bar Helen, were allowed any closer to the front than the nurses with whom they were billeted, and they still had no access to the men's amenities. But an important concession had been made, and, if Iris was planning to take every advantage of it, so too was Lee Miller when she was sent out to Brittany that summer and found that she'd lucked her way into the middle of her own private war.

The first weeks of Operation Overlord had been a period of rising frustration for Lee. Just as she'd found her niche as a home-front correspondent, she'd had to watch Dave and his colleagues being dispatched to the "real" war in Normandy. "I don't want to lose the grasp I have on work at the moment," she wrote, miserably afraid of losing her hard-won confidence.[41] But, late in July, she was offered a story about one of the evacuation hospitals near Omaha Beach, and while the more blasé of her colleagues might have dismissed this as soft news, Lee had felt nothing but excited gratitude. As her Dakota transport plane had flown over the Normandy coast, she'd gazed down on the "soft gray-skied panorama of nearly a thousand square miles of France — of freed France" and admitted to her readers she'd had to swallow very hard "on what were trying to be tears."[42]

Once on the ground, Lee could see how that soft Normandy landscape had been violated in the battle for its freedom: barbed-wire thickets had replaced the summer hedge-rows; skull-and-crossbones notices warned that wild-flower meadows had been sown with enemy mines. And, when she was given her first tour of the tented hospital wards, she could see what the soldiers themselves had suffered — men with amputated limbs and full-body burns, who barely registered her presence as they stared up "at the dark brown canvas, patiently waiting and gathering strength." Capturing these scenes with her Rolleiflex camera and notebook, Lee sensed, as Martha always had, that her own impressions, her own emotional responses were key to the story she must tell. She needed her readers to share the pity she felt for the "dirty dishevelled stricken figures" who kept arriving at the triage station, and to appreciate the awe she felt for the surgeon on duty, whose "Raphael-like face" seemed to her the archetype of professional compassion. But Lee also wanted her readers to share the hatred that had convulsed her when, allocated a tent that had formerly been used by Germans, she realized that the blanket in which she'd wrapped herself had recently been warming the body of an enemy soldier.[43]

Audrey Withers was elated by the story Lee sent home, the prose even more extraordinary to her than the images. "It was the most exciting journalistic experience of my war," she claimed. "When you think that every situation she covered was completely outside her previous experience, it makes the sheer professionalism of her text even more remarkable."[44] She titled the story "Unarmed Warriors" and ran it over two double-page spreads. Then, early in August, when *Vogue* was offered a story about an American Civil Affairs team operating in the Breton port of Saint-Malo, she unhesitatingly assigned it to Lee.

The PRO who'd proposed the idea had been assured that the city was fully secured. But intelligence wires had evidently been crossed, for, when Lee arrived on 13 August, she discovered that, far from being liberated, whole areas of Saint-Malo were still under German control. Enemy snipers were roaming the streets and enemy troops were embedded within the Fort de la Cité and its three flanking fortresses. Lee knew perfectly well that SHAEF protocol demanded her immediate retreat, but this was an opportunity too good to miss. "I was the only photographer for miles around and now I owned a private war," she gloated; speciously, she reasoned that, since it was the authorities' mistake in sending her there, she was fully within her rights to stay until ordered to leave.[45]

The American Civil Affairs team were too busy to bother with Lee's rogue presence: they had surges of vigilante violence to control, hundreds of homeless families to shelter and feed. Meanwhile, the 83rd Infantry Division who were battling for control of Saint-Malo were frankly delighted by her presence. Excited that Lee would be "putting them in the papers," individual soldiers competed for the privilege of driving her to the best vantage points, allowing her to sit beside them when firing at German snipers; and, during the five days she spent with the division, she was adopted as their friend, their pin-up girl and their mascot.

"I'm mad about the 83rd," Lee wrote to Audrey, and she was prepared to risk shells and bullets in her determination to do them justice.[46] Shortly after her arrival, the Americans embarked on what they hoped would be the final assault on Fort de la Cité, and Lee, without the luxury of a telephoto lens, wanted to get as close as possible. She found an abandoned hotel just 700 yards from the citadel, from which she could document every phase of the attack: the "swelling" of the air which heralded the approach of the U.S. bombers, the "sickly death rattle" of falling ordnance, and then the engulfing clouds of smoke, which, unknown to her, were the characteristic signature of napalm, America's new secret weapon.[47]

After the planes came the infantry, who were under orders to scale the citadel wall to dislodge the enemy. This stage of the assault was tricky to photograph; without a built-in light meter or autowind, each image had to be a matter of intuition, knowledge and luck. Yet, even as Lee concentrated on her work, she was terrified for those vulnerably exposed soldiers as they laboured up the fort, armed with grenades and guns. "It was awesome and marrow freezing," she wrote, hardly able to look when one of the men was hit by a bullet just as he reached the top, raising his arm when he fell as though "waving at death."[48]

The enemy were fighting back hard, and, as machine-gun fire came blasting out of the citadel, Lee's own position was targeted and she had to move fast. Outside the hotel, several buildings were on fire, and a swarm of feral cats and flies was already moving in on a group of American soldiers lying dead in the street. Lee ran for the shelter of a Nazi dugout, just below the city ramparts, but, as she squatted down below the line of fire, she could feel something revoltingly cold and fleshy beneath her boot. It was "a dead, detached hand" which had been severed from a soldier during an earlier engagement, and Lee cursed furiously, hating the Nazis for having started this war and for "the sordid ugly destruction they had conjured up in this once beautiful town."[49]

Although the Germans were not easily dislodged, they had suffered unsustainable losses in the citadel's defence. On 17 August, Lee was present to photograph the moment when Colonel von Aulock emerged to offer his formal surrender. He was the epitome of the Prussian officer, she thought — tall, pale and very dignified with his monocle and Iron Cross — and, when she tried to take his picture, the Colonel cursed, lifting up his hand to hide his face. At that moment, Lee could feel a reluctant stirring of pity. Von Aulock looked exhausted, but he was still behaving impeccably in defeat, shaking hands with each of his aides before being driven away, and assuring the Americans that, in gratitude for their "gentlemanly" conduct, he'd guaranteed them safe entrance to the citadel and had refrained from laying its access tunnel with mines.

Lee felt another flicker of sympathy when she was permitted inside the citadel and saw the hastily abandoned belongings, the letters and family photographs which the Germans had left behind. But, by now, she no longer owned her Saint-Malo war, for news of the citadel battle had spread and a flock of correspondents had begun to converge on the city, "like vultures for the kill."[50]

Dave Scherman was one of the first, and he was delighted to find Lee, triumphant in her scoop and looking like an "unmade unwashed bed."[51] They had a euphoric few hours together, toasting their reunion and planning to pool their best Saint-Malo shots. However, along with the press pack had come the PROs, and with them came trouble for Lee.

"I'm in the doghouse for having scooped my battle," she wrote despondently to Audrey, explaining that she'd been ordered to the press HQ in Rennes, to await whatever punishment the authorities deemed fit. As a doghouse, the HQ was reasonably luxurious. It was based in a large hotel, and Lee had a room to herself, where she could sleep off her exhaustion and begin work. Audrey was excited by the outline she sent — "a great adventure, wonderful story" — and promised to give it 10,000 words in the October issue. But, on 20 August, SHAEF announced that Lee's escapade had prompted stricter clarifications to the protocol affecting female correspondents and a new clause had been added, stating that none could be "permitted to enter a forward area *under any circumstances.*"[52] This was a blow to all those women who'd been looking for loopholes and it fell very hard on Lee. Sharing her private war with the 83rd had been a pivotal experience. She'd never felt more alert, more wholly herself than when she'd been risking her life to photograph her new soldier friends, and she'd been honoured and excited when they had insisted that she stick with them when they moved on from Saint-Malo to their next battle.

News of the additional SHAEF clause, however, had blighted Lee's hopes of becoming embedded with the 83rd, and when she looked to Audrey for help, none was forthcoming. It was 26 August when she was finally released from Rennes, and the Germans had just surrendered Paris. Enthusiastic though Audrey might have been about Lee's adventures with the 83rd, what she urgently needed for *Vogue* was a story about how the world capital of fashion was celebrating its freedom — and, most importantly, what it was wearing.

"It is very bitter to me to go to Paris now that I have a taste for gunpowder," Lee cabled sullenly back to London.[53] But, while she was personally dreading a return to hair and make-up, fabric and buttons, most of her colleagues regarded Paris as the news event of the summer. From the middle of August, as Allied troops advanced on the city and resistance groups attacked from within, journalists and photographers had begun competing for transport and travel permits. "Every international typewriter . . . every accredited war correspondent [was] wrangling and conspiring to be the first to enter Paris and file history from the great city of former lights," wrote Robert Capa. As the world's press raced towards the French capital, all of them wanted to be there in time for the tearing down of swastikas and the celebratory parades; and all of them wanted to report on a party that was certain to be on a scale more historic, more delirious than any this summer of liberation had witnessed.[54]

CHAPTER THIRTEEN:
THE LIBERATION
OF PARIS, 1944

"It was all wild, you know, and wonderful"
HELEN KIRKPATRICK[1]

Helen was staying on the island of Mont-St.-Michel when the rush for Paris began. Ernest Hemingway, Irwin Shaw and various other lords of the American press were also present, "sort of taking time off," she recalled, and "eating very well." The fighting on the Normandy mainland remained fierce: when Helen went swimming one afternoon, dressed "in what the army thought the well-dressed WAC [should wear] under her uniform, kaiser silk panties . . . and a bra," she could see smoke and flames from a last-ditch German offensive.[2] But, out on Mont-St-Michel, the only topic of interest was how they would all get to the capital. Hemingway boasted that he would fight his way there assisted by the band of impressionable young resistance fighters whom he'd just recruited to his "Hem division" of personal "scouts." Helen, however, planned to do things more ef-

503

ficiently; after she left the island, she quietly arranged a transfer from the U.S. army to the 2nd Armoured Division of the Free French.

It was the French, Helen guessed, who would be leading the march into Paris, and their commander, General Leclerc, who would be receiving the city's surrender. But her decision had also been forced on her by an American PRO who, unimpressed by Eisenhower's permit, had been trying to obstruct her freedom of movement. Like Martha and Virginia, she'd heard that the French were admirably relaxed about the division of male and female roles in the war, and once she was on the road with the 2nd Armoured Division, she discovered that their enlightened attitudes extended to cooking. Rather than being fed from a centralized field kitchen, the soldiers built their own little fires each night and cooked their own food. "Every man does for himself," she wrote to her parents, and she was shamed into improvising her own K-ration cuisine — eggs poached in a mess tin and served over rehydrated corned beef. Still, it was hard for the French to remain relaxed as news came through of the insurrections in Paris, where the FFI (Forces Françaises de l'Intérieur) were leading mass demonstrations and attacks on their German occupiers. Camped out at Ecouché, 200 kilometres away from the capital, Helen could see that the 2nd Division "were going out of their minds" with impatience. On 23 August, when their orders finally came through, the soldiers struck camp at miraculous speed to begin their "hell bent" advance on Paris.*

Helen was as exhilarated as the French, but the weather was filthy and, when she was permitted a "dash for the bushes," she slipped while clambering down from her rain-slicked jeep, and fractured her big toe. By nightfall, when the convoy stopped outside Rambouillet, just sixty kilometres short of the capital, her foot had swollen so badly she could no longer squeeze it into her boot, and it was "quite a feat," she recalled, "to tend to one's needs hopping on one foot in the mud."[3] A shot of novocaine the following morning made her fit to continue, but a new obstacle had arisen, for Leclerc was now insisting that no foreign journalist would be allowed to accompany him and his troops that night, when they made their first triumphal entrance into Paris.

It was a matter of national pride that the French, and only the French, take possession

---

* The Americans had hoped to delay the liberation of Paris, unwilling to shoulder the responsibility for supplying food and fuel to the beleaguered city. But the FFI had been so effective in destabilizing the Germans, they accepted that immediate action was necessary.

of their capital, and road blocks were already being erected. Hemingway was predictably furious, swearing that if Leclerc did not rescind the order, he and his fifteen scouts would smash their way into the city. According to Robert Capa, Ernest had cast a spell over his Hem division — all of them copying his "sailor bear walk," and his habit of "spitting short sentences from the corner of his mouth."[4] But Helen left Hemingway to his blustering and, in collaboration with an American liaison officer, Johnnie Reinhart, she found a sergeant with a captured German jeep, who was willing to find them a back route into Paris.

Leclerc entered the city just before midnight on 24 August 1944, and, at ten thirty the following morning, he formally accepted the Germans' surrender. Helen didn't arrive in time to witness that moment, but, as she and Johnnie Reinhart drove the last few kilometres to Paris, the liberation story was unfolding around them. Crowds had congregated along every stretch of the road — throwing flowers, waving at anyone in uniform — and, when their jeep crested a small rise and the capital's skyline came into view, Helen caught her breath at the wonder of it.

"Paris was still standing and looking very beautiful in the morning sun" she wrote, and the closer they got to the centre, the more riotous the street parties became. "It was all wild, you know, and wonderful," she affirmed, as men, women and children clambered into their jeep, "suffocating" them with kisses and offering bouquets and bottles of wine. Paris was not yet fully secure, and, against the raucous symphony of singing, shouting and accordion music, Helen could hear the sound of gunfire. German guerrilla units were still holding parts of the Right Bank and snipers were concealed in basements and attics, all under orders to spread fear and chaos while the rest of the army retreated north. But, as she recorded, none of the French seemed to care. "Paris is free. Its freedom is heady and intoxicating,"[5] and it was particularly sweet to be sending her first dispatch from the Hotel Scribe, the new Allied press HQ, which, until just two days ago, had been servicing the Nazi media.*

That night, Helen dined on champagne and a foie-gras omelette, and slept between freshly laundered sheets. When she woke, late

---

* Hitler had ordered General von Choltitz, commander of the German forces in Paris, to destroy the city's most historic buildings rather than relinquish them to Allied hands, but the General had defied the order, partly because he didn't want to be held responsible for such an act of vandalism, and partly because he lacked the resources to carry it out. He claimed later that he already considered Hitler to have gone mad.

the following morning, it was to a message from Hemingway inviting her for lunch at the Ritz. Ernest had always vowed he would personally liberate the city's most famous hotel, and already stories were spreading of how he and his scouts had blasted their way into the Ritz, forcing out the "Nazi scum" who'd commandeered its luxury quarters for the last four years. Fiction, however, was far more entertaining than fact; the Germans had actually been long gone by the time Hemingway appeared, and the hotel manager, Claude Auzello, had to courteously request that he and his men lay down their weapons at the door. When Helen arrived for lunch, all Ernest could claim to have "liberated" was the hotel's wine cellars — Auzello having offered to serve some of the classic vintages that he'd kept hidden from his enemy clientele.

It was a hilarious lunch, nonetheless. Johnny Reinhart, Charles Wertenbaker and Irwin Shaw were also present, and their war stories grew more colourfully self-aggrandizing with every glass. Helen enjoyed herself terrifically; she was greatly amused by Hemingway, even if she found his boasting absurd, and she knew that this lunch was making history, of sorts. But she also knew that more important history was being made outside, for the four French generals — De Gaulle, Leclerc, Koenig and Alphonse Juin — were to be leading a celebration parade through Paris that afternoon, starting at the Arc de Triomphe and ending with a brief service of blessing at Notre Dame. Hemingway was incredulous when Helen announced her intention to go and report on the event. "Daughter, sit still and drink this good brandy," he ordered. "You can always see a parade but you'll never again lunch at the Ritz, the day after Paris was liberated." But she was not to be badgered; leaving the men to their digestifs, she forced her way back into the partying crowds.[6]

Helen was right to follow her instinct, for, that afternoon, she would land a story that she came to regard as "the greatest, most exciting" of her career.[7] Threading her way through the backstreets, she found the square outside Notre Dame already packed. Most of the crowd was made up of resistance fighters and their families, and, to her pleasure, Helen could only spot one other journalist, a reporter for the BBC. At four fifteen p.m., when the generals arrived, there was a moment of high, solemn excitement as the hushed Parisians joined their generals in a collective salute. But, within a second, that moment had fractured into panic. German snipers had been lying in wait, one was even crouched behind a gargoyle on the cathedral roof, and it was as though the crowd's salute had been their signal to open fire. Suddenly, everyone was trying to seek cover inside the cathedral, and, as Helen was swept up in that frantic, animal surge, she realized, to her horror, that there were even more snipers inside. "An automatic opened up from behind us," she wrote, "it came from behind the pipes of Notre Dame's organ. From the clerestory above, other shots rang out and I saw a man ducking behind a pillar above. Beside me, F.F.I. men and the police were shooting. For one flashing instant, it seemed that a great massacre was bound to take place as the cathedral reverberated with the sound of guns."[8]

The next ten minutes "felt like hours," Helen reported, but she forced herself to memorize every detail. A man close by was shot dead; people were cowering behind pillars and under chairs; and screaming women were clutching their babies. De Gaulle, however, did not flinch, and Helen believed this was the moment when the General proved himself a national leader. Upright, shoulders squared, he walked calmly up the cathedral aisle, encouraging his fellow generals to accompany him into what appeared to be a hail of bullets. Once they reached the altar, he signalled for the priest to begin the Te Deum, even though gun fire continued to ricochet around the recesses of the building. De Gaulle's courage had an extraordinary effect on the crowd, who quietened down to listen. When the brief service was over, everyone waited respectfully for the four generals to process back down the aisle, before leaving themselves. "I could only stand amazed," Helen reported, "at the coolness, imperturbability and apparent unconcern of French generals and civilians alike, who walked as though nothing had happened. Gen. Koenig, smiling, leaned across and shook my hand. I fell in behind them and watched them walk deliberately out and into their cars. A machine gun was still blazing from a nearby roof."

"Daily News writer sees man slain by her side in a hail of lead." The following day, Helen's story was front-page news, yet, dramatic though her account had been, she later admitted that she'd underplayed the danger, acknowledging that it had been a miracle the Germans had claimed only twenty-five lives. She learned that the Notre Dame attack had actually been one of several that day, a terror campaign orchestrated with the hated Vichy police, the *Milice.* But the Parisians would not be cowed, and, on 27 August, when Helen and Johnny Reinhart went hunting for enemy snipers with a team of French police, the mission grew distinctly festive in spirit. For every German who was locked behind bars, a bottle of champagne was uncorked. By the end of the day, everyone was emotionally tipsy, and one of Helen's most precious war souvenirs was the note written to her by the officer in charge that day: *"Les partisans de la délivrance. Nous vous saluons braves soldats américains. Ce jour de notre délivrance comptera parmi les plus beau de notre vie."*[9]★

Those first three days of liberation were uniquely wonderful for Helen and she knew she'd been privileged to experience them. Sigrid, exiled in America, could only read the reports, and even as she celebrated the freedom of her childhood home, she had to endure the chagrin of not being present. As for the other women in France who'd been trying to join the race for Paris, they had frustrations of their own. Unlike Helen, they'd been forced to improvise their journeys, and their progress had not only been slower, but more dangerous. Forbidden army escorts and excluded from daily briefings, they were often travelling blind, unsure where the fighting was most intense, and unsure of where the demarcation lay between enemy and Allied lines.

Iris Carpenter, who'd teamed up with Ruth Cowan, had been trying to cadge a lift at a crossroads just outside the newly liberated city of Saint-Lô, when a wave of German

★ "The supporters of deliverance. We salute you brave American soldiers. This day of our deliverance will be among the most beautiful of our lives."

bombers flew overhead. As the ground erupted, the two women had flung themselves into a shallow crater. After the planes had disappeared, they were still shakily dusting each other down when an American command car screeched to a halt, and an officer demanded to know "what the hell were they doing" trying to hitch a ride at this exposed spot? "War correspondents don't have to do that sort of thing," he barked. "They have their own jeeps and drivers." Ruth, quick-witted even in terror, replied that, while that might be true for the men, "we happen to be women."[10]

Iris suffered a perforated eardrum from that attack, but, dizzy and half-deafened, she was still determined to reach Paris. When she and Ruth got to Rennes, however, a PRO with a "hard mouth and a hard heart" informed them that female correspondents were banned from the capital until it was fully secure, and the two of them were to be held in the same hotel where Lee Miller was already under house arrest. By now, there were nine others corralled at Rennes, among them Catherine Coyne, Dot Avery, Virginia Irwin from the St. Louis Post-Dispatch and a British newcomer, Judy Barden, contracted to the New York Sun. All twelve were obliged to conform to the same terms of imprisonment, signing themselves in and out of the hotel if they even wanted a stroll, and giving a detailed account of their every movement.

The women had to wait until the night of 26 August for their freedom to be restored, and, by the time they'd hitched to Paris, over 300 kilometres away, the liberation story was several days old. Ruth's first instinct was to find a beauty parlour where she could attend to the neglected roots of her dyed blonde hair; Lee Carson, a reporter for the International News Service who'd successfully evaded the Rennes PRO, had headed for a nightclub and found herself among a crowd of "jerking, jumping, hair-in-eyes GIs," already showing Paris their jitterbugging moves.[11] Iris, though, went straight to the Hotel Scribe. Here, for the first time in her war, she was on an equal footing with her male colleagues — free to use the same cabling and broadcasting facilities, free to order up one of the dozens of military-command cars that were parked in the road outside, free to take a room in the hotel, if her budget ran to it, and, perhaps best of all, free to socialize in the gloomy hotel basement that now did service as the correspondents' mess.[12] The food on offer was uninspired — rarely stretching beyond the dried biscuits and canned foods of basic K rations — but there was unlimited alcohol, and, to Iris, those first nights at the Scribe felt like "the greatest party of all time."[13]

■　■　■　■

Martha was not much inclined to party when she reached Paris a day or two after Iris. As soon as she'd heard the city was free, she'd hitched a flight to Lyons and, from there, got a lift in an American jeep. Half-way to Paris, the driver had lost control of the vehicle, and Martha arrived with a crop of bruises and a broken rib. It hurt even to breathe, yet what troubled her most was the seemingly un-scarred beauty of the city, which she could not help but compare to the smoking chaos of Italy. Geraniums were blooming in sunny window boxes, booksellers were lined up on the banks of the Seine and the women were parading the streets as though untouched and untroubled by war: "couture and hats, fine smooth faces, gleaming hair," she noted with dislike. "How shocked one is, absolutely beautiful clothes . . . Everything non-utility."[14]

It was a misleading first impression, and Martha would shortly appreciate how starved and threadbare Paris had become, under its picture postcard veneer. In her first rush to judgement, however, she'd assumed the city had not only prospered too well under Nazi occupation, but had been guilty of a collective act of cowardice. She was deeply offended by the first Parisians she interviewed, who scrambled to claim a fighting role in the resistance. "Everyone," she snorted, "has now become a great F.F.I. or partisan," and, contemptuously, she compared the passivity with which they had let the Germans walk into their city, with the brave fighting spirit of Madrid.[15]

Perhaps Martha was influenced by her pre-war dislike of Paris, when right-wing Parisians had been so in thrall to Hitler, and when the city had felt spiritually rotten to her. Yet, while she was correct that only a small minority had been active members of the resistance — around 3 per cent — she did not yet understand why. It had taken a year for the resistance to organize, partly because the communists, who had the physical muscle and experience to lead it, were under orders from Russia to respect the Stalin–Hitler alliance. By the time that alliance had been broken and the French had dared to hope for an eventual German defeat, the Nazis had solidified their hold on Paris. They'd begun to ship able-bodied men and boys off to labour camps, imposed newly punitive rationing and introduced systems of surveillance, interrogation and torture, against which it took extraordinary courage to act.

Martha would learn exactly how extraordinary that courage was when, in mid-October, she joined a press tour of the Gestapo's secret prisons. It took over four days to see them all

— as Martha savagely reported, there turned out to be "more torture chambers in and around Paris than you can conveniently visit" — and, by the end, she'd felt paralysed by the cumulative horror.[16] She'd been shown the interrogation cells on Rue des Saussaies, where electric shocks and water torture were used to extract information; the shooting range at Issy, where condemned prisoners were used for target practice; the frigid underground tunnels at Ivry, where inmates were simply starved to death, their scrawled messages of farewell still legible on the walls. But worst of all was the fortress at Romainville, which the Nazis had equipped with large metal-lined ovens, where prisoners could be "prepared" for interrogation by a process of slow, excruciating roasting.

Helen, who also went to Romainville, was allowed to interview one of its few survivors. Madame Lewulis had been a sturdy young woman before she was taken by the Nazis, but her body was now crooked, half-paralysed from repeated beatings, and the soles of her feet so severely burned that, even four months after her release, Helen reported that they looked as raw as "underdone beef."[17] It wasn't possible for her to write more about the awful specifics of Madame Lewulis' torture — restricted by the rules of censorship and good taste, she could only comment that the details were "best left to the imagination." But even had she been given more licence, Helen knew she would struggle to find words that were adequate to the truth. After the war, when Iris Carpenter tried to describe all that she'd seen and heard of Nazi atrocities, she listed the worst of their interrogation methods: the castration, the gouging out of eyes, the severing of hands, and the particularly awful cruelty meted out to one young resistance fighter, who was forced to watch his mother and sweetheart being raped, and his comrades being butchered, before being shot himself. But, although there was courage in Iris's blunt approach, it read like a crude cataloguing of horrors; and to Martha, in Paris, it was becoming clear that the ultimate challenge of the war correspondent was how to make human sense of so much wickedness. However doggedly she forced herself to imagine the agony of being locked inside those Romainville ovens, to imagine the shrinking and flinching and searing of flesh, she'd been unable get it all down on paper. Caught between evasion and melodrama, she finally had to accept it was impossible "to write properly of such monstrous and incredible and bestial cruelty."[18]

As Martha dug deeper into the story of the Paris occupation, she was learning to temper her criticisms, to question her own quickness to judge. Like her colleagues, she was shaken by the ferocity of vigilante groups, who were ranging freely around the city, hunting down all those suspected of collaboration. Women who'd taken Germans as lovers or clients were the easiest targets — some were not merely shaved, but had swastikas branded onto their naked backs — and De Gaulle, as head of the new provisional government in France, was trying to contain the worst of the violence by imposing a legal system of trial and punishment. But there were so many accused of collaboration — 15,000 in Paris alone — that the courts were unable to process them. Some of the accusations were backed by solid evidence, but many were motivated by spite, and, during those first months of liberation, when guilt and innocence were frighteningly fluid, people were being beaten, even murdered for crimes they hadn't committed. When Martha attempted to trace her former lover, Bertrand, she discovered that he had exiled himself to Switzerland. Despite the courage with which he'd fought at the Maginot Line, despite the fact that he'd disowned his earlier attempts to forge links with the younger Nazis, his reputation had been tainted and he feared for his life. The lines between right and wrong had begun to look hazier to Martha, and, as she prepared her liberation story for *Collier's,* she had never felt further from that high moral ground where she'd so easily, and confidently, denounced objectivity as "shit."

Meanwhile, she was having to navigate her way around Ernest, who was still in the capital, living large at the Ritz, writing for *Collier's* and meeting up with his professional cronies at the Scribe. Martha was staying more modestly at the Hotel Lincoln, and, while she had to go to the Scribe to use its facilities, putting on her uniform and trusting that no one would ask to see her non-existent AGO, she would never go drinking in the correspondents' mess. The issue of her divorce had yet to be broached with Ernest, and, although she assumed he would be equally ready to end their marriage, she wanted to meet and discuss it in calmer, quieter surroundings.

The two of them circled around each other for weeks before agreeing to meet for dinner. Martha had hoped to see Ernest alone, but when she arrived at the restaurant he was surrounded by a protective detail of friends and scouts, and was evidently determined to embarrass her. He was drunk, talking "like a cobra," and the jibes he directed at her were so poisonous that even his loyal friends sloped away. As for the divorce, he wasn't prepared to discuss it. Martha had been a lousy wife, he said; if anyone had the right to end the marriage, it would be him, not her, and, as he continued to blindside her with threats and recriminations, she could only retreat from him in tears.

Back at her hotel, though, she met Robert Capa, who was sitting at the bar, counting his winnings from the night's poker game. Capa knew Ernest well and, seeing Martha's distress, he pointed out gently that there was one simple way to manage the situation. Ernest might be trying to pin the failures of their marriage onto her, but he had recently begun an affair with Mary Welsh and could hardly claim to be blameless. Martha had not known about the affair, and winced when Capa informed her that Ernest was sharing Mary's bed at the Ritz every night. But she understood the information gave her power. Obediently following Capa's instructions, she telephoned Mary's room, then, when Ernest answered, and recognized her voice, she simply put down the receiver. "It will be all right now," Capa assured her, predicting correctly that, once Ernest had been placed so irrevocably in the wrong, he would lose his appetite for the fight.[19]

Martha had got what she wanted. Yet, for the last seven years, Ernest had been a constant in her life, and now that she'd forced their separation, she felt rudderless, confused and alone. "I am free like nothing quite bearable," she wrote desolately to Allen Grover. "Who shall I talk to, and who will tell me why I am doing what I am doing?" Irrationally, she wished she'd had a child with Ernest, wistfully reflecting on the pure "human" connection she could have had with a baby son or daughter, and she tormented herself with the thought that, at thirty-seven, she had left it too late.[20]

"I scream for kindness. Let there be kindness," Martha wrote, as the pain of her broken marriage merged with the horror of the occupation, the vigilantes, the whole horrible mess of the war.[21] Lee Miller, however, had experienced an unexpected lift of happiness when she arrived in Paris on 29 August, and her bitterness at being parted from the 83rd had been dispelled by the pageantry of "flags . . . girls, bicycles, kisses and wine." She'd cabled immediately to *Vogue*'s New York office, "TOWN LOOKED LIKE BALLROOM MORNING AFTER," and, working with two cameras, in case one got broken or a film got spoiled, she walked through the streets, tirelessly documenting the bizarre, moving and wonderful spectacle around her: the skinny children playing in burnt-out jeeps; the GI with two giggling little French girls hefted onto his shoulders; the sweating teenage boys, pedalling their bikes to work the hair dryers at a coiffure's salon; the hungry fights breaking out when the first U.S. convoys arrived with deliveries of canned food and flour.[22]

Lee's generous budget from *Vogue* meant that she could book herself into the Scribe, with a bathroom large enough to set up an improvised darkroom, and space to carve out a studio, office and general supply dump for her photographic equipment, her hoard of emergency provisions, as well as her accumulating bits of war booty — a magpie collection that ranged from Nazi insignia to odd scraps of fabric, lace or leather that had caught her eye.

Booked into the room next to hers was Dave Scherman, who'd arrived in Paris two days earlier. Yet, glad though Lee was of his reliable company, her immediate concern was to seek news of her old Parisian friends. Picasso was still in the city, having sat out the occupation in his studio on Rue des Grands-Augustins, and, when she went to find him, their embrace was tearful and fond. Picasso exclaimed that Lee was barely recognizable as the Riviera goddess he'd painted seven years ago: "This is the first allied soldier I have seen and it's you," he freely exaggerated, and demanded that she sit for a new portrait in her uniform. The two of them went for a celebratory meal, during which Picasso told the story of how he'd survived the last four years. He'd been banned from exhibiting, having been categorized as a degenerate modern, and at one point had feared arrest. But the Germans had decided not to make a martyr of the city's most celebrated artist and he'd been allowed to keep working throughout the occupation, resorting to vegetable juices when the paint ran out, using paper tablecloths when canvas became unobtainable.[23]

Picasso may have played down the fact that his situation had been improved by a few art-savvy Nazis who'd purchased a number of paintings. For him, as for so many artists, writers, and intellectuals in France, certain acts of compromise had been necessary if they were to persist with their work and, as the philosopher Jean-Paul Sartre pointed out, it was impossible not to feel morally tainted: "Everything we did was equivocal. We never quite knew whether we were doing right or wrong. A subtle poison corrupted even our best actions."[24] Sartre, at least, had smuggled mild acts of subversion into his writing, but he'd risked far less than the brave minority who had produced actively dissident material, among whom was Lee's dear friend Paul Éluard. Paul had worked with the clandestine publishing house Les Editions de Minuit, and during the final year of the occupation, he and his wife, Nusch, had to move house eight times to avoid arrest. When Lee finally tracked them down, she was shocked by the visible marks of their ordeal. "There wasn't much left of Nusch," she wrote, "so thin and delicate that her elbows were larger than her arms and her skirt hung slack."[25] Paul, equally starved-looking, had flinched when he'd opened the door; he'd lived in such fear of men in uniform that even the sight of Lee in her war correspondent's jacket and cap had triggered a reflex terror.*

Even more harrowing was Lee's reunion with the Jewish playwright Tristan Bernard. For two years, Bernard had been interned in Drancy, a deportation camp in north-eastern Paris, and even though his supporters had agitated for his release, he and his family had been left to subsist on greatly reduced rations. When Lee tracked Bernard down, he invited her to stay for supper, but the meal was so pitiful, a dish of potato pancakes followed by a dessert of raw grains, she was too choked with pity to eat. His situation was very different from that of Jean Cocteau, who had thrived during the last four years; and Lee began to think there was an interesting feature to write about the ways in which artists had coped under occupation, and the ways in which they were adapting to freedom. Like Martha, she was conscious of the darkness that shadowed the liberation story: "There are the gay squiggles of wine and song. There is the beautiful overall colour of freedom but there is ruin and destruction.

* The active collaborators were easy to condemn, among them Robert Brasillach, editor of the pro-Nazi newspaper *Je suis partout;* more slippery cases were those like Jean Cocteau, who'd simply prospered a little too well under the Germans.

There are problems and mistakes, disappointed hopes and broken promises."[26] Audrey liked the idea of this piece, and would ask Lee to return to it; however, her priority was still fashion, and what she needed now was photographs and descriptions of what the women of Paris were wearing during this celebratory autumn of 1944, and what they'd been wearing during the four preceding years.

Even though Lee had rebelled against the exchange of gunpowder for gowns, she knew enough about clothes to understand there was an issue of substance here. While Martha had been offended by the sartorial extravagance she'd seen, Lee had rightly interpreted it as a language of defiance. Unlike the British, who'd made it their patriotic duty to wear the boxy utility fashions dictated by government rationing, the women of occupied Paris had turned flamboyance and frivolity into acts of transgression. Rather than eking out the tiny allocation of fabric allowed them by Nazi regulations, they'd squander an entire year's allowance on the making of one outrageously gorgeous skirt or dress. When the Nazis issued a ban on wide-brimmed hats, the Parisiennes wore their hats with tall, twelve-inch crowns, marvellously decorated with artificial flowers, remnants of old net or even stuffed birds. When the Nazis prohibited fabrics that bore the colours of the French flag, women took to walking along the street in threes, each individually dressed in red, white or blue.

Lee was charmed by these "very queer and fascinating" statements of rebellion; and, when the last surviving fashion houses in Paris announced they would be rushing out their first free collections in early October, she saw it as her duty to celebrate their initiative.[27] "Everyone wanted to express some sort of *joie*," she wrote, marvelling at the speed and cleverness with which designers were able to conjure an illusion of luxury out of the most meagre materials — a small sparkle of sequins stitched into a velvet jacket, a witty slash cut into a skirt. She was outraged when her New York editor, Edna Woolman Chase, cabled to complain that the women who were modelling the collections lacked professional refinement. Most of them were malnourished and were moonlighting from day jobs as secretaries, shop girls or factory workers. "Edna should be told there is a war on," Lee snapped, and she made a point of underlining that fact by staging one of her shoots outside Van Cleef & Arpels, the luxury jewellers, whose shop window was still pockmarked from German bullets.[28]

Edna's cable reminded Lee of the insularity and snobbery she'd come to loathe in fashion, but her snappishness had also been born of fatigue. In addition to covering the October collections, she was volunteering practical assistance to *Vogue*'s newly reopened Paris office, and coping with Audrey's demands for features on Fred Astaire and Marlene Dietrich, who were among the celebrities now returning to the Paris stage. Lee regretted the efficiency of the Scribe's cabling service, which made it impossible for her to pretend these demands had gone astray. While it suited her to relay her own requests back to London — a new uniform from Savile Row or three cartons of tampons — she disliked being so very accessible herself.

When Roland came to Paris on leave, he was disconcerted to see the changes in Lee as she darted authoritatively around the city. He was proud of her success, especially her war stories from Saint-Malo, but he felt privately diminished by them — "they gave me a sense of inferiority when I compared my own efforts to her immensely daring exploits" — and he was aware that, however happily Lee welcomed him, she had only limited time to spare.[29] Roland was also very conscious of Dave's presence, and the degree to which Lee had become dependent on him. Writing was still hard for her. "Every word . . . is as difficult as tears wrung from stone," she moaned, and she could sit for hours at her Hermes Baby typewriter, drinking brandy, playing word games and generally "boondoggling." It was Dave who bullied and cajoled her every time a deadline loomed, and, even though he found it a tortuous process, much like having his own brain put through a "meat grinder," it brought him very close to Lee, much closer than Roland himself.[30]

For most of the correspondents who made it to Paris that autumn, it felt as though the war had turned. Living and working in a liberated city brought a gladdening foretaste of peace, even if it revealed how raw and difficult that peace might be. The break from combat reporting also created space and time for friendships. After months of being scattered across different battle zones, journalists were now attending the same daily briefings, drinking together at the Scribe. And for Lee, one of the most educative and entertaining benefits of this Parisian interlude was discovering the company of Helen Kirkpatrick.

Once Helen had reported on the liberation story, she'd been tasked with the reopening of her paper's Paris bureau, and she'd been very moved when she'd gone to the office and discovered it was exactly as her predecessor, Edgar Mowrer, had left it. Back in June 1940, Mowrer had been ordered out of Paris so fast that a copy of his final report, detailing the speed of the Nazi advance, was still lying on his dust-covered desk. And, even though Helen would have preferred to be back in the field, following the Allied armies as they pushed onwards from Paris, she felt the shiver of history in that bureau office and accepted that her immediate duty was to pick up where Mowrer had left off.

There were also local stories that still needed urgent coverage. During the final months of occupation, the Germans had slashed the ration allowance so punitively that many Parisians were now critically malnourished. A local family whom Helen had got to know had asked her to become godmother to their ten-month-old son, and, when she'd been given the infant to hold, she'd been appalled by his frailty: "he lay unnaturally quiet in my arms, his eyes dull," she reported, incredulous to learn that, for months, he'd only been fed flour and water.[31] Helen begged her readers to imagine how they would feel if their own children were starving, and she wrote an angry critique of the American government, whom she believed were not only providing criminally inadequate aid to the French, but were hampering the nation's own efforts of recovery. Washington's dislike of De Gaulle had persisted to the point of questioning his legitimacy as leader of the new provisional government; and without that endorsement, De Gaulle could not control the competing political and factional interests in France, let alone focus on feeding his country.

To Lee, Helen appeared admirable. She was as impressed by the knowledgeable thrust of her reporting as she was pleased by the self-deprecating and very American style of her wit. As for Helen, while she'd known Lee slightly in London, and had known something of her "fantastic past," it was only, now, in Paris, that she had time to see beyond the differences in their temperament and background, and get to know her as an ally and friend. She was wide-eyed and starstruck when Lee introduced her to artists like Picasso, Cocteau and Éluard. In October, when she was ordered to cover the fashion collections, and feared that, after two years in uniform, she'd lost whatever "eye for style" she formerly possessed, she drew gratefully on Lee's inside knowledge.[32] And, when Helen was offered the loan of a spacious apartment, with the rare bonus of a maid and central heating, she invited Lee to live with her for a while, offering her a refuge from the noise and clutter of her room at the Scribe. So closely linked did the two women become that, in January 1945, they were singled out by French *Vogue* as the two female correspondents who'd made the greatest contribution to France, not only by placing themselves in "the terrifying spotlight of the war," but by demonstrating their "inspired understanding of our country."[33]

Lee and Helen were also united that autumn by their growing impatience for action. Helen, at least, was able to monitor it from her desk, processing reports of the Allied advance through northern France and the Low Countries. Lee, however, was keenly aware of her exclusion, and, as early as mid-September, was reminding Audrey that her fashion duties could only be temporary. "I want to go to the wars again," she'd cabled, and, even before the collections opened, she'd hitchhiked down to the Loire to photograph groups of surrendering Germans.[34] On 18 October, when the collections were done, she then made an unsanctioned trip to Luxembourg, where her friends in the 83rd were securing the border. It was a blissful reunion: "Stow the red scarf and put on your helmet," the soldiers had shouted when they saw her, and Lee had spent a euphoric few days going out with them to survey enemy defences and hunt down enemy agents.[35]

"I was home again," she wrote, but she would have to wait until late January before *Vogue* allowed her to return full time. When she did put her helmet back on, however, the conditions under which she was reporting had undergone a radical change. The protests of female correspondents, the courage and ingenuity they'd displayed in finding their own ways into this war, had finally had their effect, and SHAEF had agreed to rewrite the exclusion orders. During the final months of the conflict, a select number of women would get equal access to the press camps, the briefings, and the transport and filing facilities; they would no longer be ducking and diving their way to the front, and they would no longer be restricted to the "soft" angles deemed appropriate to them. Some of the old prejudices would die hard. The British were still in the grip of Montgomery's antiquated views, and the small group of women to whom the War Office granted licences were still hedged around with petty restrictions. Evelyn Irons, writing for the *Evening Standard,* would be forced to switch her accreditation to the French in order to report more freely (and would subsequently be awarded a Croix de Guerre, with a silver star, for her bravery). Even those who benefited from the more liberal American accreditation would have remaining battles to fight: when the Allies crossed into Germany, in early 1945, and there was heated competition for travel orders, the men of the press corps were given automatic priority. But the change in protocol had been dramatic, nonetheless. By early March, thirty-eight women would be officially embedded with the invasion force, and, as their numbers rose, all of them would be able to regard themselves as more or less professionally equal — free to go wherever their colleagues went and free to compete for the same news.

CHAPTER FOURTEEN:
THE BATTLE OF THE BULGE,
WINTER 1944–5

"If they don't want to accredit you, you just
do it, any little lie will do"
MARTHA GELLHORN[1]

Throughout the autumn of 1944, Martha
had already been slipping out of Paris to write
unlicensed reports on the Allied advance.
She'd seen the liberation of Brussels and Ant-
werp, and, in mid-September, had travelled
to Nijmegen, a modest town on the Dutch
border, which had now turned in to a peculiarly vicious war zone, as the British and
Americans fought to wrest it from German
control. The details of the fighting were only
marginally interesting to Martha, although
she'd long ago learned how to calculate the
chances of a lone Messerschmitt, dogfighting
with three Spitfires, or to interpret the layout
of gun batteries and emplacements. What
principally concerned her was the day-to-day
endurance of Nijmegen's remaining inhabi-
tants, and the irony that what they were suffering now was a direct consequence of the

fight to set them free.

In the article she filed for *Collier's,* "A Little Dutch Town," she described the quiet stoicism with which men and women emerged from their shelters every morning to survey the night's fresh damage and to "sweep up broken glass . . . in a despairingly tidy way."[2] With bleak exactitude she noted that Nijmegen had been reduced to a place "where people sleep in cellars and walk with care on the streets, listening hard for incoming shells," yet, despite the suffering she observed, Martha was convinced that freedom from the Nazis was worth almost any price. She was seeing the effects of the occupation everywhere: in the rickety children, so weakened by years of starvation rations that they'd forgotten how to play; in the families who'd lost their fathers, brothers, husbands and sons to German factories and labour camps. As for the town's Jewish community, it had been virtually obliterated, although Martha did meet a very small number who'd managed to survive. One of them, a thin, dark, agitated woman, unhealthily pallid from four years spent hiding in a basement, was now working twelve-hour shifts as a Red Cross nurse and walking eight kilometres each day to visit her injured child in hospital.

Her situation was both tragic and heroic, yet, as Martha observed, tragedy had become so much the norm in Europe, it was hard to summon more than an abstract feeling of pity for this woman. It was especially hard once she had learned about the other twelve hundred Jews from Nijmegen who'd been transported to their deaths in a concentration camp in Poland. Martha had heard rumours of the Nazi death camps, but she was devastated, nonetheless, when a local Dutchman confirmed their truth. As she reported to her readers, her informant had heard directly from an SS guard about the specialized extermination facility with which this Polish camp had been fitted — a "clean, white tiled bathroom" with special air vents, through which lethal "blue-gas" was pumped. She had no idea, yet, of the scale of the Nazis' genocidal mission, but, trying to imagine the terror of those Jews, who'd died "in what agony we cannot know," Martha wondered about the scientists and engineers who'd willingly developed such murderous technology, and about the people of Nijmegen, over whom its shadow must always fall. "To have lived close to such evil and to have seen, heard and understood it does something to people that will never be wiped out," she mused, not yet comprehending how she, too, would become permanently marked by her own war experiences.[3]

By the second half of October, the five Allied armies had advanced so far, they were ready to make an assault on the Siegfried Line, the chain of man-made and natural defences that ran along Germany's western border. When the fortress city of Aachen was taken, on 21 October, it seemed that victory might even be theirs by Christmas. But optimism was dangerously premature. In early November, a spell of incessant rain set in, and as armoured convoys became bogged down in mud, their progress was further impeded by the dense forests and vast lakes of this border region. None of these obstacles had been properly anticipated; but the most fatal blind spot in the Allied strategy was their failure to understand the will of the enemy.

Hitler had taken a humiliating battering over the last six months: his Luftwaffe planes no longer had control of the skies, his factories were unable to crank out sufficient tanks and arms, and the majority of his generals had lost faith. But he was still prepared to stake his own life, and that of the Reich, on one last counteroffensive. "We gamble everything now. We cannot fail," he'd ordered, and his proposed campaign had a brilliance born of desperation. Teams of English-speaking Germans were tasked with sabotaging Allied communications, while intelligence agents went scouting for weaknesses in the Allied front. The most vulnerable area was the Ardennes, the 11,000 square kilometres of thickly forested plateau spanning the borders of France, Belgium and Holland, which SHAEF had opted to defend with just three and a half armoured divisions. On the morning of 16 December, when wave after wave of German bombs and paratroopers came falling out of the skies, when tanks, trucks and infantry came barrelling out of the Ardennes forest, the unprepared Allies were scattered into headlong retreat.*

Within days, four of the five armies had become encircled and tracts of recently won territory were lost. The speed and scale of the Germans' ballooning advance earned it the nickname the Battle of the Bulge; but, as was the case so often in this war, the more flippant the slang, the grimmer the reality. During a single month, the Germans killed or captured nearly 80,000 Allied troops, they seized crippling quantities of arms and fuel, and they regained control over swathes of Belgium and north-east France. Extraordinarily, however, it was at this peculiarly perilous moment in the war that women were granted equal access. On 18 December, Lee Carson was able to stand at a forward command post on the Belgian–Luxembourg border, witnessing an approaching phalanx of

* In his more rational moments, Hitler did accept that outright victory was unlikely, but he was convinced he could force the Allies to accept a negotiated peace on terms most favourable to him.

Tiger tanks and reporting that enemy planes were "zooming down from the pink-streaked winter skies to shower our frontline positions with streams of hot lead."[4] That same day, Iris Carpenter was being driven in a military jeep along a steeply winding road that her escort feared might be "lousy with parachutists."[5] Just a month earlier, both women could have been court-martialled for being so close to the fighting; now, they were reporting from the front with the full knowledge of their commanding PRO and as officially designated members of the U.S. First Army press corps.

When SHAEF had finally performed its U-turn on the issue of female correspondents, a grudging proviso had remained, which theoretically excluded them from the most forward areas of a battle zone. But the wording had been left usefully vague, distinctions between "rear" and "forward" were essentially left to the discretion of individual officers, and women would rapidly come to identify which of the latter would prove most amenable. When Iris Carpenter and Lee Carson got themselves assigned to the U.S. First Army, they were not unaware that its press commander, Colonel Andrews, had gone on record to affirm that any woman who came under his jurisdiction would be treated on equal terms. They would be free to go "wherever their reporter's conscience drives them

— same as the men do — and if they get a beat on the story and scoop the pants off the men, it's all right by me."[6]

Privately, Andrews had begged Lee and Iris not to put themselves in actual harm's way: "you'll be no darned good to your paper if you get hurt, and you'll be one hell of a big embarrassment to me."[7] But, when the Battle of the Bulge had exploded around the five Allied armies, it became impossible to predict where danger lay, and when German bombers attacked Andrews' press camp, mistaking it for a military site, it was the Colonel himself who was killed.[8]

Meanwhile, as the fighting spread and editors were rushing to get extra journalists on the ground, more women were being sent out from Paris. In late December, Helen left her office in the care of a deputy and travelled to Alsace, where the U.S. 44th Division were attempting to block the Germans' eastwards advance. Blizzards were sweeping in from the mountains and temperatures were so low that bedrolls were stiff with ice, equipment was failing and some of the men were actually freezing to death in their foxholes. Helen was horrified when she saw how badly prepared the division had been for the onset of winter; most of the troops were still in their summer uniforms and were having to use thin white cloaks, sewn out of sheets by local women, for their winter camouflage. It was incompetence that bordered on a war crime, she believed, and she sent a furiously worded report to General Hodges, commander of the First Army, to tell him so.

Helen was never sentimental about American servicemen, acknowledging that too many of them had come into this war with a meagre education and poor discipline. But she cared about their well-being. One morning, she had drunk coffee with some men from the 44th Division, listening to their combat stories, their memories of home; and a few weeks later, when she heard that many of them had been killed in the Battle of Metz, she wrote letters of condolence to their families. One of the wives responded with tearful gratitude: "Your letter brought me a picture I so much wanted to see. The homely task of brewing coffee after a night of horrors makes Leonard's experiences there so much more real to me."[9] And for Helen, the woman's note brought a piercing reminder of just how widely the war had spread, from the battlefields of Europe, into homes across America.

Thousands of Leonards were dying every week, and, for the women who'd come most recently to combat reporting, their slaughter was difficult to witness. In late December, Dot Avery and Catherine Coyne were travelling with an American division towards the Belgian town of Bastogne. In anticipation of

Christmas, the men had decorated their helmets with holly and mistletoe, and, according to Catherine, "the convoys [had turned] into huge, fantastic, noisy parades." But, once at Bastogne, their larky festivities were met with "wreckage and desolation." The U.S. 10th Armoured Division had been holding out valiantly against a German assault, but the cost had been terrible; Dot and Catherine heard of men dragged screaming from their burning tanks, of a makeshift Allied hospital being annihilated by enemy bombs. There was no glory here, just blood and pain; when Martha too reported on the defence of Bastogne, she was moved to emphasize that, behind the military accounting of losses and gains, lay the suffering of real individuals. "This was not done fast or easily; and this was not done by those anonymous things, armies, divisions, regiments. It was done by men, one by one — your men."[10]

Although the Germans had been forced into retreat, there were rumours of a renewed attack; when Martha went to interview some soldiers who'd been posted just outside Bastogne, she was struck by "how small" these pivotal moments of warfare could be. "Finally it can boil down to ten unshaven gaunt-looking young men, from anywhere in America, stationed on a vital road with German tanks coming in."[11]

For the recently liberated civilians of France

542

and Belgium, the Battle of the Bulge was no less of a hell. In Bastogne, Dot and Catherine saw silently weeping families being dug out of blasted homes; in Spa, a hysterical Jewish mother begged Iris Carpenter to take her baby to safety; in Strasbourg, where German forces were close to victory, Helen saw terrified householders pulling down recently hoisted French and American flags; and Lee Miller, arriving shortly afterwards, could find nothing in the churned and frozen landscape, the wrecked villages and milling homeless that resembled the excitement of her Saint-Malo war. "Smell of death everywhere, of corpses, of exploded shells," she wrote, and her photographs captured that same hopeless misery: the group of stricken, clumsy nuns, searching for their priest in the rubble of a church; the child's doll, flung onto a pile of rubble, its arms stuck up in a poignant parody of surrender.[12] The soldiers fighting in Alsace also looked far younger and more vulnerable than Lee's heroes in the 83rd, their faces "gray and yellow with apprehension," and they seemed to be suffering many more casualties — from the walking wounded, who "were silent and moved like sleepwalkers or drunks," to the fatally injured lieutenant whom she saw slumped by a ditch, waiting for his death with an awful quietness.[13]

One event Lee didn't record for *Vogue* was

her tour of a remote Nazi camp, which the Allies had discovered the previous November. Struthof had subsequently been converted to housing for interned German civilians, yet evidence of its former barbarities remained. And while Lee would shortly come to appreciate how modest its operations had been, in relation to camps like Dachau, her heart froze when she toured Struthof and was shown the neatly stacked pots, containing ashes of the dead, and the small improvised gas chamber, with a crude contraption for pumping gas, and meat hooks for holding the victims in place.

Throughout Lee's tour of Alsace, she'd had her own jeep and her own military escort — a young, impressionable Frenchman, who'd been happy to drive his beautiful charge wherever she wanted to go. Martha, meanwhile, was still travelling alone and on the fly, convinced that her independence from the press corps was the best guarantee of her integrity, her route into stories that others could not write. Back in late December, however, there had been a moment when Martha's principled self-sufficiency had almost cost her the war. She'd travelled to Sissonne, a small village just outside Reims, where the U.S. 82nd Airborne Division had just concluded a long and gruelling battle to relieve a trapped American unit. She'd found an abandoned house in which to lay out her bedroll and had persuaded a couple of sympathetic sergeants to let her tag along on their night patrols. But, typically, she'd pushed her luck. One evening, wandering alone through a prohibited area, she'd been spotted by a military policeman and, because she had no AGO, nor any other form of professional identification, she was taken straight to the division commander for questioning.

Fatalistically, Martha prepared herself for the worst. If Major General James Gavin turned out to be a woman-hater, a stickler for protocol, she could face a period in custody, possibly even a deportation order back to the States. She might never get to write the war's final chapters. Yet, when she was marched into Gavin's presence, she saw that he was nothing like the "over-medalled" men in power, whom she'd come to fear and detest. There was a quizzical lift to his voice, an expression of lively intelligence on his broad, open face, and when he asked for an explanation of Martha's presence in Sissonne, he seemed positively to relish the story of her rogue status. Impressed that she'd managed to get so far without accreditation, Gavin had actually applauded her initiative, joking that she would make an excellent guerrilla fighter.

Martha had known for sure she was safe, when she'd realized that the Major General not only admired her, but found her attractive. She'd felt his gaze raking over her, as "electric" as a caress, and had noted her own flushed response. But this was no time for flirtation, and, once she was dismissed by Gavin, the encounter all but faded from her mind.

She travelled to Luxembourg, diverted north to Bastogne, and was back in Luxembourg on a snowy New Year's Day to see children shrieking joyfully on their sledges while U.S. fighter planes circled overhead. Late in January, she went south to the French–Spanish border, visiting the makeshift refugee camps which had become home to half a million defeated Loyalists. The Spaniards were being fed on little more than the "soup of starvation," Martha wrote, yet they refused to abandon their fight against fascism or relinquish their "transcendent faith" in their cause. And she was holding those Loyalists very close to her heart when, late in January, she managed to talk her way onto an American Black Widow night fighter and go hunting for Nazi warplanes.[14]

Martha was scared of flying. She perfectly recalled the "twitching limbs" and "peevishly disconnected" state in which she'd flown over China nearly four years ago. Now, with an ill-fitting oxygen mask clamped to her face, the throb of the engine hammering in her bones, she simply expected to die. At 22,000 feet above sea level, the cold and the altitude pressure were ferocious: "I thought my stomach was going to be flattened against my backbone, that I was going to strangle," she wrote.[15] But these terrors paled into insignificance when the Black Widow had to swerve and tumble its way through anti-aircraft fire, and when, dogfighting with an enemy plane, it ended up flying directly above its prey, and directly in range of its guns. Yet, while Martha feared death at every moment of this mission, she didn't regret it. Flying high over Germany she'd been able to see flashes of artillery from the Western Front, the trail of a rocket bomb rising from a red ball of fire. Hitler's Reich was now battling, hard, for survival, and, for her, it was a beautiful sight.

This should have been a turning point in Martha's war. The Battle of the Bulge had finally been won, and not only were the Allies back on the offensive, she had regained her own privileged position at *Collier's,* Ernest having split from the magazine in a spat over expenses. Yet the months of solitary travelling had taken their toll. Martha could hardly remember when she'd last been properly warm; the winter freeze was exceptionally hard this year, and disrupted coal supplies meant that, even in Paris, buildings had heat for only two hours a day. Whenever she made a brief sortie back to the Lincoln, she had to wear gloves over her swollen chilblains to type up her copy. But more debilitating even than the cold was the sheer relentlessness of this war; in late January, when Martha wrote a letter to *Collier's* confessing that she did not know whether she was "simply tired to death or full of despair," she intimated that she was unsure how much longer she could continue.[16]

Her trusted editor, Charles Colebaugh, had died the previous year, and Martha was furious when his replacement chose to publish her, confidential, letter, and illustrate it with a glamour shot she greatly disliked. But she was grateful, nonetheless, to Henry La Cossitt when he suggested that she might spend some time in London, to report on how the city and its residents were surviving their fifth year of war, and how they were holding out against the new, more lethally sophisticated variant of Hitler's rocket bomb. Even though Martha was not particularly interested in the assignment itself — she'd exhausted all she wanted to say about London on her previous visit — she was very glad to have a reprieve from the fighting, and glad, too, for the opportunity to catch up with Ginny Cowles.

Virginia herself was now definitively *hors de combat:* her mysterious illness, her battle fatigue, her work for the embassy had all kept her confined to London, and she was additionally eager to spend time with her sister, Mary, who was now based in the city and working with American intelligence. Yet, even if Ginny was no longer covering the war directly, she was still Martha's closest battle "pal" — the person with whom she was able to share her own recent travails, and with whom she found it easiest to escape into laughter. It was with Ginny, too, that Martha was shocked into realizing she had no idea of what her life would be like when the war was over. As the two women had discussed how they might support themselves, they'd come up with the idea for their collaborative play — a comedy about two female correspondents, holed up in a press camp in Italy. They spent a hilarious few days at their typewriters, each writing a caricature version of the other and together inventing a cast of male characters who represented every cocky journalist and obnoxious PRO they'd ever endured. Martha had such a good time with Ginny she resolved to move to London when the war was over, and, acting with her usual decisiveness, she found "a filthy flaking little villa" in Belgravia's South Eaton Place, which she bought for a knock-down price.[17]

London was restorative, but Martha's pleasure in the city was blighted by one last encounter with Hemingway. He had agreed to begin their divorce proceedings as soon as he was back in Cuba, largely because he wanted to marry Mary Welsh. Yet, while he was prepared to be rational, he still had the power to frighten Martha. "A man must be a very great genius to make up for being such a loathsome human being," she wrote to her mother, and, flinching from the thought that she'd ever been married to him, she swore that she never wanted to hear his name again.[18]

She was still thin skinned and vulnerable in early March when she returned to her room at the Lincoln and found a message from James Gavin. He and his men were in Rouen, recuperating from their winter campaign, and he'd taken advantage of his leisure to track her down. It was his third attempt, he wrote, and so eager was he to see her again he was sending down a plane to fly her to his barracks. Martha bristled at his presumption — it made her feel, she claimed, like "a package" that had been ordered up for collection.[19] But it didn't stop her going. She was lonely for male company and she'd heard interesting things about Gavin, who was said to be one of the most inspired, and inspiring, commanders in the American armed forces. "Jumpin' Jim," as his men called him — or "Slim Jim," as he was known to the press — was unique in actually undertaking combat jumps alongside his paratroopers. He was, in fact, a hero, and, at this point of the war, Martha was badly in need of one.

Their first encounter in the dingy Rouen barracks was not encouraging. Martha felt she was being "pushed" into Jim Gavin's bed, and suspected she was far from being the first. But her wariness eased when they sat down to talk, and Jim spoke with a moving passion about his belief in this war, and about his commitment to the men under his command. "I was crazy about him as a soldier," Martha admitted. And when she eventually agreed to make love with him, she acknowledged, with a return of her old ironic humour, that it had been "on a basis of high mutual esteem."[20]

By the end of her stay in Rouen, Martha was also crazy about Jim as a man, and Edna Gellhorn, hearing news of the affair, observed shrewdly that it fell within a well-established pattern. When Martha had been in love with France, Edna wrote, she'd fallen for Bertrand, "the complete Frenchman"; when she'd been honing her craft as a novelist, she had turned to Ernest, "the finest writer" of his generation. Now, in the middle of the war, Martha had predictably found Jim Gavin, "who was considered perhaps the bravest [fighter] of all."[21]

Edna did not add that her own husband had almost certainly established this pattern — the paternal exemplar to whose high, exacting standards Martha had always tried to aspire, and against whom she'd eventually rebelled. In time, Martha would also run away from Jim; but, during the spring of

1945, in the middle of the war, she embraced him as a saving force of steadiness, inspiration and joy.

Their times together were fleeting — snatched between combat duties and reporting assignments — and they weren't always easy. During one of their reunions, Martha learned that Jim had ordered his men to make a tactical sortie, to draw fire from an endangered Allied unit. He'd done so in full knowledge of the casualties it would incur, yet, for him, it had been a necessary calculation, a sum total of lives saved set against those that might have been lost. Martha, however, could not accept that logic. She'd made good friends in the 82nd and was horrified that Jim would send them knowingly into peril. As always, when her passions ran hot, she went on the attack, storming into his office and accusing him of ordering a massacre. His response was shocking. With a military steel she'd never yet heard in his voice, he told Martha to leave his office and never question his tactics again. Later, she was able to apologize, recognizing that Jim had responsibilities she could neither measure nor judge, but the incident was a marker for her, illuminating the different worlds the two of them inhabited, and the problems they might encounter should they try to remain together after the war.[22]

All they could do was live as greedily as

possible in the present moment. When they were apart, they wrote long letters and Martha sent pictures and photographs to decorate Jim's office. When they were together, they played competitive games of gin rummy and Martha, to her intense relief, also found pleasure in their lovemaking. For the first time in her life, she felt she had been admitted into a world that others took for granted, a world where sex was not a weary duty, but "something wild and crazy and fierce like war."[23] Perhaps Jim was more skilfully attuned to her body; perhaps she trusted him more readily than her previous lovers; or perhaps it was the accelerating intensity of the war itself which had jolted Martha into these sharp, exhilarating glimmers of joy.

Love and sex acted on women in very different ways, and, if they were healing for Martha at this stage of the war, to others they seemed like dangerous complications. Pregnancy was an obvious risk, for even though Allied soldiers had been issued with supplies of rubbers, condoms broke, latex degraded, and no female correspondent wanted to find herself pregnant in the middle of a combat zone. But heartbreak and loss could be no less disabling. Back in Berlin, Sigrid had allowed herself to become emotionally vulnerable when she fell in love with Peter Ilcus, and the pain of their enforced separation, the anguish of not knowing if Peter had survived, had made the war additionally hard. It was the fear of ratcheting up their own exposure to grief that had made Virginia and Aidan draw back from marriage at the onset of war, and a comparable fear had also kept Helen on her guard. To do her job well, she knew she had to keep her emotions on a leash, to keep her love affairs casual; and her wariness had been reinforced by the example of Margaret Bourke-White, who, late in 1943, had been blindsided by the charm of an American counter-intelligence officer.

Major Jerry Parpurt had proposed marriage and when the two of them had been separated by their different war duties, they had continued their affair by army airmail. In June 1944, however, Jerry's letters ceased, and, after weeks of uncertainty, Margaret heard that he'd been wounded and taken prisoner during Operation Overlord. Frantically, she wrote a short, urgent note: "I love you, I will marry you."* But the Allies had bombed the prison camp where Jerry was held and Margaret never learned if he'd read her words.

If Margaret's loss was not warning enough to Helen, she then had a cautionary encounter with her former husband. On her way to

* The Vatican operated a system by which short messages could be delivered to some prisoners of war.

Strasbourg in December 1944, she broke her journey in Vittel, and dining quietly in the Allied HQ officers' mess, she was jolted by a slap on her back so hearty "it nearly threw me into my soup."[24] It was Vic Polachek, now in a captain's uniform, and, as Helen soon discovered, the same aggressively cocksure man she'd married. The following morning, he insisted on driving her to Strasbourg, partly because he wanted to show her an observation post which promised some lively action. Helen reluctantly agreed, but when she and Vic were spotted by Germans, and howitzer shells came hurtling in their direction, she had no desire to risk a pointless death and asked Vic to drive on. He, however, seemed to regard this moment as a contest of nerves, and, making a show of calming Helen down, he drawled, "Now, don't get excited, sweetheart."

"I'm not your sweetheart and I'm not excited," Helen snapped back. Her skin was ready to crawl with memories of how wrong she'd been to marry Vic, and, conscious of the poor choice she'd made with him, she was very far from wanting to make herself vulnerable to another man. Yet four or five months later, just as the war in Europe was winding down, she met an officer named Nigel, and, for a brief interlude, she seems to have been deeply in love. Helen herself never wrote about the affair. "I dislike so much the personal pronoun," she would state when asked why she'd never published her memoirs, and no record remains of when, where and how she and Nigel first met.[25] The depth of their mutual connection, however, was ardently disclosed in the one surviving letter Nigel wrote. "Darling, I'm not very good at expressing my feelings in writing — or verbally for that matter, I just get rather incoherent. But I can say that nothing has changed, except perhaps that this wonderful and surprising thing is getting stronger and stronger . . . Oh God, I wish you were here. I love you."

Nigel's name and his style of expression both point to him being English, but his letter reveals frustratingly little about his military circumstances, beyond the fact that he'd written it from an army base "East of Brest-Litovsk," and that he and his unit were shortly being moved to Berlin. He clearly hoped for a future with Helen, promising to join her in Paris as soon as was "humanly possible," and promising that one day they would be together "all the time." Yet that future would never materialize. It's possible Nigel was posted elsewhere, to the continuing war in the Far East, but it's equally possible that Helen drew back. She'd grown so accustomed to organizing her own life and career, and her independence was so deeply ingrained that it had become hard for her to imagine herself in a permanent relationship — and she would not, in the end, commit to a second marriage until she was forty-five, and had long retired from journalism.

Yet, if wartime intimacy felt too precarious for many, Martha was not alone in seeking it out. Lee Carson, Iris's friend and colleague in the First Army, was "quite frank" about using sex to "forget the daily horror of war."[26] Bold, generous, curvily at ease in her own body, she was as direct in encouraging the men she liked as she was in rejecting those she didn't. At this stage in the war, it was becoming a concern amongst a minority of male journalists that women were exploiting their new proximity to the troops to flirt their way to the best copy. One disgruntled male reporter, spotting Lee with a group of GIs, jitterbugging crazily in the ruins of Aachen, had sniped, "How can you work against a dame? There she was, dancing with these guys . . . that's the way a dame gets stories."[27] But his paranoia was misplaced. Lee was dancing only because she enjoyed it, because flirting was her natural element and because some of those young soldiers might be dead the next day.

Lee Miller also seems to have turned to sex for comfort and release. Although she would join up with Dave Scherman at the very end of the war, there were periods when she felt very alone and very defenceless against all that she was having to document. "I had held my eyes so rigid and my mouth so frozen that I could scarcely manage a smile," she later recalled. And, while others who encountered Lee on the road would find her as charismatic as she'd ever been — gutsy, funny, resourceful and grubbily beautiful in her khaki — it was a charisma that was also shored up by artificial stimulants and the temporary company of men.[28] Years later, an officer from the 83rd admitted he'd been one of several in the division to share Lee's bedroll, and, unlike her butterfly peacetime affairs, this warzone promiscuity seems to have been driven by a very basic instinct for survival.* Thrust into a fractured, brutalized world, the simple weight and warmth of another body was the most immediate form of solace Lee knew, and, like the other Lee, it may have felt like a simple act of charity to offer that same solace to the men risking their lives at the front.

For Clare Hollingworth, the war would take a surprisingly romantic turn. During the last five years, she'd come to regard herself as a free agent, enjoying sex where she found it, warding off any romantic entanglement with her caustic insistence that "a good gin and

* He was interviewed for the 2001 BBC documentary about Lee, *A Crazy Way of Seeing,* but chose not to appear in the finished film, for fear of wounding his wife and family.

tonic gives me more pleasure than any man."[29] But, in the middle of 1943, she met Geoffrey Hoare, newly appointed Cairo correspondent for the *Times*. "He was tall, blonde and thin," she wrote, "with an impeccable taste in tropical clothes and, far more important, a profound knowledge of Egypt and its politics."[30] He was also a seasoned womanizer and, while he was married to a red-headed journalist named Morley Lister, he seems to have regarded the obstinately unmanicured Clare — a streak of white already showing in her Brylcreemed hair — as a piquant challenge. Clare, for her part, seems to have had no compunction about the affair. She'd come to believe that adultery, in wartime, was excusable, if not morally defensible, and she hardly spared a thought for Morley Lister, dismissing her as exactly the type of journalist she'd always despised, trading on her looks and her femininity to advance her career.

Yet, as months passed, Clare recognized that she might finally have met her partner and her match in Geoffrey. As a journalist, he shared her addiction to travel and headlines; as a socialist, he shared her hopes for a rational future; and, as a lover, he was more entertaining and worldly than any man she'd known. There were long periods of separation when Clare was away from Cairo, covering political developments in the Middle East and investigating guerrilla resistance in the Balkans and Greece. But, in the autumn of 1944, she and Geoffrey were both coincidentally assigned to Athens, where the Germans were in retreat (recalled to fight more urgent battles in Western Europe), and where communist and royalist Greeks were fighting each other for control of their newly liberated county.

The six months that they spent together in Greece set the seal on their relationship. Away from the hothouse gossip of Cairo, they were able to live openly together, but they were also learning how well they worked as a professional team; many of the stories they filed from Athens were investigated by her and stylistically finessed by him. In the spring of 1945, they moved down to Crete to cover the surrender of the last remaining German troops, and this, for Clare, was one of the happiest times of her life. The lovers drove around the island "like lords," spreading news of the Allied victory to a few stubbornly resistant German units. And it was here, in the middle of their Mediterranean idyll and their own private war, that Geoffrey proposed.[31]

During those last few months of the conflict, Clare had become so absorbed in Greece and Geoffrey that she'd made no real effort to return to where the principal news was breaking. She'd been following the progress of the Allied armies as they fought their way across the Rhine in February and March — drawing inexorably closer to the Russians who were approaching Germany from the east; and it was very obvious to her that the end must be in sight. Yet, while it had meant everything to Clare that she'd scooped the outbreak of war, she was content to leave the closing chapter to others. She would only read what others had reported about the triumphant convoys that had penetrated into the heartland of the Reich, capturing one bombed-out city after another. And she would only hear, second hand, about the confusion of emotions her colleagues had experienced when they'd first found themselves standing on enemy soil. It had been disorienting enough for the press to be in Germany itself, but even more so to encounter actual German civilians: men and women whom they'd learned to fear and hate, yet who now appeared the feeblest of adversaries — stripped not only of their homes and livelihoods, but, in many cases, of their national pride.

Chapter Fifteen:
The Fall of the Reich,
Spring 1945

"It is eerie to be in Germany where the
adrenalin, stimulated by hate,
boils in the blood"

LEE MILLER[1]

"We were confronted with this intangible thing we had hated for so long as the enemy, only to discover . . . that it was made up of . . . ordinary people."[2] Iris Carpenter was not alone in discovering that the loathing which had sustained her throughout the war was now softening into something like pity. At a distance, it had been easy to regard Hitler's Reich as a single, evil aggressor; it had been easy to cheer the bombing of Hamburg, Frankfurt, Berlin as a righteous revenge for London, Coventry, and Liverpool. But, during the second half of March 1945, when the press were allowed to enter the westernmost cities of Germany, the devastation of buildings and people had been difficult to witness.

Janet Flanner, Paris correspondent for the

New Yorker, had blanched to see the magnificent medieval centre of Cologne looking "shapeless in the rubble and loneliness of complete physical defeat."[3] The RAF had flown a relentless 250 raids over the city, systematically pounding its historic architecture to a wasteland of gaping ruins, incinerating its trees to derelict stumps. Amid Cologne's desolation, the once-prosperous citizens were scrabbling for survival — half-famished mothers were begging scraps for their children; elderly couples were picking forlornly through the wreckage of their homes — and, as the Allies pushed forwards and the ruins accumulated, some of the press were conflicted between jubilation and guilt.*

Martha was not one of them. When she

* In Britain, questions were privately raised as to whether "Bomber Harris," the Air Marshal in charge of RAF strategy, was being driven less by military logic than by the bloodlust of the popular press. The carpet-bombing of German cities was creating huge logistical problems for the Allies, generating millions of homeless and blocking the roads. Meanwhile, enthusiasm for retaliation bombing was uneven. Helen reported on a survey taken in 1941 which indicated that it was the parts of Britain most unaffected by the Luftwaffe raids which showed the greatest support (76 per cent) for retaliatory bombing, while the big cities, which had taken the brunt of the Blitz, expressed least approval.

crossed into Germany, she was enraged to see healthy-looking civilians going about their business, in villages that were still smugly intact; even the bomb-blasted cities failed to touch her. She reminded her readers of the roll-call of atrocities that had been committed in the name of the German people — citing the little French village of Oradour-sur-Glane, where, in retaliation for local resistance, every woman and child had been locked inside the church and burned alive. "In Germany, when you see absolute devastation you do not grieve," Martha wrote. "We have grieved for many places, in many countries, but this is not one of [them]."[4]

She wouldn't, or couldn't, feel compassion for the individual Germans she interviewed. Deaf to their stories of misery and loss, she was conscious only of their reluctance to accept any responsibility for Hitler and his war. "To see a whole nation passing the buck is not an enlightening spectacle. No one is a Nazi, no one ever was. There may have been some Nazis in the next village . . . that town about twenty kilometres away . . . Oh, the Jews. Well, there weren't really many Jews in this neighbourhood."[5] The piece Martha filed for *Collier's* was coruscating in its contempt, and that contempt would deepen as she travelled through Germany. It became the fuel that kept her going, and, during the final weeks of the war, she would tend it, almost as a form of love.

Lee Miller was in the grip of a similarly unyielding rage. When she, too, reached Cologne, she was among a group of journalists taken to witness the liberation of the city's Gestapo-run jail. The first of the prisoners to emerge was a nineteen-year-old Belgian girl, arrested for assisting RAF pilots when their planes had been shot down; she'd been barely able to stand as she was helped, blinking, into the cobbled prison yard, every bruise, every jutting bone of her body standing out pitifully in the spring sunshine. After her came a Dutch woman, jailed for listening to banned foreign radio stations; then came a desperately fragile adolescent boy and, most heartbreakingly of all, a tiny Russian girl, so traumatized she could only whisper, over and over again, that she was very hungry and very cold.

Like everyone else at the scene, Lee was overwhelmed with pity, disgust, an existential rage; and she could barely contain herself when, interviewing a group of local residents, she was assured that none of them had been aware of the atrocities being perpetrated in their midst. She was convinced they were lying, that they were simply trying to "curry favour" with their new masters, and she felt the same contempt for the Germans in Cologne that she'd felt for those in Aachen a few days earlier.[6]

That city too had been in ruins, yet while its population were hungry and traumatized, Lee chose only to see them as a "prideless" people, who "hoarded selfishly" and "cheated in food queues." When she climbed over mounds of rubble to photograph the bomb-damaged cathedral, she had no pity to waste on the half-decaying corpses she disturbed. The scraps of flesh that stuck to her hands and knees, the "foul tomb smells" that swam up from the ruins, were simply emblematic to her of the evil at the core of Hitler's Reich.[7] "It is eerie to be in Germany where the adrenalin, stimulated by hate, boils in the blood," she wrote to Audrey, and to Roland she admitted her mood was toxic: "I'm getting a very bad character from grinding my teeth and snarling and constantly going around full of hate . . . I work myself into such a state that I have no human kindness in me."[8]

But, even though Lee could feel her moral compass swinging out of control, she had neither the will, nor the power, to correct it. Helen Kirkpatrick, however, was typically more cautious, typically more analytic. Years in the news room had trained her to weigh her facts, and she knew there had been courageous individuals in Germany who'd held out against the Nazi regime. She was even capable of feeling pity for its young army conscripts, and had quietly wept when she'd seen two women tending the body of what she assumed was their brother, carefully placing the boy's helmet over his face and covering his body "with branches from a shell torn tree."[9] His was one of the few deaths that she saw being mourned with dignity and love. So many Germans were being killed in the Allied advance that most of their corpses were simply abandoned. When Helen reached the Bavarian city of Schweinfurt, every street seemed to be littered with unclaimed and unshriven bodies. "Nobody has had time to bury them or even to glance at these odd twisted ragdoll remains of human beings," she reported, and, when she was given a tour of the city hospital, she tried to honour at least one of the German dead. He was a young soldier, barely more than a boy, and he'd served just one month in the Wehrmacht before being sent home with a bullet in his lungs. He'd died on the filthy hospital floor, laid out beside the corpse of his wife, and it mattered very much to Helen that she learned his name. It was Hans, she told her readers, and in this brief account of his death she felt she'd at least paid some respect to his pitifully short life.[10]

But the line of compassionate objectivity was difficult to tread. Helen was travelling more or less constantly throughout the spring of 1945, and the empathy she tried to summon for ordinary Germans was in conflict with all she was learning about their political masters. Almost every town and city which the Allies liberated was revealed to have some kind of Nazi work camp, in which men and women from the occupied territories had been kept as a slave labour force. Their conditions, Helen learned, were inhuman, with working days lasting twelve hours or more, and near-starvation rations of black bread and potato gruel. Many had perished, but it had been deemed "a crime against blood" for any German citizen to feel sympathy for them, and an act of treason to offer material aid.

In the city of Kessel, Helen saw 100,000 such workers being released from captivity, all of them pathetically malnourished, many with the high, hectic colour of consumptives. In Frankfurt, she saw another 15,000, lice-ridden and listless. But, Helen reported, even as the Allies were liberating the camps, they were also making problems for themselves, for, as the freed workers began trudging their way homewards, they were creating "the biggest exodus in human history," jamming up all the roads across Germany and looting food, petrol and farm vehicles as they went.[11]

Even though a network of holding camps was hastily assembled to contain the situation, it was a hopeless task. In one of the camps, Helen observed eight young American soldiers attempting to process the details of

14,000 people; and, when she interviewed the Brigadier General who was meant to be in charge of the "Displaced Persons Operation" back in Paris, she noted that very "little of what he said bore any relation to the facts," and that he clearly had no understanding of the problem's scale.[12]

Nor was it just the liberated workers who were complicating the Allied advance. Large numbers of their own captured soldiers were being freed and many needed urgent medical care. Helen spoke to one emaciated-looking group who'd been force-marched from their POW camp alongside the retreating German army and had been allowed nothing to eat beyond the scraps of animal feed they could forage on the way. Their treatment had been in blatant violation of the Geneva Convention and it inspired new levels of hatred among the active soldiers. Some of the American conscripts had come reluctantly to this war, regarding it as an abstract issue, a quarrel over alien soil. Now, it felt personal, and Iris Carpenter witnessed a hardness setting in among the men of the First Army. All they cared about was defeating the Germans, and she noticed how rarely they wrote to their families now: "Death, dirt and weariness are the familiar . . . it is impossible for them to think of a world of baths and home-cooked food when everything within eye range is broken and spoiled."[13]

■ ■ ■ ■

It was additionally dangerous for these men to think about home, given that victory was drawing tantalizingly close. Numerically, the Allies were at a huge advantage: they were invading Germany with four times more men and hundreds of times more machine power. Seven of their armies were now fanning across the Reich: the 21st Army Group (comprised of the British Second, First Canadian and American Ninth), who were fighting in the north; the 12th Army Group (American First and Third), who were in the centre; and the 6th Army Group (American Seventh and French First), who were in the south.* They were also advancing across terrain that had already been half bombed into submission, the factories and communication links of the Reich now as badly damaged as its cities.

In certain regions, the Wehrmacht was imploding; Helen reported that some divisions had become "so badly mauled and disorganised" that their officers had lost all track of the thousands of men who were simply choosing to lay down their weapons.† Civilians were also surrendering, and white flags

---

* Their respective commanders were Bernard Montgomery, Omar Bradley and Jacob L. Devers.
† Overwhelmed by the numbers of surrendering

were being hoisted over towns and villages long before the Allies got near. Meanwhile, there were rumours of frantic disarray within the Nazi high command. Hitler, holed up in his Berlin *Führerbunker* since 12 January, was said to be in a state of drug-addled denial, issuing hysterical contradictory orders to his generals, and seemingly oblivious to the fact that the city above him was being bombed twice a day.

On certain days it was impossible to believe that Germany had any fight left, but the seven armies were still encountering pockets of savage resistance. Guerrilla units were risking death to sabotage Allied supplies and communications; Nazi agents in American uniform were raping and murdering German civilians to incite rebellion against Allied troops; and, even now, the Wehrmacht's depleted ranks were being filled with new recruits. Some were women — Hitler having abandoned his vow never to let German wives and mothers become sullied by combat — but the majority were teenage boys, often so young that their uniforms flapped loose around their skinny frames.

Many of these boys had been educated in Nazi schools, regimented in Hitler Youth

---

Germans, the Allies could only send them off in the direction of a hastily assembled POW camp.

groups, and they were fighting now in an adolescent fervour of bloodlust and self-sacrifice. They were Hitler's new generation, and, while the Allied advance was essentially unstoppable, the unpredictability of this last-ditch resistance made the last few weeks of the war peculiarly hazardous. The front lines were everywhere and nowhere: it was frequently impossible to distinguish which side was in control of what terrain. As for the press, their own rules of engagement had to be radically tightened; while they'd previously been allowed to drive around battle zones with just one escort for protection, SHAEF now insisted that they travel at all times with a convoy. A sheaf of Helen's travel papers, dated between 9 March and 7 April, show her continually swapping from one division to another as she zigzagged around Germany.

Even the most battle-hardened of the press were exhausted by the distances they were covering and the furious pace of the news. All of them were living in uniforms that were stiff with dirt and sweat, and sleeping at night in half-ruined buildings, sometimes with the luxury of an army cot, but often on a dirt floor. They'd almost forgotten what it was to eat anything but the dry biscuits and pink greasy pork loaf of their military K ration and conditions were so insanitary it was impossible to recall why any PRO had ever bothered himself about the "convenience question."

Many were nursing bruises or fractured ribs from jeeps that had veered off muddy roads; and, hungry, sleep deprived, fizzing with adrenalin, the majority were smoking and drinking heavily just to keep going. If it was remarkable that they reported accurately and well under such conditions, it was also remarkable that so much of their copy — hammered out in derelict houses, on dusty, dented typewriters — actually reached its destination. A makeshift system had been developed to keep the news flowing, with each division allocated a dispatch rider to bike typewritten reports and rolls of film to the nearest functioning military HQ. If the HQ had cabling facilities, copy could be delivered electronically to the Hotel Scribe; if not, it had to be flown there by plane.* Censors were meant to check all material before it could be forwarded to the relevant desks, but, by this point, their vigilance was noticeably lax: "things had become so wide open and so sort of chaotic," recalled Helen, "that there wasn't any point in stopping stories, because by the time they [arrived] something new had developed."[14]

In the middle of fatigue, fear and frequent

* An auxiliary cabling system was also in place, using a commercial wireless company that operated a connection between London and Normandy.

isolation, the women of the press learned to prize the few moments when their reporting paths crossed. Back in Cologne, Helen had shared a billet with Lee Miller, Janet Flanner, Margaret Bourke-White, Dot Avery and Catherine Coyne. It was a chilly, abandoned house on the edge of the city, yet the women happily congregated there at the end of each day, to share their whisky supplies and to joke, gossip and bitch. Janet Flanner, at fifty-two, was the oldest of the group, her cropped white hair, sharp humour and autocratic manner a little alarming to some. Lee Miller, who'd met her in Paris the previous autumn, had found her somewhat aloof and "scratchy in places."[15] Yet Janet was very conscious of the five years she'd just spent in America, sitting out the war, and here in Cologne she was modestly quick to acknowledge how much she could learn from her younger, more experienced colleagues, especially the "splendid Helen." Janet was also the main entertainment of the billet, and in the evenings she would regale the others with indiscreet stories about the artists and celebrities she'd interviewed before the war, and share her seemingly unlimited, often quite filthy repertoire of truth-or-dare parlour games.

Not every woman was admitted to this inner circle. When Marguerite Higgins, a pretty and pugnacious twenty-four-year-old, writing for the *New York Herald Tribune,* had brought her bedroll to that Cologne billet, she'd immediately made herself unpopular. She was allocated a space in the room already occupied by Helen, Lee and a woman named Rita Vanderwert, and, while these three had agreed to leave their window open at night, Maggie had unilaterally insisted on keeping it shut. Helen conceded it had been the most minor of transgressions, yet it had mattered very much at the time — "You know, those silly things you remember." And she would come to regard it as typical of Maggie's naive but ruthless enthusiasm for getting ahead of the game, her willingness to exploit her looks in getting to a source, to skimp on research and even twist her facts to scoop herself a headline.

Helen dismissed Maggie as an "ambitious minx" and made a careful point of avoiding her; the other Maggie, though, she admired more fondly every time they met. The affection was mutual and, when Margaret Bourke-White came to write about Helen in her memoir, she would rank her as the "best of war companions," celebrating the reckless speeds with which she'd driven herself around the war, bashing up and down muddy hills and navigating uncertain terrain. "It was Helen who read the maps, charted our course and drove the lead jeep," wrote Margaret. "She loved to sail along so fast . . . that the Colonel was always in a dither knowing that before the day was over her exuberant little jeep would disappear into the distance and leave the rest of our convoy far behind."[16]

Helen and Margaret were together in Frankfurt on Easter Sunday, where the fires were still smouldering and groups of young women were stepping over corpses as they searched for lilac blossoms to decorate what remained of their homes. A band of newly liberated slave workers was scavenging for scraps in the garbage, and, later that day, when Helen interviewed a local industrialist whom she knew had profited from their labour, she was sickened by his boast of the fresh chicken he'd managed to procure for his own Easter meal. From Frankfurt, she and Margaret travelled to Kassel, where the bombing had left a miasma of thick yellow dust in the air. It was becoming hard, now, to distinguish one city from the next — the ravaged buildings, the stink of cordite and death were always the same — and it was no less hard to find new angles of the war to cover. But, on 12 April, another story broke, which briefly stole the headlines from the invasion.

Helen was at a press camp near Schweinfurt, trying to work up some enthusiasm for her K-ration supper, when a jeepful of American medics arrived, shouting out news that Roosevelt was dead. The sixty-three-year-old President had been suffering from high blood pressure, atherosclerosis and a damaged heart, yet to his army he'd always figured as their protector and war leader, and Helen was moved by the number of bewildered and bereft young GIs who came wandering into the press camp that night, "all in tears, all wanting talk and comfort. It seemed to them that they were doing so well, that the war was nearly won and then this happened."[17]

Lee Miller, meanwhile, was following the war wherever her instincts took her. While the daily news journalists had to plot their itineraries around breaking stories, Lee's monthly deadlines gave her the luxury of time, and she wanted to see all the different facets of the Reich's disintegration. In Bonn, the birthplace of Beethoven, she photographed a statue of the composer still standing with a bleak kind of dignity in a bombed-out square. In the Nazi stronghold of Leipzig, where the majority of homes were still decorated with photographs of the Führer, she was shown the bodies of the city treasurer and his wife and daughter, who'd committed suicide rather than live to see their city's defeat. The family seemed to have choreographed their deaths with a ritual staginess, especially the daughter, who lay, Ophelia-like, on the leather couch in the treasurer's office, her arms loosely crossed and her lips parted in death to reveal what Lee acerbically acknowledged to be "extraordinarily pretty" teeth.[18]

She'd placed her Rolleiflex mercilessly close to the girl, shooting one of the most macabre portraits of her career. But among the many, many rolls of film she was sending back to Audrey, there were dozens of similarly disturbing images: forensic shots of a dead German soldier, with two pairs of surgeon's forceps still dangling from his shattered wrists; extraordinary landscapes of the valley where the Nazis had stored their looted art, the sculptures so thickly swathed in camouflage netting, they looked like alien life forms. "The war has become so fluid I can't keep up with my own ideas," Lee cabled excitedly to Audrey.[19] Yet, while it was addictive to be racing around Germany looking for fresh views that others hadn't seen, she was also pushing against her limits. Physically exhausted and emotionally numbed, she might well have crashed had she not been joined, mid-April, by Dave Scherman.

During the first phase of the invasion, Dave had been stuck in Paris, under orders to photograph the spring collections, but, once he was done, he'd acquired a 1937 Chevrolet, which he'd named Jemima and spray-painted a military olive drab, before driving off to Germany to catch up with the war and look for Lee. The two of them had continued on together, Lee presumably relishing the comfort of her sporty new ride; and, faced with the choice of many different fronts to cover, they opted to attach themselves to the First Army as it fought its way east.

It was an astute decision, for the Red Army was advancing rapidly from the opposite direction and the two great forces were predicted to meet up very soon. On 25 April, news broke that Ann Stringer of the United Press had caught sight of a Soviet soldier emerging from the River Elbe in his swimming trunks, and had heard the sounds of jubilant Americans crossing over to greet him. Russia and America were within a handshake of a ceremonial encounter, and, when it was decided to stage that encounter at Torgau, a small town on the Elbe, just a hundred kilometres south of Berlin, Lee knew "there would be a terrible rat race" to cover it.

She was fully determined to be ahead of that race and, because Dave had been told to hold back (another photographer with *Life* was already much closer to Torgau), Lee had to cadge a lift with four American soldiers. The journey was rough and jolting, but the jeep caused a sensation as it roared through the quiet towns and villages: "People fleeing everywhere, thinking we were the Russians," noted Lee. "Displaced persons cheering wildly. Armed German soldiers ducking out of sight etc."[20] It also got her to Torgau ahead of most of her colleagues, and she was one of the few to photograph representatives of the two military powers making their first symbolic exchange of food — black bread and raw onions from the Russians, K rations from the Americans.*

By the time Dave caught up with her, she was in the thick of a celebratory lunch, held in the grounds of a shell-blasted villa. Pictures of Stalin and Roosevelt (the latter framed in black) had been hung from trees, but the gravity of their presence had no effect on the collective exuberance. Cheese, sausage and vodka had been produced in astonishing quantities by the Russians, outdoing the Americans' far duller contributions of chocolate and powdered eggs; the meal was accompanied by tearfully bellowed toasts, random gunfire, and music from accordions and mandolins. Afterwards, there was dancing. Lee was grabbed by a stoutly booted Russian general and whirled around the grass; Iris Carpenter and Lee Carson, also recent arrivals, were similarly spun from officer to officer.

The three Americans had assumed they were the only female presence in Torgau, until they realized there was a small contingent of women amongst the Red Army. These women

* No press had been present for the first modest encounter, when a tiny envoy of American soldiers crossed the Elbe at Torgau to make contact with the Russians.

580

looked peculiarly square and masculine in their uniforms, and when Lee made friends with some of them — the vodka doing most of the talking — she understood why. Casually stripping off their jackets and shirts, the Russians had shown her their army-issue brassieres, so solid and heavily strapped they flattened down every curve. Always game, Lee stripped off herself; but, when the Russians saw that she wore no bra, and had little need for one, they were baffled and distressed. With a concern she found both comic and touching, these war-toughened women gathered around Lee in sisterly sympathy, clucking over her meagre bosom, insisting she must fatten herself up.

It was the clinching detail for her Torgau story, and she felt additionally smug when Marguerite Higgins pitched up just as Dave and she were about to drive away. "How is it that every time I arrive somewhere to cover a story," she whined to Dave, "you and Lee Miller are just leaving?"[21]

Martha arrived even later, and all she learned about that historic day came from Jim's heartlessly enthusiastic report that the Soviets played "excellent music" and their "vodka supply was limitless."[22] She managed to jot down some lively impressions of the small Russian unit posted on the American side of the Elbe, with whom she ate delicious sausage and fresh eggs, but the "lovely sad sound" of singing which came from the men on the Soviet side of the river was the closest Martha would get to the Red Army itself.

Already, there was a strict territorial divide between the areas of Germany under Allied control and the "forbidden, unimaginable" stretches of ground that had been conquered by the Soviet force.[23] The story Martha had most wanted to cover was the battle to secure Berlin, a battle now imminent as the Red Army had all but encircled the capital. But the Russians were insisting that they and they alone would take Berlin, and, since Western journalists were banned as well as Western troops, Martha had no choice but to switch direction and follow Patton's Third Army south-west to Munich.

Lee and Dave had also planned to report on the battle for Munich, but along the way had made a detour to Nuremberg. The city's Gothic centre had been trashed to the usual chaos of rubble, spent ordnance, burnt-out vehicles and bodies, and Lee admitted she felt troubled. "This is the first German city . . . I feel sorry for having wrecked," she wrote, and she was particularly moved by the story of one young woman, a teacher, who'd been incarcerated in a work camp simply for having listened to BBC News on her radio. The photographs Lee took at Nuremberg, of families camping out in air-raid shelters, cooking river carp over little fires, had an unusual quality of empathy, as if she'd been released from the "boiling hatred in her blood." But, that same day, she and Dave heard reports that the Allies had reached Dachau — the concentration camp on the outskirts of Munich. They drove through the night to get there, and the horrors they saw as they walked around the camp meant there could be no further possibility of forgiveness.

The heaps of the dead, the starved, broken bodies of the survivors would scar Lee, as they would all her colleagues. Nothing about this war had prepared them for the evil of the concentration camps — and the enormity of what they experienced, the images that were scorched into their minds, must be dealt with, here, in a chapter of its own.

Lee and Dave, meanwhile, left Dachau "gulping for air" and actually craving a battle story to cover, which they imagined would feel like "a mirage of cleanliness and humanity" by comparison. In the centre of Munich, there was little fighting left to report.[24] However, the two of them found unexpected distraction from the horrors of Dachau when, in one of the most bizarre twists of their war, they ended up squatting for the night in Hitler's house. As the U.S. 45th Armoured Division had swept through the Bavarian capital, they'd taken possession of the large, bourgeois villa that had functioned as the Führer's Munich residence, office and bomb shelter, and when Lee and Dave made their way to Prinzregentenplatz 16, they were told they could use it as a temporary billet. To be walking through rooms where Hitler had entertained men like Mussolini and Franco, to be handling his knick-knacks, looking at his paintings and sitting on his chairs felt surreal. But strangest of all was the banality of the place. It didn't look as though "anyone more pretentious than merchants or retired clergy" had ever lived there, Lee wrote, certainly not the dictator who'd set half the world on fire.[25] And, caught between derision, horror and disbelief, her instinctive response was to take a bath in Hitler's tub, to use his personal flannel to wash away the filth of Dachau. She placed a framed photograph of the Führer on the side of the bath and dumped her muddy combat boots on the mat — and the photograph that Dave took of her sitting naked in the water, a grimace of triumph and transgression on her face, would eventually become the most iconic shot of his career.*

It was 30 April 1945, and Lee had no idea, then, that Hitler himself was no longer alive.

* Initially published in a small magazine, the image languished in the archives for years, until Lee's own posthumous fame brought it to international notoriety.

Just before midnight, however, she and Dave were drinking with the other Americans in the apartment when the BBC broadcast news of the Führer's death. During the last few days, he and his entourage had been huddled inside their Berlin bunker, listening to the encroaching thump of Soviet artillery, the shudder of explosions, and knowing the city must imminently be lost. Hitler had no intention of letting himself be taken as a trophy, however. On 29 April, he granted his mistress, Eva Braun, her dearest wish, and married her. The following day, he consecrated that marriage by giving a cyanide pill to his bride and turning his pistol on himself.

Hitler had instructed Goebbels to wrap their two dead bodies in army blankets and burn them in the little garden by the bunker's entrance. Then, because the loyal Propaganda Minister had no wish to survive his Führer, he committed suicide with his wife, Magda, and their six children. Some of the Nazi inner circle were less devoted: Göring and Himmler had already left Berlin to attempt negotiations with the Allies; Martin Bormann, Hitler's bully boy and fixer, was plotting his own escape, but would die in the attempt. It was left to Grand Admiral Karl Dönitz, nominated by Hitler to take command of the war, to decide the country's future. But, while Dönitz had been ordered to continue fighting until the Allies had agreed to a negotiated peace, the Allies themselves would only accept unconditional surrender. According to Helen, SHAEF was prepared to stay in the field "until every uniformed German has been taken prisoner."[26]

And so the war would stagger on for another few days. Hitler's death, however, had brought a sense of finality. On 1 May, Lee and Dave drove south to the town of Berchtesgaden, where Hitler had built his Bavarian alpine retreat. SS officers who'd been guarding the Eagle's Nest had attempted to torch it before they fled, and, when Lee and Dave arrived that evening, the fires on the compound were still raging out of control. When they returned the following morning, news of Berchtesgaden's capture had already spread, and not only were the war tourists already gathering, but a frenzy of looting had begun, as journalists and soldiers freely ransacked the wines, silverware, books and fine linen that had been stashed in underground cellars to service the Führer and his entourage.

"It was like a very wild party," Lee observed, "with champagne corks whizzing over the flagpole and the house falling down around our ears."[27] Although she and Dave were decently restrained — he taking a set of Shakespeare plays that were marked with Hitler's personal bookplate, and she making do with an ornamental silver tray — others were shameless. When Helen arrived, a few days later, everything of value had disappeared. She did, however, find a frying pan, abandoned in the compound's kitchen, and she recalled that one of her most satisfying meals of the war was the bacon that she and her colleague Bill Walton had managed to procure, and which they'd fried up in "Hitler's skillet," looking out over the smouldering ruins of his mountain retreat.[28]

By 4 May, the Nazi war machine had stalled to a halt: German ground troops were surrendering across Europe, German U-boats were returning to port and the Soviet flag was flying high over Berlin. So covetous was Stalin of control of the city that he would extend the ban on Allied troops, intelligence officers and journalists for another two months. Churchill, always suspicious of Stalin's motives, guessed that he wanted time to scour Berlin's labs and archives for military and industrial research, and to find the nuclear materials that were widely believed to be hidden in the city. But Churchill's protests had been overridden by the Americans, whose principal concern was concluding the war with Japan, and so, for eight weeks, the Russians had Berlin to themselves.

A very small and very reckless handful of American journalists, however, had succeeded in getting into the German capital, among them Virginia Irwin of the *St. Louis Post-Dispatch* and Andrew Tully of the *Boston Traveller.* The two of them had teamed up with an American sergeant at Torgau and had tagged alongside a Russian convoy heading for Berlin. Their jeep had barely been noticeable among the farm carts, gypsy wagons, old-fashioned pony traps, discarded American lorries and captured German trucks in which the Soviets were travelling. As for the soldiers themselves, they seemed to Virginia as carelessly jolly as a party of "holiday makers going on a picnic . . . singing their fighting songs, drinking vodka."

There was one bad moment when the convoy reached Berlin and the Americans were taken off for questioning. But the Russians were too elated to be overly concerned with a couple of foreign journalists. They were "happy," Virginia wrote, "with an almost indescribably wild joy," and, once she'd satisfied her interrogators that she wasn't a spy, she was placed in the charge of "a fierce Mongolian with a great scar on his left cheek," who presented her with a dishpan of water, a broken mirror and a handful of looted cosmetics with which to make herself pretty for the evening's celebrations. Trestle tables were being set up amid the rubble of central Berlin, with candles stuck into milk bottles, old pickle jars filled with a few miraculously surviving spring flowers.[29] Quantities of food appeared, much of it unrecognizable to Virginia, and the party that followed had a riotous, improvised munificence, which remained vivid in her memory. Innumerable bottles of vodka were drunk; and, after hours of speeches, kisses and songs, everyone ended up dancing "a wild jitterbug to music from a beaten-up Victrola."*

"It is all unreal," she wrote that night, scribbling her notes by the last guttering light of her candle; and she was too charmed by the Russians, too excited by the brilliance of her scoop to spare much thought for the defeated people of Berlin. The city's pavements might be sticky with their blood, but Virginia viewed the capture of the German capital as nothing less than the Russians' due. It was "their true revenge for Leningrad and Stalingrad," she believed — and she had no inkling of how thorough that revenge would be.[30] The women of Berlin, however, guessed all too well. They'd heard talk of the Red Army's

---

* The two journalists had to be punished for their violation of the Russian ban — their stories were spiked and their accreditations temporarily suspended. But a far worse fate was in store for their friendly Russians, who had committed the double crime of not only permitting two members of the capitalist press into Berlin, but then having unlicensed contact with them.

advance through East Prussia, during which soldiers had not only been licensed to murder and loot, but to rape every female within sight. Now, during the nightmare days in which the Russians closed in on Berlin, it was the women who most felt their approach as a terrible doom.

Dorothea von Schwanenfluegel was one of them. A young mother, living alone with her small daughter, she'd reached the point where she would only dare leave her apartment to queue for food. Even before the Russians arrived, Dorothea had been at risk from the bands of SS officers and Hitler Youth who were rounding up Berliners for the final defence of their city. Elderly men, women, even children who tried to resist were being killed and strung up from streetlamps with signs hung around their necks which proclaimed them as cowards.

But, to Dorothea, these die-hard fanatics were far less of a threat than the approaching "Ivan"; and, on the evening that the Russians smashed their way into her district, all she could do was join with her neighbours in barricading the windows and doors of the apartment building, hoping to make it look abandoned. They spent the long night huddled together in a single room, "gripped in fear" as they listened to the approaching tramp of boots, the shattering of glass, the looting of furniture. Most ghastly of all, however, had been the noise of "what sounded like a ter-rible orgy, with [raped] women shrieking for help, many shrieking at the same time."[31]

Dorothea had survived that first night, at least, and the following morning, when she ventured outside, she attempted to make herself as unattractive as possible, smearing her face with coal dust and covering her hair with an old rag. It was "our make-up for the Ivan," she recalled, but it would provide little protection. Natalya Gesse, one of a very small number of female correspondents who trav-elled with the Red Army, would later confirm the sickening extent to which rape had become the Soviets' weapon of choice. "The Russian soldiers were raping every German female from eight to eighty. It was an army of rapists."[32] Some of the victims were assaulted multiple times, and, among the 100,000 women who were raped in Berlin alone, there were many who died as a consequence. Some were fatally injured, their rapists using cud-gels and knives, but others were victims of botched abortions, syphilis infections and suicide — a tragic number of women simply unable to live with the trauma and shame.*

There were decent Russians, of course, and

---

* In East Prussia, Pomerania and Silesia, cases of rape were estimated to total 1.4 million, and ac-cording to the great Vasily Grossman, who was also travelling with the Red Army during 1945, it was

sexual assault was far from being a purely Russian war crime. Months of being frozen, hungry and scared, months of having little or no contact with women had brutalized many of the men who fought in this conflict, and while the British and Americans liked to believe their own ranks remained decent and civilized, a significant number had been guilty of rape. Iris Carpenter hadn't wanted to credit rumours that men from her own beloved First Army were routinely abusing German women as they advanced, but the truth was forced on her when a desperate mother came to beg for her help in stopping an American driver from attacking her daughter. Iris had been chilled by the terror she heard in the girl's screams and the ugliness of the man's voice as he snarled, "Stop clawing, you little bitch, or I'm gonna break your bloody neck." She managed to intervene, but was unable to convince the driver that he'd been committing any crime. Brandishing his gun, he seemed, to Iris, brutally "matter-of-fact" about his rights: "There ain't nobody who's going to stop me having her or any other German gal I want. We won 'em, didn't we?"[33]

That driver was given an official reprimand,

not merely German women whom the Red Army attacked, but Poles, Ukrainians and Belorussians.

yet it was a blot on the Allied war record that most of the rapes committed by their men were left unpunished, and that too little value was placed on German women for any widespread investigation to be made into the assaults they endured. For the women themselves, however, these things had a grim relativity. Allied soldiers were under orders, at least, to respect certain decencies in regard to those they conquered. And, when Germany finally surrendered on 8 May and the nation was divided into jurisdictional zones, it was telling how many thousands of Germans would risk their lives to get into areas that were under Allied, rather than Soviet, control.

The zoning was enforced in late July, and, when Jim Gavin arrived in Berlin to liaise with the Russians in the city's recovery, he was elated by the chance of doing something positive. "I love this work," he wrote to Martha. "At last we are doing . . . humanity some permanent good."[34] But such generosity of spirit would be beyond Martha, and it would be even more unreachable for Sigrid Schultz, whose hatred of Nazi Germany had grown even darker and more immovable during her absence. In a rage-filled polemic, *Germany Will Try It Again,* she'd written scathingly of her belief that there was something historically malign in the German psyche, an ingrained national and racial hubris; in January

1945, when she finally returned to the country, she wanted nothing more than to see it humiliated.

She'd been flown to the First Army HQ in Spa, from where she was able to report on the very last phase of the Battle of the Bulge. Sigrid was fifty-two now, her hair steely grey under her correspondent's cap, and, to the press commander, Colonel Barney Oldfield, she appeared both admirable and formidable as she acquainted herself with the essentials of front-line journalism. Sigrid herself felt boundlessly energetic as she climbed in and out of the trenches, interviewing soldiers, demanding information about strategy and weapons. It was wonderful to be covering daily news again, to be doing so without Nazi constraint, and, according to Oldfield, she was so enthusiastically fearless in the face of shelling and sniper fire that the soldiers of the First presented her with her own gun.

Once the Allies had crossed the Rhine, Sigrid was assigned to the Air Power Press Corps, which not only gave her the advantage of speed, but a bird's eye view of the invasion's growing sprawl — the smashed cities, the convoys barrelling along the roads, the columns of displaced people and surrendered Wehrmacht. Much of it she found frankly exhilarating. Broadcasting from Cologne for the Mutual Broadcasting System, she admitted how little sympathy she could muster for the city's ravaged state, given the damage the Germans had wreaked elsewhere. Nor could she waste any tears on Cologne's homeless, since they were at least being fed and sheltered by their conquerors — unlike the people of Nazi-occupied Warsaw or Paris, who'd been machine-gunned as they'd fled for safety.

It was late July when Sigrid reached Berlin, and even for this, her former home, she could feel only a twinge of regret. The war-gutted city had a particularly ghastly aspect that day. It had been raining hard and the skeletal ruins were streaked with wet; thin Berliners, trudging between mountains of rubble, looked like ghosts of their former selves, and there was a graveyard feel to the place, with its smells of untreated sewage, its misery and decay. When Sigrid went to investigate her former haunts, she found the Hotel Adlon half-sheared of its magnificent facade, and many of her favourite shops, restaurants and bars obliterated without trace. A wedge of her own life had been destroyed with them. Yet, any inclination Sigrid had to mourn was swept aside when she made a pilgrimage to Wilhelmstrasse, the administrative heart of Nazi Berlin, and saw that the monolithic hubris of Hitler's Chancellery, along with most of the Ministry buildings, had been bombed to a meaningless wreckage of twisted steel and broken stone.

For years, Sigrid had reported on the policies that had been formulated within these buildings; for years, she had tried to analyse the combination of greed, corruption and deranged paranoia that had driven their execution. She had tried to understand how Hitler and his inner circle had so successfully managed to fool, seduce, brutalize and terrorize an entire nation. But, three months ago, she'd been among the first group of correspondents to enter the concentration camp at Buchenwald, and there, in "an inferno of suffering and cruelty, stench and filth, disease and death," Sigrid had understood that the depravity nurtured within those Wilhelmstrasse buildings had descended to depths even she had failed to grasp.[35]

CHAPTER SIXTEEN: BUCHENWALD, DACHAU AND NUREMBERG, 1945

"Dachau had everything you'll ever hear or close your ears to"

LEE MILLER[1]

"We have all seen a great deal now," wrote Martha, "but nowhere was there anything like this."[2] The scale of this war had already outrun the limits of ordinary journalism — the numbers of city centres transformed into mass boneyards, the millions left dead, homeless and bereaved. But, when the gates of the concentration camps were opened, reporters had to deal with material so hideously beyond their range that even the virtuoso broadcaster Ed Murrow was silenced. Speaking from Buchenwald on 11 April, he admitted, "I have reported what I saw and heard, but only part of it. For most of it I have no words."[3]

The majority of the press had heard something of the camps' existence, long before they were liberated. Sigrid had reported what she could about Dachau, the first of them, but lawyers and activists who'd tried to investigate behind its walls had been silenced, and no one outside the Nazi inner circle had known for sure how widely these concentration camps had proliferated across Greater Germany, nor how murderously finessed they'd become.

Initially, the camps had been used to house high-value political prisoners, Jews and other categories of *Untermensch*. Many inmates had been executed for their alleged crimes, many had died from hunger and disease; but it was not until mid-1941, as the Reich expanded and shooting squads were no longer sufficient to deal with its accumulating population of "human vermin," that Heinrich Himmler and Reinhard Heydrich made the leap into proposing that certain camps be fitted with dedicated extermination facilities.

In October 1941, a camp at Belzec in Poland was constructed with gas chambers and ovens that were large enough to dispatch several hundred prisoners at a time. The following year, more death facilities were constructed across Poland and Belarus: new camps were built, like Treblinka, and older ones, like Auschwitz, were expanded — the chambers and crematoria at its Birkenau annexe so efficient that up to 2,000 could be annihilated in a single session and up to ten times that number in a single day. Jews were the principal victims — by mid-1943, an estimated two million had been gassed and incinerated — but many thousands of Bolsheviks, Roma, political activists and homosexuals had been slaughtered alongside them.

The reluctance of the Allies to bomb these camps, or at least to disable the railways and communication links that serviced them, was to become one of the murkiest issues of the war. There had been very clear intelligence about their existence, much of it smuggled out by underground groups; the BBC had reported on them and questions had been raised at the highest levels. However, it was argued by military strategists that attacking the camps would kill more inmates than it would save, and, in truth, the camps were not their immediate priority. According to Iris Carpenter, there was a widespread belief that reports had been exaggerated, that at worst the camps represented isolated extremes of German savagery. When Maggie Higgins arrived at Buchenwald, she'd been so determined not to be spun an "atrocity line" that she'd marched into the compound with a crass insensitivity, demanding to be told the real facts, before she was shamed into understanding what they were.

It was the Russians, advancing through the eastern Reich, who reached the extermination camps first. The Nazis had destroyed most of the infrastructure, before retreating, but, at Auschwitz, in January 1945, 7,000 prisoners had been discovered, some of them with just enough strength to stammer out fragmented, ghostly accounts of what the camp had been. Even now this information was not widely disseminated; only one short paragraph appeared in the Soviet press because it was Kremlin policy to emphasize only the suffering of Russians, and the majority of Auschwitz's victims were Jews. The Allies, meanwhile, were acquiring the truth piecemeal. They'd liberated Struthof, back in November 1944, but, while its primitive gas chamber had been evidence of hideous crimes, its operations had clearly been limited. On 4 April 1945, however, a division from the Fourth Army had stumbled across a recently evacuated camp at Ohrdruf, which was on a whole other scale. Piles of half-charred bodies were stacked around the grounds, and when soldiers interviewed a small group of survivors, the testimony they reported was so horrific that three of the generals — Eisenhower, Patton and Bradley — had been impelled to see Ohrdruf for themselves. Eisenhower wrote later of his own appalled response: "I have never felt able to describe my emotional reactions when I first came face to face with indisputable evidence of Nazi brutality. I have never at any other time experienced an equal sense of shock."[4] Even the famously stoic Patton had vomited. But Ohrdruf was only the beginning; a wider search of the area revealed that it was just one of several interconnecting camps, and a mere satellite of the monolith that was Buchenwald.

As soon as Patton grasped what he was seeing, he ordered a select group of journalists to be flown in to Buchenwald immediately. Among them were Sigrid Schultz, Helen Kirkpatrick and Ed Murrow, and all reported that they'd been similarly poleaxed, nauseated by what they were shown. Thousands of corpses had been left behind by the fleeing Germans, who had run out of petrol to incinerate them, and they looked so grey and brittle, were stacked so high, Sigrid's first reeling thought was that they must be piles of wood. No less hallucinatory was the appearance of the 17,000 prisoners left alive. Some were little more than walking skeletons, gaunt and hollow-eyed in their filthy prison garb; the sickest and weakest had been dumped in with the corpses and were only able to signal for help through the faintest flicker of an eyelid, the feeble wave of a hand.

Although 56,000 had died at Buchenwald, it had not been categorized as an extermination camp, and inmates who'd also experienced Auschwitz would insist that Buchenwald had been paradise by comparison. To the newly arriving journalists, however, it was as though they had entered the gates of hell. Helen forced herself to make a tour of the entire location, taking in the hundreds of noxious dormitories, the gallows, the firing range, the ovens, but eventually her brain and her senses had shut down: "when you see thousands and thousands of corpses and half-burned bodies . . . you lose your perspective . . . you can't absorb any more."[5] She needed to find some small human details on which to focus, and, during the two weeks she remained at Buchenwald, she chose to follow the work of the Allied medical teams as they attempted to coax the camp's survivors back to some semblance of health.

A page torn from her notebook — the one memento she kept from Buchenwald — reveals the care Helen took in monitoring the fluids and vitamins that were drip-fed into wasted bodies, the slow gradations by which life returned to the almost dead. At moments, she admitted that the assignment she'd set herself was "pretty awful," especially when she was summoned to the bedside of a patient who turned out to have been one of her professors.[6] He'd spotted Helen, tried to whisper her name, but he was so cadaverously altered she'd been unable to recognize him as the man who taught her International Affairs, back in Geneva. By her twelfth day in Buchenwald, however, her endurance was rewarded: the death rate had declined from one hundred a day to thirty, and in the piece she filed back to Chicago — "3000 skeletons come slowly back to life" — she was able to salvage a cautious note of humanity.[7]*

Sigrid had known something of Buchenwald back in 1938, when she'd written about its satellite camp, Buchfart, and it was terrible for her, now, to see the obscenity into which it had grown, to understand the futility of her own reporting. But, like Helen, she attempted to numb her distress with practical activity. She'd been entrusted with a list of Jewish students who'd been deported to the camps from Paris, and was hoping to track some of them down. A young French inmate whose assistance she'd begged had been bleakly pessimistic, however. He'd known two of the boys, but both had died, and, if others had been at Buchenwald, he doubted their chances of survival. The Nazis had worked them like horses, he said, sending them out for fourteen hours each day to haul rocks at a nearby quarry, and shooting all those who were too injured or weak to work.

But, while Sigrid had to abandon her list, the boy asked if she might talk to some of the other French inmates, who hadn't yet fully understood they were free. Later, she wrote about her painstaking tour of the camp

* The tone of her piece was also influenced by her paper's new publisher, who was far less serious than Colonel Knox and was pressuring his staff to put a more upbeat spin on their war reporting.

dormitories, where she saw men lying on wood-slatted bunks, so closely packed that "blood and everything else [was] dripping from tier to tier." Gently she tried to explain that their nightmare was over, and, as she did so, one "pitiful bearded creature" raised himself from his bunk and "stuck out a groping hand." He looked so wasted, so ghastly that Sigrid doubted he would leave the camp alive, but she took his hand and, with as much cheerfulness as she could feign, she talked to him about home — "about the chestnuts that were in bloom in Paris" — and assured him that, even now, there were planes being sent out to the camp to fly him and his compatriots back to France. "I was rewarded by a wonderfully peaceful smile," she wrote, "as he let go of my hand and sank back on his bunk."[8]

That smile brought Sigrid, too, a little peace, but she was helpless against the rage that convulsed her when she reported on the 2,000 civilian Germans from nearby Weimar who'd been ordered by General Patton to make a tour of the camp. Others who were present would claim that some of the Germans expressed shame and horror, but Sigrid insisted she saw only evasion and denial. "They tried to look everywhere — at the treetops or the sky — rather than at the dead," she wrote, adding that one smartly dressed woman had actually curled her lip with distaste, muttering, "All of this is not a concern of ours."[9] And if Sigrid was allowing moral contempt to prejudice her judgement, she had every excuse, for she'd recently learned that some of those Weimar residents had actually profited from the camp, using inmates to do odd jobs — plumbing and carpentry — in their homes, and betraying them to the camp guards if ever they dared to beg a slice of bread or a glass of milk.[10]

"Their only crime was to be hungry," Sigrid wrote, and, to her, this insidious normalizing of evil was one of the most grotesque features of Buchenwald. It was beyond her comprehension that the ordinary people of Weimar had come to accept the camp's existence, as part of daily life; just as it was beyond comprehension that the Nazis who ran it, whose job was to de-humanize and torture, had seen fit to plant flower beds around the compound, and to build wooden hutches where they bred dozens of sleek, well-fed angora rabbits.*

Every correspondent who came to the camps would struggle with what they witnessed, and nearly all of them would feel that they, and everything they held dear, had been

* Sigrid would shortly learn that these rabbits had been bred across a network of camps, their exceptionally fine fur making excellent insulation for Luftwaffe flying jackets.

desecrated. Lee Miller had not seen the worst of Buchenwald, since she'd arrived days after its liberation and the clearing-up process had begun. But she and Dave had only been hours behind the 42nd and 45th divisions when they'd opened up Dachau, on 29 April, and the camp was still exactly as the Germans had left it.

The stench had hit them first, the putrid sweetness of death and decay, and initially it led them to a freight train parked outside the compound, which was crammed with the bodies of the last prison transport to reach Dachau. All were dead. But, as Dave and Lee walked through the gates, the stench only grew fouler, and it was then that they saw the mass of corpses heaped around the compound, and the hundreds of mortally sick who were lying in pools of their own vomit and excrement.

A small group of the 33,000 inmates who'd been left alive by the Nazis were strong enough to volunteer information as Lee and Dave were shown around the entire site, around the degradingly crammed dormitories, the interrogation rooms and isolation cells, the warped "medical centre," where experiments were conducted on prisoners to see how long they were able to survive extreme temperatures, oxygen deprivation or the effects of deliberately injected streptococcus germs.[11] The intricacy and the scale of the place was overwhelming: "Dachau had everything you'll ever hear or close your ears to about a concentration camp," Lee reported back to Audrey, but she was stubbornly determined to record every aspect of it.

A French army doctor, Jacques Hindermeyer, who'd been tasked with collecting visual evidence of Dachau, was both shocked and impressed by her tenacity. "Lee took photographs that I could not," he admitted, as he watched her clamber right inside the stink and flies of the abandoned freight car, capturing the sickened, incredulous expressions of two smooth-cheeked American medics, as they stared down at the withered face of a corpse.[12] She was prepared to hover over the recently slain body of an SS guard which she spotted "slithering" in an adjacent canal, to insert herself in the middle of a starving group of inmates, capturing their blind, avid hunger as they awaited a distribution of food. Every photographer would document the piles of the dead, but Lee was one of the few to zoom in on their faces — faces that were little more than skulls, but which were still a reminder of all those individual lives which had been disposed of like so much trash.

Even Dave was taken aback by the calm deliberation with which Lee forced herself into the middle of these horrors. But he knew her well enough to understand that the calm could only be temporary and that the trauma had simply gone "underground." Margaret Bourke-White, who reached Dachau shortly afterwards, recalled that she, too, had tried to "keep a veil" over her emotions, to concentrate only on the camera in her hands; and she had dissociated herself so effectively from her surroundings that, only later, when her photographs were printed, did she realize exactly what she'd seen.[13]

Martha, however, was incapable of distance. She'd waited until the initial press scramble had died down before making her own approach to Dachau, for she'd had friends, personal heroes, who'd been interned there and she wanted time and space to fully understand what they'd endured. Even so, it was far worse than she'd believed possible: "We all lack imagination, and I hadn't imagined anything like this."[14] Although the clearing up had begun, heaps of the dead were still stacked around the compound, and many of the survivors still looked barely human. Martha stared at one group of men who were sitting listlessly in the early May sunshine, searching their bodies for lice, and realized she could tell neither their age nor their nationality. "They had no faces left, only yellowish stubbly skin stretched across bone . . . They all look alike and like nothing you will ever see, if you are lucky."[15]

Her own emotions ricocheted between nausea, rage and guilt. "It took twelve years to open the gates of Dachau. We were blind and unbelieving and slow," she wrote, and the penance she set herself was to record all of it in meticulous detail.[16] She noted the excruciatingly cramped dimensions of the camp "punishment box," no bigger than a telephone booth, in which four prisoners might be confined together for three days and nights; she noted the number of lashes a prisoner could receive — twenty-five to fifty — simply for the crime of possessing a cigarette butt; she observed the mass of shirts, jackets, trousers and shoes that had been taken from the recently dead, and that had been sorted neatly into piles for subsequent use.

But, as always, Martha looked for the human stories onto which those facts and figures could be pegged, and one of the central figures in her Dachau article was a Polish inmate to whom she talked in the camp infirmary. He was so emaciated that his jawbone "seemed to be cutting through his skin," yet he was still strong enough to tell Martha that he'd come to Dachau on the last transfer from Buchenwald, and that he'd been the only one of its doomed human cargo to survive. He'd been discovered, dehydrated and starved, under a crush of bodies, yet it seemed to Martha that this lost wraith of a man would have preferred to have perished alongside the others. "Everyone is dead. No one is left. I cannot help myself," he'd wept, and his wasted features had twisted into an expression that lay somewhere unreachable, beyond "pain or sorrow or horror."[17]

"Aside from the terrible anger you feel, you are ashamed," Martha wrote. "You are ashamed of mankind."[18] She could barely make herself listen to the "mad-eyed" woman who talked over and over again of the moment she'd arrived at Auschwitz and she and her sister had been ordered into separate lines — she for the work squad, her sister for the gas chamber. Martha understood that she would never be able to forget these tragedies, but only later would she understand how fundamentally she was changed by them. "Looking back," she wrote, "I know I have never again felt that lovely easy lively hope in life which I knew before, not in life, not in our species, not in our future on earth."[19]

On 4 May, when word came through that the Germans were surrendering, Martha could only respond with a vague, weary relief. She was in the camp infirmary at the time, which seemed to her "the most suitable place in Europe" to hear the news.[20] Lee, meanwhile, was in a press camp south of Munich, typing up her visit to the Eagle's Nest at Berchtesgaden. And, when a soldier informed her the Allies had won the war, Lee had murmured an absent-minded, "Thanks," before realizing what she'd heard. "Shit. That's blown my first paragraph," she swore. And then she wondered where she should go next.[21]

The war in Europe would not officially be over until the Americans, Russians and Germans met to sign the surrender document, and Nazi Germany was formally dismantled.* But, during the intervening four days, Lee and Dave decided to head for Paris, in time for the victory celebrations. Janet Flanner was already there, and, on the afternoon of 8 May, when De Gaulle broadcast his victory speech to the French, she watched the Parisians take to the streets. "They streamed out onto their city's avenues and boulevards and took possession of them from curb to curb," she reported. "They paved the Champs Elysées with their moving serried bodies . . . The babble and shuffle of feet drowned out the sound of the stentorian church bells clanging for peace and even the cannon firing from the Invalides . . . All anyone cared about was to keep moving, to keep shouting, to keep singing snatches of the Marseillaise."[22]

By midnight, when American planes flew over the city amid an exploding cacophony of

* The first signing took place at Reims, at one minute past midnight, on 7 May, but a mistake in the wording meant it then had to be re-signed, twenty-four hours later, in Berlin.

fireworks, the majority of those still partying were the very young. Their lack of inhibition as they "ran free and mixed on the streets" struck Janet as a wonderful portent, the hope of a better, brighter future. But Martha had been unable to share the joy, and had spent most of VE day alone, walking unseeing among the crowds. When she eventually bumped into a friend and took him back to the Hotel Scribe, she could only lie weeping in his arms, incapable of talking about anything except Dachau and the "insane wickedness" she had witnessed there.

The camps drew Martha like a terrible magnet. After Paris, she went to the Bergen-Belsen compound in northern Germany to watch bulldozers burying the dead; from there, she travelled to the women's camp at Ravensbrück, whose surviving inmates looked shrivelled and bent beyond their years. These were women "who had lived with death too long," she wrote, and all she could do was listen to their stories and suffer through them a tiny fraction of what they'd endured.[23]

Everywhere Martha went in Germany, she saw a nation broken in defeat: towns and cities were without electricity or running water; fields were stripped of vegetation; men, women and children were begging for food. When she eventually reached Berlin, she noted the desperation with which skinny young girls were bartering themselves for chocolate or cigarettes; the "desolation" of the older women, the *Trümmerfrauen,* who were paid a pittance to sort through rubble for reusable construction materials. The writer George Orwell was moved to horrified pity when he witnessed these scenes: "To walk through the ruined cities of Germany is to feel an actual doubt about the continuity of civilization."[24] But, for Martha, none of it was adequate punishment; all of Germany should be made to suffer and starve, she wrote grimly, because that was the only way it could "catch up" with the misery it had inflicted on the rest of the world.

Sigrid was travelling similarly long distances during that summer, looting books from the ruins of Hitler's library at the Eagle's Nest, celebrating the end of the war, but also looking for evidence that Germans might be capable of some collective act of contrition. Hardly anyone she spoke to, however, seemed willing to accept guilt for the crimes committed by their leadership, and she claimed she was even having a hard time "scaring members of the Hitler Youth organizations into acknowledging their former faith."[25] One of the men whom Sigrid interviewed was the brother of a childhood friend, whose construction firm had been employed in the original conversion of Dachau from munitions factory to prison camp. Sigrid needed to understand how this seemingly decent man could have dirtied his hands with such a project, especially since the Nazis, in 1933, were new to power and "still pretty unsure of themselves." But Karl Storir had responded with a self-absolving shrug. "What could I have done about it?" he said, pointing out that the camp would have been built anyway, with or without his involvement.[26]

Sigrid encountered that same cynical shrug over and over again. It hardened the beliefs that she'd argued in the pages of *Germany Will Try It Again:* that these were a blighted people; so ingrained with an extreme, racist nationalism, they would remain primed for any resurgent Nazi movement, for decades to come. Contempt and moral despair settled as deep in Sigrid as they had in Martha. Yet, back in the spring, she'd at least had one redemptive moment of happiness when she discovered that her dear friend Johannes Schmitt was still alive.

Johannes' luck had been astounding. Just as Sigrid had always feared, his work as a press informant and resistance worker had led to his arrest, and he'd been taken to Sachsenhausen, where political dissidents were routinely executed. But he'd been kept alive at the behest of two very powerful men, both of whom had been on his pre-war patient list. One was the conductor Wilhelm Furtwängler (allowed by Sigrid to have been one of the few "good Nazis"), who'd insisted that Johannes was the only doctor in Germany with the osteopathic skills to keep him fit for the podium. The other was Heinrich Himmler.

The SS Reichsführer also suffered from back problems and he too had come to swear by Dr. Schmitt's healing hands. More specifically, in January 1945, he needed his skills for a Berlin general, who'd suffered a severe stroke. Johannes had been released from the camp and put under house arrest in the Bavarian town of Gmund; he was still there when the town was taken by the Allies, and he was elected its new, post-Nazi mayor. Sigrid was overjoyed to see her old friend again, and almost as pleased to discover he was still the same impeccable source. It was Johannes who took her to Himmler's nearby villa, to show her the large photo album which contained secret records of the Nazis' angora rabbit breeding project. It may have been one of Johannes former contacts, too, who, later in the summer, supplied Sigrid with evidence for her final scoop.

The story had started to take shape in June 1945, when the Kremlin had issued the bizarre claim that Hitler had not actually shot himself in his bunker, but had fled abroad, leaving behind the charred remains of a "very poor double." This was a blatant contradiction of the Russians' previous statement that the Führer's dental records had been used to identify his corpse — however, Stalin was no less free with the truth than his enemy had been. Faced with the challenge of rebuilding Russia and consolidating its new territories, Stalin had calculated it would be politically expedient to resurrect the world's most hated man, creating a scapegoat around which to unite his people and to keep alight the flame of the Great Patriotic War.

The British and Americans were furious, knowing that rumours of Hitler's miracle escape could become a focus for Nazi resistance. Yet, as the world's media played out the story, it was Sigrid who published the most evidence-based rebuttal. Having picked up the remaining threads of her and Johannes' network, she traced a dental assistant, Kaethe Haeursemann, who was able to confirm that the corpse near the bunker had indeed had dental work identical to "two of Hitler's dental bridges," and that, back in May, the Russians had appeared to accept this as confirmation of Hitler's death.

Post-war Europe was becoming an ideological battleground, with Britain and America intent on bringing democracy to the formerly occupied territories, while Russia hoped to annex them as satellite communist states. When Helen drove around Austria and Czechoslovakia, she saw refugees so desperate to escape from Soviet jurisdiction they were prepared to risk being drowned or shot. Her views were politically biased, of course, but even though conditions were atrocious in the Allied-run zones and refugee camps, those in the Soviet-run zones were said to be far worse. The aid provision was meagre, and a vindictively sectarian system was also being used to process the displaced; it was rumoured that former slave workers who were unable to demonstrate proof of Communist sympathies were being accused of having serviced the Nazi regime, and were being sentenced to years of hard labour in Soviet gulags.

There was no map, no blueprint for making the transition to peace, and, for Lee Miller, it had become a struggle just to get through the days. Exactly as Dave Scherman had predicted, the trauma of Dachau had gone very deep, and shortly after they arrived in Paris, the reaction set in. Lee was haunted by everything she'd seen, and when she heard that *Vogue* had decided against publishing all her photographs from the camp ("it seemed unsuitable to focus on horrors," Audrey explained, now that the world was celebrating), Lee felt that the dead of Dachau had been betrayed all over again.[27] "I am encased in a wall of hate," she wrote. By mid-May, when Audrey proposed she might travel to Denmark and report on how the country was embracing its freedom, Lee was desperate to find some distraction from her poisonously churning thoughts.[28]

During the long drive to Copenhagen, she passed columns of Wehrmacht marching back to their homes, and "arrogant German officers whisking around in super charged cars." She still could not look at them without revulsion; however, once in Copenhagen, she found a city so "drunk on laughter and fun and freedom" that her nerves began to settle and her faith in the world was slightly restored. The Danes, she learned, had acted with dignity and courage during their years of occupation, and had resisted the Nazis in whatever ways were possible. Businessmen had protected their workers from deportation to labour camps; citizens of all faiths had helped Jews escape to neutral Sweden; and even the royal family had taken a stand — wearing yellow stars in solidarity with their Jewish subjects. Here, at least, were people whom Lee could unequivocally admire, and she celebrated them in some of the most charming lyrical photographs she'd taken in years.

But Lee was still aware that she hadn't yet learned the trick of how "to relax, to go from war to peace."[29] After Denmark, she went to London, where an effusive welcome awaited her. There was a film crew at Downshire Hill to record her reunion with Roland, and at

Vogue she was treated like a returning celebrity, toasted with champagne, garlanded with
kisses and told she could continue working
for the magazine under whatever terms she
chose. The accolades barely touched her,
though. War nerves and war fatigue still made
her jumpy, and all that she'd seen of the
peace so far — the ruthless jockeying for
political power in Britain, the chaos and corruption in mainland Europe — made her fear
that the "real nobility" of the last five and a
half years of fighting was being erased.[30]

Roland was very sensitive to Lee's fragile
state, but he assumed that, with careful nursing, she could be restored to the woman with
whom he'd first fallen in love — the beautiful
creative playmate who'd stood with him
against bourgeois convention. He couldn't
understand that Lee had outgrown that
woman, that she'd learned too much about
herself and the real world to go back to her
former life. Nor could he understand that his
attempts to cosset her were stifling. "I'm not
Cinderella," she shouted during one of their
increasingly bitter rows, and, in the second
week of August, she fled back to Paris.

Here, with Dave and with the grizzled core
of war journalists still based at the Hotel
Scribe, Lee tried to ride out her nightmares
and her rages. "Really great groups of humans
are suffering the same shock symptoms
caused by peace that I'm combatting," she

wrote, in one of her earnest attempts at self-analysis. It was hard work: the combination of wartime adrenalin and post-war despair had jangled her body clock so that she was unable to get up in the morning without Benzedrine and coffee, unable to sleep without alcohol and pills. There were days when she felt so "lethargic and useless," she stayed in bed and wept. But she was also convinced that work was her best therapy and her best salvation, and, in the third week of August, she persuaded Audrey to sign off on a series of articles exploring the reconstruction of some of the formerly occupied territories. She planned to travel east though Austria, Hungary, Romania, possibly all the way to Russia, and she was pinning all her hopes on the fact that this assignment would keep her on the road — and in flight from her jitters — for months to come.[31]

Martha had been living through her own version of Lee's distress, blitzed by nightmares and hopped up with a restlessness that made her feel "shredded up inside." The past kept returning to her in "small amazed snatches," yet, however bad the war had been, however "hated, perilous and mad," it had also become her home. It was a place, as she put it, where she'd always "had something to do that looked necessary," and she admitted to her diary that she feared she had become "really unsuited for anything else." A short visit back to her mother convinced her that she could never settle in America, but she could no more easily imagine a life with Jim Gavin. Throughout the summer, he'd been sending her long, ardent letters: "Darling, I love you, I love you, I love you. It is a good love now. It is sturdy, dependable and solid, something that one can count on." But, while he was clearly angling for marriage, the idea of setting up home on an American air base with Jim was impossible to contemplate. "How & where will I ever live normally?" Martha fretted, and she was very afraid that the independence she'd always prized had now become a curse.[32]

Clare Hollingworth had long predicted that she would become displaced and deracinated by the war, that she would feel like "a strange foreigner" by the time she returned home. In September, when she was reunited with her family, she was able to put on a convincing show: "I'm your aunt, so you've got to like me," she briskly informed her sister's two small children, and proceeded to hold them spellbound as she unpacked the war booty she'd brought home in her trunk.[33] To Richard, aged five, she presented a dagger, some watches and a military cap, which she claimed to have looted from the battlefields of North Africa. But, even though her family had welcomed her back with joy, had been pleased by the news of her engagement, Clare had only come home to perch. By the beginning of 1946, she was off again with Geoffrey, the two of them summoned back to Greece to report on the continuing civil war.

Travel, crises and deadlines were Clare's life now, yet her haste to resume that life was also a reflection of the distance that had grown between her and her family. Albert, Daisy and Edith had sat out the war in the relative safety of Middle England, and they could not begin to picture what Clare had seen and done. A wedge of incomprehension had separated them, just as it had Roland and Lee. And this same wedge was replicating itself across the world as journalists, soldiers, nurses and auxiliary workers returned to their homes. Divided from families and friends by all that they'd experienced, many of them lacking either the will or words to explain, they had become what the historian Nancy Caldwell Sorel described as a "post-war fraternity of the psychically displaced."[34]

Even Virginia Cowles had been momentarily speechless when, in the middle of May, she'd opened the door of her London flat and found Aidan back from the war. The shock was physical. Aidan looked nothing like the confident broad-shouldered pilot from whom she'd parted nearly six years ago: his clothes hung loose around his once-sturdy frame; his handsome smile was marred by stained and broken teeth. But Virginia was a war professional; once she'd shaken off her bewilderment, she knew what questions to ask, and could guess what answers she was likely to receive. For Aidan their reunion had been closer to a homecoming than the meeting with his parents, which had felt "so unreal" that none of them had known what to say. With Virginia, he recalled, "we [simply] started where we had left off in 1939. There was so much to talk about. She took as great an interest in my doings as I in hers."[35]

Aidan's war had mostly been spent in prison camps. After he'd been shot down in Libya, he'd spent three weeks in a Greek transit camp, where he'd doubted his chances of survival. The camp commander was trigger-happy and the heat in the verminous huts had been intolerable. But he'd been moved around, after that — first to Stalag Luft III in east Germany, then to Schubin in Poland, then back to Stalag Luft III — and, throughout that period, had managed to keep relatively healthy and sane. Twice he had tunnelled his way out, once getting to within fifteen kilometres of the Swiss border. But he had been fortunate not to be part of the "Great Escape," which had been attempted from Stalag Luft III in March 1944, and which had resulted in fifty RAF officers being shot, on Hitler's orders. Aidan had been lucky, too, that, when the retreating Germans had packed up his camp, he and his fellow POWs had been allowed to pack whatever clothes and provisions they still possessed onto improvised sledges, and that they'd been allowed to beg and barter for food during their long forced march to a new camp near Hanover. On 2 May, when a British patrol appeared at the camp to announce they were free, all of the men were in sufficiently good health to be flown immediately back home.

Aidan had thought a lot about Virginia during his incarceration, and when he arrived at her flat he had a proposal of marriage fully rehearsed. She, however, had spent the past four years braced for his death, and, elated though she was by Aidan's return, she couldn't immediately adjust to the idea of becoming his wife. She asked for a fortnight to make up her mind, joking that he would certainly have to get his teeth fixed before she could walk down the aisle with him. Tactfully, Aidan removed himself to Scotland to stay with friends and to prepare his campaign for the forthcoming general election. But, before the fortnight had passed, Virginia telephoned to accept his proposal. On 26 July, Aidan was elected Labour MP for North Buckinghamshire, and, four days later, the two of them were married by Aidan's father, the Reverend Stafford Crawley.

For Virginia, the future had already begun to assume a solid, hopeful shape when the war in the Pacific was brought to its final cataclysmic conclusion. On 6 and 9 August, America dropped atomic bombs on the Japanese cities of Hiroshima and Nagasaki, killing 120,000 people and consigning thousands more to a slow death by radiation poisoning. The U.S. generals had judged it the only clean way to end hostilities, given the barbarity of Japanese ground troops and the lethal recklessness of their suicide pilots. Yet, while there was international consternation over the implications of this new technology, while Helen would regard it as morally unjustifiable, the world had become too saturated with disaster for the majority to care. Lee, writing to Roland from Paris, admitted that this final chapter of the war felt unreal: "We celebrated VJ day several times before we finally gave up and decided we'd invented the atomic bombs ourselves and dreamed up the Jap surrender."[36]

Before those bombs had flattened Hiroshima and Nagasaki, Iris Carpenter had been among the small number of female correspondents applying for accreditation to the Pacific. This most distant region of the conflict had never been welcoming to women, and the nearest that most of them had got to the action was the upper deck of a hospital ship. As always, there had been the brave or lucky exceptions: the photographer Dickey Chapelle who'd secured a posting with the U.S. marines in the spring of 1945, and managed to document the amphibious invasion of Okinawa; Patricia Lockridge, a journalist for *Woman's Home Companion,* who'd persuaded a U.S. naval officer to let her report on the battle to secure Iwo Jima.

Yet, while some in the European press corps had hoped to use their hard-won contacts to finagle a route into the Pacific War, the bombs had been dropped before they'd even begun to arrange their reaccreditation, and the only news left to report was the trials in which the Nazis and their high-level collaborators were brought to account. In late July, Helen was in Paris, sitting in the dark, overcrowded public chamber of the Palais de Justice to see Marshal Pétain stand accused of his crimes as leader of the Vichy government. She had a very clear view of the Marshal and could see the stubborn hauteur with which he was gazing "contemptuously and frigidly" around the courtroom, "his eyes small, very cold and hard," with only a "slight trembling of the hand [that] betrayed his eighty-nine years."[37] Pétain had never deviated from his belief that in yielding to the Germans he'd saved his country from annihilation; and so convinced was he of his own patriotic rectitude that he refused to say anything in his own defence. But Helen could see that the jury was stacked against him; his collusion with the crushing of the French resistance, with the deportation of men and women to labour camps, with the rounding up of 75,000 French Jews were crimes too despicable to forgive.

Although Pétain was sentenced to death, De Gaulle requested that the judgement be commuted to life imprisonment, in acknowledgement of the Marshal's distinguished record from the previous war. No such mercy could be shown to the Nazi leaders, however, when they took the stand in Nuremberg, in November 1945. These were the trials on which the world's eyes were focused, and, when Helen arrived for the opening sessions, she was among 250 correspondents, all vying for accommodation and access.*

As always, she reported, the women took second place. While the men were billeted in a vastly ornate schloss, the forty-two female journalists, stenographers, typists and clerks were consigned to the dower house in the grounds. They slept on camp beds in improvised dormitories, which rapidly became frowsty with the smell of too many bodies and unlaundered clothes. They also shared a single filthy bathroom, which, perversely, had

* It was around this time that Helen discovered the Nazis had kept a dossier on her, and that she was on their blacklist of correspondents deemed hostile to the regime.

been fitted with two male urinals. When Helen protested at the billet's inefficient squalor, she was reprimanded for being difficult. Yet her recollections of those first days at Nuremberg were fond. There were lively evenings in the press bar, where many of the war correspondents were being reunited for the first time in months; and, afterwards, in the women's dower house, Janet Flanner was at her most inventively wicked, making everyone play a game in which they had to choose which Nazi leader they would have sex with, if placed under extreme duress.

But, as the trials ground on, month after month, the reporting became onerous. Helen was not in Nuremberg all the time — the Paris bureau still required her presence — but the unvarying grimness of the prosecutors' evidence, the shuffling evasions of the accused wore her down. She distracted herself by observing the body language of the Nazi prisoners who, seated together on one side of the dark brown courtroom, were listening intently to the progress of each other's cases. "They were being tried for their lives and they knew it," she wrote. And the Nazi who most fascinated her, the one who still clearly regarded himself as the star of his Party, was Hermann Göring.[38]

Six months in prison had shrunk the swaggeringly corpulent *Reichs-marschall* to a physical shadow of himself, and the reduction of his morphine intake, after years of addiction, had left him with an old man's tremor.* Yet, even though he was stripped of the flunkies, the medals, the hair dye and cosmetics with which he'd bolstered his power, Göring's ego remained undiminished. In his testimony to the court, he boasted theatrically of his power and influence within the Nazi Party, but at no point would he accept any guilt. His narcissism, his disregard for the truth, his indifference to his past crimes were astonishing: when questioned about the bombing of Guernica, he'd replied in a tone of affable regret, "It was a pity, but we could not do otherwise as we had nowhere else to try out our machines."

Martha was also in Nuremberg, and she'd made a point of attending the sessions in which Göring was questioned about Spain. As she'd winced at his inhuman testimony, she'd tried to work out if the blackness of a man's soul could be read in his face. In Göring's case, she concluded it could — he had "possibly the ugliest mouth I have ever seen." Studying the other Nazis in the dock, however, she found it harder to discern their

* Helen reported that, by the end of the war, Göring had been injecting himself with doses twenty times higher than those his doctors considered safe, and his withdrawal from the drug had to be done slowly in order not to induce a "manic state."

moral character. Rudolf Hess looked "weird, inquisitive and birdlike"; von Papen "shockingly weak"; and Hans Fritzsche, with his "sensitive fox's face," had, Martha thought, the romantic air of "a minor poet who has killed his mistress."[39]

Faces had always haunted Martha. Her war had been defined by the blank-eyed children of Barcelona, by the frozen fortitude of the Finns, by the nutcracker-jawed complacency of Chamberlain, and by the skeletal inmates at Dachau, who'd had no faces at all. It bothered her that so few of the Nazis on trial looked like the monsters they actually were, and that fact became emblematic of her own accumulating frustrations in Nuremberg. However probing the prosecution, however stark the witness testimony, it seemed impossible to break these men down, and, while Helen would find relief from the courtroom in the company of friends or the pressure of work, Martha tended to spend her two-hour lunch break wandering alone around the centre of Nuremberg, walking off her anger, but also canvassing the residents for their own local view of the trials.

A few of those to whom she spoke did appear glad that the Nazi high command were being held to account, and even expressed some shame on their behalf, but there were others who insisted that the crimes of Göring and the rest had been exaggerated. One young soldier assured Martha that he'd personally seen inmates returning from the concentration camps looking "fat and brown" with good health; and, while he agreed it had been wrong to kill so many Jews, he believed that they'd never been anything but a parasite on the Reich, never doing a proper day's work, only changing money "in a tricky way."[40] The squalid stupidity of the soldier's views was proof, had Martha needed it, of the culpability of the regime to which he'd so blindly adhered. Yet, when the trials were concluded the following year and eleven of the accused were sentenced to death, Martha still felt she'd been denied a final resolution, a final dispensing of justice. Göring, entitled to the end, had taken a cyanide pill the night before his hanging, and the most heinous of the Nazi leaders — Goebbels, Himmler, Heydrich, Bormann and Hitler himself — had died long before they could be put in the dock.

Martha was oppressed by the same angry, defeated cynicism when she reported on the concluding phase of the Paris Peace Conference, early in 1947. The promises that had been agreed during the conference were exemplary; the newly formed United Nations, the International Monetary Fund and the World Health Organization were designed to create binding ties of friendship between their member states, to herald a new world order of cooperation and progress. Yet, as post-war treaties were negotiated between the victorious Allies and the defeated Axis powers, it seemed to Martha that the same mistakes were being made that had blighted the Versailles treaty, little more than a quarter of a century ago.* "No compromise — only distrust and fear — more cynicism than in 1919 — no one cares about human rights," she jotted in her notebook. "More like preparation for another war than making a peace."[41]

Helen feared much the same when she too reported from Paris. Not only were the participating countries divided along familiar atavistic lines of nationalism, ideology and greed, but their discussions were replaying exactly the same issues that she'd reported in Geneva, back when the League of Nations had begun to implode. "The more I covered [Paris], the more I thought, This is where I came in. I know exactly who is going to argue what. Who is going to answer what. And this is stale. I'm burned out on this one."[42]

Helen would never deny that the war had been necessary, that it had been fought with idealism and glory. She believed that she and her colleagues had been on the right side of

* These negotiations dealt with the settling of war reparations, the protection of minorities and the handing over of war criminals for trial.

history as they reported on the fighting and the politics of the last six years. But twenty-five million soldiers had been slaughtered, fifty-five million civilians had been killed, national economies had been broken, cities laid waste, and it was unbearable to think no lessons had been learned from that carnage. It seemed to Helen that she'd spent most of her adult life obsessed with war — debating its evils, predicting its inevitability, then living its exigencies day by day. She'd been formed by the war, but constrained and damaged by it too. And, now that it was over, she not only had to worry about what kind of future awaited the world — but like Martha, Sigrid, Clare, Virginia and Lee, she had to question what her own place in that future might be.

Chapter Seventeen:
Aftermath

"This is what makes life worth living"
CLARE HOLLINGWORTH[1]

Lee Miller would build her own peace-time future on secrets and silence. The war had liberated her finest qualities, as a photographer, and as a woman, but it had blighted her too, and afterwards she preferred to bury all memory of it. To her son, Antony Penrose, she rarely spoke of the past; and when she died, in July 1977, it was both a revelation and a tragedy for him to discover the 60,000 prints and negatives that she'd stashed away in boxes and trunks, along with sheaves of manuscripts, diaries, letters and war memorabilia.

Here lay the story of Lee's life and work, and Antony's first reaction, as he began piecing it together, was to feel himself cheated. He'd never known that his mother was such an "exceptional person," nor had he known she was so deserving of sympathy. For most of his life, Lee had been an angry, drunk, withholding presence, and it was only now, as he learned the facts of her childhood rape and of her gruelling war, that Antony understood she hadn't so much been neglecting him as struggling to stay clear of her own demons.[2]

In 1978, just a year after Lee died, psychiatrists would recommend post-traumatic stress disorder as a diagnosis for patients in whom trauma had burrowed so deep that it remained active for years, manifesting itself in flashbacks, insomnia, anxiety, addiction and an emotional disconnection from the outside world. Lee knew full well that she'd been damaged by the war — "I got in over my head. I could never get the stench of Dachau out of my nostrils" — yet she was too distrustful of psychiatrists to seek professional help, and she was too proud, lonely and lost to confide in family and friends.[3]

When the war first ended, she was convinced that, if she could carry on working, she would simply outrun the pain. It was late in the summer of 1945 when she embarked on her extended tour of Central Europe and the Balkans, and she admitted to Audrey that she felt "about as rational as a scattered jigsaw puzzle."[4] In Vienna, she sat for an hour beside a baby who was dying because the medicine he needed had been stolen by black marketeers, and, during that long, bitter vigil, Lee despaired. The war seemed to have ended in a morass of waste and corruption, and for the sake of her own sanity she felt she had to keep on travelling, until she saw signs of a more positive future.

For seven months, Lee drove around Hungary, Bulgaria and Romania, observing the settling of old political scores, hoping against hope that the "modern minded" Russians might bring some kind of progress. But, as she wailed to Dave Scherman, she felt like the cursed heroine of a fairy tale: "It's my damned itchy feet, they just won't let me stop moving." By 16 February 1946, when Roland met her in Paris, she'd become exhausted, "inarticulate with shock."[5] Her gums were badly infected, her skin was blotchy, her once beautiful hair was lank and she was so racked with sharp, restless pains that she didn't attempt to argue when Roland insisted on taking her home.

This time, Lee was ready to accept her husband's care, but, while she recovered sufficiently to crank out a ten-page article for *Vogue,* her friends and colleagues remained anxious. Alex Kroll, the art director at *Vogue,* said it was as though "a screen" had been thrown up between Lee and the world — "I couldn't get through" — and Dave was convinced that she was heading for a complete collapse, grimly predicting that "sooner or later she [would] break all to pieces like a bum novel."[6]

Lee did not actually break. While her depressions and rages became darker and her periods of inertia more prolonged, there were periods of boomeranging energy during which she was able to work and travel, to refocus her camera on people, places and art. And it was during one of these bright periods of remission, early in 1947, that Lee discovered she was pregnant.

"Darling," she wrote to Roland from Switzerland, "This is a hell of a romantic way to tell you that I'll shortly be knitting little clothes for a little man . . . So far, no resentment or anguish or mind changing or panic, only a mild astonishment that I'm so happy about it."[7] Lee was so beguiled by this unexpected twist in her life that she agreed to marry Roland (the ever-saintly Aziz travelling to London to give her a divorce). And, even though Antony, soon to become Tony, was a colicky baby, even though Lee struggled through his first months, there were the usual milestones of delight — the first "awfully cute" smile, the first babbled words — which made her believe she could enjoy being a mother.

Around the time that Tony was eight, however, Lee entered a period of profound and frightening darkness, during which she lost all sense of herself. She was disgusted by her body, which had thickened with pregnancy, she could not bear to pick up her camera and she no longer had any idea of how to deal with her child. Although Tony was sent away to boarding school and there was a nanny, Patsy Marray, to take charge of him during the holidays, Lee had lost her first easy delight in her lively little boy, and instead came to resent his presence.

In Tony's memory, she became a "raging alcoholic," and he learned to dread the speed with which she could pivot from sourly aggressive gaiety to icy rage.[8] Inevitably, he looked to his nanny for love, but, close though he became to Patsy, regarding her as his surrogate mother, she was unable to shield him from Lee. As his relationship with his mother deteriorated, he recalled that the two of them learned to hate each other "with such attention to the fine points that it became an art form." Tony remained mystified by the depths of his mother's hostility: "I don't know what I represented to her, I may have reflected her own self-loathing." But Lee was so suicidally miserable, she confided to a friend that the only reason she didn't kill herself was knowing how happy it would make her husband and son.[9]

While it was the effects of the war and of her own buried history that were pushing Lee to the brink of collapse, it was also the sensation that she was no longer in charge of herself, now, but was floundering in the slipstream of her husband's life. Back in

1948, Roland had bought a modest rural estate called Farley Farm, where he planned to fulfil his fantasy of becoming a gentleman farmer. He and Lee only went down during long weekends and holidays (the Downshire Hill house was eventually replaced by a rented two-room London flat), but, although Lee could embrace the beauty of the East Sussex countryside, and the novelty of being on a farm (she was typically curious to see how a pig was slaughtered), she was intrinsically an urban creature; and when Roland first acquired the farmhouse it seemed to her cold and primitive, a burden to run.

Audrey Withers believed Lee was being buried alive: "[She] came into her own during the war. Afterwards nothing came up to it. She was not meant to be married, have children or live in the country."[10] Meanwhile, as Lee's star faded, Roland's was on the rise: in 1947, he co-founded the ICA, London's first dedicated museum of modern art; in 1955, he was appointed the British Council's fine-art representative in France; he curated exhibitions, including a major Picasso retrospective; he wrote several biographies; in 1966, he would be distinguished by a knighthood. And while there were perks to Roland's eminence — the British Council appointment came with a Paris flat, and there were always interesting guests down at Farley Farm — they were Roland's perks, not Lee's. Partly through choice, partly through circumstance, she was no longer her husband's equal, and there was a diminishing number of people, now, who knew her as the brilliant artist and photojournalist to whom the world had formerly gravitated.

When Lee was at her most miserable, when she thought her marriage to Roland was over and when she could do little but slope around the farm in her shabby gardening clothes, she begged her personal physician for help. Dr. Carl Goldman knew Lee's history and had some idea of what she was going through, but he'd seen far more extreme cases of combat stress and he'd diagnosed boredom and self-pity as the root of her problems: "we cannot keep the world permanently at war," he'd said brusquely, "just to provide you with entertainment."[11]

In the end, what saved Lee was not another war, but cookery. Although she'd always been prone to faddish diets and slimming regimes, she was fascinated by the colours, textures and flavours of food; and down in Sussex, where there was a large vegetable garden and permanently hungry guests, the kitchen became her creative domain. All the inquisitiveness and invention she'd once expended on her photography was focused on recipes and kitchen gadgets. The meals she cooked were a fearless, ongoing experiment with ingredients and cuisines, and, according to the artist John Craxton, she was at her entertaining best when standing at her stove, surrounded "with open bottles of booze and a potent cider anyone could swig at."[12]

Word of Lee's cooking spread; she was interviewed by magazines, invited on culinary tours, and, in January 1966, when she entered a competition held by the Norwegian Tourist Board, her variations on the concept of *smørrebrød* won her not only first prize, but second and third as well. As she regained her health and confidence, she came to a wary accommodation with Roland — accepting his affairs with younger women while becoming more attentive to her own appearance. She continued to keep her professional past buried — when the Chicago Art Institute asked for access to her photographs, she said they'd nearly all been destroyed, "thrown away by the Germans in Paris, bombed and burned in the London Blitz . . . or scrapped by Condé Nast."[13] But she was beginning to travel more widely again and she was renewing contact with some of her oldest and dearest friends, especially Picasso, Man Ray and Aziz.

There were new friends, too, many of them much younger women, and it was with them that Lee eventually trusted herself to disclose more of her past. Mostly, she talked about the parties, the travels, the famous names, but very occasionally she talked about the war. One night, she was sitting up late with the teenage daughter of a friend, and, after several glasses of whisky, she fetched out some of the photographs she'd taken of Dachau. They were shocking, of course, but the tears Lee wept as she leafed through the images seemed to be principally for herself. "She was crying from loneliness as well as from drink, from never really sharing that experience with anyone," observed Anne-Laure Lyon, who, young though she was, had intuited Lee's desperation, and understood that she was a woman marooned by her own history.[14]

As Lee got older, she found her best company, her best solace in classical music. Those who'd once seen her scintillating at parties, or had known her during the war as the one person everyone had wanted to be around, because she always had "whisky, cigarettes and a plan," would barely have recognized Lee Miller in her sixties: sitting very quietly, with a pair of headphones clamped to her ears, listening hour after solitary hour to her two favourite composers, Mozart and Beethoven.[15]

During the very last years of her life, Lee did find her way back to happiness. She slowly mended her relationship with Tony, who'd gone travelling after college and had returned three years later with a wife, Suzanna. They had a baby daughter in the spring of 1976, and Lee was pleased to discover how much simpler it was to be a grandmother than a mother. But time was against her. In May 1977, she was diagnosed with pancreatic cancer, and had only weeks in which to make her final peace with her husband and son. Tony was moved by the courage with which she joked her way through to the end of her illness, embracing death as though it was her final adventure. And with Roland, too, Lee returned to a simple loving affection. When she died on 21 July, it was in the embrace of her husband's arms.

Afterwards, as Tony pieced together the fragments of his mother's life, it grieved him that neither she nor Roland had trusted him with the truth about her troubled, turbulent and brilliant past. But he could at least share that past with the world. Over the following decades, he worked first with Suzanna, then with their daughter, Amy, to build up an archive of Lee's work. He researched and wrote his mother's biography, *The Lives of Lee Miller,* and he collaborated with Dave Scherman on a collection of her war journalism. As the ripples of interest spread, Lee's reputation was boosted by new research into the hidden histories of women artists and writers. Exhibitions, documentaries, books all followed, and, by the turn of the century, Lee's work, the portraits that had been taken of her, and Dave's wartime shot in Hitler's bathroom, had become part of the photographic canon.

If Lee had never got over the war, if she'd never got rid of the stench of Dachau, she was not alone. Martha Gellhorn had felt "shredded up inside" during the first months of peace; and, when she looked back at her life in the decades to come, she realized the damage had been permanent: "it was as though I fell off a cliff at Dachau, and suffered a form of concussion ever since."[16]

Martha, however, had a sufficiently robust temperament to ride out the depressions which periodically threatened. In April 1946, she was already writing about how good it was to laugh again, especially with women like Ginny Cowles, "who were glad to be alive because they knew about death," and who seemed to Martha, "so worldly and so funny, disabused, unexcited, uncomplaining and a pleasure to look at."[17]

Yet, there was another crucial factor driving her recovery. She needed, simply, to earn money, and when her long association with *Collier's* foundered, she was obliged to reinvent herself or, as she cheerfully admitted to Diana Cooper, to go "literary whoring."[18] She discovered she had a talent for popular short stories, lurid romances about titled ladies and gigolos, about innocent Americans abroad, and, trashy though she considered these "bilgers" to be, they were easier and far more lucrative work than her literary fiction, which had always been written in "blood" and self-doubt.

They also gave her the means to travel wherever her curiosity and her instinct took her. She lasted only a few months in her Belgravia house, defeated by the London drizzle and smog, and from there moved on to Washington, offsetting her distaste for American politics with the pleasures of good food, games of tennis and a companionable love affair. In 1949, she visited the newly created state of Israel, which she regarded as one of the best and brightest outcomes of the war — "a new country full of young, brave, gay people" and an act of reparation for the six million Jewish dead.[19]* Shortly before that visit, she also found what she believed could be her own new home — a brightly painted house in the small Mexican town of Cuernavaca.

Perched in the mountains, with high blue skies and hot vivid colours, Cuernavaca

* So passionately did she identify with the Israeli people she would never accept they were, in any way, guilty of crimes against their Palestinian neighbours. Victims of fascism themselves, she could not regard them as oppressors, capable of murder, theft and persecution.

seemed to Martha the idyll to which she'd aspired and failed in Cuba. She met an American doctor there, with whom she had the most joyful sex of her life. And then, in 1949, she adopted a baby.

Writing to Diana Cooper, Martha admitted she had come to accept that her life would not feel complete without a child: "It's what one needs, someone who can take all the love one is able to give as a natural and untroublesome gift."[20] Now aged forty, she assumed she was too old to get pregnant herself, but, as a woman of independent means, she could adopt, and, thinking back to all the starving abandoned war children she'd seen in Italy, she made it her mission to rescue one of them.

After scouring no fewer than fifty-two orphanages, she found a chubby blond toddler, named Alessandro, with whom she fell "fatally in love."[21] "I have never wanted anything so much," she told Eleanor Roosevelt, and, after three months of anxious paperwork, she was able to take little Sandy back to Mexico.[22] "He is bliss bliss bliss," she wrote ecstatically to the author Sybille Bedford, and she believed she would never feel anything for him but pure unconditional love. "He may grow up to be very short and stout and of moderate brightness but I think he is always going to be happy."[23]

As yet, Martha had no idea that Sandy's

requirements for happiness might not conform to her own. When she eventually decided that life in Cuernavaca was too limited, she moved on to Italy, borrowing a friend's farmhouse just outside Rome, where she planned to create an elegant "instructive" new life for them both. Four-year-old Sandy was enrolled in the local school, yet, while he learned to speak Italian impressively fast, he was unable to settle, and, to Martha's mystified irritation, started to become "prissy and finicky," disliking his new nanny, fearful of playing outdoors.[24]

It was dawning on Martha, as it had dawned on Lee, that loving a baby was no preparation for the years of iron-clad responsibility to come. She'd sprung a "giant trap" for herself and, with a sense of doom, she returned to London in 1953, reluctantly accepting that Sandy might need a more solid, dependable childhood. There, she met Tom Matthews, the handsome, patrician editor of *Time* magazine, who'd recently arrived to set up a London office. Tom was a widower with four sons, three of them adult, but one aged twelve, and a possible companion for Sandy. When Tom finally proposed marriage to Martha after a courtship of dancing, dinners and expensively well-chosen gifts, she decided she had found the perfect domestic situation, one in which her life would become "easier, just less damn trouble."[25]

She made no pretence of loving Tom, yet the pragmatism with which she'd embarked on this relationship brought unexpected contentment: "It turns out that wedlock is the easiest thing I have so far undertaken," Martha congratulated herself.[26] In May 1954, she and Tom bought a six-storey house in Chester Square, Belgravia, and, although Tom's youngest son, also a Sandy, had trouble settling into the household at first, Martha's own Sandy became immediately attached to his stepfather. As for Martha herself, now that she'd provided a family for her son, now that she'd freed herself from financial worry, she was able to put the literary whoring behind her and re-focus on serious fiction.

The marriage lasted for nine years — a long time, for Martha. But, towards the end, she grew predictably restless, resenting the loss of her independence, pulling at the faulty threads of the relationship like a fidgety child. Tom played too much tennis, demanded too much sex, was too intrinsically glum, she complained; yet, as she withdrew from her husband, she also became progressively disenchanted with her son. Sandy was a chatty, lively, affectionate boy, but he was not particularly clever, and, far more troubling to Martha, he was starting to get fat. Hypercritical of her own appearance, and always quick to associate physical flaws with moral weakness, Martha tried to put Sandy on a stringent diet. But food had always been a comfort for the vulnerable teenager, and, as he carried on eating, guiltily, in secret, he not only grew plumper, but more miserable.

The fight over food would come close to destroying Martha's relationship with Sandy, but what he remembered as the "knockout punch" of his childhood was the moment he returned from boarding school, in the summer of 1963, to learn that Chester Square was no longer his home. Martha had discovered Tom in the middle of an affair, and, motivated by a scalding, perverse jealousy — as well as the knowledge that she'd been handed an excuse to leave — she was insisting on a divorce. Sandy was heartbroken to lose both his London life and his stepfather, but Martha was already poised, impatiently, for flight. As soon as she'd got Sandy enrolled in an American boarding school, she embarked on an exploratory tour of East Africa, and in the coastal village of Nyali found a beach house for rent, where she resolved to spend her days writing, swimming, relearning how to be free.

Martha was now approaching sixty, however, and the prospect of ageing was making her anxious. She realized how carelessly she'd depended on her youth and beauty to ease her way through life, and — even though she'd begun an intermittent but happy affair with a rich American, whom she simply called "L" — she was haunted by fears of a "withered . . . sex-starved" old age. She was equally frightened that her writing might never have time to blossom into greatness. Although she remained as disciplined as ever, she was conscious that a younger generation was outpacing her, that novelists like Saul Bellow and John Updike were writing with a moral daring, a stylistic reach, and an understanding of the modern world she was unable to match.

But, if her fiction was failing, she could always return to journalism and, in the summer of 1966, Martha dedicated herself to a new campaigning cause. The war in Vietnam had been festering for years, as the U.S.-backed regime in the South attempted to bring down Ho Chi Minh's communist republic in the North. Martha had always considered it a bad war, but, when America escalated its military involvement, she judged it to be an evil one — and she was so angered by her own position as an "unwilling, revolted, powerless accomplice," she felt compelled to fly out to Vietnam and bear witness.[27]

Two decades had passed, however, since she'd last reported from a battle zone, and a disconcerting number of publications turned Martha down before the *Guardian* agreed to take six articles, on condition that she covered her own expenses. These were virtually the same terms on which she'd first gone free-lance to Spain, but Martha, at fifty-eight, knew exactly how she wanted to write, now, and where she needed to go. Flying out to Saigon, she spent three weeks searching for the human faces of this war, touring hospitals, refugee camps and orphanages, and discovering, to her anguish, how much more lethally efficient American weapons had become at killing, maiming and obliterating civilian lives.

The reports Martha filed on her return were as blisteringly, viscerally angry as any she'd written, and, while they got her black-listed from Vietnam, they thrust her briefly into the media spotlight. She was interviewed on television, and her 1959 collection of combat journalism, *The Face of War,* was reissued along with her Vietnam stories. Politics had reignited the fire and fury of her prose, yet, even as she re-immersed herself in a public battle, Martha was having to defend herself against private loss. Edna, the "north star" of her life, was failing, and when she died in September 1968, the grief Martha felt was compounded by knowledge that she'd all but lost her son as well. Sandy had never fully recovered from the collapse of his London family; he'd dropped out of college, become heavily involved with drugs, and Martha, despairing that she'd made "every known mistake" in his upbringing, feared he might soon refuse to have anything more to do with her.[28]

Depression washed over her, and, for the first time in her life, she was unable to heal herself through work. Every idea she had for a novel, a story or even an article came up against a "writer's block made of solid concrete," and she remained unproductive for a terrifying five years.[29] But Martha despised self-pity — in herself, as much as in others — and, if she could not write, she could at least divert her formidable energy and will into her appearance. Now in her mid-sixties, she refused to fade into a graceless, invisible old age, and, putting herself on a punishing regime of diet and exercise, she had her face lifted, her hair styled, and began trawling the smarter charity shops for second-hand couture.

She also went travelling, following the sun to foreign beach resorts: "I mean to keep moving," she told Diana Cooper, "guaranteed cure for accidie." Looking and feeling better than she had done in years, Martha at last found her way back to writing.[30] In 1975, she went to Madrid to report for *New York Magazine* on the death of Franco; a stalled collection of novellas began to take shape; then, in 1978, she published her one and only memoir. *Travels with Myself and Another* was structured around the most comically disastrous journeys of her career (including the trip to China, in which Ernest was referred to simply as "UC," the "unwilling companion"), and it brought Martha a new and appreciative audience. Two of her earlier novels were republished, along with a new edition of *The Face of War,* and she gained a new circle of friends, a much younger group of writers, broadcasters and journalists, among whom she found herself holding court as a grande dame, mentor and confidante.

Back in 1970, she'd bought an elegant two-floor flat in Knightsbridge, and it was here, at 72 Cadogan Square, that she began entertaining her "chaps," as she affectionately called them. The doubting self-image she'd formed of herself — a crotchety old woman with the temperament of a "hurt, greedy twenty-five-year-old" — was exorcised by the figure she now saw reflected in the chaps' admiration: a woman of sardonic glamour, worldliness, wisdom and wit. Invigorated by her new eminence, Martha sought to repair her relationship with Sandy, striving to accept her son for who he was, and she pushed even harder against the encroachments of age, continuing to write, travel and comment on the world until she was well into her eighties.

Eventually, and inevitably, Martha's body rebelled. Her sight and hearing were failing, her back was too painful to endure another plane flight to yet another beach, and, when she was diagnosed with late-stage cancer, she conceded it was time for her to die. She grieved for herself — wishing she could have written one truly great novel in her life, wishing that she could have had one truly close relationship with a man — and she admitted she was frightened of death: "it *is* the totally unknown risk."[31] But she had, typically, made sure that the time and manner of her passing would be under her control. As a naively confident twenty-one-year-old, she'd sworn it was possible to do "anything you like if you are willing to pay the full price for it."[32] It was the creed into which she'd poured all the courage and all the moral absolutism of her life, and she planned to die by it too. Back in 1961, Ernest had shot himself, giving way to his black dogs of paranoia and depression, and, while Martha would not turn a gun on herself, she was able to get hold of a pill — very probably a cyanide capsule — to do the job.

On 14 February 1998, she made tidy preparations for what she had decided would be her final day: she spoke to her brother, Alfred, on the phone; she put out the rubbish; and she attached labels to particular possessions that she wanted to leave to friends. When her body was discovered the following morning, it looked almost as though she had passed away in her sleep; and in her will she'd left instructions that she be mourned as calmly and efficiently as she'd died. There was to be no funeral, no fuss. All Martha required of her family and friends was that they gather together for a drink in her memory, and that they scatter her ashes on the Thames. It was to be the last of "my travels," she wrote, as the ebbing tide washed her cremains out to sea.

In 1966, while Martha was being feted for her writing on Vietnam, she was causing unwitting grief to Clare Hollingworth, who at that point was the *Guardian*'s staff defence correspondent and very protective of her rights of coverage. Clare admired Martha: no one else looked so good in combat reporter's gear, she acknowledged, and no one wrote about the human issues of war with her distinctive passion. But she minded very much that the space which the *Guardian* had allocated to Martha had prevented her own return to Vietnam, and that the paper had preferred Martha's grasp of the war's "larger story" to her own more "limited view of military strategy."[33] Ever competitive, ever susceptible to the professional slight, Clare felt that Martha had been little more than a tourist — reporting from the front for a mere three weeks — whereas she had dedicated most of her own career to the reporting of revolutions, international crises and wars.

In the period immediately after the Second World War, Clare and Geoffrey Hoare had carried on living and writing together as a professional team. From the conflict in Greece, they'd moved on to Jerusalem, where Geoffrey had been appointed chief correspondent for the *News Chronicle* and Clare had worked as a stringer for the *News of the World* (at that point, a reasonably respectable paper still). Tensions between the incoming Jewish refugees and the native Arab population were at a tipping point, and, in 1948, when the newly created state of Israel went to war with its Arab neighbours, Clare found the story emotionally and politically challenging to report. Only a decade earlier, she'd been helping European Jews escape from Nazi persecution, yet these former victims of fascism were now the aggressors — and she feared they were manifesting the same aggressive traits of territorial and racial entitlement as those from whom they'd recently fled.

When Jerusalem became too dangerous, Clare and Geoffrey moved to Cairo, but, in 1950, he was invited to run the *Chronicle*'s Paris bureau, and, for her, this meant a certain professional sacrifice. Clare understood the promotion was irresistible, and at first she was happy to move to France, using her temporary furlough from news-reporting to work on a newly commissioned book on the Arab world and some freelance pieces for *The Economist*. She was also Geoffrey's unofficial collaborator, still, and the following year they would lead the field together, with their coverage of Guy Burgess and Donald Maclean, the two British spies who defected to Russia.

But time hung heavy. While she decorated the Parisian apartment, went to the theatre and began collecting art, Clare still had long empty hours to fill and, untypically introspective, she began to question the choices she'd made in her life. Up until this point, she had been convinced that she didn't want children; she was only a stepmother in name to Geoffrey's teenage daughter, and she assumed that a baby of her own would be impossible to manage with her career. Suddenly, however, she was assailed by feelings of maternal yearning and loss, and, in a crisis of self-doubt, she began to question whether her work as a journalist was sufficiently distinguished, or valuable, to justify her decision to remain childless.

Clare could never quite suppress her feelings of professional insecurity. Even though she had scooped more war action than most of her male colleagues over the last twelve years, she had never been rewarded with a full-time job, never been given a medal, or an honour. Sometimes she worried that she lacked the right educational background, sometimes she feared that her pedestrian prose style would remain an obstacle to professional greatness. At some point, she even started to keep a file — labelled "Moral [*sic*] Boosts" — in which she kept copies of her most positive citations and reviews.[34] Yet in Paris, the doubts that nagged at Clare's confidence ratcheted to a new level of pain when she was forced to confront the stability of her marriage. Clare had known from the start that Geoffrey was insatiably curious about women, and she'd accepted that he would always indulge in the occasional peccadillo. But when she discovered he was having an affair with the young woman who was both their housekeeper and friend, she panicked. Not only did she threaten divorce, but she turned to religion, and, in October 1957, converted to Catholicism.

Geoffrey was alarmed by this change in Clare, as were many of her friends; yet while she remained true to her new faith, maintaining that it brought her "internal strength and happiness," it was almost certainly work that saved her marriage.[35] In the spring of 1958, the *Financial Times* approached Clare with a commission to report on the rise of Arab nationalism and Islamic fundamentalism in the Middle East, and so thorough was her coverage that, two years later, she was poached by the *Manchester Guardian* to cover the civil war in Algeria.

Finally, Clare was back on a professionally equal footing with Geoffrey, and back in the places where she thrived. Algiers was a particularly vicious war zone, rife with sniper attacks and terrorist bombs. Yet, according to one of her colleagues, Clare seemed impervious to risk as she strode around the "blood-streaked" city, looking like "a county lady determined that the vicarage fete shall proceed despite the arrival of Hell's Angels."[36] She filed some remarkable stories, and when she returned home, it was to a couple of major awards and, better yet, to her first full-time staff job, as defence correspondent for the *Guardian*.

Clare embraced her new reporter's beat with unembarrassed zeal. "I love weapons," she admitted to one interviewer, and her writing was never so immediate or so engaged as when the job took her on a tour of a nuclear submarine, or out to Aden, to witness an RAF Shackleton dropping 1,000-lb. bombs on a rebel position.[37] Even though she no longer wore an army-issue uniform, Clare was rarely seen in anything, now, but the khaki safari suit that was her own civilian version of battledress.

In the spring of 1965, she was one of the first journalists to fly out to Saigon and among the first to challenge America's claims that the Vietcong guerrillas would easily be crushed. She sensed, rightly, that the war in Vietnam would become pivotal, and she was hoping for a long assignment. The *Guardian*, however, could not give her the budget for an extended stay and she was also worried about Geoffrey, who was experiencing pains in his arm and was going to London for a consultation. By now, Clare — used to keeping her work and her marriage separate — had come to accept that the periods when she and Geoffrey were apart were necessary for both of them. "I wonder," she wrote later, "whether we should have been quite so happy had we been together all the time." But suddenly she sensed that Geoffrey needed her, and "for the only time in my life requested my editor for permission to take immediate leave."[38]

Her instinct was right, for, by the time she reached London, her husband was in hospital, having suffered a heart attack. For ten days, Clare sat by his side, watching him recover, and because the doctors were so positive, assuring her that she would soon be able to take him home, she was utterly unprepared when, on 28 May, he had a second, and fatal, attack. "I am at the moment stunned, and in the state of believing or half believing it is not true," she wrote to a friend. Even though she'd struggled at times with her husband's infidelities, he'd been her truest friend, her closest advisor and collaborator, and without him, she admitted, she felt lost.[39]

The only thing she knew how to do was work, and colleagues at the *Guardian* were confounded when, within hours of Geoffrey's funeral, Clare returned to the office, asking for her next assignment. Over the next few years, she would, as she put it, "keep away the tears" by reporting from Algiers, northern India, Aden, Turkey, Pakistan, Zambia and Saudi Arabia. She knew that some of her friends were concerned by the "desperate energy" with which she was hurtling around the world, yet it was her best way of riding out her grief.[40] Tom Pocock from the *Evening Standard* was with Clare in northern India, and, when the two of them were driving over a disputed bridge, a volley of Pakistani bullets whistling over their heads, he saw her face light up like a child's birthday cake as she exclaimed, "This is what makes life worth living."[41]

When the *Guardian* could no longer afford Clare's demanding travel budget, she switched to the *Daily Telegraph,* covering the Six-Day War in Israel, returning to the conflict in Vietnam and breaking news of the secret peace talks between America and North Vietnam. But, after seven years, even she began to run out of steam; acknowledging that she needed to be settled in one place, she accepted the *Telegraph*'s offer to become their first bureau chief in Beijing.

In the autumn of 1972, China was just emerging from the political and economic convulsions of the Cultural Revolution and only just beginning to engage with the Western world. Clare, aged sixty-one, was having to adapt to an entirely alien world and one whose rigid state control made her job almost impossible to do. All of her usual strategies for hunting news — grooming sources, travelling to prohibited places — were frustrated, and, even though Clare was fascinated by the political battles between the reformist Deng Xiaoping and the hard-line Gang of Four, she could report very little of them. After three and a half years, she was happy to cede Beijing to a younger colleague, and apparently happy to accept the *Telegraph*'s suggestion that she see out the remaining years of her contract as their London-based defence correspondent.

Everyone assumed Clare would retire once her contract was done, and, in the spring of 1981, her seventieth year, the *Telegraph* threw a party for her, presenting her with a replica rifle as a parting gift. But Clare had no intention of settling down with her books and her art collection. Her other parting gift from the *Telegraph* had been a short-term assignment in the Far East, and, during that time, she'd become very taken with Hong Kong, and had decided she could not only live there, but use it as a base for prolonging her career. Only weeks after her retirement party in London, she'd moved into her Hong Kong flat, ready to begin yet another new job, as stringer for the *Sunday Telegraph.*

For the next decade, Clare remained in business, waking promptly at six every morning when her alarm clock sounded a military reveille. Her passport and her "T and T" were always close to hand, for she was covering China and Japan, as well as Hong Kong, and she was writing for a spread of other publications, including the *International Herald Tribune.* Meantime, she kept abreast with the rest of the world news, and, in 1993, eight years before the Twin Towers fell, she wrote a prescient piece for the *New York Times,* analysing the likely spread of Islamic fundamentalism to the West. In 2000, the same year that she travelled to London to receive a Lifetime Achievement Award, Clare went on a press trip to Saigon, to mark the twenty-fifth anniversary of Vietnam's full transition to communist rule.

Reporting had been Clare's life, she couldn't imagine any other, but, during the late 1990s, her body began to let her down. She suffered a couple of minor strokes, a possible heart attack, and, more frustratingly for a reporter, she was diagnosed with macular degeneration of her eyes. As the new millennium turned and her sight degenerated, she could no longer manage without carers; when her great-nephew, Patrick Garrett, came to stay with her, he also noted that, while she had a startlingly clear recall of the past, her short-term memory was muddled.

Still Clare resisted any suggestion that she was old: even when she was celebrating her hundredth birthday in 2011, she claimed to feel like a "much younger" woman still. On the morning of 10 January 2017, however, when she was recovering from a very bad cold, she whispered to her carers that she felt tired. None of them had ever heard Clare admit to a weakness before, but, at 105, she was ready to let go.

The response to her death could have filled Clare's morale-boosting file many times over. Obituaries appeared in the international press, on radio and television, and publishers hounded Patrick Garrett for the biography he'd begun to write. It wasn't simply that Clare had lived and reported through so much history, she'd also embodied a style of journalism that now seemed endangered, if not extinct. In a world where facts could be found on the Internet and eyewitnesses sourced through multiple social media, there were diminishing numbers of correspondents who shared her tenacious integrity — her insistence on being out in the field, doing her research, or, as she always put it, on "smelling the breezes."[42]

In the affectionate, ironic cartoon with which the *Daily Telegraph* chose to celebrate Clare's career, two hacks in a newsroom were shown asking each other who would scoop the stories for them now that she was dead. The speech bubble over their heads — "Who's going to tell us when Trump starts World War Three?" — was one that Clare would have found amusing, but alarmingly topical, given the unpredictable, combative style with which the then American President was conducting himself in office.[43]

Sigrid Schultz had hunted out the truth with the same moral doggedness as Clare, and, even though the two women never met, they would have recognized each other as kindred spirits. Both were competitive, both had an absolute commitment to work, which drove them to put reporting ahead of safety and comfort. But, while Clare had been able to sustain her career until close to the end of her life, Sigrid's days of journalism were all but over when she returned to America at the end of 1945.

She had just come from Nuremberg and her emotions were raw. Listening to the lying testimony of Göring — the Nazi she'd known and hated most intimately — she'd been forced to relive the fear, disgust and frustration of her final years in Germany; and when she'd met with Colonel McCormick to discuss her coverage of the trials, she'd been stricken by his comment that the Nazis were not the only ones at fault and there were guilty Allied officers who should also be held to account. For the last two decades, Sigrid had schooled herself to accommodate the crassness of McCormick's political views, but this was beyond bearing. "Colonel, I'm sorry I can't go along with that," she'd blurted, and had walked down the long stairs at the *Tribune* office, "weeping my head off," as she later recalled, because she knew she could no longer work for McCormick or his paper.[44]

Sigrid was weeping, too, because, in cutting her ties with the *Tribune,* she guessed she was probably ending her career. Most American newspapers were reducing their foreign coverage, now that the war was over, and, in a harshly competitive job market, a fifty-two-year-old woman was not likely to thrive. Even the legendary Dorothy Thompson was being put out to grass, writing soft news and comment for the *Ladies' Home Journal,* and Sigrid would have to consider herself lucky with the small freelance jobs that came her way — the occasional article and book review for *Mc-Call's* magazine and *Collier's,* the occasional spot for Mutual Broadcasting System.

With her reporting prospects all but terminated, she busied herself with lecture tours, talking to women's clubs and civil organizations about her life in Nazi Germany. She also wrote proposals for several books. But a literary career would never blossom for Sigrid. Like Clare, she was essentially a news writer, and her pithy factual style was not suited to book-length prose. A far more fundamental problem, though, was her subject matter. All Sigrid wanted to write about was Germany, about why she considered the nation to be an enduring threat. And, in a world that was trying to find its way towards global rapprochement, no publishers were interested in dark predictions of a resurgent Nazism waiting in the wings.

But, if Sigrid felt silenced, she was too resourceful to be miserable. After she'd resigned from the *Tribune,* she joined her mother in Westport, Connecticut, setting up home in the renovated barn that stood behind Hedwig's prettily gabled house. "Mommy Schultz," as Hedwig was locally known, had already become part of the community, famous for her extended family of stray cats and dogs, for the jar of cookies she kept ready for passing children. Now, as Sigrid resumed the care of her mother, as she planted vegetables, quince and walnut trees, for the re-cultivation of her cooking skills, she too made herself a small, busy niche in Westport life.*

It was here that she managed to reconnect with Peter Ilcus. The history of their relationship remains difficult to determine, not only because of Peter's long periods of incarceration, but because, shortly after Sigrid died,

---

* Her one successful book was an edition of recipes, collected from members of the Overseas Press Club.

her house was demolished by the town of Westport, to make room for a municipal car park, and boxes of her personal papers were inadvertently destroyed. By the time they resumed contact, and Peter begged Sigrid to join him, it's clear that she felt too old, too settled to risk a new life. Although she would always refer to him fondly as "my boyfriend," and although she kept his photograph hung above her dining table, she never once saw him again.

Her refusal to go to Peter must also have been dictated by her mother's failing health, but, when Hedwig died in 1960, Sigrid was freed up to travel more locally, and she began to make the regular journey between Westport and New York, to attend meetings of the Overseas Press Club. For the next decade and a half, the Club became her mainstay, restoring her to the gossipy, stimulating world of the foreign press room, which for so many years had been her natural element. In November 1969, when the OPC put up a brass plaque in honour of her achievements, Sigrid could believe that, even if she'd been forgotten by newspaper editors, she was still loved and admired by her peers.

But a new generation was also starting to pay court. Now that a quarter of a century had elapsed, the war and Nazi Germany were becoming topics of research interest and historians were identifying Sigrid as a formidable resource. One of them, John Toland, claimed that she'd provided invaluable background for his book about Hitler's rise to power, supplying him with far more telling insights into "the spirit of the times" than anyone else he'd consulted. He couldn't understand how her own story had been forgotten — she'd clearly been "one of the greats," he thought.[45] But, shortly after Toland's visits, Sigrid was approached by a young historian called Cynthia Chapman, who was very much interested in the remarkable "guts and accuracy" of Sigrid's professional life and wanted to collaborate with her on an autobiography.*

Even as Chapman sifted through Sigrid's papers, however, and encouraged her to piece together her memories, the essential secret of her life, her Jewishness, remained hidden. In theory, Sigrid should have been free to disclose her true identity once she'd left Germany — she had, in fact, every excuse for boasting about it. Yet, for a complication of reasons, she remained silent. Back in 1938, when she'd bought her mother's house in Westport, she'd been forced to conceal the fact of Hedwig's Jewishness because there were still historic zoning restrictions in place, which discriminated against Jews. Even when

* The material was never published, but Chapman used it as the basis of her PhD thesis.

those restrictions were lifted, however, Sigrid didn't speak up. Perhaps she was afraid of legal repercussions — she must have lied about her and Hedwig's identity on several official forms — but perhaps the secret itself had become too large, too guilty to tell. So many millions had suffered and died on account of their Jewishness that Sigrid might simply have felt ashamed of disavowing her own ancestry for so long, ashamed perhaps of having survived.

As it was, she only acknowledged the truth four years before she died, and only then in a casual aside to a teenage girl, who was interviewing her for a high-school project. It was 1976, and Sigrid was physically very frail — she'd had a heart attack, and was so severely arthritic, she was all but confined to a wheelchair. When she started to tell Pamela Wriedt the much-repeated story of her first encounter with Hitler, it may have been pain, forgetfulness or fatigue that made her add the simple, clinching detail — "he didn't know I was Jewish."[46]

Unfortunately, Pamela was too young to grasp the explosive import of that detail, or to press Sigrid to elaborate. Many years later, however, Pamela's husband and a group of Westport historians began to investigate the veracity of that tantalizing revelation, and they uncovered two compelling pieces of evidence. One was the email testimony of

670

Sigrid's nearest descendant (a first cousin twice removed, from Herman's side of the family), which affirmed that he and his family had always known Hedwig, and thus Sigrid, were Jewish; the other was a copy of the passenger manifest for the SS *Statendam,* the boat on which Hedwig sailed from Rotterdam to New York, in 1938. Her name is clearly printed, and beside it, the racial designation, "Hebrew."

If Sigrid had worried, back in 1976, whether revealing the secret of her Jewishness might make her the target of Westport gossip or malice, she had nothing to fear. She'd become a local dignitary, wheeled into parties in her best kimono, with an admiring audience always ready to hear her stories, and always hopeful that she might tell their fortunes (Sigrid's experience with the Nazi astrologers having apparently inspired her to work up a convincing act of her own). She still liked to host her own soirées, serving the best champagne and wine she could afford, although she'd otherwise become very frugal in her habits — and, according to her nurse, Clarence Doore, she was notorious for having "the most godawful coffee" in town.* It was

* Sigrid's only income was the meagre $100 monthly pension paid out by the *Tribune,* plus the money she got from the rental, and eventual sale, of Hedwig's house.

a measure of the love Sigrid had earned from her community that, when she was too ill to travel to New York for a dinner which the OPC had arranged in her honour, a neighbour offered to host the event in Westport.

Back in 1969, when the OPC had honoured Sigrid with her plaque, they'd described her as a "tough competitor, staunch friend [and an] honest reporter [who] worked like a newspaperman." Eleven years later, several members of the Club took issue with the citation's wording, disliking its implication that a woman had to work "like a man" to achieve respect. They wrote to Sigrid, enquiring whether she had been similarly offended, but, when she responded to that query, in a note to the writer, Julia Edwards, she politely, but briskly, refuted its logic. "Yes, I certainly believe in the rights of the female but I insist that the only thing that counts is efficiency, which is a fact that leading newspaper men believe."[47]

This was the principle by which Sigrid had lived and worked for as long as she remembered. But the argument would no longer be hers to pursue, for just hours after writing her note, on the night of 14 May 1980, Sigrid died.

Sigrid herself never doubted the value of her work. In 1965, she donated most of her professional papers, and some of her personal correspondence, to Yale University and the Wisconsin State Historical Society. She subsequently arranged for the bulk of her estate, aside from small bequests to Peter Ilcus, carers and friends, to fund a scholarship for aspiring journalists, at Central Connecticut State University. Yet, the abruptness with which she'd been exiled from her career would always pain her, and it would remain a private, baffling tragedy for Sigrid that the professional skills for which she'd been acclaimed had so suddenly been judged worthless and out of date.

Virginia Cowles, by contrast, felt no lasting regret in putting her combat career behind her. By the time the war had ended, she was happy to be swept up in Aidan's vision — his euphoric conviction the Labour Party could be in power "for the next thirty years" and that he and his fellow MPs were "going to build a new world."[48] Virginia, as an American liberal of Republican descent, could never fully embrace Aidan's socialism, but she admired his moral principles, and was happy to be involved in some of his work, travelling around Europe with him and learning from Diana Cooper how to be a good political hostess — juggling a guest list so that the more preachy of Aidan's colleagues could be leavened with her own more amusing friends.

Between 1947 and 1950, Virginia also

produced three children — Andrew, Harriet and Randall — and, in 1948, when she and Aidan bought a farm in Buckinghamshire, she developed a Marie-Antoinetteish enthusiasm for the land — learning how to drive a tractor, helping to bring in the harvest. "The very fact of being on English soil has a magic of its own," she wrote, rooting herself deep into motherhood and marriage with an enthusiasm that had eluded both Martha and Lee.[49] Yet, Virginia never stopped working, and, since regular journalism was not compatible with family duties, she turned to history instead, writing biographies of Winston Churchill, Kaiser William II and David Stirling (founder of the SAS), researching the histories of family dynasties like the Astors and the Rothschilds, and publishing a study of Russian foreign policy. Although there were critics who challenged her scholarship, Virginia never lost her talent for telling a good story, and most of her books sold very well.

Her talent for reinvention was also a saving grace for Aidan when Labour's political momentum faltered and, in 1951, he lost his parliamentary seat. At first, he'd been unable to see past the crushing disappointment, but Virginia reminded him of the documentary he'd made about Palestine, before the war, and encouraged him to contact his friend George Barnes, who was now head of BBC television. It was inspired advice. Aidan was given the budget for a six-programme series about post-independence India, and Virginia, leaving the children with their French au pair, insisted on travelling with him, as his researcher and script editor.

India's Challenge was a popular and critical success, and it launched Aidan on a decade-long career as both television presenter and newspaper pundit. Virginia remained intimately involved: "She was my severest critic," Aidan wrote, adding that she was always quick to "spot a false note . . . or a false gesture" in his television performances, and no less ruthless in editing his articles. Years later, he would still wince at her dismissal of one of his sketchier first drafts: "You should never show me anything as badly written as that."[50]

If Virginia ever thought that she too might have performed well for television, that she too might be writing opinion pieces for the *Guardian* or the *Times,* she kept her regrets to herself. She seems to have been content with the professional battles she'd already won, and sexual politics *per se* didn't interest her. When her daughter, Harriet, tried to argue the case for Women's Lib, Virginia was unresponsive, inclined to dismiss both the movement and its members as "aggressive and humourless and loud."[51] Loyally and happily, she continued to cheer on Aidan's career as he became the first editor-in-chief of ITN News, helped to launch the new TV franchise LWT, and made a brief return to politics, as a newly centrist Tory.

Virginia, of course, was still busy and ambitious with her own projects. Harriet recalls her writing, most of the time, lying in bed, wrapped in her fur coat against the English cold, tapping away furiously on her typewriter and very much not to be disturbed. But she also recalls her as a ferociously energetic, chivvying, supportive mother, a mother who took her and her brothers on exotic, exhausting foreign holidays, ensured they went to the best schools and universities, cultivated their friends, developed their confidence.

It's possible that Virginia was compensating for her own fractured childhood, exorcising the memory of her six-year-old self as she lay beneath her dormitory bed, and screamed for home. But to Martha, her former war comrade, Virginia appeared to have become the dullest of matriarchs, and grown unforgivably smug. During the immediate post-war years, the women had remained close; Virginia had asked Martha to be godmother to Andrew, and the two of them had had larky times together when their play, *Love Goes to Press,* had premiered on the London stage, and had then mourned together when it flopped on Broadway. But, although Virginia would have liked to have continued the collaboration with a second play, Martha was poised to migrate from London; and, as their lives diverged, the women themselves drifted out of touch.

Then, in 1956, Virginia and Aidan decided to move house, and, searching for one that was large enough (and affordable enough) to accommodate their children, their guests and their individual working lives, they found a house for sale in Chester Square. Coincidently, it was right next door to Martha and Tom Matthews, and for a while there was a great deal of neighbourly coming and going: the Crawley children played with the two Sandys, and the two women dropped by for chats — Harriet remembers there was always a feeling of excitement when Martha "came through the front door" because she was "always so fun and outrageous."

But the friendship never recovered its old easy tolerance. Martha complained that Virginia bored her, that she was too quick to boast of her children's achievements, too prone to name-drop her grand, famous friends. The fundamental issue on which they split, however, was politics. Back in the war years, when the two women had been comrades, it hadn't mattered that Virginia's views were pitched in the pragmatic middle ground, that Martha staked out the extremes. Now, the gulf between them was glaring, especially to Martha, and seeing Virginia so cosily ensconced with her biographies, her clever children and her Establishment husband, she grew touchily judgemental. Not only did she make no effort to stay in touch once she'd divorced Tom and left London, she disloyally rewrote the truth of their war years together, minimizing their former closeness, and dismissing Virginia's journalism as "high-level gossip."[52]

If Virginia was hurt by Martha's coldness, she had other, more urgent worries. Unlike most of her war peers, she'd never developed a taste for alcohol, but she'd smoked as heavily as the rest of them and, in the late 1960s, was diagnosed with emphysema. The prognosis was uncertain — the condition might kill her within months or she might survive several years — either way, however, Virginia was resolved to make the most of her remaining time. She travelled as much as she could, accompanying Aidan to the Himalayas and the Philippines, and, in 1974, the two of them became semi-nomads, selling their London house and setting up a series of temporary homes in Andalusia, Tuscany and Provence. Finally, it was in a remote village in southwest France that Virginia wrote her last biographies, one about the doomed Romanovs of Russia, the other about the Duke and Duchess of Marlborough. By now she'd outlived her doctor's prognosis by nearly sixteen years, yet her strength was exhausted, and simply to get dressed in the morning cost her an hour-long struggle. In the summer of 1983, when every breath was a labour, the family had to accept the end was close.

At Virginia's request, they took her on one last holiday, to the south of Spain; then, on the drive home, she begged Aidan to make a detour to Sierra de Guadarrama, the hills around Madrid, where she'd served her apprenticeship as a war correspondent. It was thrilling to remember those tumultuous, formative months, but navigating the steep and narrow roads had been tiring for Aidan and, driving back into France, he'd fallen asleep at the wheel. The car somersaulted off the road, and, as Aidan went into shock from a fractured neck, he remained conscious long enough to hear the ambulance men pronounce that his wife's condition was *très grave.* [53]

In fact, she had died almost instantly, and, to her sister, Mary, it seemed that life's final gift to Virginia had been the massive brain haemorrhage that spared her the painful last stages of emphysema. Mary Cowles would be even more thankful five years later, when Virginia did not have to bear the tragic loss of her two sons, both of whom were killed in the same plane crash. In September 1983, when the family gathered in Arcachon for a small agnostic service of mourning, Harriet recalled that there had been tears for Virginia, but also sunshine, laughter and toasts.

Afterwards, Harriet received a "beautiful letter" from Martha, her hostility apparently forgotten as she reminisced about what a "great friend" Ginny had been to her during the war. There were few others left to remember that friendship now, few to remember that Virginia had once been almost as well known for her combat reporting as Martha. But, in 2010, a new edition of *Looking for Trouble* was published, and Virginia's own account of her war years was brought back to the public domain. One of the most detailed and admiring of the memoir's reviews came from Martha's own biographer, Caroline Moorehead, who celebrated the buccaneering reach of Virginia's journalism, the vivid immediacy of her writing, and above all the empathy with which she'd reported on the suffering she'd seen, "the ordinary people whose lives were ruined by war."[54] Moorehead would have been aware that Martha, at her least forgiving, might have begrudged Virginia such praise, but it was a graceful act of literary reconciliation, and an overdue salute to Virginia's war career.

In 1946, when Helen Kirkpatrick was honoured with the Médaille de la Reconnaissance for the insight and humanity of her war coverage, she was acclaimed by *Harper's Bazaar* as "the smartest newswoman in Paris."

This accolade would be matched by several others, yet, in less than three years' time, Helen would be walking away from her reporting career. It was the death of Colonel Knox, back in 1944, which had first made her doubt her future in journalism. Under its new proprietor, the *Chicago Daily News* was becoming a more parochial and a more populist publication. Helen had actually been asked to slant her Nuremberg coverage from a more "Chicago point of view," and, in May 1946, when she accompanied an American diplomatic team to Moscow, she was appalled by the paper's lack of interest in the dispatches she sent back, describing the degeneration of U.S.–Soviet relations. The realization, too, that she was being steadily downgraded in favour of young male colleagues forced her hand, and, towards the end of the year, she handed in her resignation.

"I have been feeling in a coma [ever] since," she wrote miserably to her parents.[55] Given the professional respect she'd earned, she had little trouble getting another job with the *New York Post*. But while the work was challenging, and she spent the next two years reporting on the reconstruction of Western Europe, the birth of Israel and preparations for Indian independence, Helen's heart and mind were not fully engaged. Everywhere she travelled, she saw the same destructive effects of tribalism, ignorance, greed; and, in India, where clashes between Muslim and Hindu factions were creating yet another refugee crisis, she succumbed to the same existential despair she'd suffered over Munich, the fall of Paris, and Buchenwald. It seemed to Helen that she could stand no more wars. Yet, when she was summoned home, to become the *Post*'s Washington correspondent, the political climate in America was no less sickening to her.

By the summer of 1948, Joe McCarthy's witch-hunt against communism was spreading a toxic climate of paranoia and prejudice across the States. Helen despised McCarthy as a violent bigot, a proto-fascist, and she would later discover that she herself had been under investigation. Yet, she was almost as troubled by the response at the *Post*, which was to repudiate McCarthyism with an uncritically pro-Russian line. Several of her articles were being rewritten to conform with the paper's stance, and — reminded all too sharply of how Chamberlain had tried to muzzle the press over Munich — Helen once again handed in her resignation.

She worked freelance for a while, had two or three "really happy" months reporting for Voice of America radio, and lent her name to the campaign to get women admitted into the National Press Association. Then, in September 1949, she was approached by the

Economic Cooperation Agency to become its chief of information in Paris. The ECA had been set up to implement America's Marshall Plan in Europe — to facilitate the economic and cultural regeneration of war-ravaged countries and, in the process, to promote American values and counter Russian influence. Helen's job was to report on the Plan's progress in France, and, if there were occasions when she questioned the underlying political agenda of her work, she was conscious of the respect she'd been afforded as the one female chief in the ECA.

An even more prestigious appointment followed eighteen months later, when Helen was made a Public Affairs Officer in the U.S. State Department at Washington. "I had the best time," she recalled, for the job not only entailed regular diplomatic trips to Western Europe, but a privileged proximity to the State Department itself.[56] Leonard Miall, Washington correspondent for BBC radio, came to regard Helen as his most trusted inside source; when asking for her opinion on the latest U.S. ambassador to be appointed to London, he'd coveted her disdainfully trenchant response — that the man had "a closed mind and an open fly."[57]

So high was Helen's standing in Washington that there was talk of moving her into the diplomatic corps, even appointing her Assistant Secretary of State for Public Affairs.

In the end, however, it was decided that America was not yet ready to accept a woman in so senior a post, and, in retrospect, Helen believed that, even if Congress had ratified her appointment, "it would have been a thankless job."[58] She would have had to work directly with the Secretary of State, and the post's current incumbent, John Foster Dulles, she regarded as a dangerous fanatic. His hatred of communism was no less crude than McCarthy's and, when dealing with any suspect or recalcitrant foreign state, his policy was simply to threaten force if they failed to toe the American line.

"The Dulles line of brinkmanship was abhorrent to me," Helen wrote, the early 1950s were "a fearsome time," and when an offer from Smith College "came out of the blue," she was more than happy to leave Washington behind. Her new job was secretary to the college president, and it ranged from domestic issues, like the hiring of a new cook, to the challenging task of protecting five members of staff who'd been fingered in the McCarthy trials. It was, Helen recalled, "a lot of fun," but, far more important, it introduced her to her second husband.[59]

Robbins Milbank was a trustee of Smith, a widower with two nearly grown-up children, with family money and a history of voting Republican. His life could not have been more different from Helen's; yet he was a man of simple, steadfast goodness, a wonderful companion, and, when he proposed marriage in June 1954, she joyfully accepted: "there aren't enough words to describe him," she wrote to a friend, "except to say that I'm the luckiest woman in the world. Everyone loves him, especially me."[60]

Helen might perhaps have flinched at the wedding notice which appeared in the *Washington Star,* its description of her as "an attractive and brainy blonde who's been a foreign correspondent" casually relegating her professional life to the past tense.[61] Six years earlier, when she'd visited Hemingway and Mary Welsh in Idaho, she had noted with wry disappointment that Mary, a "very bright girl and able writer," was doing little now but "running the house and looking after Ernest. He is the boss, first, last and always. Hence her success as a wife."[62] Helen herself had no intention of becoming such a wife. She worked for another year at Smith, conscientiously training up her successor, and, when she and Robbins set up house together in San Francisco (the two of them returning each summer to New Hampshire), she launched herself into public life, sitting on the World Affairs Council in San Francisco, the President's Commission on Trade, a number of school and museum boards and the California Coordinating Commission on Higher Education.

Even now, there were moments when she hankered for the life of travel and deadlines, when she read the latest headlines and thought, "Boy, if only I could get to Prague or Warsaw or the Soviet Union." There were the moments, too, when she felt bewildered by the domestic hinterland of marriage, the relentlessness of wondering "whether the laundry has come back, and what about the groceries." Yet, these were fleeting regrets; Helen knew she'd burned herself out as a journalist and she was genuinely excited to be discovering a new way of life: "I was delighted to get into all these other things that I'd never been able to do — I'd never had time to do."[63]

One of those things was getting to know her stepchildren and grandchildren. Although Helen had liked the idea of becoming a mother, although she had been a doting aunt to her brother Kirk's children, the moment had never come for her. To have "acquired a family ready-made" was another of the blessings Robbins had brought to her, and their life together passed busily and contentedly.[64] The two of them travelled widely, across Europe and the Far East; they became early adopters of the environmental movement and, when they moved full time to New Hampshire, Helen became "mildly involved in state politics." After Robbins died, in 1985, she moved to Williamsburg, in Virginia, from where her family had originated, and it was now that her own past began to resurface, as war historians and researchers interested in women's journalism came knocking at her door. In 1990, the Washington Press Society sent an interviewer to tape an exhaustive account of her life and career, and Smith College established the Helen Paull Kirkpatrick Collection, archiving many of her papers, photographs and clippings. Five years later, she was the only woman on a panel of six journalists, sharing their war recollections for a C-Span broadcast.[65] And at eighty-four, she was still formidable, funny and astute — when asked to comment about her success, as a woman, in becoming one of the most distinguished correspondents in the field, she responded, "Well, you'd have to ask the field about that." Mentally and physically alert to the end, Helen's death, on 29 December 1997, came with benign abruptness, apparently just hours after she'd returned from the hairdresser's.

In the years following Helen's death, her place in history, like that of her peers, has become more and more widely acknowledged. Janine di Giovanni, whose own recent career has taken her to conflicts in the Balkans, Africa and the Middle East, has commented that the generation of women who covered the Second World War now stand like "guardian angels" over today's female correspondents. Not only did they deal admirably with "the fear and loneliness that are an inevitable part of the job," writes di Giovanni, but they set an absolute standard of courage, commitment and craft. "War correspondent is not an ordinary profession," she claims, "and yet I was fortunate enough to be exposed to older women who shone a light on the path ahead of me, and made me understand what it means to be chosen for this role."[66]

That path, however, had never become a straight highway to progress. The relaxing of military protocol, for which women had battled so hard between 1939 and 1945, turned out to be a temporary concession, and, in 1950, when Marguerite Higgins tried to report from Korea, she came across the same breed of obstructive officers, and the same bigoted arguments about toilet facilities, safety and sexual unrest, which she thought she had left behind. It was during the war in Vietnam that the U.S. army were forced to take a more enlightened position, and that position was largely forced on them, because so many female correspondents had begun flying out to Saigon on civilian planes that their numbers became difficult to control. At the height of the war, there were seventy women among the official press corps. And, for Edith Lederer — a novice reporter for Associated Press who would go on to cover wars in Egypt, Afghanistan, the Falklands and the Gulf — Vietnam would prove no less formative an experience than Spain had been for Martha and Virginia.

A second milestone on the path to equal rights was the acceptance of women into most of the world's armed forces. Once female soldiers were serving alongside men, it was harder to argue a case for excluding female correspondents on the grounds of decency; and harder still to patronize them as the weaker sex. Half a century later, however, certain combat conditions have remained peculiarly inimical to women. It is never easy, writes the British reporter Kate Adie, to "crouch down . . . in the open desert . . . and pee in front of 2,000 blokes."[67] The changing nature of warfare has also created new and localized difficulties. Rapid advances in drone technology and long-range missiles have made a number of war zones dangerously volatile, and, for women, the risks of rape and harassment have become correspondingly greater. In the conflict-ridden Middle East, where public life is heavily segregated, it has also become radically harder for female correspondents to do their job — simply because they are unable to move around, cultivate sources and interview officials with the same freedom as men.

The fact that those women who report on

wars, revolutions and catastrophes are still roughly outnumbered by men three to one is also a measure of the skewed attitudes that have lingered, both in the media and the wider public. In 1980, when Kate Adie was covering the Iranian embassy siege in London, viewers were startled, even offended, to see a female reporter on their screens, crouched behind a car door, bullets flying over her head. They were just as resistant to the idea of a woman reporting from a crisis as the more conservative readers of the *Chicago Daily News* had been, four decades earlier, when they complained about Helen Kirkpatrick being assigned to the war news.

However, even if women still remain a minority on foreign news desks, even if their qualifications are weighted differently from men, a significant number have risen to the top of their profession. Adie became a household name with her coverage of the Tiananmen Square massacre, kneeing a Chinese policeman in the groin and running through bullets to ensure the safe delivery of her report. Marie Colvin, who repeatedly risked her life to report on the besieged city of Homs, and who died from a Syrian rocket attack, achieved post-humous celebrity when her life and career were made the subject of a Hollywood film.

Orla Guerin, Lindsey Hilsum, Lyse Doucet and Christiane Amanpour are among the many other women now currently feted for their war coverage; and Amanpour, a stellar reporter for CNN, believes it no longer makes sense for them to be viewed as a case apart. That women should no longer put up with discrimination is a given, but, by the same token, Amanpour suggests they should no longer be accorded privileged sympathy on the basis of their sex. "Women can do exactly what men can do," she argues. "Journalism is about rigorous adherence to the truth. That's what you're going out to report . . . Women have more than made their mark in this profession and there should be no more divisions of attention, labour, or rewards."[68]

Perhaps Amanpour's statement remains one of hope, more than fact. But, in calling for an end to the narrative of female exceptionalism, she is simply echoing the hopes and beliefs of the women in this book, who, when they went with the boys to the front lines of the mid-twentieth century, aspired to be treated as reporters first, and women second.

Certainly, their motivations for going to war were little different from those of their male peers. When Sigrid Schultz faced off the Gestapo in Berlin, when Lee Miller brazened out her private war in Saint-Malo, when Clare Hollingworth reported on the invasion of Poland, or Virginia Cowles risked prison in Spain, they were all driven by a basic hunger for action — a desire to be living their lives on a razor edge, or, as Martha Gellhorn put it, to be "getting something out of history that is more than anyone has a decent right to hope for."[69]

Like the best of their colleagues, they also went to war with a sense of vocation — with a commitment to the truth, and a pledge to speak out for the "silent millions." High on thrills and adrenalin, yet dedicated to making themselves the eyes, ears and hearts of their readers, these women didn't strive to be the best female journalists, but simply to be among the best in their profession.

And yet. Despite their reluctance to be treated as a special case, the achievements of these six female correspondents should not be separated from their experiences as women. The history of the Second World War, like that of all wars, has traditionally been told by, for, and about men; and the story of how this small group of journalists found their way to the battle zones of Europe and North Africa stands as an important corrective. In the reports they filed, in the memoirs, diaries and letters they kept, Sigrid, Martha, Virginia, Clare, Helen and Lee were not only writing history, at the moment it was being made; they were also writing a version of history that was theirs, a version that was shaped by the realities of being a woman, and was inflected by a female voice.

NOTES

Introduction

1. Cowles, Virginia, *Looking for Trouble* (London: Faber and Faber, 2010 [first published 1941]), p. 266.
2. Ibid, p. 270.
3. Ibid, p. 267.
4. Shirer, William, *Berlin Diary: The Journal of a Foreign Correspondent, 1934–1941* (e-book version, New York: Rosetta Books LCC, 2011 [first published 1941]), pp. 193–4.
5. Helen Kirkpatrick, interview with Anne Kasper for the Washington Press Club Foundation, 3.4.1990. Session 1, p. 47. Online at beta.wpcf.org.
6. Thompson, Dorothy, *Ladies' Home Journal,* March 1944.
7. Moorehead, Caroline, *Gellhorn: A Twentieth-Century Life* (New York: Henry Holt and Company, 2003), p. 243.

693

Chapter One

1. Sigrid Schultz, in a letter to George Scharschug, 1 October 1930. The State Historical Society of Wisconsin, Madison.
2. Cited in Chapman, Cynthia, "Psychobiographical Study of the Life of Sigrid Schultz," unpublished thesis, p. 184.
3. Ziemer, Gregor, "Let us Sing the Praises of Sigrid Schultz," *Lost Generation Journal,* vol. IV, 1976, p. 4.
4. Schultz, Sigrid, unpublished memoirs, 1959, p. 15, cited in Chapman, p. 59.
5. Sigrid Schultz, interviewed by Harold Hutchings for the *Chicago Tribune,* 1977, tape no. 3, p. 10. SHSW.
6. Ibid.
7. Ibid, tape no. 4, p. 1.
8. Ibid.
9. Ibid, tape no. 4, p. 3.
10. Ibid, tape no. 4, pp. 3 and 4.
11. Ibid, tape no. 1, p. 1.
12. Sigrid Schultz, interviewed by Alan Green for the *Oral history of anti-Semitism* for the American Jewish Committee, New York, 1971. SHSW, cited Chapman, p. 88.
13. Schultz, Sigrid, *Germany Will Try It Again* (New York: Reynal and Hitchcock, 1944), p. 54.
14. From a letter written in 1932, cited in Chapman, p. 71.
15. *Chicago Tribune* interview with Sigrid

Schultz, 1977, tape no. 4, p 1.

16. Quoted in Edwards, Julia, *Women of the World: The Great Foreign Correspondents* (Boston: Houghton Mifflin Company, 1988), p. 61.

17. Chapman, p. 58.

18. *Chicago Tribune* interview with S. Schultz, 1977, tape no. 1, p. 1.

19. Ziemer, p. 3.

20. Chapman, p. 98.

21. Garvey, Kerry J., "The Byline of Europe: An Examination of Foreign Correspondents' Reporting from 1930 to 1941," unpublished thesis, p. 97 [etheses.lse.ac.uk].

22. Ibid, p. 7.

23. Edwards, pp. 63–4.

24. Ibid, pp. 37 and 67.

25. *Chicago Tribune,* 15 September 1930.

26. Sigrid Schultz, in a letter to McCormick, 29 October 1930. SHSW.

27. Edwards, p. 64.

28. *Chicago Tribune* interview with S. Schultz, 1977, tape no. 1, p. 14.

29. Chapman, p. 96.

30. Undated letter from Sigrid Schultz to Scharschug. SHSW.

31. Sigrid Schultz, in a letter to McCormick, 23 November 1932. SHSW.

32. *Chicago Tribune,* 8 April 1933.

33. Edwards, p. 65.

34. Sigrid Schultz, in a letter to McCormick, 1 December 1933. SHSW.

35. Ibid.
36. Unsigned report by Sigrid Schultz on the harassment of the foreign press: First Division Museum, *Chicago Tribune* archive, I-62 Foreign Correspondents 1914–55, box 8, folder 6.
37. *Chicago Tribune* interview with S. Schultz, 1977, tape no. 2, p. 4.
38. Sigrid Schultz, in a letter to George Scharschug, 13 August 1934. SHSW.
39. Shirer, William, *Berlin Diary: The Journal of a Foreign Correspondent, 1934–1941* (e-book version, New York: Rosetta Books LCC, 2011 [first published 1941]) p. 329.
40. Chapman, p. 197.
41. Ibid, p. 273.
42. *Chicago Tribune* interview with S. Schultz, 1977, tape no. 4, p. 11.
43. Edwards, p. 66.
44. Ibid.
45. Shirer, p. 55.
46. Sigrid Schultz, in a letter to George Scharschug, 1 October 1930. SHSW.
47. S. Schultz diary, the State Historical Society of Wisconsin.
48. Shirer, p. 70.
49. Ibid, p. 38.

Chapter Two

1. Moorehead, Caroline, *Gellhorn: A Twentieth-Century Life* (New York: Henry

Holt and Company, 2003), pp. 128–9.

2. Ibid, p. 111.
3. Ibid, p. 101.
4. Ibid, p. 105.
5. Vaill, Amanda, *Hotel Florida: Truth, Love and Death in the Spanish Civil War* (London: Bloomsbury, 2015), p. 103.
6. Martha Gellhorn, in a letter to Eleanor Roosevelt, 13 January 1937, cited in Moorehead, *Gellhorn,* p. 105.
7. Gellhorn, Martha, "The War in Spain," *The Face of War* (London: Granta Books, 1993), p. 13.
8. Martha Gellhorn, in a letter to Betty Barnes, 30 January 1937, reprinted in Moorehead, Caroline (ed.), *Selected Letters of Martha Gellhorn* (New York: Henry Holt and Company, 2006), pp. 46–7.
9. Moorehead, *Gellhorn,* p. 29.
10. Ibid.
11. Ibid, p. 33.
12. Ibid, p. 37.
13. Ibid, p. 38.
14. Ibid, p. 42.
15. Ibid, p. 52.
16. Ibid, p. 60.
17. Ibid, p. 70.
18. Gellhorn, Martha, "The War in Spain," *The Face of War* (London: Granta Books, 1993), p. 11.
19. Moorehead, *Gellhorn,* p. 70.

20. Ibid.
21. Martha Gellhorn, in a letter to Allen Grover, 6 August 1950, cited in Moorehead, *Gellhorn,* p. 100.
22. Moorehead, ibid, p. 71.
23. Sebba, Anne, *Battling for News: The Rise of the Woman Reporter* (London: Hodder and Stoughton, 1994), p. 87.
24. Moorehead, *Gellhorn,* p. 80.
25. *Spectator* review, cited in Sebba, p. 87.
26. Martha Gellhorn, in a letter to Eleanor Roosevelt, 11 November 1936, cited in Edy, Carolyn M., *The Woman War Correspondent, the U.S. Military, and the Press 1846–1947* (Lanham, Maryland: Lexington Books, 2016), p. 90.
27. Moorehead, *Gellhorn,* p. 89.
28. Ibid, p. 90.
29. Gellhorn, Martha, "The War in Spain," *The Face of War* (London: Granta Books, 1993), p. 12.
30. Ibid.
31. Ibid.
32. Moorehead, *Gellhorn,* p. 113.
33. Ibid, p. 114.
34. Vaill, p. 150.
35. Gellhorn, Martha, "The War in Spain," *The Face of War,* (London: Granta Books, 1993), p. 13.
36. Gellhorn, Martha, "High Explosive for Everyone" and "The Besieged City," *The*

Face of War (London: Granta Books, 1993), pp. 15–31.
37. Ibid, p. 18.
38. Sebba, p. 89.
39. Moorehead, *Gellhorn,* p. 154.
40. Vaill, p. 155.
41. Moorehead, *Gellhorn,* p. 123.
42. Ibid, p. 121.
43. Ibid, p. 120.
44. Ibid, p. 125.
45. Ibid, p. 99.
46. Vaill, p. 161.
47. Moorehead, *Gellhorn,* p. 114.
48. Ibid, p. 127.
49. Ibid, p. 118.
50. Vaill, p. 152.
51. Ibid.
52. Moorehead, *Gellhorn,* pp. 119–20.
53. Cowles, Virginia, *Looking for Trouble* (London: Faber and Faber, 2010 [first published 1941]), p. 61.

Chapter Three

1. Sebba, Anne, *Battling for News: The Rise of the Woman Reporter* (London: Hodder and Stoughton, 1994), p. 97.
2. Cowles, Virginia, *Looking for Trouble* (London: Faber and Faber, 2010 [first published 1941]), p. 253.
3. Ibid, pp. 252–3.
4. Ibid, p. 254.

5. Ibid, p. 258.

6. Ibid, p. 253.

7. Ibid, p. 254.

8. Hearst, "March of Events" supplement, 17 November 1935.

9. Cowles, p. 13.

10. Ibid, p. 16.

11. Ibid, p. 19.

12. Ibid, p. 20.

13. Cowles, unpublished war diary, Virginia Cowles Papers, Imperial War Museum.

14. *New York American,* 27 June 1937.

15. Sebba, p. 97.

16. Reported by Vincent Sheean in an article titled "Covering Hell's Corner," October 1940 (publication title missing), Helen Paull Kirkpatrick Papers, box 8, Sophia Smith Collection, SSC-MS-00103, Smith College Special Collections, Northampton, Massachusetts.

17. Cowles, pp. 27–8.

18. Ibid, p. 34.

19. Ibid, p. 47.

20. Ibid, p. 49.

21. Ibid, p. 50.

22. Ibid, p. 53.

23. Ibid, p. 54.

24. Ibid.

25. Ibid, p. 61.

26. Ibid, p. 68.

27. Ibid, p. 71.

28. Ibid, p. 75.

29. Ibid, pp. 96–7.
30. Ibid, p. 98.
31. Ibid, pp. 98–9.
32. Moorehead, Caroline, *Gellhorn: A Twentieth-Century Life* (New York: Henry Holt and Company, 2003), pp. 128–9.
33. Ibid, p. 139.
34. Ibid, p. 134.
35. Vaill, Amanda, *Hotel Florida: Truth, Love and Death in the Spanish Civil War* (London: Bloomsbury, 2015), p. 258.
36. Moorehead, *Gellhorn,* p. 136.
37. Vaill, p. 256.
38. Ibid, p. 297.
39. Moorehead, *Gellhorn,* p. 145.
40. Ibid, p. 146.

Chapter Four

1. Helen Kirkpatrick, interview with Anne Kasper for the Washington Press Club Foundation, 3.4.1990. Session 1, p. 4. Online at beta.wpcf.org.
2. Gellhorn, Martha, foreword, *The Face of War* (London: Granta Books, 1993), p. 11.
3. Hollingworth, Clare, *Front Line* (London: Jonathan Cape, 1990), p. 3.
4. Garrett, Patrick, *Of Fortunes and War: Clare Hollingworth, First of the Female War Correspondents* (London: Two Roads Books, 2017), p. 10.

5. Hollingworth, p. 4.

6. Garrett, p. 14.

7. Hollingworth, p. 4.

8. Garrett, p. 16.

9. Hollingworth, pp. 6–7.

10. Garrett, p. 33.

11. Helen Kirkpatrick interview, Session 1, p. 42.

12. *New York Herald,* 18 November 1936.

13. Helen Kirkpatrick interview, Session 1, p. 4.

14. Ibid, Session 1, p. 1.

15. Helen Kirkpatrick oral history, Helen Paull Kirkpatrick Papers, box 1, Smith College.

16. Helen Kirkpatrick unpublished writings, 3 December 1931, Helen Paull Kirkpatrick Papers, box 1, Smith College.

17. Helen Kirkpatrick oral history, Helen Paull Kirkpatrick Papers, box 1, Smith College.

18. Helen Kirkpatrick, in a letter to Lyde Kirkpatrick, 10 September 1931, Helen Paull Kirkpatrick Papers, box 1, Smith College.

19. Helen Kirkpatrick, in a letter to Lyde Kirkpatrick, 10 December 1931, ibid.

20. Unpublished papers, Helen Paull Kirkpatrick Papers, box 1, ibid.

21. Ibid.

22. Helen Kirkpatrick interview, Session 1, p. 12.

23. Ibid, p. 13.
24. Ibid, pp. 13–14.
25. Ibid, p. 15.
26. Undated letter, Helen Paull Kirkpatrick Papers, box 1, Smith College.
27. Helen Kirkpatrick, in letters to Lyde Kirkpatrick, 3 September 1935 and 29 September 1935, Helen Paull Kirkpatrick Papers, box 1, Smith College.
28. Helen Kirkpatrick, in a letter to her parents, 9 November 1935, Helen Paull Kirkpatrick Papers, box 1, Smith College.
29. Helen Kirkpatrick interview, Session 1, p. 12.
30. Ibid, Session 1, p. 41.
31. Abrams, Irwin, "The Multinational Campaign for Carl Von Ossietzky," paper presented at International Conference on Peace Movements in National Societies 1919–39, held in Stadtschlaining, Austria, September 1991, and published on Irwin Abrams' website.
32. Helen Kirkpatrick interview, Session 1, p. 41.
33. Helen Kirkpatrick, *New York Herald Tribune,* 27 October 1936.
34. Helen Kirkpatrick interview, Session 1, p. 25.
35. Helen Kirkpatrick, in a letter to her family, 3 October 1933, Helen Paull Kirkpatrick Papers, box 1, Smith College.

Chapter Five

1. Gellhorn, Martha, "Come Ahead, Adolf!," *Collier's* magazine, 6 August 1938, cited in Moorehead, Caroline, *Gellhorn: A Twentieth-Century Life* (New York: Henry Holt and Company, 2003), p. 148.
2. Cowles, Virginia, *Looking for Trouble* (London: Faber and Faber, 2010 [first published 1941]), p. 113.
3. Ibid.
4. Ibid, p. 103.
5. Ibid, p. 104.
6. Ibid, p. 111.
7. Kirkpatrick, Helen, unpublished BBC radio script, Helen Paull Kirkpatrick Papers, box 8, Smith College.
8. Cowles, pp. 114–15.
9. Ibid, p. 117.
10. Ibid.
11. Ibid, p. 121.
12. Ibid, p. 124.
13. Moorehead, Caroline, *Gellhorn: A Twentieth-Century Life* (New York: Henry Holt and Company, 2003), p. 148.
14. Gellhorn, "Come Ahead, Adolf!," cited in Moorehead, *Gellhorn,* p. 148.
15. Ibid.
16. Cowles, p. 132.
17. Ibid, p. 133.
18. Undated article, *Sunday Times,* Virginia

Cowles scrapbook, Imperial War Museum.

19. Moorehead, *Gellhorn,* p. 149.

20. Cowles, p. 144.

21. Shirer, William, *Berlin Diary: The Journal of a Foreign Correspondent, 1934–1941* (e-book version, New York: Rosetta Books LCC, 2011 [originally published 1941]), p. 126.

22. Cowles, p. 147.

23. Ibid, pp. 157–9.

24. Ibid, p. 153.

25. Ibid, p. 173.

26. Ibid, pp. 175–6.

27. Ibid, p. 178.

28. Ibid, p. 185.

29. Moorehead, *Gellhorn,* p. 150.

Chapter Six

1. Cowles, Virginia, *Looking for Trouble* (London: Faber and Faber, 2010 [first published 1941]), p. 188.

2. Helen Kirkpatrick, in an undated letter to Mary Chase, Helen Paull Kirkpatrick Papers, box 1, Smith College.

3. Kirkpatrick, Helen, *Under the British Umbrella: What the English Are and How They Go to War* (New York: Scribner's Sons, 1939), p. 83.

4. Personal letters, Helen Paull Kirkpatrick Papers, box 1, Smith College.

5. Shirer, William, *Berlin Diary: The Journal of*

a Foreign Correspondent, 1934–1941 (e-book version, New York: Rosetta Books LCC, 2011 [originally published 1941]), p. 147.

6. Cowles, p. 188.

7. Ibid, pp. 188–9.

8. Ibid, pp. 190–2.

9. Moorehead, Caroline, *Gellhorn: A Twentieth-Century Life* (New York: Henry Holt and Company, 2003), p. 151.

10. Sebba, Anne, *Battling for News: The Rise of the Woman Reporter* (London: Hodder and Stoughton, 1994), p. 115.

11. Moorehead, *Gellhorn,* p. 152.

12. Vaill, Amanda, *Hotel Florida: Truth, Love and Death in the Spanish Civil War* (London: Bloomsbury, 2015), p. 331.

13. *Daily Telegraph,* 11 November 1938.

14. Moorehead, *Gellhorn,* p. 160.

15. Ibid, p. 158.

16. Schultz, Sigrid, syndicated in the *Richmond Item,* 16 September 1938.

17. Chapman, Cynthia, "Psychobiographical Study of the Life of Sigrid Schultz," unpublished thesis, p. 280.

18. *Chicago Tribune,* 11 November 1938.

19. Edwards, Julia, *Women of the World: The Great Foreign Correspondents* (Boston: Houghton Mifflin Company, 1988), p. 68.

20. Chapman, pp. 73–4.

21. Ibid, p. 293.

22. Cowles, p. 195.
23. Ibid, p. 204.
24. Sebba, p. 119.
25. Cowles, p. 212.
26. Ibid, p. 207.
27. Sebba, p. 119.
28. Crawley, Harriet, *Profile of Virginia Cowles,* p. 9, Virginia Cowles Papers, Imperial War Museum.
29. Cowles, p. 242.
30. Garrett, Patrick, *Of Fortunes and War: Clare Hollingworth, First of the Female War Correspondents* (London: Two Roads Books, 2017), p. 45.
31. Ibid, p. 36.
32. Shirer, p. 182.
33. Ibid, pp. 182 and 186.
34. Cowles, pp. 269–70.
35. Ibid, p. 267.
36. Ibid, p. 272.

Chapter Seven

1. Hollingworth, Clare, *Front Line* (London: Jonathan Cape, 1990), p. 22.
2. Garrett, Patrick, *Of Fortunes and War: Clare Hollingworth, First of the Female War Correspondents* (London: Two Roads Books, 2017), p. 59.
3. Ibid, p. 60.
4. Hollingworth, p. 13.
5. Garrett, p. 64.

6. Hollingworth, p. 15.
7. Garrett, p. 67.
8. Ibid, p. 69.
9. Ibid, p. 72.
10. Hollingworth, p. 20.
11. Ibid, p. 22.
12. Ibid, p. 28.
13. Ibid, p. 31.
14. Garrett, p. 81.
15. Hollingworth, p. 33.
16. Ibid, p. 34.
17. Ibid.
18. Garrett, p. 83.
19. Ibid, p. 116.
20. Hollingworth, p. 43.
21. Cowles, Virginia, *Looking for Trouble* (London: Faber and Faber, 2010 [first published 1941]), p. 276.
22. Ibid, p. 275.
23. Ibid, p. 281.
24. Crawley, Aidan, *Leap Before You Look* (London: Collins, 1988), p. 206.
25. Ibid, p. 406.
26. Kirkpatrick, Helen, *Under the British Umbrella: What the English Are and How They Go to War* (New York: Scribner's Sons, 1939), p. 303.
27. Helen Kirkpatrick oral history, Helen Paull Kirkpatrick Papers, box 1, Smith College.
28. Helen Kirkpatrick, in an undated letter to her family, Helen Paull Kirkpatrick

Papers, box 1, Smith College.

29. Helen Kirkpatrick, interview with Anne Kasper for the Washington Press Club Foundation, 3.4.1990. Session 1, p. 23. Online at beta.wpcf.org.

30. *Chicago Daily News,* 18 September 1939.

31. Helen Kirkpatrick interview, Session 1, p. 35.

32. *Sunday Times,* Virginia Cowles scrapbook, Imperial War Museum.

33. Cowles, p. 297.

34. Ibid, p. 297.

35. Ibid, pp. 300–1.

36. Ibid, p. 301.

37. Ibid, p. 304.

38. Ibid, pp. 304–5.

39. Ibid, p. 343.

40. Moorehead, Caroline, *Gellhorn: A Twentieth-Century Life* (New York: Henry Holt and Company, 2003), p. 159.

41. Gellhorn, Martha, *The Face of War* (London: Granta Books, 1993), p. 48.

42. Ibid.

43. Moorehead, *Gellhorn,* p. 163.

44. Cowles, p. 332.

45. Moorehead, *Gellhorn,* p. 165.

46. Ibid, p. 169.

47. Helen Kirkpatrick interview, Session 1, p. 40.

48. Ibid.

49. *Chicago Daily News,* 17 April 1940.

50. Helen Kirkpatrick, in a letter to her

parents, 3 May 1940, Helen Paull Kirkpatrick Papers, box 1, Smith College.

51. Helen Kirkpatrick interview, Session 1, p. 35.

52. Helen Kirkpatrick, in a letter to her parents, 3 May 1940, Helen Paull Kirkpatrick Papers, box 1, Smith College.

53. Cowles, p. 360.

Chapter Eight

1. Cowles, Virginia, *Looking for Trouble* (London: Faber and Faber, 2010 [first published 1941]), p. 386.

2. Ibid, p. 333.

3. Ibid, p. 368.

4. Ibid, p. 373.

5. BBC News, 30 May 1940.

6. *B.Z. am Mittag,* 1 June 1940.

7. Shirer, William, *Berlin Diary: The Journal of a Foreign Correspondent, 1934–1941* (e-book version, New York: Rosetta Books LCC, 2011 [originally published 1941]), p. 342.

8. Sigrid Schultz, in a letter to McCormick, 25 October 1939. The State Historical Society of Wisconsin, Madison.

9. *Chicago Tribune,* 9 April 1940.

10. Sigrid Schultz, in a letter to McCormick, 10 February 1940. SHSW.

11. Chapman, Cynthia, "Psychobiographical Study of the Life of Sigrid Schultz," unpub-

lished thesis, p. 462.

12. *Chicago Tribune* interview with S. Schultz, 1977, tape no. 2, p. 6.

13. *Völkischer Beobachter,* 14 June 1940.

14. Cowles, p. 379.

15. Ibid, pp. 380–1.

16. Ibid, p. 383.

17. Ibid, p. 386.

18. Ibid, p. 388.

19. Ibid, p. 390.

20. Ibid, p. 391.

21. Ibid, p. 396.

22. Ibid, p. 400.

23. Ibid, p. 408.

24. Ibid, p. 412.

25. Helen Kirkpatrick, in a letter to Amy Lois, June 1940, Helen Paull Kirkpatrick Papers, box 10, Smith College.

26. Garrett, Patrick, *Of Fortunes and War: Clare Hollingworth, First of the Female War Correspondents* (London: Two Roads Books, 2017), p. 93.

27. Hollingworth, Clare, *Front Line* (London: Jonathan Cape, 1990), p. 47.

28. Clare Hollingworth, oral history recorded for the Imperial War Museum. Online at iwm.org.uk.

29. Hollingworth, *Front Line,* p. 61.

30. Garrett, p. 119.

31. Garrett, p. 122.

32. Clare Hollingworth, oral history recorded for the Imperial War Museum. Online at

iwm.org.uk.

33. *Chicago Daily News,* 18 August 1940.
34. Reported by Vincent Sheean in "Covering Hell's Corner," October 1940, clipping held in Helen Paull Kirkpatrick Papers, box 8, Smith College.
35. Cowles, p. 426.
36. Ibid.
37. *Sunday Times,* 25 August 1940.
38. *Chicago Daily News,* 14 August 1940.
39. *Sunday Times,* 2 September 1940.
40. Chapman, p. 285.
41. Cowles, p. 435.

Chapter Nine

1. Carter, Ernestine (ed.), *Grim Glory: Pictures of Britain Under Fire* (London: Lund Humphries/Scribners, 1941)
2. *Chicago Daily News,* 9 September 1940.
3. *Chicago Daily News,* 26 October 1940.
4. Helen Kirkpatrick, interview with Anne Kasper for the Washington Press Club Foundation, 3.4.1990. Session 2, p. 58. Online at beta.wpcf.org.
5. *PM,* 11 December 1940.
6. "War and a Woman," undated clipping from *Chicago Daily News,* Helen Paull Kirkpatrick Papers, box 2, Smith College.
7. *Chicago Daily News,* 30 November 1940.
8. Sigrid Schultz, in a letter to McCormick, 8 October 1940. The State Historical

Society of Wisconsin, Madison.

9. Cowles, Virginia, *Looking for Trouble* (London: Faber and Faber, 2010 [first published 1941]), p. 440.
10. Ibid, p. 439.
11. Ibid, p. 459.
12. Ibid, p. 463.
13. Burke, Carolyn, *Lee Miller: On Both Sides of the Camera* (London: Bloomsbury, 2006), p. 274.
14. Ibid, p. 62.
15. Ibid, p. 15.
16. Ibid, p. 22.
17. Ibid, p. 43.
18. Ibid, p. 40.
19. Ibid, p. 50.
20. Ibid, pp. 21–2.
21. Ibid, p. 50.
22. Ibid, p. 56.
23. Ibid, p. 65.
24. Ibid, p. 74.
25. Ibid, p. 83.
26. Ibid, p. 79.
27. Undated letter, Lee Miller Archive, cited in Burke, p. 89.
28. Burke, p. 129.
29. Ibid, p. 146.
30. Ibid, p. 164.
31. Ibid, p. 177.
32. Lee Miller, in a letter to Aziz Eloui Bey, 17 November 1938, cited in Burke, p. 190.
33. Ibid.

34. Burke, p. 206.

35. Penrose, Antony, *The Lives of Lee Miller* (London: Thames and Hudson, 1988), p. 99.

36. Burke, p. 206.

Chapter Ten

1. Garrett, Patrick, *Of Fortunes and War: Clare Hollingworth, First of the Female War Correspondents* (London: Two Roads Books, 2017), p. 186.

2. Ibid, p. 111.

3. Ibid, p. 129.

4. Ibid, p. 134.

5. Hollingworth, Clare, *Front Line* (London: Jonathan Cape, 1990), p. 97.

6. Ibid, p. 98.

7. Garrett, pp. 130–1.

8. Hollingworth, pp. 78–9.

9. Garrett, p. 145.

10. Ibid, pp. 147–9.

11. Ibid, p. 151.

12. Ibid, p. 147.

13. Hollingworth, p. 120.

14. Garrett, p. 162.

15. Hollingworth, p. 130.

16. Sebba, Anne, *Battling for News: The Rise of the Woman Reporter* (London: Hodder and Stoughton, 1994), pp. 152–4.

17. Penrose, Antony, *The Lives of Lee Miller*

(London: Thames and Hudson, 1988), p. 20.

18. Hollingworth, p. 130.
19. Garrett, p. 174.
20. Ibid, p. 131.
21. Bourke-White, Margaret, *Portrait of Myself* (New York: Simon and Schuster, 1963), p. 118.
22. *Chicago Daily News,* 10 October 1941.
23. Hollingworth, p. 138.
24. Garrett, p. 177.
25. Hollingworth, p. 139.
26. Garrett, p. 179.
27. Hollingworth, p. 122.
28. Ibid, p. 135.
29. Ibid, p. 139.
30. Garrett, p. 170.
31. Ibid, p. 186.

Chapter Eleven

1. Burke, Carolyn, *Lee Miller: On Both Sides of the Camera* (London: Bloomsbury, 2006), p. 212.
2. *Chicago Daily News,* 27 June 1942.
3. Caldwell Sorel, Nancy, *The Women Who Wrote the War* (New York: Perennial, 2000), p. 192.
4. Shirer, William, *Berlin Diary: The Journal of a Foreign Correspondent, 1934–1941* (e-book version, New York: Rosetta Books

LCC, 2011 [originally published 1941]), p. 505.

5. Sebba, Anne, *Battling for News: The Rise of the Woman Reporter* (London: Hodder and Stoughton, 1994), p. 154.

6. Ibid, p. 155.

7. Ibid.

8. Nigel Nicolson, in a letter to Aidan Crawley, 26 November 1987, cited in Sebba, p. 153.

9. Penrose, Antony (ed.), *Lee Miller's War: Beyond D-Day* (London: Thames and Hudson, 2005), p. 1.

10. Burke, p. 212.

11. Ibid, p. 222.

12. Ibid, p. 213.

13. Penrose, Antony, *The Lives of Lee Miller* (London: Thames and Hudson, 1988), p. 116.

14. Moorehead, Caroline, *Gellhorn: A Twentieth-Century Life* (New York: Henry Holt and Company, 2003), p. 173.

15. Hardy Dorman, Angelia, *Martha Gellhorn: Myth, Motif, and Remembrance* (Charleston, South Carolina: JettDrive Publications, 2015), p. 154; Moorehead, p. 193.

16. Moorehead, *Gellhorn,* pp. 172 and 180.

17. Ibid, p. 177.

18. Ibid.

19. Ibid, p. 178.

20. Hardy Dorman, p. 121.

21. Caldwell Sorel, p. 144.
22. Moorehead, *Gellhorn,* p. 179.
23. Ibid, pp. 181, 183 and 187.
24. Ibid, p. 187.
25. Ibid, p. 202.
26. Ibid, p. 204.
27. Ibid, p. 207.
28. Ibid, pp. 207–8.
29. Gellhorn, Martha, "The Bomber Boys," *The Face of War* (London: Granta Books, 1993), p. 89.
30. Moorehead, pp. 199 and 207.
31. Ibid, p. 208.
32. Ibid, p. 210.
33. Ibid, p. 211.
34. Gellhorn, introduction to *Love Goes to Press* (Lincoln and London: University of Nebraska Press, 2008), p. vii.
35. Hardy Dorman, p. 160.
36. Moorehead, *Gellhorn,* p. 212.
37. Ibid.
38. Ibid, p. 214.
39. Helen Kirkpatrick, interview with Anne Kasper for the Washington Press Club Foundation, 3.4.1990. Session 2, p. 67. Online at beta.wpcf.org.
40. Ibid, Session 2, p. 49.
41. Helen Kirkpatrick, in a letter to her parents, 12 June 1943, Helen Paull Kirkpatrick Papers, box 1, Smith College.
42. Helen Kirkpatrick, oral history, Helen

Paull Kirkpatrick Papers, box 1, Smith College.

43. All the above paragraphs are Helen Kirkpatrick, in a letter to her parents, 13 October 1943, Helen Paull Kirkpatrick Papers, box 1, Smith College.

44. Kirkpatrick, Helen, *The Listener,* 9 December 1943.

45. Helen Kirkpatrick interview, Session 2, p. 22.

46. Kirkpatrick, Helen, *The Listener,* 9 December 1943.

Chapter Twelve

1. Gellhorn, Martha, "The First Hospital Ship," *The Face of War* (London: Granta Books, 1993), p. 111.

2. Edwards, Julia, *Women of the World: The Great Foreign Correspondents* (Boston: Houghton Mifflin Company, 1988), p. 110.

3. Carpenter, Iris, *No Woman's World* (Boston: Houghton Mifflin Company, 1946), e-book, loc. 283.

4. Helen Kirkpatrick, interview with Anne Kasper for the Washington Press Club Foundation, 3.4.1990. Session 1, p. 22. Online at beta.wpcf.org.

5. Caldwell Sorel, Nancy, *The Women Who Wrote the War* (New York: Perennial, 2000), p. 222.

6. Moorehead, Caroline, *Gellhorn: A*

Twentieth-Century Life (New York: Henry Holt and Company, 2003), p. 307.

7. Ibid, p. 214.

8. Ibid, p. 216.

9. Ibid.

10. Ibid, p. 217.

11. Ibid.

12. Ibid, p. 218.

13. Eckhertz, Holger, *D Day Through German Eyes* (DTZ History Publications, 2015), e-book, loc. 874–7.

14. Moorehead, *Gellhorn,* p. 218.

15. Gellhorn, "The First Hospital Ship," *The Face of War,* p. 111.

16. Ibid, p. 107.

17. Ibid.

18. Ibid, p. 84.

19. Moorehead, *Gellhorn,* p. 221.

20. Sebba, Anne, *Battling for News: The Rise of the Woman Reporter* (London: Hodder and Stoughton, 1994), p. 176.

21. Gellhorn, "The Carpathian Lancers," *The Face of War,* pp. 116–19.

22. Nigel Nicolson, in the private collection of H. Crawley.

23. Moorehead, *Gellhorn,* p. 223.

24. Gellhorn, "The Gothic Line," *The Face of War,* p. 127.

25. Ibid, p. 126.

26. Ibid, p. 124.

27. Ibid.

28. *Chicago Daily News,* 22 June 1944.

29. Carpenter, chapter 2, e-book, loc. 518.

30. Helen Kirkpatrick interview, Session 1, p. 48.

31. *Chicago Daily News,* 14 July 1944.

32. Helen Kirkpatrick interview, Session 2, p. 72.

33. Helen Kirkpatrick, in a letter to her parents, 19 July 1944, Helen Paull Kirkpatrick Papers, box 1, Smith College.

34. Helen Kirkpatrick, in a letter to her parents, 28 July 1944, ibid.

35. *Chicago Daily News,* 5 August 1944.

36. Ibid.

37. *Chicago Daily News,* 19 February 1942.

38. *Chicago Daily News,* 15 August 1944.

39. Carpenter, chapter 2, e-book, loc. 663.

40. Edwards, p. 157.

41. Burke, Carolyn, *Lee Miller: On Both Sides of the Camera* (London: Bloomsbury, 2006), p. 219.

42. Miller, Lee, "St. Malo," *Vogue,* September 1944, in Penrose, Antony (ed.), *Lee Miller's War: Beyond D-Day* (London: Thames and Hudson, 2005), p. 15.

43. Ibid, pp. 15–30.

44. Burke, pp. 223–4.

45. Ibid, p. 222.

46. Ibid, p. 228.

47. Penrose, *Lee Miller's War,* p. 48.

48. Ibid.

49. Ibid, p. 51.

50. Ibid, p. 63.

51. Ibid, p. 10.

52. Burke, p. 228.

53. Ibid, p. 228.

54. Capa, Robert, *Slightly Out of Focus* (New York: Henry Holt and Company, 1947), p. 178.

Chapter Thirteen

1. Kirkpatrick, Helen, BBC script, Helen Paull Kirkpatrick Papers, box 6, Smith College.

2. Helen Kirkpatrick, interview with Anne Kasper for the Washington Press Club Foundation, 3.4.1990. Session 2, p. 73. Online at beta.wpcf.org.

3. Helen Kirkpatrick interview, Session 2, p. 74.

4. Capa, Robert, *Slightly Out of Focus* (New York: Henry Holt and Company, 1947), p. 179.

5. Kirkpatrick, Helen, BBC script, Helen Paull Kirkpatrick Papers, box 6, Smith College.

6. Mazzeo, Tilar J., *The Hotel on Place Vendôme* (New York: HarperCollins, 2014), p. 153.

7. Helen Kirkpatrick interview, Session 3, p. 110.

8. *Chicago Daily News,* 27 August 1944.

9. Helen Paull Kirkpatrick Papers, box 1, Smith College.

10. Carpenter, Iris, chapter 2, *No Woman's World* (Boston: Houghton Mifflin Company, 1946), e-book, loc. 984-5.

11. Caldwell Sorel, Nancy, *The Women Who Wrote the War* (New York: Perennial, 2000), p. 271.

12. Ibid, p. 262.

13. Ibid, p. 276.

14. Moorehead, Caroline, *Gellhorn: A Twentieth-Century Life* (New York: Henry Holt and Company, 2003), p. 224.

15. Ibid.

16. Caldwell Sorel, p. 269.

17. *Chicago Daily News,* 14 October 1944.

18. Caldwell Sorel, p. 269.

19. Moorehead, *Gellhorn,* p. 229.

20. Ibid.

21. Ibid.

22. Burke, Carolyn, *Lee Miller: On Both Sides of the Camera* (London: Bloomsbury, 2006), p. 228.

23. Penrose, Antony, *The Lives of Lee Miller* (London: Thames and Hudson, 1988), p. 122.

24. Cited in Ousby, Ian, *Occupation: The Ordeal of France 1940–44* (London: John Murray, 1997), p. 153.

25. Penrose, *The Lives of Lee Miller,* p. 123.

26. Miller, Lee, "Pattern of Liberation,"

Vogue, January 1945, in Penrose, Antony (ed.), *Lee Miller's War: Beyond D-Day* (London: Thames and Hudson, 2005), p. 113.

27. Penrose, *The Lives of Lee Miller,* p. 122.
28. Burke, p. 235.
29. Ibid, p. 234.
30. Penrose, *The Lives of Lee Miller,* p. 126.
31. *Chicago Daily News,* 29 August 1944.
32. *Chicago Daily News,* 5 October 1944.
33. Burke, p. 247.
34. Ibid, p. 233.
35. Penrose, *The Lives of Lee Miller,* p. 130.

Chapter Fourteen

1. Sebba, Anne, *Battling for News: The Rise of the Woman Reporter* (London: Hodder and Stoughton, 1994), p. 176.
2. Gellhorn, *The Face of War* (London: Granta Books, 1993), p. 130.
3. Ibid, p. 134.
4. Caldwell Sorel, Nancy, *The Women Who Wrote the War* (New York: Perennial, 2000), p. 285.
5. Ibid, p. 286.
6. Ibid, p. 283.
7. Ibid.
8. Ibid, p. 291.
9. Letter to Helen Kirkpatrick dated 20 February 1945, Helen Paull Kirkpatrick Papers, box 1, Smith College.
10. Gellhorn, "The Battle of the Bulge," *The*

Face of War, p. 142.

11. Ibid, p. 140.

12. Miller, Lee, "Through the Alsace Campaign," *Vogue,* February 1944, in Penrose, Antony (ed.), *Lee Miller's War: Beyond D-Day* (London: Thames and Hudson, 2005), p. 150.

13. Ibid, p. 233.

14. Moorehead, Caroline, *Gellhorn: A Twentieth-Century Life* (New York: Henry Holt and Company, 2003), p. 223.

15. Edwards, Julia, *Women of the World: The Great Foreign Correspondents* (Boston: Houghton Mifflin Company, 1988), p. 131.

16. Moorehead, *Gellhorn,* p. 234.

17. Ibid, p. 237.

18. Ibid, p. 230.

19. Ibid, p. 235.

20. Ibid.

21. Ibid, p. 231.

22. Ibid, p. 237.

23. Ibid, p. 236.

24. Helen Kirkpatrick, interview with Anne Kasper for the Washington Press Club Foundation, 3.4.1990. Session 1, p. 29. Online at beta.wpcf.org.

25. Helen Kirkpatrick, oral history, Helen Paull Kirkpatrick Papers, box 1, Smith College.

26. Caldwell Sorel, p. 322.

27. Ibid, p. 277.

28. Burke, Carolyn, *Lee Miller: On Both Sides of the Camera* (London: Bloomsbury, 2006), p. 268.

29. Garrett, Patrick, *Of Fortunes and War: Clare Hollingworth, First of the Female War Correspondents* (London: Two Roads Books, 2017), p. 187.

30. Hollingworth, Clare, *Front Line* (London: Jonathan Cape, 1990), p. 134.

31. Garrett, p. 199.

Chapter Fifteen

1. Burke, Carolyn, *Lee Miller: On Both Sides of the Camera* (London: Bloomsbury, 2006), p. 249.

2. Carpenter, Iris, chapter 8, *No Woman's World* (Boston: Houghton Mifflin Company, 1946), e-book, loc. 2358.

3. Caldwell Sorel, Nancy, *The Women Who Wrote the War* (New York: Perennial, 2000), p. 318.

4. Gellhorn, *"Das Deutsche Volk,"* in *The Face of War* (London: Granta Books, 1993), p. 154.

5. Ibid, p. 151.

6. Burke, p. 249.

7. Ibid, p. 248.

8. Ibid, p. 249.

9. *Chicago Daily News,* 7 April 1945.

10. *Chicago Daily News,* 16 April 1945.

11. *Collier's* magazine, April 1945.

12. *Chicago Daily News,* 11 April 1945.

13. Carpenter, chapter 12, e-book, loc. 3540.

14. Helen Kirkpatrick, interview with Anne Kasper for the Washington Press Club Foundation, 3.4.1990. Session 2, p. 78. Online at beta.wpcf.org.

15. Burke, p. 241.

16. Caldwell Sorel, p. 335.

17. Ibid, p. 333.

18. Penrose, Antony (ed.), *Lee Miller's War: Beyond D-Day* (London: Thames and Hudson, 2005), p. 177.

19. Burke, p. 250.

20. Penrose, *Lee Miller's War: Beyond D-Day,* p. 155.

21. Penrose, *The Lives of Lee Miller,* p. 138.

22. Moorehead, Caroline, *Gellhorn: A Twentieth-Century Life* (New York: Henry Holt and Company, 2003), p. 236.

23. Gellhorn, *The Face of War,* p. 163.

24. Burke, p. 261.

25. Ibid, p. 262.

26. *Chicago Daily News,* 2 May 1945.

27. Burke, p. 264.

28. Helen Kirkpatrick interview, Session 2, p. 77.

29. Caldwell Sorel, p. 367.

30. Ibid.

31. "The Battle of Berlin, 1945," Eyewitness to History, www.eyewitnesstohistory.com/berlin.htm (2002).

32. Beevor, Antony, *Berlin: The Downfall 1945* (London: Viking, 2002).
33. Carpenter, chapter 14, e-book, loc. 4127.
34. Moorehead, *Gellhorn,* p. 242.
35. Schultz, Sigrid, "Concentration Camps," unpublished paper (1945), State Historical Society of Wisconsin, p. 2.

Chapter Sixteen

1. Burke, Carolyn, *Lee Miller: On Both Sides of the Camera* (London: Bloomsbury, 2006), p. 261.
2. Gellhorn, "Dachau," *The Face of War* (London: Granta Books, 1993), p. 171.
3. Moorehead, Caroline, *Gellhorn: A Twentieth-Century Life* (New York: Henry Holt and Company, 2003), p. 238.
4. Eisenhower, Dwight D., *Crusade in Europe* (New York: Doubleday, 1949), pp. 408–9.
5. Unpublished lecture, 1945, Helen Paull Kirkpatrick Papers, box 13, Smith College.
6. Caldwell Sorel, Nancy, *The Women Who Wrote the War* (New York: Perennial, 2000), p. 350.
7. Kirkpatrick, Helen, "3000 skeletons come slowly back to life," *Chicago Daily News,* 24 April 1945.
8. Caldwell Sorel, p. 348; Chapman, Cynthia, "Psychobiographical Study of the Life of Sigrid Schultz," unpublished thesis, p. 112.

9. Caldwell Sorel, p. 351; Chapman, p. 112.

10. Caldwell Sorel, p. 340.

11. Burke, Carolyn, *Lee Miller: On Both Sides of the Camera* (London: Bloomsbury, 2006), p. 239.

12. Ibid, p. 239.

13. Ibid, pp. 253 and 260.

14. Sebba, Anne, *Battling for News: The Rise of the Woman Reporter* (London: Hodder and Stoughton, 1994), p. 178.

15. Gellhorn, "Dachau," *The Face of War,* p. 167.

16. Moorehead, *Gellhorn,* p. 239.

17. Gellhorn, "Dachau," *The Face of War,* pp. 167–8.

18. Ibid, p. 168.

19. Moorehead, *Gellhorn,* pp. 240–2.

20. Gellhorn, "Dachau," *The Face of War,* p. 173.

21. Penrose, Antony, *The Lives of Lee Miller* (London: Thames and Hudson, 1988), p. 144.

22. *New Yorker,* 11 May 1945; also see Caldwell Sorel, p. 375.

23. Moorehead, *Gellhorn,* p. 241.

24. Orwell, George, "Future of a ruined Germany," *Observer,* 8 April 1945.

25. Schultz, Sigrid, radio script for MBS, cited in Chapman, p. 287.

26. Chapman, p. 114.

27. Burke, p. 265.

28. Ibid, p. 268.
29. Ibid.
30. Ibid, p. 274.
31. Penrose, *The Lives of Lee Miller,* p. 147.
32. Moorehead, *Gellhorn,* pp. 242–3.
33. Garrett, Patrick, *Of Fortunes and War: Clare Hollingworth, First of the Female War Correspondents* (London: Two Roads Books, 2017), pp. 147 and 199.
34. Caldwell Sorel, p. 390.
35. Crawley, Aidan, *Leap Before You Look* (London: Collins, 1988), pp. 205–6.
36. Burke, p. 271.
37. *Chicago Daily News,* 21 July 1945.
38. Helen Kirkpatrick, interview with Anne Kasper for the Washington Press Club Foundation, 3.4.1990. Session 2, p. 79. Online at beta.wpcf.org.
39. Moorehead, *Gellhorn,* p. 244.
40. Ibid, p. 243.
41. Ibid, p. 250.
42. Helen Kirkpatrick interview, Session 2, p. 80.

Chapter Seventeen

1. Garrett, Patrick, *Of Fortunes and War: Clare Hollingworth, First of the Female War Correspondents* (London: Two Roads Books, 2017), p. 313.
2. Burke, Carolyn, *Lee Miller: On Both Sides of the Camera* (London: Bloomsbury,

2006), p. 371.
3. Ibid, p. 367.
4. Ibid, p. 281.
5. Penrose, Antony, *The Lives of Lee Miller* (London: Thames and Hudson, 1988), p. 168.
6. Ibid, p. 299.
7. Ibid, p. 300.
8. Antony Penrose, in conversation with the author.
9. Burke, p. 325.
10. Ibid, p. 313.
11. Ibid, p. 311.
12. Ibid, p. 338.
13. Ibid, p. 364.
14. Ibid, p. 345.
15. *Life* photographer John Philips, quoted by Penrose in conversation with the author.
16. Moorehead, Caroline, *Gellhorn: A Twentieth-Century Life* (New York: Henry Holt and Company, 2003), p. 246.
17. Ibid, p. 248.
18. Ibid, p. 266.
19. Ibid, p. 278.
20. Ibid, p. 269.
21. Ibid, p. 275.
22. Ibid, p. 274.
23. Ibid, p. 292.
24. Ibid, p. 307.
25. Ibid, p. 309.
26. Ibid, p. 311.
27. Ibid, p. 347.

28. Ibid, p. 376.
29. Sebba, Anne, *Battling for News: The Rise of the Woman Reporter* (London: Hodder and Stoughton, 1994), p. 240.
30. Moorehead, *Gellhorn,* p. 380.
31. Ibid, pp. 29 and 424.
32. Ibid, p. 424.
33. Garrett, p. 318.
34. Ibid, pp. 270–1.
35. Ibid, p. 252.
36. Ibid, p. 265.
37. Sebba, p. 226.
38. Hollingworth, Clare, *Front Line* (London: Jonathan Cape, 1990), pp. 197 and 239.
39. Garrett, pp. 307–8.
40. Ibid, pp. 316 and 303.
41. Ibid, p. 313.
42. Ibid, p. 454.
43. Ibid, p. 470.
44. *Chicago Tribune* interview with S. Schultz, 1977, tape no. 2, p. 14.
45. Chapman, Cynthia, "Psychobiographical Study of the Life of Sigrid Schultz," unpublished thesis, pp. 250–2.
46. Quoted by Morley Boyd, Pamela Wriedt's husband, in conversation with the author.
47. Edwards, Julia, "Dragon Lady," *Chicago Tribune,* 11 September 1988.
48. Crawley, Aidan, *Leap Before You Look* (London: Collins, 1988), p. 209.
49. Cowles, Virginia, unpublished diary entry,

cited in Crawley, p. 217.

50. Crawley, p. 265.

51. H. Crawley, in conversation with the author.

52. Sebba, p. 103.

53. Crawley, p. 422.

54. Moorehead, Caroline, "Days of Wine and Shrapnel," *Spectator,* 11 September 2010.

55. Helen Kirkpatrick, in a letter to her parents, 22 July 1946, Helen Paull Kirkpatrick Papers, box 1, Smith College.

56. Helen Kirkpatrick, interview with Anne Kasper for the Washington Press Club Foundation, 3.4.1990. Session 2, p. 86. Online at beta.wpcf.org.

57. Leonard Miall, Helen Kirkpatrick obituary, *Independent,* 8 January 1998.

58. Helen Kirkpatrick, oral history, Helen Paull Kirkpatrick Papers, box 1, Smith College.

59. Helen Kirkpatrick interview, Session 3, p. 98.

60. Letter, 25 June 1954, Helen Paull Kirkpatrick Papers, box 8, Smith College.

61. *Washington Evening Star,* 23 June 1954.

62. Helen Kirkpatrick, in a letter to Mary Chase, January 1948, Helen Paull Kirkpatrick Papers, box 8, Smith College.

63. Helen Kirkpatrick interview, Session 3, p. 89.

64. Ibid, Session 3, p. 109.

65. "Reporting World War II," 18 September

1995, c-span.org.

66. di Giovanni, Janine, "The Women Who Report on War," British *Vogue,* 26 January 2019, www.vogue.co.uk/article/women-who -report-war.

67. Sebba, p. 270.

68. Amanpour, Christiane, "How I get it done," *The Cut,* 10 April 2018, www.thecut .com/2018/04/christiane-amanpour-cnn -interview.html.

69. Moorehead, *Gellhorn,* p. 154.

BIBLIOGRAPHY

Archives

Papers of Virginia Cowles, Imperial War Museum, London.

Helen Paull Kirkpatrick papers, Sophia Smith Collection, SSC-MS-00103, Smith College Special Collections, Northampton, Massachusetts.

Papers of Sigrid Schultz: The State Historical Society of Wisconsin, Madison.

Lee Miller Archive, Farley Farm, Sussex.

Books

Alexievich, Svetlana, *The Unwomanly Face of War,* London: Penguin Classics, 2017 (first published 1985).

Beevor, Antony, *Berlin: The Downfall,* London: Viking Press, 2002.

Beevor, Antony, *The Second World War,* London: Weidenfeld & Nicolson 2012.

Bourke-White, Margaret, *Portrait of Myself,*

New York: Simon and Schuster, 1963.

Bowen, Elizabeth, *The Heat of the Day,* New York: Knopf Doubleday, 2002 (first published 1948).

Burke, Carolyn, *Lee Miller: On Both Sides of the Camera,* London: Bloomsbury, 2006.

Caldwell Sorel, Nancy, *The Women Who Wrote the War,* New York: Perennial, 2000.

Carpenter, Iris, *No Woman's War,* Boston: Houghton Mifflin Company, 1946.

Cowles, Virginia, *Looking For Trouble,* London: Faber and Faber, 2010 (first published 1941).

Crawley, Aidan, *Leap Before You Look,* London: Collins, 1988.

Eckhertz, Holger, *D Day Through German Eyes: The Hidden Story of June 6 1944,* DTZ History Publications, 2015.

Edwards, Julia, *Women of the World: The Great Foreign Correspondents,* Boston: Houghton Mifflin Company, 1988.

Edy, Carolyn M., *The Woman War Correspondent, the U.S. Military, and the Press 1846–1947,* Lanham, Maryland: Lexington Books, 2016.

Garrett, Patrick, *Of Fortunes and War: Clare Hollingworth, First of the Female War Correspondents,* London: Two Roads Books, 2017.

Gellhorn, Martha, *The Face of War,* London: Granta Books, 1993.

Gellhorn, Martha, and Virginia Cowles, *Love Goes to Press,* London and Lincoln: University of Nebraska Press, 2008 (first published 1946).

Hilsum, Lindsey, *In Extremis: The Life of War Correspondent Marie Colvin,* London: Chatto and Windus, 2018.

Hollingworth, Clare, *Front Line,* London: Jonathan Cape, 1990.

Kershaw, Ian, *Hitler 1936–1945: Nemesis,* London: Penguin, 2001.

Kirkpatrick, Helen, *This Terrible Peace,* London: Rich and Cowan, 1938.

Kirkpatrick, Helen, *Under the British Umbrella: What the English Are and How They Go to War,* New York: Scribners, 1939.

Manning, Olivia, *The Balkan Trilogy,* London: Arrow Books, 1992 (first published 1960).

Manning, Olivia, *The Levant Trilogy,* London: Penguin, 1992.

McNamara, John, *Extra! U.S. War Correspondents in the Fighting Fronts,* Boston: Houghton Mifflin Company, 1945.

Moorehead, Caroline, *Gellhorn: A Twentieth-Century Life,* New York: Henry Holt and Company, 2003.

Moorehead, Caroline, *Selected Letters of Martha Gellhorn,* New York: Henry Holt and Company, 2006.

Oldfield, Barney, *Never a Shot in Anger,* New York: Duell, Sloan and Pearce, 1956.

Penrose, Antony, *Lee Miller's War: Beyond D-Day,* London: Thames and Hudson, 2005.

Penrose, Antony, *The Lives of Lee Miller,* London: Thames and Hudson, 1988.

Roberts, Andrew, *The Storm of War,* London: Allen Lane, 2009.

Sands, Philippe, *East West Street,* New York: Knopf, 2016.

Schultz, Sigrid, *Germany Will Try It Again,* New York: Reynal and Hitchcock, 1944.

Sebba, Anne, *Battling for News: The Rise of the Woman Reporter,* London: Hodder and Stoughton, 1994.

Sebba, Anne, *Les Parisiennes: How the Women of Paris Lived, Loved, and Died in the 1940s,* London: Weidenfeld and Nicolson, 2016.

Shirer, William, *Berlin Diary: The Journal of a Foreign Correspondent 1934–41,* New York: Rosetta Books LCC, 2011 (first published 1941).

Vaill, Amanda, *Hotel Florida: Truth, Love and Death in the Spanish Civil War,* London: Bloomsbury, 2015.

Waugh, Evelyn, *Sword of Honour* trilogy, London: Penguin, 2001 (first published 1965).

Wineapple, Brenda, *Genet,* London: Pandora Books, 1989.

Unpublished Theses

Chapman, Cynthia, "Psychobiographical Study of the Life of Sigrid Schultz," 1991. Copies held at Göttingen University and The State Historical Society of Wisconsin, Madison.

Garvey, Kerry J., "The Byline of Europe: An Examination of Foreign Correspondents' Reporting from 1930 to 1941," 2017. https://ir.library.illinoisstate.edu/cgi/viewcontent.cgi?referer=&httpsredir=1&article=1671&context=etd

Online Material

Helen Kirkpatrick Milbank Interview, Washington Press Club Foundation, 1990. http://beta.wpcf.org/oralhistory/kirk

PERMISSIONS ACKNOWLEDGEMENTS

Women in Journalism Oral History Project Interview with Helen Kirkpatrick Milbank, Washington Press Club Foundation. Reprinted with permission. All rights reserved.

Helen Paull Kirkpatrick papers, Sophia Smith Collection, SSC-MS-00103, Smith College Special Collections, Northampton, Massachusetts.

Permission to quote from *Front Line* by Clare Hollingworth provided by Patrick Garrett / *Of Fortunes and War: Clare Hollingworth, First of the Female War Correspondents.*

Fortunes of War © 2017 Patrick Garrett. Reproduced by permission of Two Roads, an imprint of Hodder and Stoughton Limited.

Looking for Trouble by Virginia Cowles © Faber and Faber Ltd.

Excerpted from *The Face of War* copyright ©

ABOUT THE AUTHOR

Judith Mackrell is the critically acclaimed author of *The Unfinished Palazzo* and *Flappers*. She is also a celebrated dance critic, and her biography of the ballerina Lydia Lopokova, *Bloomsbury Ballerina,* was shortlisted for the Costa Biography Award. She also coauthored *The Oxford Dictionary of Dance.*